MW01616599

CARIBBEAN TRAILBLAZERS:
ST. VINCENT AND THE GRENADINES
VOLUMES I AND II

EDITED BY BALDWIN KING AND
CHERYL PHILLS KING

KINGS - SVG PUBLISHERS
ST. VINCENT AND THE GRENADINES

PUBLISHED BY

KINGS-SVG PUBLISHERS
BOX 2713, ST VINCENT AND THE GRENADINES
AND
BOX 702, MADISON, NJ 07940, USA
www.kingsinn-svg.com
kingba@aol.com

**CARIBBEAN TRAILBLAZERS:
ST. VINCENT AND THE GRENADINES
VOLUMES I AND II**

COPYRIGHT 2012 BY KINGS-SVG

ISBN: 0-9778981-9-9

PUBLICATION DATE: JUNE 2012

PRINTED IN THE USA

COVER PHOTO: SALT POND, OWIA, ST. VINCENT AND THE
GRENADINES; COURTESY OF CHERENE KING

PUBLISHED BY

KINGS-SVG PUBLISHERS

CARIBBEAN TRAILBLAZERS:
ST. VINCENT AND THE GRENADINES

VOLUME I

COPYRIGHT 2010 BY KINGS-SVG

ISBN: 0-9778981-5-6

PUBLICATION DATE: JULY 2010

CONTENTS

CONTRIBUTORS

Peggy Antrobus

Andrea Punnett Boos

Jean M. Dorsinville

Ann Eustace

Adrian Fraser

Hazeldene Phills Hercules

Bertram A. John

Catherine John

Baldwin King

Cheryl Phills King

Sir Fred Phillips

Elizabeth Punnett

Anne Samuel

Vin Samuel

Adrian Saunders

Joan Samuel Simien

Monica Thomas Woodley

PREFACE

In 1979, Sir Rupert John wrote a book entitled "Pioneers in Nation-Building in a Caribbean Mini-State". In the preface, he said: *"**Pioneers** ... is an attempt to consider in one small volume the lives of twenty two Vincentians and the contributions they made during the earlier years of the twentieth century to the political, economic, social or cultural development of their native land ... All of the people ... were born in St. Vincent and the Grenadines ... With one exception, all of those whose lives are sketched herein have already passed away. None of them was born before the year 1836 ... Only one of them had the opportunity of receiving any formal secondary education and none of them ever pursued studies for a university degree".*

Pioneers ...was republished in 2009 by KINGS-SVG Publishers and included in the new edition is a biography of Sir Rupert himself written by his son Karl John. We thought it was time to follow up on Sir Rupert's effort and continue his ground-breaking work. So we have profiled in this volume fifteen people (twelve men and three women) who have made substantial contributions either to St. Vincent and the Grenadines (SVG) directly or in the SVG diaspora. We have broadened the scope also to include persons who were not born in SVG but who lived and worked in SVG and made substantial contribution to its development. We have also included persons who are still alive because we feel strongly that such persons should be recognized and honored in time for them to enjoy such recognition. With one exception, all of the persons profiled here were born in the twentieth century so we cover individuals between 1905 and 2010. All of the persons (except one) have had a secondary education and a number of them have had a university education.

We have used as our mantra "History through Biography" so we have used the lives of some of these persons to tell the history of St. Vincent and the Grenadines as far as possible. In other cases, we have simply told the story of fascinating lives and paid tribute to many of them for their extraordinary accomplishments. A number of them may be labeled "unsung heroes" but some are not so unsung having been recognized formally by government or organizations. We regard all of them as trailblazers.

Of course, the people considered here represent only a small fraction of those who deserve recognition. We hope to cover another set of persons in a second volume, provided we can find writers
.In addition to the acknowledgments in individual articles, we wish to express our thanks and gratitude to all seventeen authors in helping us to bring this project to fruition. We hope, along with Sir Rupert's book, that this volume brings inspiration to all its readers especially to the youth who

need to know more about the people on whose backs much of the progress of SVG has fallen and to whom we dedicate this volume.

Finally we wish to thank our three children, Bryan, Cherene and Debra, for their considerable help in the technological aspects of putting this volume together.

Baldwin King
Cheryl Phills King
(Editors)   July 2010

1.   **JOSEPH CHATOYER**
                              By
                        Adrian Fraser

" Until the Lions have their historians, tales of hunting will always
glorify the hunters" (African proverb)

On March 14, 2002, at a ceremony at the Victoria Park, Joseph
Chatoyer, the paramount chief of the Black Caribs (Garifuna), was officially
declared the first National Hero of St.Vincent and the Grenadines in
accordance with sections 11 and 12 of the National Heroes Act No. 7 of
2002 and following the publication of a Notice in the Government Gazette of
Tuesday, March 12, 2002. This came after a long period of advocacy by the
National Youth Council, voluntary associations and individuals in the
country. In fact, in 1985, the National Youth Council spearheaded the
erection of an obelisk at Dorsetshire Hill in honour of Joseph Chatoyer and
on March 14, 2001 a public holiday was declared that paved the way for the
establishment of National Heroes Day as a permanent national holiday and
the declaration of the country's first national hero. The efforts of a single
masquerader has also to be singled out for on two different occasions, at
Carnival 1963 and 1973 "Mas Man", Louis Boucher, depicted Chatoyer as
national hero as part of his presentations for 'Individual Mas' of those years
at the annual Carnival festival. This reflected the fact that the feats of
Chatoyer had reached the consciousness of ordinary people of the country.

The singling out of Chatoyer for recognition however began long before
this. The "Drama of King Shotaway", a play written and produced by a
gentleman named only as Mr. Browne was performed in New York in 1823.
This play has the distinction of being the first play performed in that city
about a black person and the author is lionized as the father of the Black
Theatre in the United States of America. Copies of the play cannot be
located but the Playbill depicts it as "Founded on facts taken from the
Insurrection of the Caravs in the Island of St. Vincent written from the
experience of Mr. Browne."[i] It is certainly a mark of distinction that a
member of the indigenous community from one of the far 'flung colonies'
could have been lionized in that way at a time when the Caribs were still
regarded as savages and when colonialism reigned supreme.

Chatoyer's elevation to the rank of National Hero followed efforts by
the country after its attainment of independence from Great Britain in 1979,
to continue the process of reconstructing its history, a process that started
before Independence and informed the quest to break the colonial bondage.
The British colonial empire of which we were a part had provided us with
heroes carved out by the euro-centric framework of that time. Colonial
education was a key instrument in this colonization. The 'heroes' who were

featured in our colonial education were normally persons who had been prominent in the decimation of the indigenous peoples, in the slave trade and in the colonization of the countries that made up what we now call the Caribbean basin. Chatoyer on the other hand was depicted in the colonial literature as "ruthless and sanguinary" and his conduct was said to be marked by "cruelty rather than courage." (Shephard p. 74)

Chatoyer was a 'Black Carib', today commonly referred to as Garifuna. His ancestors emerged from the inter-breeding of the indigenous Yellow or Red Caribs (as they were called then, and now referred to as Kalinagos) and Africans who consisted largely of slaves who escaped from plantations in Barbados and Martinique, from raids carried out by the indigenous peoples on European plantations in colonies to the north and from a slave ship that was shipwrecked off Barbados, presumably in 1635. He is recognized mainly for his role in the struggles of his people to defend their land from incursions by the Europeans. This struggle did not begin with him but he played a prominent part at a significant period in those struggles and continued what his Kalinago ancestors had begun.

Chatoyer really epitomized those struggles. Early efforts by the Spaniards and then the British and the French to establish themselves in the smaller islands of the Caribbean resulted in the decimation of most of the Carib peoples through war and European diseases. Those who remained took refuge in the colonies of Dominica and St. Vincent which up to then had resisted the settlement of Europeans and remained the last defence of the Carib peoples. In the 1620s and 30's the British and French had begun to establish colonies in most of the Lesser Antilles. St. Vincent remained fully in the hands of the Caribs, and was considered the headquarters of the Caribs (The Memoirs of Pere Labat, p.137) So even before the emergence of the group now recognized as the Garifuna, the Kalinago peoples of St. Vincent had been firm in the defence of their land.

It was this stubborn defence of their land that prompted an ideological battle that led to them being referred to as cannibals, that has done such psychological damage to them and still to some extent "defiles their name and defames their memory" (Richard Moore, pgs 1-2) . Richard Moore, whose research on reputed Carib cannibalism was prompted by a statement on a poster at Nelson's dockyard in Antigua, strongly challenges that claim and quotes Juan de Castellanos, described as a Literary Spanish Conquistador, to the effect that:

"They were called Caribs not because they would eat human flesh but because they defended their homes well." (Richard Moore, p. 15).

Moore, after doing significant research on the issue, has concluded that there is no evidence to justify that claim. Jean Baptiste Labat, a Jesuit Priest who served in the French islands between 1694 and 1705 dismissed the idea of Carib cannibalism. He writes:

"It is true that when they kill someone, they cure his limbs and fill up calabashes with his fat, which they carry away to their homes; but this is as a trophy and a mark of their victory and of their valour…" (Jean Baptiste Labat, "A Sojourn on Dominica (1722)[ii]

Long after sugar was established in the Caribbean colonies and the so-called 'sugar revolution' had started, St. Vincent remained in the hands of the Caribs, even though they allowed some French people to live on the leeward side of the island.

Joseph Chatoyer entered the historical literature after St. Vincent passed into the hands of the British following the Seven Years War that ended in 1763. In 1768 when the Commissioners of Land announced their intention to move into the Carib territory to survey and dispose of lands, Chatoyer, as Chief of Grand Sable described as "the richest and principal settlement of the Charaibs" (Young, p. 38) led the resistance of his people. They knew of no King of Great Britain who could sanction any encroachment on their land. Chatoyer was then not paramount chief but was obviously one of the major figures. He was, later, one of 28 chiefs who signed the treaty with the British following the end of the 1772-1773 war and had apparently begun to assume the mantle of 'principal chief'. (Nancie Gonzalez, p.19; Robin Fabel, p.193)

Chatoyer's Elevation to First National Hero

The Order of National Heroes Act, 2002 established the criteria for the selection of national heroes and in this case the first National Hero:

(10.2). "In determining the qualification …the Committee (the National Heroes Advisory Committee) shall have regard to whether that person:

a) Has given outstanding service to Saint Vincent and the Grenadines and his contribution has altered positively the course of the history of Saint Vincent and the Grenadines.

b) Has given service to Saint Vincent and the Grenadines which has been exemplified by visionary and pioneering leadership, extraordinary achievement and the attainment of the highest excellence which has redounded to the honour of Saint Vincent and the Grenadines; or

c) Has, through his heroic exploits and sacrifice, contributed to the improvement of the economic, social or political conditions of Saint Vincent and the Grenadines and Vincentians generally"

It might be argued that the Advisory Committee in drawing up the criteria had Chatoyer firmly in mind. The advocacy for his elevation to that position had started a long time ago and at that time, there were virtually no other contenders, so much had he been in the consciousness of those who had been leading the charge.

There were problems associated with building a case for Joseph Chatoyer. The first was the paucity of literature on Chatoyer and the fact that whatever we knew about him was penned by his enemies who had been determined to paint him in a particular way. The Caribs left no writings of their own and the Europeans who wrote about Chatoyer saw him largely as an enemy who was leading the resistance to their occupation of what were considered prized sugar lands. St.Vincent is a mountainous country with a mountain range running through the centre of the island. Flat lands ideal for planting sugar cane were at a premium. Planters, their allies, and others seeking a fortune in sugar recognized that the Caribs occupied most of the flat land. Their main objective was to have the Caribs removed from the colony and to do so they had to paint a picture of the Caribs as ruthless, as obstacles to British colonization and the establishment of the sugar industry. In a letter of July 17, 1769 sent to the Lords of Trade and Plantations, the Commissioners argued:

"...the experience now shows us that it will be impossible, without imminent danger to the colony, to complete any settlement or arrangement with the Charaibs; let the terms proposed be ever so tender or advantageous without a force sufficient to restrain and awe them into obedience." (Young, pgs. 52-53)

. Chatoyer, as initially one of the major Carib personalities, and later the Principal Chief, would obviously have featured as a major obstacle.

When one looks at the context of the encounter between the British and the Caribs and understand what was motivating those who laid claim to the country and who argued for the expulsion of the Caribs, then their arguments and the pictures they painted, have to be examined carefully. Much of what we know about Chatoyer came from Charles Shephard's **An Historical Account of the Island of Saint Vincent** and Sir William Young's **An Account of the Black Charaibs in the Island of St.Vincent's.** Shephard's work was dedicated "To the Survivors of the Carib War". He states clearly:

"The Work now offered to the Public was undertaken at the request of several Gentlemen of the Colony, who were anxious that the particular circumstances attendant on the Insurrection in 1795, should be preserved in a convenient form, and with more minuteness, than has hitherto been done in the Historical Narratives of the West Indian Islands." (Shephard, xiii)

In her **Historiography of the British West Indies**, Elsa Goveia has the following to say about Young's work:

"His book may, without injustice, be described as a piece of settler history. It is full of the righteous indignation which inevitably prevailed at a time when the settlers found themselves threatened by the continued existence and hostility of a strong tribal enclave within the island...The colonists in St. Vincent were petitioning that the Black Caribs be removed, since they could never be trusted; and Young, in his book, gives a vigorous support to this request, citing the constant 'perfidy' of the tribes, their strong attachment to the French, and their endemic hostility to the settler interest...Let them therefore be removed, that the settlers, true subjects of the Crown might be safe." (Goveia, p. 37)

Bernard Marshall was also very critical of William Young's work. He writes in the **Caribbean Quarterly, Volume 19, No. 4, December 1973**:

"To date, this work which has completely distorted the picture has remained virtually unchallenged... no one has yet attempted to refute Young's arguments by a thorough re-examination of the available data. Indeed, throughout the work, Young views the Black Caribs as a group of 'savages' whose sinister designs against the lives and properties of 'innocent' British subjects created a situation in which there was no alternative but to use force against them and remove them from the island at all costs." (p. 5)

The pictures the colonists painted of Chatoyer must therefore be seen against this background. Peter Hulme and Neil Whitehead captured it best when they argued that many of the accounts of the period were written either by planters "who wanted Carib land" or by colonial officials "for whom the Caribs were a 'problem'." (Fraser, p 21-22) Accounts written by Catholic missionaries, many of whom lived among the Caribs tended to be more sympathetic and balanced. They were largely written in the 17th or early 18th century before Chatoyer emerged as a major figure among the Caribs.

The images we have of Chatoyer are mainly those related to resistance and war, to the efforts to defend his people and prevent the encroachment of Europeans on their land. It is, however, in the defence of this country that Chatoyer is heralded and gained recognition as the first National Hero. In a tour of the islands in 1791 William Young detailed a visit to him by Chatoyer and Du Valle, another of the Chiefs. Gifts were exchanged and Young notes:

"We had much conversation with them ... Chatoyer and Du Valle were well dressed...Chatoyer and his sons dined at the villa and drank each a bottle of claret."

This certainly is not the picture of a savage and should bring some comfort to those Vincentians who resented the fact that someone who is a national hero of this country is mainly depicted in loincloth. One assumes from Young's reference to their dress that they were dressed in a manner that found favour with the Europeans. One of the problems encountered with those persons who have refused to accept Chatoyer as a national hero is that they are trying to take him out of the historical context in which he existed. In any event the encounter between Europe and the indigenous people would have guaranteed changes on both sides, so that Chatoyer and Du Valle could well have adopted European garb or perhaps wore the ceremonial garb of their people or 'office'.

There is no doubt that Chatoyer had a significant impact on the people with whom he came into contact and those who were writing about his life. He was the subject of at least one of the engravings of Agostino Brunias who it is believed might have travelled to St. Vincent with William Young. This engraving was featured in Bryan Edwards, **The History, Civil and Commercial, of the British Colonies in the West Indies**, 1801. Even his death took on some significance. The traditional story relates the death of Chatoyer to his defeat in a duel with the British Major Leith. Many historians and other commentators are skeptical about this account. The account of his death as stated was likely to have been a propaganda tool to be used against the Caribs in an effort to convince them about the superiority of the British by showing them that their Major Leith was able to defeat their Chief. The Caribs fought guerilla-style. They avoided direct confrontation. The evidence suggests that the Caribs were ambushed. The British soldiers crept up on them unobserved. This took place after midnight. It was under these circumstances that Chatoyer was killed. There is no description of a duel but simply a statement to the effect that Chatoyer was killed.

E. L Joseph in his novel "**Warner Arundell: The Adventures of a Creole,** that was supposed to have been based on real figures, "openly or thinly disguised," describes the attack on the Caribs who were in camp at Dorsetshire Hill:

"We passed without noise into the fort and surprised the enemy in the midst of their carousal. It was no fight – it was a mere regular slaughter." *(Vol. 1, p.57).*

The book was published in 1838 and showed that the question of the death of Chatoyer had been in the consciousness of the people of that time. E.L Joseph is known for his **History of Trinidad** which was also published in 1838. The Diary of Stipendiary Magistrate John Colthurst, also provides support for this position.

The event of major significance to this country that was celebrated on October 27, 1979 should more accurately be described as the date on which St. Vincent recovered its independence. Chatoyer was among the early fighters for the retention and preservation of the independence of this country. In a manuscript written in 2002 to commemorate the declaration of Chatoyer as this country's first national hero I commented on the importance which was given to Chatoyer at that time by those who opposed him. I stated:

"The fact that Sir William Young singles out Chatoyer for attention suggests that he recognized his importance and his position within Carib society. Chatoyer was then undoubtedly Paramount Chief and is described by William Young as "The Charaibe Chief of all."

It has to be pointed out too that other chiefs had at different times visited Young's home, but more attention seemed to have been paid to Chatoyer. William the Younger, commented on this in recognizing what he considered to be "the most flattering attentions and hospitality" given to Chatoyer by his father." (**Young,** p. 107.)

Chatoyer stood out as Diplomat and Chief Strategist. He clearly understood the geo-politics of the time and was aware of the uneasy relationship between the English and French. It was stated by Sir William Young that when Chatoyer died, a 'proclamation' was found in his pocket. It was published under the caption "Copy of the Declaration of Joseph Chatoyer, Chief of the Caribs". It was said to have been written at Chateaubelair on March 12, 1795. It reads in part:

"Where is the Frenchman who will not join his brothers, at a moment when the voice of liberty is heard by them? Let us then unite, citizens and brothers, round the colours flying in this island; and let us hasten to co-operate to that great piece of work which has been already commenced so gloriously..."(p. 117)

The tactics of Chatoyer and his men quite often had the British baffled. In negotiations with them in the late 1760s, Chatoyer indicated that some of them were willing to accept the terms they were offered but others were against it. Young in commenting on those tactics, argued as follows:

"There is reason to suppose, that appearing divided among themselves was a settled design of the Charaibs; and it was the most artful that could be devised..."

He noted later:

"Fatal experience had not yet taught 'that perfidy is the policy' of the Charaib: that he is most submissive when he meditates revolt, most complacent when he designs outrage; and prepares for devastation and murder by acts of conciliation and professions of attachment." (p. 422).

It says something for the respect with which Chatoyer was held and the confidence in his ability as a strategist that some Frenchmen actually served under him.

Chatoyer died in the early stages of the final British-Carib war but his presence loomed so large that he stood out as a major figure in the war and at that time. The fact that St. Vincent was among the last of the countries in the Caribbean to have been colonized is testimony to the struggles of the Caribs. The 18th century was a period of intense warfare between the British and the French with some of the islands/colonies being used as pawns. Chatoyer was a figure of major importance at this critical stage in the struggle by both Britain and France to seize lands for the cultivation of the sugar cane. He made the ultimate sacrifice, dying for his country in attempting to deny conquest by the Europeans. It should be of some significance to us today that the Caribs, with inferior military technology, (although at times they were able to get arms and other support from the French in their struggles with the British) were able for a long time to have withstood the persistent efforts by the Europeans to colonise their lands. The struggle started before Chatoyer and there were other dominant figures in that struggle but Chatoyer took control at a critical period and the respect with which he was held even by his enemies, says a lot about him. The reconstruction of Chatoyer is a remarkable feat and the result of excellent detective work by different people, working through the pictures of savagery and primitiveness that some contemporaries had attempted to paint. It is also of some significance that this country has gone back to the 18th century to select as its first national hero a man who had been so vilified by those who wrote our early history.

We salute the Right Excellency Joseph Chatoyer, Paramount Chief of the Caribs as our first National Hero.

[i] See Fraser, Chatoyer (Chatawae) National Hero of St. Vincent and the Grenadines, pgs. 7-8
[ii] Hulme and Whitehead (ed), p. 164-166. For a brief discussion of this, see Fraser, pgs. 18-19

BIBLIOGRAPHY

1. Eaden, John (ed), The Memoirs of Pere Labat 1693-1705, Frank Cass and Co. Ltd, 1970

2. Edwards, Bryan, The History, Civil and Commercial of the British Colonies in the West Indies, 4th edition, Vol. 1, John Stockdale, London, 1807

3. Fabel, Robin F.A, Colonial Challenges: Britons, Native Americans and Caribs 1759-1775, University Press of Florida, 2000.

4. Fraser, Adrian,Chatoyer (Chatawae) National Hero of St.Vincent and the Grenadines, Galaxy Print Ltd., 2002

5. Gonzalez, Nancie, Sojourners of the Caribbean- Ethnogenesis and Ethnohistory of the Garifuna, University of Illinois Press, 1988.

6. Goveia, Elsa, A Study on the Historiography of the British West Indies to the end of the 19th Century, Instituto Panamericano De Geografia E Historia, Mexico, 1956

7. Hulme, Peter and Whitehead, Neil (ed). Encounters with Caribs from Columbus to the Present Day – An Anthology, Clarendon Press, 1992

8 .Joseph, E. L, Warner Arundell- The Adventures of a Creole, University of the West Indies Press, Mona, 2001. (Originally published, London: Saunders and Otley, 1838.)

9. Marshall, Bernard, "The Black Caribs- Native Resistance to British Penetration into the Windward Side of Saint Vincent- 1763- 1773", Caribbean Quarterly, Vol. 10, No. 4, December, 1973

10. Moore, Richard, Caribs and Human Relations, Pathway Publishers, New York, 1972

11 .Shephard, Charles, An Account of the Island of Saint Vincent, Frank Cass, 1977 (originally, London, Nicol, 1831)

12. Young, Sir William, An Account of the Black Charaibs in the Island of Saint Vincent- with the Charaib Treaty of 1773 and other original documents- compiled from the papers of Sir William Young, Frank Cass and Co. Ltd, 1971. (First published 1795)

Dr. Adrian Fraser is Director of the University of the West Indies Continuing Education Centre (Open Campus) in St. Vincent and the Grenadines.

2. EDGAR JULIAN DUNCAN
By
Baldwin King

The following article is based on an interview I had with Dr. Edgar Julian Duncan on July 4, 2008 at his home in Trinidad and Tobago.

What causes me great concern now is our education system, which is training children to learn facts, but not to think. The students are very good at learning facts, but understanding concepts causes them great difficulty. Something has gone wrong... They are pumped with information and are not allowed to think for themselves. I think some of the exam types, multiple choice, for example, do not allow for developing their ability to synthesize. I think multiple choice serves a certain purpose, a quick test, but I don't think it should be part and parcel of a final exam.

Those are the words of one of the Caribbean's leading science educators - Dr. Edgar Julian Duncan.

Edgar Julian Duncan was born in Kingstown, St. Vincent and the Grenadines on December 9, 1933. His parents were Alphonse Duncan and Elaine Duncan nee Porter; they had five other children - Jean, Greta, Lennox (deceased), Hayden and Hildred (deceased).

Julian started his primary education at what one would today call a kindergarten run by Miss Jennie Jacobs. From there, he went to the Anglican Primary School. He later spent some time at the Roman Catholic Primary School. Eventually he moved to Miss Louise John's private school on Bay Street.

Among the primary school teachers he remembers fondly were Miss Lucille Cato (later Mrs. Eustace) who taught him at the Anglican School, Miss Norma Kirby who taught him at the Roman Catholic School as well as Sister Edna, an Irish nun who is still alive and living in Trinidad. In the John school, he was taught principally by Miss Louie John.

The Anglican School and to a lesser extent, the Roman Catholic School, in those days were very strong on discipline. As children, they were very firmly disciplined. This was not abusive discipline; one was taught to toe the line. This served him in good stead in his later life. At Miss John's school, the atmosphere was a little more relaxed, but still, she was herself a disciplinarian. Discipline was not a problem for Julian because he came from a home where discipline was the watchword. His father was quite a strong disciplinarian.

He remembers very little of his primary school days, apart from the fact that he thoroughly enjoyed it.

For his secondary school education, Julian attended the Boys' Grammar

School (BGS). He arrived there in January1945 at the age of 11 and left in 1953. During his sojourn there, W. M. Lopey was the headmaster. Some of his teachers there were Mr. Harley Moseley who taught Latin and Mathematics and Mr. Crick, who also taught Mathematics. Then there was Mr. J L Eustace (Sir Lambert Eustace) who had a tremendous influence on his students. He was unorthodox, but very effective, in his method of teaching. Julian remembers that when he took the Cambridge School Certificate exams, everybody passed English, which was taught by J. L. Eustace.

Julian says that his secondary school career was not particularly stellar. He was indifferent to learning and claims his performance was very inconsistent in that he skipped a form but he also repeated two forms. However he did pick up some prizes, two of which were important: the Junior Old Boy's Prize awarded for overall performance at the fourth form level, awarded by the Old Boys Association and the Blackman Memorial prize which was awarded for the best performance in Geography at the School Certificate level He thinks at that time, his attitude to learning was all wrong. He says:

"I disliked some subjects because of who taught them. Take for example, Latin. I remember getting 4% in a Latin exam because I disliked the subject I hated it because of the way it was taught and who taught it. On the other hand I just did well in the, subjects that I enjoyed,."

Unlike many school boys, Julian did not play cricket at BGS. He did play House football as a member of Orange house. However, after he left school, one of the masters who had come from Trinidad, Eugene Moore, started badminton and Julian took up badminton in a serious way. .He continued to play the game through university days and when he went to the University of the West Indies in Trinidad as a Lecturer, he continued to play badminton, even at the competitive level.

Julian was a cadet in BGS, achieving the rank of Lance Corporal in the Cadet Corps. His first cadet officer-in-charge was Mr. Ali from Trinidad and then Mr. Eugene Moore. He was also a scout. His first scoutmaster was Mr Rupert John (later Sir Rupert John) followed by Mr. Norris (Toby) Antoine

In BGS, apart from English, Julian liked science subjects and excelled in those areas. That laid the foundation for his future life as a scientist.

Julian did not go to university right after Grammar School. Instead he taught for four years in St. Vincent before embarking on his university education. He taught for a term at the Grammar School. Then he went to the Emmanuel High School where he taught for a year. He then returned to the Grammar School where he taught mainly Geography.

Then in 1957, Julian began his tertiary education by enrolling at the

University College of the West Indies (UCWI) as it was then called, at Mona, Jamaica. He had hoped at the time to study Geography, but Geography was not offered. So he ended up doing Chemistry, Botany and Zoology as his first year subjects and majored in Botany and Zoology in his finals in 1960.

From the point of view of his undergraduate years, two experiences stand out in his mind. One was that his self confidence was boosted because he met scholarship winners from different islands of the Caribbean at UCWI and although he did not consider himself scholarship material, he found that he was able to keep pace with the island scholars.

. Secondly he discovered at university something that is difficult to articulate. He encountered two types of students which he categorizes as bright or intelligent. The difference is that the bright ones are good learners and can perform well on certain exams. However the intelligent ones think and when one gets to university, one begins to see the difference. Given a problem to solve, many of the learners seem to have difficulty with it, whereas people who think, rather than learn by rote, seem better able to deal with the problem. In his lecturing career, he has seen it. Some students who enter with good A levels seem not to perform as well as some who do not have similarly good A levels. But when one looks at them carefully, one realizes that some the latter are really intelligent. They think outside of the box, and are good at problem solving.

Julian topped the class of his final year at UCWI and was awarded the first Sir James Irvin Memorial Scholarship to do post graduate work. Sir James Irvin was the chairman of the committee set up to look into the establishment of the UCWI. He was principal of St. Andrews University in Scotland. Sir Harold Mitchell endowed a scholarship in Sir James' memory. Julian was awarded the first scholarship which took to him to St. .Andrews in September 1960. The scholarship was for a two year period so Julian was registered for an M.Sc., but after two terms his supervisor had his registration upgraded to the Ph. D. He left St. Andrews in August 1963, two years and ten months after he began his studies there, having completed the PhD in Botany. Julian always liked Botany. It was always one of his favorite subjects. So when he got to Mona, he enjoyed it even more because it was more expansive and intriguing than at Secondary school level.

About his postgraduate days at St. Andrews, he thinks those were among some of his happiest days in that he was involved in something in which he was truly interested. The problem he worked on was one of trying to solve the intricacies of nuclear division in fungi. This was something that had apparently been worked on by many biologists for years and yet there were differences of opinion about what really occurred during nuclear division   The title of his thesis was "A Study on Marasmius androsaceus (L. ex Fr.)Fr. and M, rotula (Scop. Ex Fr) Fr.". Some significant results came from this work. For example Julian was able to advance a theory on how the nucleus of the fungi divided. Dr. Carl Lindgren, emeritus professor from Southern Illinois University in commenting on the work wrote:

'For the last forty years I have studied the division of the fungal nucleus and I have recently written a book on this subject. I devote a large share of one chapter to Dr. Duncan's work on his theory of the nature of nuclear division in fungi. I believe that his solution to this problem is definitive.'

And, as Lindgren has said, this was done at a time when certain fancy bits of equipment were not available. Lindgren thought it was quite commendable that, with what was available, Julian was able to accomplish so much. That theory is still very much in existence at this time but Julian believes there might have been modifications because it seems now that the theory is specific to a certain group of fungi.

After his Ph.D., he was offered a post at St. Andrews, which he actually accepted, but turned it down the day he got a cable from Mona informing him that they were offering him a position at UWI. So his first job proper after his PhD was at UWI in St. Augustine. He got there in October 1963 as the only botanist in the then developing College of Arts and Sciences. He was put into a department with agricultural botanists. Because he was the only pure botanist, he was given just about every botany course to teach. So he has taught everything in Botany except Plant Physiology and Plant Pathology..

Julian was able to continue his research on fungi at UWI but after 1975, he changed his research focus because the dean was of the opinion that his research was rather academic and had very little practical applicability. Julian disagreed but he decided he would change the focus somewhat. He still dealt with fungi as organisms, but he went into their histopathology, looking at the pathological effects, from an anatomical point of view, that fungi had on plants during the diseased state. One of his first research students worked on Witches Broom disease which affects cocoa. They found that the fungus existed in two phases:. a monokaryotic phase in which the cells of the mycelium possess one nucleus and a dikaryophase, in which the cells contain two. In the earlier phase the organism is parasitic and eventually kills the parts of the plant infected. It then converts to the dikaryophase which is saprophytic and lives on the dead tissue nuclei. .

Now, he wanted to maintain the monokaryotic phase and that can be maintained only on living tissue. So he thought it would be useful if they could produce calluses. In 1975, Julian got a Deutsche Akademische Austauschdienst Dienst (DAAD) Fellowship to Freie Universitat, Berlin, Germany to upgrade his knowledge of plant tissue culture with the intention of coming back to UWI and working on Witches Broom disease. However after leaving Germany, he went to Reading University in Britain on a lectureship exchange and lectured there until September 1976. While at Reading, he introduced a course in tissue culture.

On his return to St. Augustine in October 1976 he started a program in plant tissue culture. Part of the goal was to train Caribbean nationals to become proficient in plant regeneration initially, then plant transformation. Not with exogenous genes, but through somaclonal variation and selection from variants developed on media in which there was pressure for selection of a particular characteristic. For example, one can select for tolerance to high salt levels in the soil or tolerance to herbicides. The process involves regenerating plants from pieces of tissue of a donor plant. There is no genetic homogeneity in plant cells (at least about 5% of cells are not of the same genetic type as all the others) and it is possible to exploit this heterogeneity. One does not know what those cells will necessarily express under certain conditions. They might express a characteristic that is valuable. Under a specific pressure, a cell that is competent to exist under this pressure could be the progenitor of a regenerated plantlet in the system, which .will then have the capacity to survive under the particular pressure.. So that if you put herbicide in the medium, most of the cells would die, but if some survive then they will be resistant to herbicide. In addition, mutagenesis was used to obtain variants. For example, banana meristems were treated with either chemical or physical mutagens and the plantlets regenerated were then tested for resistance to Moko Disease. Those were the initial stages of the programme during which he was able to train some ten students at the post graduate level, three to PhD level in this area.

In 1980, Julian then received a fellowship from the International Atomic Energy Agency (IAEA) in Geneva to go to Brazil for a six week training course where he did some more work in tissue culture. Having, in a sense, become adept in regeneration and the production of variants , the next step was to get into genetic engineering of these plants. So a young member of staff who was a plant breeder was sent to the Scripps Institute in the USA to bone up on certain aspects of molecular biology. When he returned, he was asked to spearhead the approach to genetic engineering. However to date a lot of success has not been achieved in this area for certain practical constraints. None the less the work in that area has continued and is progressing slowly but surely as additional expertise in the area has been recruited.

Julian was instrumental in setting up the UWI Biotechnology Research Program, initially with a grant of TT$150,000,00 from the National Institute of Higher Education, Research, Science and Technology (NIHERST) of Trinidad and Tobago.

Julian has served as the National Coordinator of the Organization of

American States (OAS) Multinational Project in Biotechnology in Trinidad. He also served as the Trinidad and Tobago representative on the board of the International Center for Genetic Engineering and Biotechnology based in Italy and has attended meetings in Trieste, Italy and New Delhi, India, where there are branches of the Institute.

On another area I asked Julian what were his thoughts about the relative importance of teaching versus research and whether he had a preference for one or the other. He replied:

No, not really, but I think that the teaching has been more effective than the research from the point of view of the numbers of students with whom you deal. I have taught more students, as you'd expect, than I've supervised. in research. So that I think I have had greater influence in the undergraduate area than the postgraduate area although I'm quite satisfied with my postgraduate students.

Apart from teaching, Julian had been heavily involved in administration, serving on various university committees He was Head of the Department of Biological Sciences from 1976-79 and Head of the new Department of Life Sciences from 1991-98. He achieved the rank of Professor in 1990.

As a result of his excellent leadership of the department, he was awarded the Vice Chancellor's Award for Excellence in Teaching and Administration in 1994. For his pioneering work in plant tissue culture, he received a life achievement award in agriculture from NIHERST in 2000. .

He was named an icon in Science and Technology in Trinidad as well as a Caribbean Icon in Science, Technology and Innovation (Another Vincentian, Dr. Cecil Cyrus, was also named a Caribbean icon for his work in Medicine)

Julian has supervised a number of students at the postgraduate level. He has supervised some ten students in tissue culture, two in floral biology, two in pathology and one in anatomy. He has co-supervised (with Dr. Pathmanathan Umaharan) two persons, one doing work with cocoa transformation, the other on Anthuriums

. He was also deputy dean for postgraduate studies in the Faculty of Science and Agriculture. He also served as a Warden of Milner Hall for a period. He was fully involved in University life.

I asked him if he cared for administration, especially vis-à-vis teaching. He replied:

Yes and no. I think there are two aspects of administration that I found, not difficult, but would rather not have done. One, I discovered things about my colleagues that I'd rather not have known. And, the second is, that because you're their friend , they think you mustn't be honest. As head of department, I had to write a confidential report on all members of my staff, which they had to see and sign.. Some persons felt that some of the things I said, I need not have said it. But I feel that, if you're going to be honest, you have to mention not only the person's strong points, but also the weaknesses and point out how you think those weaknesses can be addressed. But, there are people who don't like that because they think you're their friend...

The other thing, when somebody's up for promotion, you have to be really honest, because, it's unfair to someone who gets promotion through honest means and really is deserving of it, if you pad somebody else's resume. It makes you unpopular, but the amusing thing is, when you demit office, they tell you, you should be back with us. The other thing I found, was that a lot of people couldn't understand why I never sought to do anything that was in the best interest of just this section or that section, but the department as a whole. It meant that there were some people who did not agree with the decision because it affected them adversely. But you just can't think of sectional interest, you have to go with what's best for the whole and some people just can't take that..

Julian retired formally from UWI in 1998 and was conferred with the title of Professor Emeritus in 1999. He continues his research in a limited way, and also continues to supervise students. His latest PhD student graduated in 2007. There is a bit of research he started in 1980 and completed after he retired. The material was published in March 2006, being the sole article in a volume of Caribbean Marine Studies. It was a checklist of the marine algae of Trinidad and Tobago. Julian was the senior author with a staff member from the Institute of Marine Affairs as junior author. Students from classes at the University during the 1980s did the illustrations which were of a very high artistic quality. The original drawings are now lodged in the West Indian Section of the Library at the St. Augustine campus of the UWI.

.   Julian has also done a review of *Warszewiczia coccinea*, the national flower of Trinidad and Tobago. He has done a lot of work on its floral biology and some of its pathology and plans to write a monograph on it. He has also done, with his research students, work on a number of food crops such as bananas, breadfruit, cassava, cocoa, dasheen, pigeon peas as well as on ornamental plants.

Some of Julian's work goes beyond the University and this is where Trinidad, Jamaica, and Barbados with UWI campuses have an advantage over the other Caribbean islands. The schools there have drawn quite heavily on university personnel like Julian to give lectures, for example, to their Sixth forms on specialized topics. This is something that always pained Julian in that his native country, St. Vincent and the Grenadines where all his initial formal training was done, has had very little direct benefit from whatever expertise he has to offer. But, in a sense, his involvement with

UWI has been of indirect benefit to St. Vincent.

Julian has served on the board of management of the Caribbean Industrial Research Institute (CARIRI)., the Board of management of the Institute of Marine Affairs (IMA) in Trinidad and Tobago; the Textbook Selection Committee (Trinidad and Tobago); and the Museum Committee. He serves presently as an honorary life member on the board of the Asa Wright Nature Centre, for whom he wrote the book "*A Guide to Wild Flowers of Trinidad and Tobago*". *He has served on the* board for over 30 years, serving as Vice President for a couple of years..

He serves today on the advisory board of the Environmental Studies Committee of the College of Science, Technology and Applied Arts of Trinidad and Tobago (COSTAATT) and on the Advisory Committee on Environmental Education of the Cropper Foundation.

Next I asked Julian about his religious background and his views on religion. Julian is an ardent Methodist. He has taught Sunday School and was superintendent of the Sunday school at Tunapuna for 33 years. He was, until recently, a property steward at the church and does a devotional session with the Women's League of the church on the first Monday of every month. I asked Julian what he thought might have been the effect on his personality from all that churchgoing. He replied:

I feel the discipline that my father enforced, plus my religious leanings, taught me to know just when to pull the reins when I was abroad on my own. I had a sense that if things were going too far, I should pull the reins.

Theologians/preachers he admired included Rev. J .B Broomes who was a Methodist Minister and a very humble man despite his great prowess in preaching. And then there was a Dominican by the name of William Whatty who was the minister of the church he attended when he went to Trinidad. He was very influential in Julian's religious life.

I asked Julian how he felt about politics and especially about Caribbean politics. He replied:

I'm concerned about the political situation. I live in Trinidad and Tobago, therefore, the politics of Trinidad would affect me more than that of any other place. What disturbs me about politics in Trinidad is that it's heavily polarized based on race. I find the politicians tend to behave immaturely in that, an opposition party opposes, regardless of the issue. They seem to think that they're there to oppose. I do not belong to a particular party I don't vote for a party; I vote for the person in my constituency from whom I think I will get best representation. You know, Eric Williams is supposed to have said that if you put a crappo up in a PMN area, people will vote for it. I vote for the person I feel will best represent the constituency, which is probably not the best approach. In the next to last elections a new party emerged, the Congress of the People and I had great hopes for that party because they seem to be trying to embrace both ethnic groups and in their campaign dealt with issues, pointing how they intended addressing them.. Apart from that, they had some fresh ideas, but they did not win a seat because people are ingrained in this tribal voting. I think in Trinidad now, we have to get away from the concept of maximum leader. I think this is one of our greatest problems now.

I went on to ask Julian how he would label his political philosophy - social democrat, conservative, progressive…He replied:

I'm not Conservative. I would say I am leaning towards Social Democrat... I see too many governments concerned only about themselves and their supporters and not the people as a whole. For example, take here in Trinidad. Trinidad is a very rich country, yet you have the rich and you have the poor. And there are things the poor cannot afford, like good health care. The public health leaves a lot to be desired and the transport system likewise. The education system need to be revamped The government talks about developed status by 2020. To me, developed status means having a good education system, health, housing, and nobody should be below the poverty level. I know we will always have the poor, but nobody should be living below a subsistence level. And I'm not seeing that happening. There are lots of promises made but little follow through.

I asked if there are any political leaders that he admired in Trinidad and Tobago or the wider Caribbean. He said:

I wouldn't say leaders, I would say there are some politicians I admire. And one of these is Keith Rowley because he stands up for what he considers to be right. And, he has suffered for it. Now, I admire somebody who is prepared to put his head on a block for what he believes in, regardless of the consequences. I admire such people.

I asked Julian about his hobbies and he informed me that he is a wood-worker who makes all of his own furniture. He finds it satisfying, therapeutic and of course it saves money. And you get exactly what you want, not what is there to be sold. In that context, I asked what he thought about merging academic learning with vocational skills in terms of making the person a more holistic person, so to speak. He replied:

I feel that it's sad when I see somebody devoting his total life and being to academia. I've seen too many of my colleagues retire and in a sense

19

vegetate because they have no other interests. Their interests (academic matters) have, in a sense, pulled away from them on retirement. I think there must be a blend and you must have some interests other than just academic, whatever that interest may be.

My last question to Julian was: "If you can encapsulate your philosophy of life, what would that be? What is the recipe for a good, successful life as you visualize it?" He believes, first of all, that you should say only that which you are not ashamed to admit later. Secondly, you should live as honestly as you can, so that you can look every man straight in the face. And thirdly, you should do everything to the best of your ability. He does not believe in the word "can't". His wife jokingly tells him that this was conceit. But he says you shouldn't say I can't do this or that. Instead you should recognize you just haven't tried hard enough. You might not do it perfectly but with effort, you'll get it done.

Julian married the former Ann Isabel O'Neill - a Trinidadian with Vincentian connections - in 1965. The union produced three daughters: Elspeth Blanche; Kathryn Angela and Vanessa Julie-Ann. Ann and Julian are blessed with one grandson, Liu.

When the youngest of the girls was 8, Ann returned to the world of work and was employed at the then Department of Extra-Mural Studies until her retirement in 2001.

Elspeth studied English at the St. Augustine campus of the University of the West Indies (UWI), after which she completed an M. Phil. in Criminology at the University of Cambridge (UK). Unable to find employment that would allow her to use her training in Criminology, she went into the world of advertising where she was able to put her creative talents to good use. After a few years with leading advertising firms in Trinidad, she branched out on her own and is now a multi-media artist producing, music and videos. She won an award in a Commonwealth-wide competition for the production of a video on Education.

Kathryn studied French and Linguistics at the UWI (St. Augustine), subsequent to which she obtained an M. Phil., in Library Studies at the Mona campus of the same Institution. She has been working with the Inter-American Institute for Cooperation in Agriculture (IICA) for the past 10 years, where she is the Information Specialist. Her fluency in both French and Spanish has been an asset to her in that capacity.

Vanessa joined the staff at the St. Augustine campus of the UWI, first in the office of Admissions, but is now an Admissions Assistant in the School of Graduate Studies with responsibility for M. Phil.. and Ph. D candidates across the faculties.

To sum up, Professor E. Julian Duncan has had an illustrious career as a lecturer, researcher and administrator at the University of the West Indies.

He has also played a significant role in the growth of the agricultural sector especially of Trinidad and Tobago. It is fitting that we should pay tribute to this native of St. Vincent and the Grenadines for his outstanding contributions to science education and research.

Dr. Baldwin King is a chemical educator and researcher. He is Professor Emeritus and Research Professor of Chemistry at Drew University in New Jersey, USA.

Caribbean Trailblazers: St. Vincent and the Grenadines

3.   **JOSEPH LAMBERT EUSTACE**
                                    By
                              Ann Eustace

INTRODUCTION

The gods were profligate with their gifts on that day in 1908 when Joseph Lambert Eustace came into the world. Seldom are so many of what we usually think of as disparate abilities combined in a single individual.

With his intellectual endowment, he could have been an architect or engineer, a lawyer or doctor, an aviator or mariner. Circumstances dictated that he follow his father into teaching and preaching. In those days teaching was a vocation not a career. In those days young men thought about where they could best make a contribution to society rather than what is the quickest way to "make a dollar". The children of privilege (as some would have it) were brought up to recognize that this position carried with it responsibilities and duties.

He was known variously as "JL" by his associates and colleagues, as "Parkie" by family and friends and as "Poose" to his numerous students.

He devoted the first 25 years of his adult life to teaching, concentrating on preparing succeeding generations to take advantage of the gradually expanding range of opportunities in various professions. In many respects ahead of his time, he was an advocate of lifelong learning and was one of the most widely-read men of his generation. He was always ready to engage in discourse on a wide variety of topics. Consequently he was in great demand as an orator and attained renown as an inspiring speaker.

Although decidedly authoritarian, he took a surprisingly enlightened view of the equality of the sexes. He believed in the equality and brotherhood of man (as befits one with French ancestry) as well as respect for all men – but particularly those who agreed with him. He was a man of strong opinions which were always vehemently expressed.

His career after teaching progressed through business management, entrepreneurship and politics, culminating in his appointment as Governor-General in 1985. He, however, would not have deemed that his crowning achievement.

In all things he was guided by the Word of God and was by and large faithful to His commandments, rare though this may be in preachers and politicians alike. His quick temper was well-known and he was subject to periodic outbursts of rage.

In general he defied stereotyping, being at once a traditionalist and a non-conformist. Some of his teaching methods were decidedly unorthodox. He was a thinker and talker as well as a doer; a man of intellect who was never ashamed to work with his own two hands.

He was proud of the various strands of his lineage and heritage but saw himself essentially as a Caribbean man and he remained committed to the cause of Caribbean integration throughout his life.

ANTECEDENTS/FAMILY BACKGROUND

Like many West Indians the Eustace family can trace its roots back to both Europe and Africa. There are indications that the Eustace line originated in France (where the name is spelled "Eustache") and migrated to England. Details are sketchy regarding the move from England to the Caribbean but it is known that JL's grandfather, Ashton Eustace came to St.Vincent from Barbados around 1860. Ashton married Sarah Foster and produced one daughter and four sons, the eldest of whom, Massiah, was the grandfather of Arnhim Eustace, and the youngest, Reynold Lambert, was JL's father.

In 1898 Reynold Lambert Eustace was dispatched to the Grenadine island of Mayreau as headteacher of the primary school. There he met and wooed Beatrice Alexandrine St.Hilaire, the daughter of the owner of the island, Paul Henry St. Hilaire. The earliest known St. Hilaire ancestor arrived from France in the wake of the French revolution and settled in Carriacou. His son later purchased the island of Mayreau from the Marquis de L'Isle in the 1820s.

JL Eustace was born on 28 February 1908 at Montrose in St. Vincent. He was the fourth child of Reynold Lambert and Beatrice Alexandrine, being preceded by two sisters and a brother (John Parmenas). Two more sisters and another brother followed.

THE EARLY YEARS, 1908-1926

Joseph Lambert Eustace did not speak very often about the past; he preferred to look always to the future. He had had a very strict, even puritanical, upbringing as father Reynold Lambert was not only a teacher but also a charismatic preacher and leader in the evangelical Christian sect known as the Plymouth Brethren or simply Brethren. The Gospel Hall in Kingstown was where they worshipped. Beatrice Alexandrine had renounced the Catholic faith of her birth after meeting Reynold.

In their household there was little room for frivolity. Calypso and carnival were anathema and even sports were frowned upon. The daughters were virtually cloistered. Yet the Eustace brothers showed quite an aptitude for sports and the young Joseph Lambert had a fondness for pranks which continued into adulthood. He also had a keen sense of humour. But the father's severity was tempered by the warm, spirited devotion of his mother. The family lived at Montrose and Georgetown before acquiring a house at the Quarry (Upper Kingstown). Much of their leisure time revolved around the sea, not only through frequent trips to Mayreau but also on a small sailboat which the boys would sail around the Kingstown harbour.

He attended the Kingstown Preparatory School and later the Boys Grammar School (BGS) from 1920-1925 when Mr. Frederick W. Reeves was headmaster

THE YOUNG ADULT, 1926-1946

JL Eustace grew up somewhat in the shadow of his taller, handsome older brother John Parmenas, known as JP or Parmie. Inevitably there was competition between the two; nonetheless their lives followed a remarkably similar trajectory until the mid-1940s. They both excelled academically at the BGS, both preached at the Gospel Hall; together they founded the Intermediate School where JL succeeded JP as Headmaster, they both moved on to teach at the BGS, married in their 30s and in each case their first child was a daughter.

JL was far and away the more unconventional of the two with a greater intellectual curiosity and had none of JP's austerity of view. It was this curiosity which caused him to become a voracious reader with a quite remarkable collection of books on a wide variety of subjects.

The Intermediate School was founded in 1926 by the Eustace brothers with JP as Headmaster and 12 students. It was initially located at Kingstown Park. It was a bold venture aimed at making secondary education more widely available at a time when the only existing institutions, the Boys Grammar School and Girls High School were both too expensive for most and inadequate to meet the increasing needs of the population. Within a few years as the school expanded rapidly, they moved to the Forester's Court building in Kingstown on the corner of Back St and Murray's Rd and later still to Middle St. premises between the bridge and Egmont St. It eventually took students from Class 4 primary to Form 5 and the Cambridge School Certificate examinations. Their results at the external examinations were outstanding.

When JP left the Intermediate School in 1931 to teach at the BGS, JL took over the running of the school. This is not to say that JP left everything up to him. However after his marriage in 1935, JP began to devote more of his time to missionary activities so that the school became increasingly JL's responsibility. Then in 1941 JL too accepted a teaching appointment at the BGS (JP was by this time pursuing studies in the US) while continuing to oversee the Intermediate School. Gradually over the next decade, Bertram "Timmy" Richards took over the responsibility of managing the Intermediate.

JL's students found him to be a gifted teacher and stern disciplinarian who set out not merely to impart knowledge but to inculcate a love of learning as well as to mould character. His greatest delight was when a student excelled and he was known to reward exceptional performance out of his own pocket. It is also recalled that on more than one occasion he would throw the blackboard eraser...or any other handy object...at a student who seemed inattentive, to recall his wandering mind. He taught almost all of the subjects in the curriculum at various times as needed...from English Language and Literature to French, Mathematics, Geography and Mechanical drawing. Always an innovator, he introduced classes in woodworking at the BGS in the face of opposition from the Barbadian Headmaster, William M. Lopey who felt that the school should be producing academic scholars and not handymen. In other words he believed that the responsibility of a teacher was to form the whole man and not just the mind. He continued to have a keen interest in sports throughout his life being wholeheartedly committed to the British tradition that sports were a vital part of the curriculum. Among his other duties he taught physical education at the BGS and was Housemaster for Green (later Millar) House. Even in his sixties he was rash enough to challenge a former student to a high hurdle contest...at which he was of course bested. He followed cricket avidly and was an excellent chess player becoming National Champion in 1947. He also had an interest in theatre arts...an activity that would have been deplored by his siblings given the association between the theatre and lax morals in Victorian England and her colonies. Many remember the BGS production of Shakespeare's 'As You Like It' in the mid 1940s for which JL was the producer and no doubt set-designer.

Sometime between 1939 and 1941 he designed and built with his own hands (and the help of two loyal assistants in Walter Cummings and Robert Wilson) a solid and spacious stone house on the family property at Montrose and furnished it with mahogany furniture which he also constructed himself. Having completed this, he felt ready for family life and shortly thereafter he married Elaine Harold aged 22 a fellow-teacher and former student at the Intermediate school. In May 1943 a daughter, Elaine Marjorie (called Eppie from the initials Elaine and Parkie) was born. Cutesy nicknames appear to have been something of a family tradition. Tragically his wife died when the baby was just 4 months old and two weeks afterwards his mother also passed away in Mayreau. For the last months of 1943, therefore, he was submerged in grief.

Throughout the 1930s and 40s he continued to preach at the Gospel Hall, but when JP returned from the USA in 1946 there came a rupture in their fellowship with the Brethren. While JP went on to establish his own church in Mesopotamia, JL shunned organized religion thereafter only occasionally worshipping at the Kingstown Methodist Church. It was the beginning of a parting of ways.

THE MATURE MAN - A NEW PHASE, 1946-1966

The five years following 1946 brought a number of significant changes in the life of JL Eustace. First he gave up preaching entirely. However he never gave up speaking as if with God's authority. In April 1947, he embarked on a second marriage, this time to Faustina (Fossie) Gatherer who had been a student at the Intermediate school some 9-10 years earlier, and was then working in the Civil Service. They were devoted to each other. A son, Reynold Lambert Mountbatten (known as Monty) was born in 1948 just one week after the death of his grandfather and namesake. Another daughter, Margaret-Ann, followed in 1952. Rather curiously his second wife, like the first, was a devout Anglican, some 12 years his junior.

JL was very fond of children and doted on his offspring who lacked for nothing that a father could provide. He spent many long hours when he was not making furniture, etching his wife's name into glass-topped tables or making wooden toys, swings, dollhouses and later, the table-tennis board. New sides to his character were constantly emerging and he discovered a fine eye for fashion, often buying for his wife dresses that were invariably a perfect fit and in superb taste. He even enjoyed cooking and baking, presiding in the kitchen whenever the household help disappeared without notice. He took great pride in his bread-making and in later years his guava jelly and callaloo soup were much praised by the many guests at the table. His younger daughter was an especial delight especially when after the age of 8 or so she showed an inclination to spend all her pocket money on books at Robertson's Bookstore or SPCK.

When the children were in their formative years, the day would begin with a family bible-reading and a homily. Although never one to spare the rod, it was not brought into play with undue frequency. While he could never be accused of leniency, his children grew up with a considerable degree of freedom. There was for example no stipulated bedtime...yet discipline was not lacking. Certainly life in JL's household was never dull. He had so many varied interests and his enthusiasm for boats, cars, aeroplanes and machinery of any kind was infectious. It often seemed that he could make just about anything and fix anything that was broken. He regarded anything that was not working as a challenge and not as a chore. At one point his home was a veritable farm with chickens, guinea fowl, ducks, goats, pigs and cows in addition to the dogs and cats. In the 1960s he even built an incubator for hatching eggs. He had at some time purchased an electric hand-engraving tool and for many years was the sole engraver in the country for all sporting trophies, plaques or other awards. It did not occur to him to charge for this service.

In 1951 he finally gave up teaching at the BGS and took up the post of Manager of the Government Cotton Ginnery at Richmond Hill. He, however, continued to teach classes occasionally at the Emmanuel High School which was founded by his brother, JP in 1952. He also arranged tours of the ginnery for groups of BGS students. By this time cotton was already starting to decline as a viable crop and planters were beginning to switch to bananas. The ginnery employed about 60 persons and as a by-product of the cotton which was packed into huge bales for export, the separated cotton seeds were crushed to provide cooking oil for local consumption. Unfortunately in November 1959 the ginnery burned to the ground being full of highly combustible cotton and oil.

Since the government of the time showed no inclination to rebuild that industry and hundreds of acres still remained in cotton cultivation, JL Eustace decided to step into the breach and build a replacement ginnery on his own property at Montrose. So as to make fullest use of the crop, machinery was also installed for producing the cottonseed oil and animal feed. In addition, a soap-making operation was combined with this enterprise and Robert Wilson who had just returned from Aruba was put in charge. Although there was some resurgence of interest in cotton as a cash crop at this time with the introduction of the unique "sea-island cotton" which produced a very fine, silky fabric, there was no sound business plan or economic projection underpinning this venture. It was undertaken with a view to sustaining local agriculture and with the goal of contributing to regional self-sufficiency in the hope that sea-island cotton would find a niche market in Europe. These expectations did not materialize and with the collapse of the short-lived West Indies Federation in 1962, the enterprise was similarly doomed to failure.

Meanwhile, JL had decided to build another house on his beachfront lot at Indian Bay which he had purchased from Syl DeFreitas in the late 1950s. He designed this one in the shape of an aeroplane and set about constructing it in 1964-65, again doing much of the work himself. Although he was looking forward to living near the sea, he allowed his brother-in-law to occupy the house upon his return to St. Vincent in early 1966.

Also in the mid-1960s, a group of mostly younger men with whom he had sporadically discussed philosophical or metaphysical subjects coalesced into a study group which met regularly at his house. After 1967, somewhat different groups came to the house and the subject would be politics.

FORAY INTO POLITICS, 1966-1974

As the year 1965 unfolded, the St. Vincent Labour Party (SVLP) was looking ahead to the next general election which was due in 1966 and began sounding out new faces for its slate of candidates in an attempt to defeat the populist People's Political Party led by then Chief Minister, Ebenezer Theodore Joshua. It is beginning to look as though whenever political leaders in St. Vincent feel the need to add lustre to a jaded party, they turn to a Eustace. The initial overtures were rejected out of hand, given that JL had never seen himself in the role of politician and his family was unanimously opposed to the idea. Eventually after several months of pleading and ego massage, he made the decision that he could advance the development of the country through the political arena. In some sense it meant returning to familiar roles of preacher and teacher, except with a rather different text. Moreover it would chime with his fondness for laying down the law. Still, his bluntness and the directness with which he expressed himself were not assets to a politician.

At any rate he duly became a member of the SVLP, agreed to run in the South Leeward constituency and took to the campaign trail with gusto. His family having resigned themselves to supporting this new endeavour, frequently accompanied him to political rallies all over the country. With his skill at oratory, he was under pressure to appear at meetings in every constituency as the featured speaker.

Coincidentally, James Fitz-Allen (Son) Mitchell returned to Bequia in January 1966 from his studies in Canada, determined to enter the political fray. He made sure to visit his former teacher early on to pay his respects and to discuss his plans and ideas. Soon thereafter, Mitchell was drafted into the Labour Party as the candidate for the Grenadines seat. The two became firm political allies united both by their vision for the future of the country and their status as newcomers in the party as well as their roots in the Grenadines. Both successfully contested the general election of 22 August 1966 but the SVLP again lost out to the canny Joshua's PPP which held a slender majority of one seat. Thus JL took his place in Parliament on the Opposition benches. The electoral defeat was a bitter blow to Robert Milton Cato, the leader of the SVLP. However after some months of machinations and behind-the-scenes manoeuvering, Sam Slater, the PPP member for North Leeward, crossed the floor, thus bringing down the government. Fresh elections were called in May 1967 and this time the Labour Party won convincingly by 6 to 3. Eustace was named Minister of Education and Health in a cabinet which included R .Milton Cato, James.F. Mitchell, Hudson Tannis, St.Clair Dacon and Levi Latham.

The first order of business for the new government was constitutional talks in London as a prelude to the transition towards Independence. Both

Eustace and Mitchell accompanied Chief Minister Cato to London. Two years later, on 27th October 1969, St. Vincent (henceforth known as the unwieldy St. Vincent and the Grenadines) became an Associated State with the Head of Government, Milton Cato, designated Premier, and the Head of State (Hywel George) formerly known as the Administrator, became the Governor. All matters of administration of the country now rested in the hands of Vincentians except for Foreign Affairs and Defence.

Being in Government transformed JL Eustace from someone who had been a critic and challenger of the system to a defender of the status quo, notwithstanding the differences that rapidly developed between himself and the Premier. It is a blot on the Labour administration that during their tenure a number of books and individuals were proscribed. Moreover, the members of the Educational Forum of the People, a quasi-political grouping of young progressive intellectuals, most of whom had recently returned from university studies, were mercilessly persecuted, largely on grounds of their avowed atheism. Indeed the Public Services Commission was coerced into terminating the employment of two who were teaching at the BGS. Human rights activism was not yet in vogue. It did not augur well for our decision-making potential as an independent state.

Given JL's lack of patience, inability to compromise, intolerance for the peccadilloes and moral lapses of others, it was predictable that relationships within the party grew increasingly strained. Matters came to a head in 1971 when the Premier in a cabinet reshuffle, relieved him of his Ministerial portfolio over the protests of Mitchell and Latham. Not long thereafter, Mitchell also resigned, deciding to contest the 1972 election as an Independent candidate. JL quit the Labour Party and continued to lend vocal support to Mitchell.

By 1970, both JL's younger children were abroad at University and the eldest was suffering from an incurable illness. She died in March 1972. In the meantime his wife had become Executive Director of the St. Vincent Planned Parenthood Association.

The 1972 election resulted in a tie between the two political parties with Mitchell as an Independent holding the balance of power. With Labour forced to eat humble pie, Mitchell emerged as Premier in an alliance with the PPP. JL Eustace was then appointed as Speaker of the House. With Joshua as Finance Minister it was obvious that the centre could not hold for very long and in 1974 the Alliance fell apart when both Joshua and his wife switched their support to the Labour Party. This precipitated another premature election in which the combined PPP-SVLP captured all 12 seats on the mainland. Rather than have Mitchell named as Leader of the Opposition, the Parliament engaged in constitutional chicanery and named Ivy Joshua as Opposition Leader. The farce deepened.

LATE MATURITY, 1975-1988
PHASE 1 – SEMI-RETIREMENT

The summer of 1975 saw further political developments with the birth of the New Democratic party of J.F. (Son) Mitchell. To quote Mitchell himself: "a group of us had got together to put some kind of party structure in place at the home of JL Eustace at Montrose". Although not a member of the new party, JL continued to make appearances on the NDP platform starting with its launching in the Market Square, Kingstown in December 1975. His treatment at the hands of Milton Cato continued to rankle. It had been an unsettling year with his daughter suffering a career-threatening injury in April and he himself hospitalized in June following an altercation with a trespasser. Both spent some time together in Barbados recuperating. For much of 1976 he continued to brood and grew increasingly morose and irascible.

In 1977 JL realized his long-deferred dream of relocating from Montrose to the beachfront home at Indian Bay. He busied himself with the necessary repairs to the house, relaxing with a daily swim. Throughout the 1970's his relations with his brother JP grew more fractious primarily over the question of selling part of Mayreau to which JP was adamantly opposed.

Full independence for SVG came on 27 October 1979 closely followed by a general election on 5th December which returned the SVLP to office. The run-up to the election was marred by violence and even attempts on the lives of Opposition candidates. In the immediate aftermath came the Union Island uprising and the threat of secession by the Grenadines. JL had by now reverted to type, being inclined to side with the rebels – the Grenadines people – with whom he identified.

The election of July 1984 saw a resounding victory for the NDP fielding a slate of mainly newcomers to politics, with James Mitchell becoming Prime Minister – a position he would hold for the next 17 years. The population was thoroughly disenchanted with the SVLP and JL and his family were elated at this triumph of his protégé and former student.

PHASE II - GOVERNOR-GENERAL

In gratitude for his support over the preceding 18 years, Prime Minister Mitchell asked JL to become the country's second Governor-General. After careful consideration, JL agreed and was sworn in on February 1985 replacing Sir Sydney Gun-Munro. It was not without regrets that he moved into Government House. He chafed at not being allowed into the kitchen, which the staff considered unthinkable although they were much amused at the idea. It was typical of JL that he declined to go to Buckingham Palace to receive his KCMG from the Queen. He and his wife did, however, attend the wedding of HRH Prince Andrew in July 1986, returning via the USA. HM the Queen and HRH Prince Philip paid a visit to SVG in September 1985 on the royal yacht Brittania; and in 1987 HRH Prince Edward visited and was entertained at Government House.

As time went on, however, Sir Lambert began to find life at Government House too restrictive. He missed his freedoms, informal interactions, going into town and the sound of the sea. Moreover, on occasion the Prime Minister tended to usurp the prerogatives of the Governor-General and consequently friction developed between the longtime allies. JL was always a stickler for correct procedure and was not inclined to bend the rules, or to turn a blind eye when others did so. He therefore resigned the post in February 1988 after serving just 3 years.

THE TWILIGHT YEARS, 1988-1996

At 80 years of age, JL was still vigorous, active, mentally alert and combative. He still did the grocery shopping and the Sunday cooking. Regrettably there were no grandchildren but he and his wife 'adopted' the many children in the neighbourhood in an effort to fill that void. He did not begin slowing down somewhat until 1994. In August 1996 he was hospitalized with bronchitis/pneumonia. Three months later, after a second hospitalization, he died at home of pulmonary edema.

He is best remembered for his contribution to broadening both the reach and the scope of education in St. Vincent; as someone who pushed his students to the highest standards of excellence; as an orator and an exemplar; and for his erudition. More a patriot than a politician, he lifted the level of political discourse, was an advocate for regional integration and contributed to the development of tourism in the Grenadines. Without a doubt he served his country well.

ACKNOWLEDGEMENTS

The author would like to express gratitude to the many people who provided information about the influence of JL Eustace in their lives or otherwise assisted with this endeavour. These include Dr. Edgar Adams, Bertram Arthur, Sir Frederick Ballantyne, Agnes Cato, Dr. Cecil Cyrus, Grace Eustace, Syd Hazell, Yvonne Harold, June Phills, Edmund Sealey, Elsa Velox, Winston Venner, Douglas Williams, Eileen Williams.

Dr. Ann Eustace is a retired physician and lives in St. Vincent and the Grenadines.

4.   **JOHN PARMENAS EUSTACE**
By
Vin Samuel

A Most Unlikely Vincentian Hero

At the dawn of the 20th century, St. Vincent and its satellite Grenadines existed primarily to produce food and fiber for export to England. The population, a majority of whom descended from African slaves, worked as laborers on plantations/estates owned and operated by descendants of European settlers. As a subject people, not afforded the benefits of British citizenship, the masses had limited exposure to opportunities for educational development beyond rudimentary arithmetic, reading and writing. Brawn rather than brains was essential to field work. It was in this environment that a son, John Parmenas (JP) Eustace, was born to Reynold and Beatrice Eustace in Mayreau on December 17, 1905. Through faith in God, self-sacrifice, a penchant for hard work and the desire to serve God and country, the young Eustace made a marked difference in human resource development and the socio-economic advancement of his homeland.

While a student at The St. Vincent Boys Grammar School (BGS), J.P. accepted Jesus Christ as his savior. This meant that he could "do all things through Christ who was his strength". Consequently, following the example of the apostles, Eustace took on the arduous task of an evangelist and Sunday school teacher. At some point, he had an epiphany: It was not enough to teach others about the Christian life. A person needs spiritual, physical and academic education. Therefore, after graduation from the Boys Grammar School with high honors in the overseas examination and serving two years in the civil service, J.P. Eustace decided to take on a monumental challenge – investing in the creation of the first private secondary school on the island. Thus, in 1926 the Intermediate High School was born. To appreciate the significance of this bold decision in the history of St. Vincent and the Grenadines we need to consider the following:

1. When the Intermediate High School opened in 1926, J.P. Eustace was barely 21 years old.
2. The existing Boys Grammar School and The Girls High School served the children of the wealthy landowners and the administrative elites of the island that was a colony in the British West Indies. He had to draw his students from the poor.

3. Eustace had no government, religious institution, or private business entities to sponsor and underwrite the cost of operating a secondary school.

4. While serving as Principal of the Intermediate High School he continued a full regimen of preaching and Sunday school teaching.

5. His brother, Joseph Lambert Eustace, also a Grammar School graduate, was among the few persons he could afford to employ as teachers.

To some people, this venture might have appeared as the "Eustace's Folly". After all, the Eustace brothers appeared to be privileged sons of the Plantocracy and the administrative elite of twentieth century St. Vincent. Being the grandsons of a white plantation owner and the sons of an educated black father, the brothers might have faced some small discomfort among both black and white Vincentians. However, in a class and color conscious society their light skin and Grammar School education positioned them well for employment in the civil service, appointments to political office, or to pursue careers in law, medicine, engineering or other professions favored by the elite class. In fact, Joseph Lambert Eustace went on to become Minister of Education and Governor General of St. Vincent and the Grenadines.

But J.P. Eustace, a man of high intellect and Christian fortitude, had a higher calling. He directed his skills towards the betterment of mankind. It didn't matter whether he had to work 16 hour days, he would give his all to God and country.

At the end of 1930 J.P Eustace left the Intermediate High School (IHS) to become Mathematics Master at the Boys Grammar School. This was the early years of the worldwide economic depression that started in the United States of America in 1929 and spread throughout Western Europe and the rest of the world. Therefore, the financial condition of the Intermediate High School suffered as the ability of parents to pay school fees declined. Consequently, Eustace could have taken the Grammar School job in order to subsidize the operations of the school. At this time, J.L. Eustace became Principal of the IHS.

J.P. Eustace resigned from the Boys Grammar School position in 1935 to expand his religious work. The next year he married a young Canadian missionary, Minnie Hubble, and moved to carry out missionary work in Bequia. Their sojourn on Bequia was fraught with much hardship. This experience contributed to a decision to return to St. Vincent. Grace Eustace, their daughter was born in St. Vincent in 1940.

In 1938, J.P. and Minnie Eustace founded the New Prospect Mission School. This school catered to students who would otherwise have to travel to Mesopotamia or Biabou to attend primary school. And in 1940, they established the Sandy Bay Mission School.

At age 37, Eustace left St. Vincent with his wife and young daughter to study for the Doctor of Optometry degree in Philadelphia, Pennsylvania, USA. But for the Second World War that began when Hitler invaded Poland in 1939, he would probably have gone to London to study. But travel across the Atlantic by ship was quite hazardous at the time. At this time, he turned over the responsibilities for management of the Intermediate High School to Bertram "Timmy" Richards. Later on the school was unofficially called Timmy Richards High School.

On September 14, 1945 Eustace received the Certificate of Optician from the Brooklyn School of Optics and on November 17th of that same year he graduated with the Doctor of Optometry degree from the Philadelphia Optical College. Instead of setting up his practice in the USA, he returned to St. Vincent in 1946. Shortly thereafter, the Eustace Patriarch, Reynold Eustace died and J.P. now affectionately called Doc became executor/manager of the family estate in Mayreau. Additionally, he operated his medical practice, worked as Refractionist at the Kingstown General Hospital and continued his evangelical work. As if this was not enough work for The Doc and his family, J.P. Eustace opened the Emanuel High School in Kingstown in 1952.

The decade beginning with 1951 was a truly transitional period in the history of St. Vincent and Vincentians. Some of the Moyne Commission's [1] recommendations for changes in the British West Indies were implemented; universal adult suffrage was instituted; George Charles and E.T. Joshua emerged as trade unionists and politicians; banana farming was introduced to replace sugar; there was a pressing need for the expansion of elementary and secondary education. This was the dawning of modern life in our homeland as the masses of the people became politically enlightened through involvement in island politics and village councils. Additionally, the move from commercial sugar cane farming to banana farming combined with the infusion of wealth earned by Vincentians who worked in the oil refineries of Aruba, Curacao and Trinidad into the local economy creating a progressive

---

[1] For more on the Moyne Commission see the Life and Times of Dr. John Parmenas Eustace page 77.

climate for education, housing improvements and advancements in small farm ownerships.

Under the banner Nisi Emmanuel Frustra: "Except the Lord Build the house, they labor in vain that build it", the Emmanuel High School, Kingstown came to fruition in April, 1952 (the Easter term). The school opened with only 11 students but grew to be one of the largest institutions of secondary education even after experiencing much problems. By 1960, Doc was looking for space to open another school as the demand for secondary education was too much for the existing schools to accommodate. Every year, applicants were turned away for lack of space.

The Emmanuel High School, Mesopotamia opened its doors in May 1963. Housed on the ground floor of the Marriaqua Community Center, the school was centrally accessible to prospective students in the valley and by foot or bus to outlying areas such as Biabou, Windward Lowmans, Greggs, Chapmans and even as far north as Georgetown, Sandy Bay, Owia and Fancy.

According to its mission statement: "Emmanuel High School exists to help students prepare for a productive, rewarding, and enjoyable life of service in the home, the community, the nation and the world. .. Emmanuel hopes to achieve its objectives by providing an environment where students are motivated to develop academically, physically, spiritually and socially through a course of study in the arts, sciences, humanities, technical and physical education, daily devotional time relating to the study and application of biblical principles, and a variety of opportunities for the development of personal relationships that will enrich life." This was the first secondary school to open in Rural St. Vincent. Under the leadership of Doc Eustace and his daughter Grace, this school grew to be one of the most comprehensive schools in St. Vincent and the Grenadines.

Conclusion

Dr. J.P. Eustace's accomplishments must be seen in the context of the possibilities of twentieth century St. Vincent and British administration of its West Indian colonies. With little financial resources, he made heroic contributions as a preacher, educator and doctor. Through the tireless efforts of Grace Eustace and some devoted partners in Christ, the work started by Dr. Eustace continues to bear fruits in St. Vincent and the Grenadines and elsewhere. But as today's world is a much more complex place than when J.P. Eustace was alive, there is a need to evaluate his contributions and to decide upon strategies that will build upon the basic foundation that now exists. To this end, we must consider the following:

1. How has St. Vincent and the Grenadines advanced since the death of Dr. J. P. Eustace?
2. What innovations were introduced to benefit the citizens?
3. How are we mobilising our education for the common good? It is well and good to have an increasing number of college and university graduates. However, how do we measure the benefits accruing from this knowledge?
4. How do Vincentians wean themselves from an over-reliance on elected officials and foster the entrepreneurial development of the private sector
5. What skills/knowledge/abilities do we need to transform our agricultural economy?
6. What industries must we target in order to develop the economy and create jobs?
7. Do we have the capacity to assemble and market solar panels?
8. Can we develop for-profit educational and health services that will bring in students and clients from overseas?
9. Are there opportunities in sports, music and entertainment than can be exploited for jobs creation in SVG?

These and other initiatives would do homage to the contributions of progressive Vincentian innovators such as Dr. J.P. Eustace.

This article is based on information published on the biography of Dr. J.P. Eustace. You can read the entire biography in the book entitled: The Life and Times of Dr. John Parmenas Eustace by Vin G. Samuel; ISBN1-55395-298-1

Vin G. Samuel is a 1970 graduate of the Emmanuel High School in Mesopotamia. He is a trained economist as well as an attorney and lives in Lawrenceville, New Jersey, USA..

5.   **CIPRIAN BERNARD "CHES" GIBBS**
1910 - 2006[2]
By
Peggy Antrobus

Introduction

At the turn of the 20th Century the islands of the British West Indies were still under colonial rule. The enslaved African population had been emancipated in 1830 and following Abolition in 1834, the Government of Grenada approved schemes to import workers first from Malta and Madeira, Portugal (1839) and later from India (1857). However, living conditions for the majority of the population remained largely unchanged.

For the disenfranchised, education was to be the means of social mobility. At Emancipation the British government provided a grant for the education of ex-slaves that was divided between the Anglican and Methodist churches. In 1857 an Education Act was passed and the Board of Education was chaired by the Lieutenant-Governor himself. It prescribed the establishment of a Boys' Grammar School (BGS) and a Girls' Grammar School, both for the education of middle and upper class children. It also prescribed the establishment of "a Model School for the training of teachers, and a Normal School for children of the lower classes whose parents wished to educate them."(Steele, 2003:207). (a normal school was for the training of elementary school teachers)

The first Principal of the BGS, Mr. John J. Noble, "viewed the elementary school teacher as an "agent of social change" and an "instrument of progress", though he was of the opinion that the middle and upper classes saw the role of the teacher as simply to instill in their pupils a respect for authority and for the status quo (and) regarded it as a mistake to educate the lower classes, as they thought that this would make them averse to estate labour, and make them ambitious to improve themselves." (ibid, 207- 208).

By 1900, there were three (private) secondary schools on the island – the St .Joseph's Convent, the St .Georges Girls High School and the St. Georges Grammar School (SGGS). SGGS was taken over by the government and opened as **The Grenada Boys' Secondary School** (GBSS) on September 11, 1911. The first Headmaster of the GBSS was Mr. Hallam Massiah. All teachers were European and the pupils were either white or coloured children of parents of "moderate means"; wealthier parents sent

---

[2] He would have celebrated his 100th birthday this year.

their children to school in England or Barbados. The curriculum was based on that of English schools and was so divorced from the reality of the pupils as to foster a "mistaken cultural identity". Indeed, "many Grenadians at this time believed that they were British in exile regardless of their ancestral origins.... The aim of the aspiring middle classes was to be as British as possible" (Steele pp. 261-262)

An Island Scholarship was instituted in 1916, providing for 3–4 years of training at a university in Europe, Canada or the USA. Selection was based on the results of the Senior Cambridge Exam and the winner had to pass with honors and in those subjects that would exempt him (only boys qualified) from the London Matriculation. But the scholarship was seen to reward more than the winner: "the benefits will best be seen in the dominating incentive given to make school life a serious affair all round, thus serving to build up for Grenada a studentry (sic) worthy of the colony, and ensuring for us men better qualified to take up positions in various spheres of local activity" (an editorial in The West Indian newspaper for April 2, 1916, quoted in Steele, 2003:256).

The series of riots across the West Indies in the 1930s, described as "an age of revolutionary nationalism within the colonized world" (Beckles op.cit.), led to the establishment of a West India Royal Commission to investigate social and economic conditions in [its colonies] ... and to make recommendations. The composition of Royal Commissions reflected the significance of the matter under investigation, therefore the fact that this Commission was a high-powered one headed by a member of the aristocracy, Lord Moyne, and including members of parliament and leading academics, indicated the seriousness with which the British government viewed the riots. They could not allow events in the Caribbean to get out of hand and serve as encouragement to restless populations in other parts of the British Empire. Although according to Beckles (op.cit. p.33) "Public relations success rather than social and economic development were paramount on the agenda of the Colonial Office at this time,"[iii] the Commission nevertheless made a major impact on the countries of the Caribbean and set a pattern of socio-economic development that shaped policy-making and practice for decades to come. Its recommendations were taken seriously by the British government and implementation ensured by the enactment of a Colonial Development and Welfare Act (1939).

The Report shone a light on colonial education and the extent to which it created a class structure that served to maintain the status quo of colonialism is graphically described by Barbadian novelist, Austin Clarke in his classic, *Growing-up Stupid Under the Union Jack* and by scholars such as Eric

Williams (1950) and Kathleen Drayton (2009). Primary school education was intended for a disciplined and compliant working class, while secondary education, based on a British classical education, aimed at creating an elite that would work alongside the colonial administration to govern the colony. When the process of 'de-colonization' started, no doubt prompted by declining profits from sugar and increasing costs of administering the colonies, the new educated elite was ready to take over from their colonial masters. Bernard Gibbs was among these.

Ciprian Bernard Gibbs: The Early Years

Widely known as "Ches"[iv], Ciprian Bernard Gibbs was the first child of Matilda and Thomas Gibbs of St.Georges, Grenada, and one of 9 children. As was typical of these islands, Matilda and Thomas were the offspring of mixtures of African, European and Indian racial groups.

Thomas Gibbs' grandparents were teachers [v] and education was highly valued in this family. At the Grenada Boys Secondary School (GBSS) Bernard was one of the brightest students. His studies included British History, Geography, English and English Literature, Mathematics and Latin. He also excelled in sports and engaged in a number of extra curricula activities including the cadet corps and coaching the netball team of the Anglican Girls' High School.

Bernard sat for the Island Scholarship three times (1925, 1926 & 1927) and came second on each occasion. This probably says less about his academic abilities than about his priorities! As a result, he never went to university. In those days, there were none of the opportunities available to bright young minds as there are today. Failure to win an island scholarship meant the loss of opportunity to attend university, unless your parents had the resources. After failing at his second attempt, therefore, Bernard became a teacher and a housemaster[vi] at the GBSS before joining the staff of the Customs Department in 1935.

According to some of his students, he was an excellent teacher. One of them, Lamuel Stanislaus, a former Grenadian Ambassador to the UN, wrote in a testimonial to him in 2000:

As a student...I profited immensely from his tutorial, counseling and athletic skills. I credit Mr. Gibbs among others for much of what I have accomplished in my boyhood, adolescence and manhood.

Mr. Stanislaus was not alone. Bernard Gibbs continued as a 'teacher' outside the classroom and helped the careers of many young men in his time. One of these, Vincentian Sir Fred Phillips, who went on to an illustrious career in the public services of many countries in the region, wrote of him as follows:

I remember with particular affection one of my superior officers, Bernard Gibbs, a Grenadian with a robust personality... He was very well-read, well-spoken, competent and thorough, but never reached the heights he should have attained in the administrative field... I learnt a great deal from him (1991:15, Phillips, Heinemann, Kingston)

The Family

In 1935, Bernard married Kathleen Lucille Comissiong, another Grenadian of mixed parentage. Her mother was from Scottish ancestry and her father the grandson of an Italian sail-maker, Comissione, and an African woman. They had five children: Peggy, Betty, Tony, Jenny and June[vii], all but June, were born in Grenada. A sixth child, Tommy, was born after Bernard ended his marriage to Kathleen.

His relationship with his family was complex: he was a wonderful father paying as much attention to the physical care of his children as to their social and intellectual development, surrounding them with books, music and interesting people from whom they learned about the world beyond the boundaries of the Caribbean. He instilled in them values of respect for everyone regardless of class, commitment to public service and a work ethic evident in the way they live their lives. He was a great authoritarian and a strict disciplinarian, but never used physical punishment. He inspired their affection, but was sparing with praise for their accomplishments and demanding more of them than he did of anyone else.

The youngest of the children, Jenny and June, died young, murdered by a jealous boyfriend. Peggy won the St. Vincent Island Scholarship in 1953 and went on to obtain a degree in Economics from the University of Bristol, a Certificate in Social Work from the University of Birmingham, and a doctorate in Education from the University of Massachussets, Amherst. Returning to St. Vincent with her husband, Dr. Kenneth Antrobus[viii], in the 1960s, she worked for the Commonwealth Save the Children Fund and later established the Community Development Department for the Milton Cato Administration on the eve of Statehood. For the past 35 years her work has focused on women's rights and development. She lives in Barbados. Tony also lives in Barbados. He was awarded a Colonial Development & Welfare

(CD&W) Scholarship and obtained degrees in Engineering from Queen's University, Belfast; later, a Commonwealth Scholarship led to a postgraduate at the University of Leeds. He is an award-winning expert on wind and earthquake resistant design, and works as a consultant to the Pan American Health Organization specializing in the structures of medical facilities throughout the region. Betty lives in Trinidad. She has had a varied career including working as governess to the children of the Administrator of St.Lucia, a bank clerk, an extra in the film *Island in the Sun*, one of the first coloured air hostesses with British West Indian Airways (BWIA), and as the Personal Assistant to the wife of the Governor-General of the Federation of the West Indies. She has recently published a children's book, *Brown Sugar and Spice*, about their childhood. Tommy, currently lives in New York and takes care of Bernard's 99-year old sister. Longevity is one of the characteristics of this family. There is another sister of over 90-years living in the UK.

The Civil Servant

During most of Bernard's working life, these islands were Crown Colonies, under the control of the Colonial Office. In this period of our history "the Civil Servant existed mainly as a private assistant to an important public official holding office under the Crown. Against this background, it is easy to understand why public officers... were assigned by patronage..." (Iton, 2006:193) A bright young man like Bernard Gibbs, of a certain complexion[ix] and with clear potential for taking leadership was bound to attract the attention of those looking for candidates who could carry forward the legacy of the Colonial Civil Service. Once selected, they were nurtured by those for whom they worked. If they worked diligently they progressed steadily through the ranks of the civil service. In addition to this if, as Bernard did, they exhibited special qualities such as the ability to write and speak with clarity and wit, to be loyal, to dress elegantly and to operate comfortably among the elite, their promotion could be accelerated.

Bernard Gibbs did not remain long at the Customs. He was one of those young men who thrived in this system. Intelligent, personable and efficient he gained the confidence of those for whom he worked and was rewarded with steady promotion. After failing[x] to enlist in the Royal Air Force at the start of World War 11, he was appointed to the post of Confidential Clerk, in St.Lucia in 1943, and spent the war years there. St.Lucia was of strategic importance, not only because of its proximity to the French colonies of Martinique & Guadeloupe, and the presence of a US base, but because its protected deep water harbor made it an ideal coaling station for the ships of the Allies.   From that vantage point, Gibbs witnessed some of the major operations of the Allied Forces and the Germans in this part of the world [xi].

Gaining experience in administration in St.Lucia, he went on to hold a number of senior administrative posts in the colonial governments of St. Vincent and Grenada and with the governor of the Windward Islands[xii] to become one of the first West Indians to serve as the crown's representative – as acting Administrator of St. Vincent and Grenada between 1952-1955.

In 1943 he was transferred to St. Vincent to the post of Chief Clerk and after a brief stint as Chief Clerk to the Government of the Windwards, he was promoted, in 1944, to the post of Government Secretary in the St. Vincent Administration.   In 1946 he was commissioned by the administrator of St. Vincent, Ronald Garvey, to prepare a Development Plan for the Colony (sic). Without any degree or training in economics he produced a document that served as a blueprint for St. Vincent's development in the period 1947 through the 1950s.

The Development Plan

The Plan for the Development of the Colony of St.Vincent (1947-58), which he compiled, was his magnum opus, his pride and joy.   It was part of a series of Plans occasioned by the CD&W Act of 1945 (following the Moyne Commission). The Act provided the sum of one million, eight hundred & fifty thousand pounds[xiii] for Windward Islands development schemes, to be financed by a combination of CD&W funds, tax revenues and loans.   The Plan was divided into 3 parts:
1.   The "Master Plan"
2.   The "Practical Plan, and the
3.   The "Hypothetical Plan".
The "Master Plan" included "all existing schemes and other desirable projects, and (would) serve the purpose of keeping within view the Colony's main overall requirements for the next decade or two at least." (p.iii)

The "Practical Plan" set out the schemes that it was hoped would be possible to execute within the decade with the resources available from the CD& W grant, government revenues and loans.

The "Hypothetical Plan", underlined the limitations of the Practical Plan, but showed how it "grew out of the Master Plan" (p.iv).
Some of the schemes in the Practical Plan were already being implemented.   These included Land Settlements, Small Town Improvements, Stud Centres, Agricultural Experiment Stations, Rural Dispensaries and Health Centres, School Building Programmes and Teacher

Training (p.v), overlapping with the previous, post-Moyne Commission, plan of 1938-48.

The Plan, which included a number of expert reports and memoranda on St. Vincent's problems and detailed recommendations for dealing with these, was "intended to serve as a work of reference and a guidebook... in respect of development schemes for the 'Colony' (sic)" (p.iii) not only for the 10 years covered but for future years. In that sense, it provided invaluable information for future plans. Indeed, these documents (reports and memoranda) are an invaluable resource, not only for planning but for historical research on a wide range of topics. The list includes, among others:
- Reconstruction of the Telephone System
- Agricultural Policy
- Land Settlement
- Forestry
- Arrowroot Industry
- Marketing of Local Produce
- Medical and Public Health Services
- Housing and Slum Clearance
- Education
- Social Welfare
- Economic reports, including reports by Professor Frederic Bentham,
the Economic Adviser to the Comptroller for Development & Welfare in the West Indies.
- Volcanic Investigations
- Scientific Surveys

The Foreword of the Plan also includes a "Preliminary Examination of the Economic and Fiscal Structure of St. Vincent" by Dr. A. Jolly, Lecturer in Economics at the Imperial College of Tropical Agriculture (ICTA), fore-runner of the Faculty of Agriculture of UWI, St.Augustine Campus. It is particularly revealing for a number of reasons, including the insight it provides into the thinking of economists and colonial administrators of the day on socio-economic development. The following quotes from Jolly's piece are illustrative:

As economic expansion [growth] takes place, social expansion can follow, but there is no reason for believing, and there have been no examples in the past, that Government sponsored social expansion will result in economic expansion large enough, and rapid enough, to carry the burden. (p.xvi)

The standard of earnings and the standards of living in any community depend on the efficiency with which the available resources of production are utilized. These resources do not consist only of land, or, for that matter of physical manpower; they include also the natural gifts of individuals, their capacity to manage, organize and invent; and their ability to accumulate capital.... Efficiency is achieved by the best balance of the factors of production so that there is no wasteful over-application of one factor that is limited by a shortage of another... With a reasonable balance of the factors of production the standards of living of the whole community can be immeasurably raised...

The lack of balance is most marked in the shortage of enterprise (managerial and inventive ability) and a surplus of human manpower. There is indeed too little competition between managers of agricultural and industrial enterprise and too much competition among the wage earning labour. As a result, the earnings of managers are high in relation to the services they render in making their business ever more efficient, by European standards; the wages of the workers judged by the same standards are low for their services in sweat and toil.

This glaring economic defect of West Indian populations cannot, however, be remedied artificially by reducing the earnings of the managing class and directly or indirectly increasing the earning of the worker. Such a step would disorganize the economy even more, since fewer managers still would be induced to remain. The solution, paradoxical as it may seem, is to make the scope of living and earnings of the managing class even more attractive; the more managers the greater competition between them for the other factors of production, labour, capital and land; and competition will result in more progressive business. (pxvii)

Since this is not a thesis on the colonial economy, or thinking, I will resist the temptation to continue this revelation, and to simply point out that we have here some of the fundamentals of a neo-classical economics that cannot conceive of the extent to which power is embedded in transactions between labour and capital, especially in plantation economies.

The reports and memoranda included in the 821-page tome provide a picture of the scope of British Colonial administration, its access to some leading scientific/ academic resources and the focus on broad-based socio economic development. Notwithstanding the moral outrages, the economic exploitation and socio-cultural indignities of colonialism, the British in the Caribbean created a foundation on which nationalist leaders were able to build. It stands in contrast to the militaristic approach of some of today's empire-builders as well as a blueprint of what must go into nation-building. That it was compiled by a civil servant, with no academic training, is a tribute to the native intelligence and commitment to duty of ordinary West Indians; a example of the unrealized potential of ordinary folk just waiting for an opportunity to serve.

The Testing Time

The years that Gibbs served in St.Vincent were some of the most tumultuous   in the political and constitutional development of the country[xiv]. Agitation for representative government following World War 1, and the appointment of a commission (headed by Edward Wood, Parliamentary Under Secretary of State for the Colonies) led to a semi-elected legislature and ultimately to a new constitution which increased the number of elected members. However, the dissatisfaction with this arrangement continued. In 1932, George McIntosh started the Workingmen's Association and he led the riots leading to his imprisonment.   In 1938 a high-level Royal Commission, headed by Lord Moyne was appointed by the British Government to inquire into the social and economic conditions in the region.

Its landmark Report was comprehensive and recognized the links between the socio-economic and political factors that had led to the unrest. It acknowledged the "growing political consciousness" of the masses and the legitimacy of the claims "that the people should have a larger voice in the management of their own affairs", but its recommendations regarding constitutional reform left initiatives for policy formulation in the hands of the Governor in Council.   However, following the Report, more concerted efforts were made to 'prepare' West Indians to take over leadership roles in all areas of the socio-economic and political development of Britain's West Indian colonies.   These efforts included training at the newly established University College of the West Indies, as well as in Britain for a number of administrative officers in the civil services of the region.   The so-called Devonshire courses were among these.

In 1947–48 Bernard Gibbs attended one of these courses at Keble College, Oxford University, working in the Colonial Office during the vacations. By the time of his return to St. Vincent, the island was on the eve of the major constitutional changes that would lead to adult suffrage in 1951.

In the midst of this, Gibbs was recommended by the Governor, Sir Robert Arrundell, for the post of Assistant Administrator and Establishment Officer.   According to Arrundell's letter (dated May 22, 1951), "The Administrator reports that Mr. Gibbs has worked well and conscientiously during the last 2 years [following the Course] and exhibits considerable powers of concentration and initiative". However, he had begun to make enemies and in that same month the Vincentian newspaper published a "defamatory" editorial (May 26th) in which his official position was challenged. He sought, and received permission to sue the newspaper. Nothing came of it and he was appointed to the post, which carried with it a seat in the Executive Council (November 1951) as one of its ex-officio members. In 1952, he held the post of Acting Administrator on two occasions.

In this capacity, he presided over the introduction of adult suffrage, a development of which he felt a great deal of ambivalence. His ideas of governance and his work ethic were strongly influenced by the values of the colonial service. He believed in hard work and merit and inherited the arrogance of the formally educated toward those without these credentials. He had a hard time accepting the authority of the early elected representatives of the people who rose from the ranks of the working class and advocated on their behalf. His on-going struggles with the newly elected Chief Minister Ebenezer Joshua and his wife Ivy, Minister of Health and Welfare, well publicized by the couple in their public meetings, would make an interesting story.

These years in St. Vincent were probably his most difficult. At a time when he should have been reaping the rewards of his hard work and recognized ability he was given responsibility, as Assistant Administrator and Establishment Officer, for maintaining the high standards set by colonial administrators for the public service. He made enemies of those he had to discipline, and those whose new authority he tried to curb. These years were not a happy time for "Ches" Gibbs.

In October 1952, Governor Arrundell recommended him for a transfer to the same position of Assistant Administrator and Establishment Officer in Grenada. In his letter to Gibbs he describes "Government Office and administration in general [as being] in a deplorable shape and the key to recovery is the caliber of the Assistant Administrator." He ends by stating, "I do not know of anyone other than yourself who could tackle the job effectively." Gibbs tried to decline the offer in a letter dated November 29th 1952 describing his work in this position in St. Vincent as "a fairly long period of grueling and distasteful jobs" and requesting "transfer to some distant post in the colonial civil service at the expiration of long leave [after his service in St. Vincent] …which I am not at all keen on continuing beyond the end of 1953."

Evidently this heartfelt plea fell on deaf ears because he ultimately accepted the post in Grenada where he was rewarded by intermittent appointments as Acting Administrator (up to 1957) and an opportunity to lead the relief and rehabilitation efforts in Carriarou, which had been devastated by Hurricane Janet.

Hurricane Janet

Though hurricanes had not been much cause for concern on Grenada, Hurricane Janet broke the rules when it stormed into the region on September 22/23 1955 as a Category 3 event, passing directly between Grenada and Carriacou, killing 122 people (including 35 in Carriacou) and causing extensive damage. The experience of heading relief and rehabilitation efforts was probably one of the highlights of his career. His capacity for hard work and organizing and his ability to connect with ordinary people must have brought him the deep satisfaction that had eluded him in the rarified and conflicted environment of senior administration where he would have to perform a role that was antithetical to his nature. There he endeared himself to the people, earning their recognition with the naming of a water tank "Gibbs' Tank". In his retirement, he spent some months in Carriacou and never tired showing the tank to his friends who visited him there. It was an honour more appreciated than the Queen's Birthday Honour that he was never awarded.

In 1957, when his assignment in Carriacou ended, he left the Windward Islands Civil Service to take up a post in the Ministry of Home Affairs in Jamaica, where he worked until 1960, retiring at age 50 to take up residence in the UK.

The Ending of an Era

His early years of retirement brought him face to face with the realities of the British class system and racism. Anonymity as just another West Indian in London and his inability to get the kind of employment to which he had been accustomed placed him in a position that was often hurtful and demeaning. He felt betrayed by the 'rulers of Empire' and must often have questioned his decision to take early retirement from the civil service. In that sense his situation could not have been very different from that of the hundreds of former colonial civil servants returning to an unwelcoming and unappreciative public service in Britain at the End-of-Empire. The only record of paid employment in those early years of his retirement, the decade of his 60s, was temporary employment in the Post Office.

What saved his sanity in that period were opportunities to return to Grenada on several occasions to undertake special official assignments.

These always required the skills of someone who could tackle difficult and complex tasks, such as dealing with the controversial political leader, Eric Gairy, and in 1967, assisting the newly elected Herbert Blaize in his unsuccessful efforts to integrate Grenada into the state of Trinidad and Tobago.

Back in the UK, between 1977 and 1982 he became Head of Administration of the Regional Office for the East and West Midlands and Wales of the Commission on Racial Equality (CRE) set up by the British Government to address the tensions between the hosts and expanding communities of immigrants. It must have restored his self-respect to be appointed to a position that measured up to his ability. According to one of his co-workers, Aaron Haynes, Regional Principal for the Office, "It was a new office and it was immensely valuable to have his experience and skill to draw on. You could be proud of his contribution." (Personal correspondence from Mr. Haynes)

The Sunset Years

After this, he again returned to the Caribbean to spend his sunset years, enjoying the beaches of Carriacou, Grenada, Bequia and St. Vincent – his beloved Windwards.

His final official assignment was 1983–84 when he served as Secretary of the Grenada Constitutional Review Commission under the Chairmanship of his old colleague, Sir Fred Phillips. The assignment drew on his experience in administration and his love of and facility with language and *la juste mot*. The elegance of his prose in numerous minutes and communications with the Colonial Office was legendary. The Latin scholar was in his element and the mentor reaped the rewards of working with one of the young men who had "sat at the feet of Gamaliel" and who showed appreciation and respect. My father was finally restored to the regard due to someone of his stature and experience in the "evening of his days".[xv]

After this final assignment he returned to St. Vincent, moved to Florida with his second wife, Sybil, for a few years before returning to St. Vincent to take up residence in the Thompson Home. In 2003 he moved for surgery to Barbados where his son, Tony, and daughter, Peggy, lived. He spent his last years there. In the seniors' home in Barbados, he had the good fortune to meet a Barbadian teacher, Clayton Harewood, who shared his love of Latin. They argued about classical texts and took great pleasure in making remarks about the staff in Latin. He died in September 2006 at the age of 96.

Summary and Conclusion

Born in 1910 of parents of mixed African, Indian and European ancestry, educated at the Grenada Boys Secondary School, selected by the colonial administrators and nurtured for senior positions in the civil service, it can be argued that the significance of Bernard Gibbs' life is less about his achievements than about the times in which he lived and worked.

His work in senior administrative positions in the colonial civil service in Grenada, St. Vincent and Jamaica, and on the staff of the Governor of the Windward Islands covering the period of the emergence of an educated, coloured middle class that identified with their British masters, even as some of their members, influenced by the socialist tendencies in the British Labor Party and driven by British racism, made common cause with the working class in the struggle against colonialism and the inhuman living conditions that characterized the plantation societies of the Caribbean. He represents that generation of West Indians who were the first to rise in the ranks of the Colonial Civil Service, mentored by Colonial administrators to take over the reins of government even as this dying breed tried to respond to the social unrest of the 1930s, World War 11, the last days of colonialism, the introduction of adult suffrage, the rise and demise of the ill-fated West Indian Federation, the introduction of the Ministerial System, Statehood and Independence.

In thinking of the life of this West Indian, one is struck by the complexities and contradictions that defined him: the dedicated public servant and the pleasure-seeker; the senior civil servant who fraternized with junior members of staff, treating everyone with respect and winning the devotion of an assortment of drivers, messengers and orderlies and the "trouble-shooter" and "problem-solver" enlisted to sort out disorganized civil service departments and inefficient civil servants. However, in one area there was no contradiction: he was a loyal servant of the Crown. He had completely internalized the values and attitudes of his British masters and mentors. In 1954 he stood squarely with the British Prime Minister's decision to invade Egypt when his Egyptian counterpart, Colonel Nassar dared to claim the Suez Canal for the benefit of the country[xvi].

As Sir Fred Phillips pointed out, he never reached the heights he should have attained in the administrative field, given the opportunities that came his way. However, it is clear that he never aspired to these heights, never allowed the possibilities of promotion to the highest ranks stand in the way of his pursuit of pleasure. His son-in-law's words on the occasion of his 80th birthday capture the spirit of this complex man:

> Your kith and your kin and your friends all salute
> A colourful life – that none will dispute.
> Details we'll eschew, it's the substance we count –
> And the fun and the wisdom that pour from your fount.
> (Ken Antrobus 8/1/90)

"Ches" Gibbs may never have risen to the top echelons of public service in the region that he loved, never identified with the struggles against colonial domination, but he is remembered as a great teacher and public servant by those who knew and worked with him, and he left a legacy of hard work and dedication that few can match.

[1] Beckles quotes Gerald Chapman, Economic Planner at the Colonial Office: "There have been two motives behind this proposal; the one a desire to avert possible trouble in certain colonies, … the other a desire to impress this county and the world at large with our consciousness of our duties as a great Colonial Power". (from the Public Record Office 1939)

[2] The nickname was given by school friends because of his habit of thrusting out his chest. Many people think that the 'C' in his initials stands for 'Chester'.

[3] A marriage certificate from my father's great-grandparents show that they were Indians, Suenaryan, and described as "coolies" although they were teachers. Both designations were recorded on the certificate.

[4] It was typical that bright students became teachers on leaving school, in order to complete their education, before moving on to other fields.

[5] Bernard gave each of his children one name only, and the shorter version.

[6] Vincentian Ken Antrobus won the Island Scholarship in 1951 and studied medicine at the newly established University College of the West Indies.

[7] Cedric Harold and Kenneth John state in their analysis in *Flambeau* #6, Nov 1966 that although the color/class structure of colonialism was "never hard and fast, but tempered by all sorts of personality considerations

…when all is told, it remained a fact that a black skin was a distinct liability under the old dispensation." (King et al 2006: 163)

[8] He gave up the idea after the boat that was to transport him to England was torpedoed.

[9] There are vivid accounts of those years, from a child's perspective, in Betty Peter's book *Brown Sugar and Spice.*

[10] The Windwards – Grenada, St.Vincent, St.Lucia and Dominica – were in those days a 'unitary state', administered by the Governor of the Windward Islands. In the late 1960s, in the lead up to the West Indian Federation, this arrangement ended so that each country could have their own representation in the Federal Parliament,

[11] Of this sum, three hundred & forty-five thousand, eight hundred & fifty-eight pounds was allocated to St.Vincent, in addition to the island's share of the sum of two hundred & eight thousand pounds allocated for joint development schemes for the Windwards and Leewards, and an additional hundred thousand pounds for the construction of an airfield.

[12] See Kenneth John's excellent analyses of the political and constitutional developments in St.Vincent, first published by Flambeau, the publication of the Kingstown Study Group (1964-68) and reprinted in the publication *Search for Identity: Essays on St.Vincent and the Grenadines*

[13] The phrases used here were some of his oft-repeated favourites.

[14] It was my first political quarrel with him, and marked the beginning of my own political consciousness..

Selected Readings

Barriteau, Eudine. 2001. *Stronger, Surer, Bolder: Ruth Nita Barrow: Social Change and International Development.* Kingston: University of the West Indies Press.

Clarke, Austin. 1980. *Growing-up Stupid Under the Union Jack: a memoir.* Toronto: McClelland& Stewart

Drayton, Kathleen. 2009. "Lessons from my Life", Presentation at the Opening of the 2009 Caribbean Regional Institute on Gender and Development", IGDS Cave Hill Campus, UWI, Barbados

Gibbs, Bernard. 1947. *A Plan of Development for the Colony of St.Vincent.* Guardian Commercial Printery: Trinidad.

King, Baldwin; John, Kenneth; King, Cheryl A., 2003. *Search for Identity: Essays on St.Vincent and the Grenadines.* KINGS-SVG Publishers, St. Vincent.

Miller, Errol, Ed. 1991. *Education and Society in the Commonwealth Caribbean.* Mona, Jamaica: ISER

Phillips, Sir Fred. 1991. *Caribbean Life and Culture: A Citizen Reflects.* Heinemann: Kingston.

Report of the West Indian Royal Commission 1938. (The Moyne Commission). Reprinted 2000, Barbados: Government Printing Department Report.

Steele, Beverley A. 2003. *Grenada: A History of its People.* McMillan Caribbean: Oxford.

Williams, Eric. (1950). Reprinted 1994. *Education in the British West Indies.* NY: A & B. Book Publishers.

I want to acknowledge the help I received from Paul Lewis in providing information about my father from official files. I am grateful to him and those who assisted him in this effort

Dr. Peggy Antrobus is a leading scholar of women issues in the Caribbean. She lives in Barbados.

6.   **FITZ ALLEN JOHN**
                                  By
                           Catherine John

"BRETHREN, THY WANDERING SHEEP BEHOLD!"

When Fitz Allen John returned to St. Vincent and the Grenadines for a visit in March of 2003 he was 74 years old. Although he had visited his home on many occasions since his departure in 1954, it was the very first time he was coming with his entire family consisting of his wife Fay, his elder daughter Catherine, and his younger daughter Julia, all of whom hailed from the island of Jamaica. While Fay had come with Fitz repeatedly to St. Vincent over the years, and Catherine had accompanied him in 1998 to the funeral of his brother Clyde Agard, this was, however the very first trip for Julia and the family as a whole. Yet this native son, who had not realized when he left at 26 that it was not his destiny to return to his homeland permanently, spent the next fifty years of his life using the homegrown ethics and values that he acquired at an early age as a foundation for the immense impact that he would make on the places and people he worked in and amongst.

Early Beginnings

He was born in Brighton, St. Vincent on December 16, 1928. to Helen Charles and Alfred John. His father left St. Vincent for Trinidad early in his life and died there before he got to know him. Later in life he learned that a local man of darker hue was rumored to have been his real father, but his mother never admitted otherwise.[3] When Fitz was quite young, his mother departed St. Vincent to become a domestic worker in Barbados leaving him with his grandparents, Urias and Amelia Charles. As a young man he traveled with a friend to Barbados to see his mother after not having seen her for a long time. Upon arrival the two young men jokingly asked her to identify which of them was her son; she proceeded to identify the man who was not Fitz. On another occasion Helen Charles sent her son a pair of shoes as a gift; unfortunately the shoes were too small. These two oral tales are indicative of a painfully strained and underdeveloped relationship between Fitz and his biological mother. The real parents in his life were his grandparents, Urias and Amelia Charles, as well as his aunt, Catherine Charles Chance.

---

[3]Fitz John mentioned this information to his daughters on the trip they made to St. Vincent in 2003.

His grandfather Urias, known as Worthy to some and Daffo to others, was born in 1878 to Eunis and Hue Charles, former slaves. As a teenager, Urias and his friends decided to swim the 9 miles from St. Vincent to Bequia with the aid of a floating banana tree bark. The tides were too strong, however, and instead of reaching Bequia, they drifted to another part of St. Vincent. They returned home at dusk to parents and relations who were overjoyed to see them alive, having presumed them drowned. Later on in his youth, Urias traveled to Venezuela to work for six or seven years. While there, he and his fellow working companions got lost in the forest. As the story goes, Urias recalled learning how to make a clearing for the sun to come through thus creating a compass on the ground. The rays of the sun fell on the ground at such an angle that it showed the cardinal points and Urias was able to help himself and his companions find their way home. Throughout his life Worthy was entrepreneurial, specializing in the transportation of goods. For a long time he transported goods from place to place with a donkey cart and then he worked as a transporter on one of the big estates. Later he became an overseer for a nearby farm and his final job of record was as a transporter of goods by sea from St. Vincent to Trinidad. He had an adventurous spirit and was also a jack-of-all-trades.

In the village Worthy was revered. He was an outstanding lay preacher in the Plymouth Brethren Gospel Hall and it was his lay preaching in part which later inspired Fitz to enter the ministry. Urias was also a dispute-settler in the village; all the little quarrels and arguments were brought to him. He was the village storyteller, one who is often also the local historian, and he is said to have told many a story in his lifetime. Although he lived during a period when education was hard to come by he was not illiterate and he read and wrote many letters for community residents who could not do so for themselves. In 1902, shortly after he returned from Venezuela, he married Amelia Adams of Mesopotamia, St. Vincent. Amelia and Urias had ten children between them; six boys and four girls. She was an ardent Methodist, a disciplined woman, and a preparer of some of the most delicious fish dishes; she was also a woman who never went to bed leaving any pots or pans unwashed. While Fitz remembers his grandfather's "laissez-faire" attitude with regards to boy-girl adolescent affairs, his grandmother had no such inclination and would intervene if she saw a relationship developing of which she did not approve. Their daughter Catherine, who was well known in her adult years as an excellent baker of birthday and wedding cakes grew extremely fond of her nephew. She gradually took over the responsibility for his upkeep and care, functioning as mother to him and mother-in-law and grandmother to his wife and children later on.[4]

As a young boy Fitz Allen liked the sea. He was a strong swimmer and spent a lot of time down at Salt Pond beach. Fitz's cousin Belfied Castello remembers that he often walked the 10 to 12 miles before school began in the mornings from Brighton to Hopewell to Richland Park to see his maternal family and bring ground provisions back from the countryside. He recalls that early in life, Fitz exhibited signs of extreme discipline and a passion for learning. His spiritual upbringing was split between the Plymouth Brethren Gospel Hall of his grandfather and the Brighton Methodist church that his grandmother attended. He was an excellent student yet his familial responsibilities and social life never interfered with his schooling. He attended Brighton school which was housed in the same building as the Methodist church and after getting out of Sunday school at three in the afternoon he and his cousins went on to the Brethren Sunday School.

Fitz eventually cleaved to the Methodist church because of the thriving Wesley Guild organization. He became a Sunday school teacher when he was sixteen and later on became the Sunday School Superintendent. The Wesley Guild was organized around four principles: devotion, literary studies, cultural learning, and social activity. Guild activities ranged from prayer and bible study to outings, games, and organized debates. Fitz and his closest friends all were members of the Guild and then became full members of the Methodist church. He names Victor and Carlisle Adams, Neville Sandy, and Donald Brown as part of his inner circle. He describes the elders in the church as not being afraid to train the youth, stating, "They would train you and then yield the leadership to you while giving you guidance. They would eventually ease out and leave you in charge."[5]

Besides school, church, swimming at Salt Pond beach, and Wesley Guild activities, Fitz's other passion like most of the men of his youth, was cricket. Under the guidance of their beloved teacher Mr. Herbert Jack (whom the boys secretly called "little head") Fitz, Victor, Sandy, Carlisle and various others developed a cricket team they called The Rugby Boys. They got the idea for the name from the famous English novel *Tom Brown's School Days*. There was a junior and senior segment of the team. Legend

---

[4]Much of the information about Fitz John's grandparents was gathered from Fitz John for a high school report on ancestry done by Catherine John for an Advanced Placement History course at Medford High School in Massachusetts, submitted on February 27, 1984.
[5]This information was gathered in interview with Fitz John on January 6, 2001 in Nassau, Bahamas. The interview was conducted and recorded by Catherine John.

has it that they were invincible and never lost a match. As they returned home they would sing boastful songs about their skill and prowess leaving people in Brighton wondering how they won so often and if they were working obeah. Fitz describes the Guild and The Rugby Boys as developing in him a humanitarian spirit that was useful later in life. He and his friends had a brotherhood philosophy of the highest order. They would write plays together for the Guild and give various among them credit even if only one person actually wrote the play. Furthermore this communal spirit carried over into their playing of cricket. "[We] had a philosophy in cricket that no matter how we were cheated by another team we would not walk away; we would come from behind and win."[6] When Teacher Jack was with them, this did not work out as he loathed unfair play and if he suspected his team was being cheated he would walk out even before the prepared meal was served – his departure being signaled (much to the dismay of Fitz and his teammates) by him brusquely putting on his jacket.

Coming from too poor of a family to afford high school, Fitz went through an alternative educational structure in which advanced students were trained as assistant grammar school teachers. A specialist teacher would come to the schools once a month and assign all the part-time teachers work that was the equivalent of what was done in the regular high schools. Fitz states, "After two years all these part time teachers would go to Kingstown and do a big exam and if you passed you became a student teacher and you would teach [full time]. On [Saturdays] the student teachers met in a particular school to study for the Senior Cambridge exam," later replaced by the GCE or Ordinary level exams.[7] For students who had less academic talent or opportunity, there were primarily two other options. One involved some form of employment on one of the three big white owned estates: Brighton, Prospect and Diamond. This involved work in a factory or out in the field picking cotton, sugarcane, or reaping arrowroot. On the other hand there was a Methodist technical school where one could learn various trades including architecture. Additionally, many parents would send their sons to apprentice with master carpenters, masons, or tailors.

Fitz easily passed the required six subjects and was then sent to Gomea Elementary School which had recently lost its headmaster; there he became principal for a year. But another significant event had begun to happen in his life. As a young child he received as a Sunday school prize the book, *Twelve Brave Boys* containing the story, "Cyril of Caesarea." The power of this story alongside the influence of his grandfather's local preaching inspired Fitz to consider a profession among the clergy and attempt the difficult process of becoming a candidate as a Methodist minister. At that

---

[6]Ibid.

[7]This information was also obtained from the 2001 Interview with Fitz John.

time, almost all the Methodist ministers throughout the Caribbean were white British men and the process and procedure for inclusion in their ranks was an arduous one. First he had to become a local preacher which itself required a recommendation from the minister, a vote by the local preacher's committee, and training in Methodist doctrine, bible study and written exams on the Old Testament. If a person was successful in all of this then Fitz states, "A report [was] brought to the… local preacher's meeting and if the report was good then at a future meeting you [were] brought before the [group] and other ministers and other local preachers would question you extensively on Methodist doctrine."[8]

Fitz describes the latter end of the process in his own words. "You had to be a fully accredited local preacher to be a minister and you had to be recommended by the local preacher's meeting. Then you were under the guidance of the clergy in your circuit. Once you were approved you had to go back and do, at a…rigorous level, [more] Old and New Testament exams as well as a preaching exam and a Methodist doctrine exam. The papers you had to pass did not come from your circuit but from the theological school in Jamaica. When you were ready they would send the [exam] papers to the superintendent minister [in your circuit] and then you would [have] a week to do the exam...[T]hey would send your test papers back to Jamaica where they were corrected. If you got through all of this, then you were brought before the annual synod and there you had to do a preaching exam before all the ministers and local preachers who had not heard you before. Then you were called before the ministerial session at synod and you were grilled orally about your sense of call, and basic knowledge of the church. Finally, if you passed all of these tests then you were sent to the theological school in Jamaica."[9] Under the guidance of the Rev. Errol Wiltshire and the Rev. J.B. Broomes he became a candidate for the Methodist Ministry and was sent to the Caenwood United Theological College in Kingston, Jamaica. While he was not the first Black man to attempt to become a candidate specifically from St. Vincent, he was the first to succeed.

Caenwood and the Ministry

At Caenwood Fitz excelled both in his studies as well as in his beloved sport of cricket. He became captain of the Caenwood Cricket team. While in St. Vincent, his excellence as a cricket player had led him to play on one occasion for St. Vincent's national team in a game against St. Lucia. Academically, he walked away with the lion's share of prizes at his 1958 graduation including one for excellence in Hebrew and another for

---

[8]Ibid.
[9]Ibid.

excellence in Old Testament scholarship. Despite being a four year institution, Caenwood was not a degree granting school and those students interested in acquiring a formal Bachelor's degree had to do a correspondence course through the University of London. Fitz was the first SVG student to successfully complete the Inter BD, a kind of associate's degree that was a halfway point to the Bachelor's. He attempted later on to get the full Bachelor's degree but failed the exam – which was questionable given his academic talent.

At the end of the four years at Caenwood, the Methodist tutor H.J. Cook came to inform the students of their first pastoral assignments. Fitz presumed that he would be sent back home to the South Caribbean and eagerly awaited his appointment. He had come to Caenwood with three other young men from the South Caribbean circuit – three Barbadians and himself. He was convinced, therefore, that if one of the four of them had to remain in Jamaica, it would be one of the 'Bajans.' At the end of the day, however, it was he, the lone Vincentian who was left behind and stationed in Jamaica. Ironically, it was his skill as a cricketer that prevented him from returning home. One of the senior clergy of the era, Rev. Hugh Sherlock had seen Fitz play cricket. He had seen him make a 100 runs, as well as spin bowl in a game against Sherlock's own Boys Town cricket team. Sherlock wanted Fitz for the Boys Town team and so requested that he be stationed in Jamaica. On the other hand, one of Fitz's Barbadian colleagues was eager to stay in Jamaica. Fitz states, "He came to me and he pleaded with me saying, 'Look mahn, Fitz mahn, Fitz John mahn, you know I want to stay in Jamaica.' And I said 'I know that yes. And I don't want to stay in Jamaica.' He said 'Alright. Let us agree to swap. Let us go to Cook.' So we went to Cook mahn, but Cook for some reason did not too much like [him]. So they wouldn't budge."

Fitz John's career as a Methodist Minister began in the Bensonton circuit in St. Ann, Jamaica where he worked from 1958 to 1961. On the personal front, he had become enamored with and engaged to Imogene Power, a fellow Vincentian who was also from his home district of Brighton. The relationship did not work out and the engagement ended shortly after he took up his appointment in Bensonton. But Fitz in many ways was married to the church. In 1961 at age 33, he was transferred to the Falmouth circuit in the Jamaican parish of Trelawny where he worked from '61 to '64. In his work life he established a reputation early on as a strong leader and master fundraiser. As fellow Methodist minister Nymphus Edwards recalls, "I had the good fortune of spending a weekend with [Fitz] in his manse in the Beechamville and Bensonton Circuit in St. Ann. I soon realized that he was a very gifted person for Christian ministry. He was full of ideas and was not afraid to express them. He…gave me much encouragement as a young man, and shared [his] theological and practical wisdom with me. He had a reputation as an innovative and hardworking pastor, and it was a delight to see the loving relationships shared between the members of the various churches in his Circuit and himself... Fitz was also an excellent fund-raiser and... an efficient administrator. Little did I know then that within another few years I would follow in his footsteps in the Falmouth Circuit of Methodist Churches on the north coast of Jamaica, West Indies, from 1967 to 1972. It was there that I learned so much about the Rev. Fitz Allen John and the impact that his ministry had on that Circuit. His shoes were hard to fill, and I had to remind myself that I was not Fitz John! I began to use some of his methods and found that they worked effectively as I did ministry in the various churches."[10]

His future wife Fay Bailey describes some of these methods and strategies in detail. She states, "[His] leadership and fundraising strategies were very successful, largely because he was committed to transparency and clear explanations. He would describe in detail how he envisioned the task at hand being accomplished. He would write everything down on paper and give everyone a copy and he would state, for example, 'We need to raise $5000. [Our church] rally will raise us $2000 and the [fundraising] dinner will raise us $500...and so on and so on.' After any event or goal had been achieved he would return with printed information with the results [made plain for everyone to see]. One of his favorite statements was something along the lines of 'Let people see their possibilities.'"[11] During his years in Falmouth, at the encouragement of a former seminary tutor, Fitz decided to apply for a scholarship to a school in the United States. Up until this point, Baptist ministers and various others had taken advantage of such fellowships but the Methodists, partial to their British education, had thus far shunned American institutions. Fitz applied and was admitted to Pittsburgh Theological Seminary in Pennsylvania. When he requested study leave however he was denied. Being strong willed and independent, he decided to go anyway. Despite not having formally received his Bachelor's degree, the placement exams at Pittsburgh revealed his level of knowledge to be far above the Bachelor's degree requirements. In a year he had acquired the STM degree, a Masters in Sacred Theology. He was as always a pathbreaker, and his enrollment at Pittsburgh was not only the first for a Methodist minister from the Caribbean but the church subsequently softened its policies and other ministers attended Pittsburgh and other U.S. instutions with both official leave and pay as well.

---

[10]This information was acquired from written tributes to the late Fitz Allen John that were written to his wife Fay after his death.
[11]Information here was gathered from interviews conducted with Fay John in July of 2007.

Marriage, Work & Family

During his year in Pittsburgh he pursued and became engaged to the love of his life, the Jamaican Fay Bailey, whose older brother Eric Bailey was one of his best friends, and whose eldest brother C. Evans Bailey preceded Fitz in the ministry in both age and prominence. Fay was a graduate student at McGill University in Montreal, Canada at the time. After a courtship of several months and their respective graduations from McGill and Pittsburgh, Fitz asked Fay's father Cyril Bailey for her hand in marriage and they were married in Jamaica in 1965 before Fitz was assigned to his third ministerial appointment in Black River, St. Elizabeth. While Fitz put his all into each district and community to which the church assigned him, he was aware that the remote Black River appointment would have been perceived by some in his situation as a form of punishment for his willfulness in going to Pittsburgh without official church consent and approval.

When he and his wife arrived in Black River the house that was being used as a manse was broken down and old. For all the years prior to his arrival, the ministers assigned to this circuit were living in a house belonging to an organization known as the Daly Trust. Daly was a man who had left a lot of houses in trust for the Methodist church to use. The church could use the profits from the trust as long as they maintained a school for training domestic science students – these were the terms of the trust. In an attempt to remedy the situation, the district renovated one of the other houses in the Daly trust, for Fitz and Fay to live in. However, when Fitz saw the faulty wiring in the supposedly renovated house, he refused to live there and rented yet another house instead. This was a new expense for a circuit that was already going hat in hand to the headquarters in Jamaica for its support. The ministers in that circuit had to be paid from the headquarters in Kingston because the circuit was not making enough money to pay their own ministers and keep up with their expenses.

Fitz got the Board that oversaw the Trust to meet and he proposed that the circuit would raise funds in order to purchase the land upon which the house which was being used as the main manse was located. He additionally proposed that after the purchase of the land, the church would raise the funds to build their own manse – this would from henceforth belong to the circuit and not to the Daly trust. The Trust sold the property and land to the church for what was called "peppercorn price" and then the circuit had the project of raising funds to build a new manse. Under his leadership and within his first year in Black River, the circuit raised the funds to build the new manse. They also started paying their own ministers as well as giving apportionment (money) from the circuit to the district. For years the Black River circuit had paid no apportionment. Additionally, Fitz John spearheaded raising the funds to build a proper church in Vineyard, one of the areas within Black River's jurisdiction. He was only in Black River for two years. After he left Black River it continued to be one of the foremost circuits in paying apportionment.[12]

On July 26, 1967, a few weeks before Fitz was relocated to the May Pen circuit of the Methodist church, Fitz and Fay's first child Catherine Amelia was born. She was named by Fitz after his beloved aunt Kate as well as his grandmother Amelia Charles. The May Pen circuit needed a new church and Fitz got the people enthusiastic about rebuilding. Although he did not see this project completed he laid the foundation for the fundraising that eventually made the new building possible. In May Pen as he had done in the Black River and Falmouth circuits he spearheaded the organizing of a big annual fair as the main fundraising event. The important thing about his organizing of the fair was that the congregation never spent any money up front. Everything was donated. So in many of the circuits he worked he came to be known and referred to as "the big beggar" and he was not ashamed to do it. If a farmer in the area had cattle, even if the farmer was not a Methodist, Fitz would go and demand a head or two and he would get it. While the big church in a circuit would host the annual fair, some of the smaller churches would have rallies. Again, no matter how small the rally, every church in the circuit would be expected to attend and to make their donation to that particular rally.

'EXPECT GREAT THINGS FROM GOD, ATTEMPT GREAT THINGS FOR GOD'

On April 4, 1968, while Fitz and Fay were still stationed in May Pen, Martin Luther King Jr. was assassinated. He was exactly one month younger than Fitz John in age and his death happened during a decade of turmoil on a worldwide scale. In October of '68, Guyanese scholar Walter Rodney was banned from returning to Jamaica due to "his advocacy for the working poor."[13] The political events of the 1960's which included the Cuban and Algerian revolutions as well as Jamaica's independence and that of other African and Caribbean countries strongly influenced Fitz and his generation. The migration of many Caribbean people to England, both pre and post independence had resulted in a rise in racial tensions. It was during this political moment that Fitz was sent by the Methodist church to Birmingham, England to be a Race Relations Officer. He arrived in England in 1969 and was employed by both the city of Birmingham and the Methodist church

---

[12]Information acquired from 2007 interviews with Fay John.
[13]This information is cited on the Wikipedia online entry relating to Guyanese intellectual Walter Rodney.

circuit to help to bridge the divide between these Black Caribbean and white British Christian populations. Harold Jones, the British layperson who was assigned to be Fitz's circuit steward writes:

"The arrangement was that he would be working from a specific church which already had a Caribbean membership, [he would also work] with a team of Methodist minister colleagues as well as with a support group in the form of an existing Community Relations Committee. It had to be a cultural change for Rev. Fitz John but he quickly identified with both the black and white community within which he was working, preaching to mostly totally white congregations within the circuit. He also travelled widely across the greater Birmingham District, including rural areas, bringing a clearer understanding of the community relations that had to be developed. It was pioneering work for at that stage some of the churches that he visited in the outlying districts had never had a black minister taking a service there before and had probably never met a black brother. He was [also] able to assist the police in understanding the reaction that they sometimes experienced when dealing with Caribbean young people and in turn support the parents of children who had grown up in Birmingham…In the three years that Rev. Fitz John spent in the Birmingham District from 1969 to 1972, he was able, in a special dedicated way, to improve the understanding between two communities and his pioneering work has been continued so that today the integration that has taken place would have amazed him. During his life time, Rev. Fitz John achieved much--and amongst it--his work in the Birmingham District of England must be regarded as outstanding. For although he most likely did not recognize it as such, at that time, he was laying the foundations for the harmony and friendships that subsequently developed between black and white people, both in the church and the community, and continues to grow today."[14]

While in England, Fitz added to his already full roster of activities, acquiring a second Master's degree in Theology from Birmingham University. His thesis entitled, **"Re-Mythologizing the Christian Message"** was completed in 1971, and early in 1972, he, Fay and his daughter Catherine moved to Belize where he became the Chairman of the District. He was stationed in Belize until 1975 when he was re-assigned to Jamaica and took up one of the most significant career appointments of his life at St. John's Methodist Church in Montego Bay. In 1973 while he was stationed in Belize, his second daughter Julia Erica, named after Fay's mother and her elder brother Eric, was born. Fay moved back to Jamaica in advance of Fitz, and Julia was born in Kingston. Once Fitz was assigned to Montego Bay, the family reunited and moved into the church's relatively

---

[14]Taken from a tribute written to Fay John in honor of Fitz John by Harold Jones.

recently built manse on Upton Hill, one that had a spectacular view of both the city and the bay where cargo and cruise ships docked. In Montego Bay, the big project was retaining the land next to the church that had been purchased prior to Fitz's arrival, but due to the debt that was still owed on the land, the church was considering re-selling the property. Fitz organized the church to raise the money to pay off the land debt and then they planned and began to raise the money for what eventually became a community center that was finally completed in the 1990's and dedicated to his memory in 2006. A stone plaque installed in the community center in his honor reads:

Rev. Fitz John, a Vincentian, superintended the Montego Bay-Mt. Ward Circuit from 1975-1980. St. John's Methodist Church agreed to sell a parcel of land to repay its debt. On his arrival he counseled the church against the sale and encouraged the establishment of a facility for outreach ministries. Today the St. John's Methodist Community Action Centre (CAC) occupies this site. Motivated by William Carey's words, "EXPECT GREAT THINGS FROM GOD, ATTEMPT GREAT THINGS FOR GOD," Rev. John initiated the $250,000.00 project. He used his zeal, passion, and ability to organize and encourage massive fund-raising drives for the project. Rev. John's successors, Rev. Dereck Stanworth, Rev. Dr. Rupert Young, and Rev. Lindley Rankine supported the project.

Ground was broken on Monday, December 15, 1980 and the building dedicated on February 21, 1991. Mr. K.D. Watson, Chief Architect, Mr. Don Daley, Contractor and Builder, Mr. Leonard Parkin, Landscaper, church members, work teams, and members of the community constructed the building. The members wanted St. John's to be "a servant community of faith to respond to urgent human needs." Hence Ministries at the CAC included:

- *A feeding program for the sick, the shut-in and street people*
- *A clinic for Medical, Optical and Dental Care*
- *A citizen's advice bureau for counseling*
- *Library facilities*
- *Rental of the hall for civic and religious functions.*

Central to Rev. John's ministry was an "advocacy for the poor, and disenfranchised, justice and fair-play in church and society." His deep desire was that the CAC would be "A concrete symbol reminding one and all of God's love."

The Centre was renamed The Fitz John Methodist Community Action Centre on May 21, 2006. "The God Whom Christians Worship and Serve is Concerned with Human Wholeness." – REVEREND FITZ ALLEN JOHN

In each circuit that Fitz worked he helped the church to pay off any existing debts, he developed new projects and he got involved in the development of the surrounding community. He was abruptly transferred from Montego Bay to Coke Methodist Church in Kingston before the Community Center was finished. Dissatisfied with Coke for various reasons he decided to leave the Caribbean all together and took up an appointment in Boston, Massachusetts where he was assigned to pastor **The Morgan Memorial Church of All Nations** in downtown Boston. While he was there from 1981 to 1984, he helped to create a program to feed the homeless called *Saturday's/Sunday's Bread* which fed an average of 200 people every weekend. The program is still in existence. In 1984 Catherine graduated from Medford High School and shortly thereafter the family was transferred to Greenwood Methodist Church in the heart of urban Dorchester in Boston. Julia attended Pierce Junior high school in Brookline, Catherine enrolled at Boston College and Fay began work at Boston Gas Company. Fitz set himself to the task of developing his new and predominantly Caribbean church set in an urban and dilapidated area. The Four Corner's neighborhood where the church and the manse were located was known at the time for urban violence, an absence of commerce, and underdevelopment. Youth unemployment, loitering, abandoned buildings and litter, were the norm.

In order to respond to the community's needs, Fitz and the church members founded **The Greenwood Family Life Center** which taught English as a Second Language (ESL) classes to Haitian immigrants and worked in coalition with other Dorchester youth organizations to help control crime on the streets. To this end the center taught computer literacy to youth, ran summer school programs, and helped place young people in jobs. Additionally, Fitz worked with several organizations in the area to found **the Four Corner's Coalition** – a group of several organizations in the community devoted to improving the life of youth in the area. Fitz also taught voluntary citizenship classes at the **Codman Square Health Center** which was less than a mile down the street from the church, and he was a founding member of the **Methodist Black Pastors Association**. Working with the Rev. Richard Harding among others, Fitz founded a sister relationship between urban Greenwood and two other suburban Methodist churches in Wellesley and Sudbury respectively. He was also involved early on in the statewide organization **Health Care for All** which went on to create healthcare for Massachusetts residents generally. At Greenwood church specifically, Fitz raised approximately $300,000 in surplus funds over the course of his twelve year ministry. These funds helped to re-shingle the roof, purchase a new organ, buy a minivan and install an alarm system.

'BRETHREN, THY WANDERING SHEEP BEHOLD!'

In 1996 Fitz Allen John retired from the United Methodist church in the United States. In 1998, Fay took early retirement from Boston Gas Company where she had worked for over 14 years and they relocated to Palm Bay, Florida. In Florida, Fitz became a member of the **Brevard Caribbean American Sports and Cultural Association** (BCASCA) where he started a building fund and continued his ministry which he described in his own words as his being "here and there for God." He ministered to the sick, worked with community organizations, taught adult Sunday school classes, and continued to travel far and wide, attending conferences and visiting family and friends.

Fitz's visit to St. Vincent and the Grenadines in 2003 was the first and last visit he would make with his whole family, and it was his last visit to his homeland. The family stayed with his long time friend and mentor, Mr. C.D. Hercules and visited with the family of his childhood friend Mr. Festus Toney, among others. They walked through Brighton village and went to Salt Pond Beach and on a tour of Bequia. They visited his maternal family in Richland Park and they went to see Gomea Elementary School where he was once the principal. They saw him preach at Mt. Coke, Arnos Vale and Kingstown Methodist churches where he greeted his fellow Vincentians with the phrase, "Brethren, thy wandering sheep behold!"

In late August of 2005 he was suddenly diagnosed with colon cancer. He was admitted to Palm Bay hospital and was in good spirits as his wife, and many friends visited with him. After his surgery, Catherine arrived in town the weekend of the 17th and spent time with him in the hospital. On September 20th in the early afternoon, Julia arrived into town and joined the family. After spending a good portion of that day with him, Catherine and Fay left Julia in the hospital to spend the night with her father. Shortly after 9:00pm she called them at home to say that he was having difficulty breathing and the medics were in the room working on him. He suffered a heart attack and passed away that night.

Fitz Allen John was among that generation of Vincentians who had a strong sense of pride in nation, culture and community. His pioneering legacy is a testament to his ancestors and their culture. His commitment to uplift his downtrodden brothers and sisters was an example for those who were witnesses as well as those to come.

Dr. Catherine John is an Associate Professor of English at the University of Oklahoma in Norman, Oklahoma, USA

Caribbean Trailblazers: St. Vincent and the Grenadines

7.   NESTA LUCY "CLARIE" PAYNTER
By
Anne Samuel and Joan Samuel Simien

<u>Serving her Community, Preserving its History</u>

She was a loyal Vincentian through and through
Born on the lands where bananas grew.
Park Hill and Glen are just two of the names
Of places she lived, played and enjoyed island games.

Nesta Lucy was her name given at birth,
But Clarie they called her and the name just stuck.
Moving to Kingstown changed the girl
Into the woman who was willing to learn.

Independent and strong,
Before women's movements began,
She forged forward, a woman
Entering the world of a man.

As stenographer and photographer
She diligently worked,
Owning photo studios and guesthouses,
Meeting people of the world.

The Red Cross, Girl Guides,
Save the Children's Fund
Are some of the volunteering
Work she has done.

Clarie Paynter was born in 1905. By the time of her death in 1998, she had served the community that she so loved in a variety of capacities, most notably as civil servant, photographer, innkeeper, and community volunteer.

THE EARLY YEARS

Clarie, whose birth name was Nesta Lucy, was the third of ten children born to Robert E.A. Paynter and Margaret Ross Paynter. Robert was a schoolteacher and headmaster for forty-five years, retiring from the profession in 1934, while Margaret was a stay-at-home mother, who also oversaw the maintenance of the household and the family's farmlands during Robert's teaching assignments away from home.

Clarie's siblings included Amy, Hinford, Jack, John, May, and Val. Three others died before reaching adulthood. John celebrated his 100th birthday on June 24, 2009, in New York, USA but sadly passed away on June 15, 2010. He had lived in Brooklyn with his daughter, Rhona Craig for many years.

Along with various members of her family, Clarie grew up in the locations where her father was teaching, such as the Bellevue-Park Hill area, the Calliaqua-Glen area, Kingstown, and Mayreau.

During her early life, Clarie followed the normal path of so many other West Indian children, attending school while living and playing on the lands her family owned in Park Hill and Glen. She enjoyed music, and throughout her life played the violin, guitar, and quattro, performing classical as well as Hawaiian music. She was active in the Music Council. She played the violin in the Literary League Band, performed in concerts for charity, and sang with the choir of St. George's Cathedral, where she also attended church services.

CIVIL SERVANT

Clarie (or Nesta as she was officially known on the job) initially worked for the St. Vincent Government during a short period in 1935, taking depositions for the riots in Kingstown that year. Prior to that, she was employed for several years as solicitor's clerk in the offices of Barrister Stanley G. Defreitas. During her earlier years she had worked in the accounting department at Corea and Co. Ltd.

In 1943, Clarie resumed her public service, as acting clerk to the Crown Attorney. The following year, in a communication addressed to His Honor the Administrator, the Crown Attorney cited her "wide knowledge of legal matters" in his recommendation that she be assigned to a permanent position in that office. In that position, she was paid a beginning annual salary of 80 pounds with projected annual increases of 10 pounds to a top salary of 100. pounds. She worked for the government for sixteen years.

A letter of recommendation signed in February 1948 by the Acting Administrator attested to the high regard in which Clarie was held by that incumbent for the quality of her work and her character.

Clarie's desire to serve almost took her well beyond the everyday routine of a clerk within the safe confines of an office building in her local community onto a larger, potentially dangerous stage: During World War II she sought to enlist in a branch of the Canadian Armed Forces. However, on April 19, 1944, she received a letter from the Canadian Government Trade Commissioner, whose office was located in Port of Spain, Trinidad, stating that they had deferred her application because they were unable to proceed with the necessary and required interview due to a lack of time, as the representative was returning to Canada.

PHOTOGRAPHER

It is in Clarie's more independent and entrepreneurial—one might even say trailblazing—endeavors that her contributions to the community are most visible and numerous. Prior to 1935, with instruction from family friend Robert M. Anderson, author of the *Saint Vincent Handbook*, Clarie began a career in photography. With the skills and knowledge passed on to her by "Andy," as he was fondly called, Clarie became the island group's first female photographer, operating her own photographic studio for some thirty years. Through that enterprise, Clarie provided an invaluable service to a wide range of customers, from private individuals, to local politicians and officers of the government, to World War II soldiers stationed in neighboring islands, and countless others.

Clarie's photographic work included the 1939 plane crash at Grand Sable Estate, Georgetown, during World War II; E.T. Joshua, together with the Eighth Army political party; and Royal visits to St. Vincent by Princess Alice and the Earl of Athlone, and by Princess Margaret. She also photographed many Carnival Queen contestant shows, as well as a new entertainment venue—the Lyric Cinema—when it opened under the proprietorship of Henry Wilson around 1948 The Lyric theatre had a colorful history. After Henry Wilson, it was taken over by Randolph Russell in 1952 and for the next twelve years was the center of social activity for many a movie fan. In 1964 Luther Robertson , one of the shareholders of the company, took over the management of Lyric. It gradually faded away over the next twenty years or so.

A talented artist, some of whose watercolor paintings could be seen on the walls of the guesthouses she operated, Clarie also used this ability to transform black-and-white photographs and postcards of scenic locations in the island group into color. Many photographs attributed to *C. Paynter* are still available today, thereby preserving images of St. Vincent and the Grenadines from an era long past to be experienced, if only on paper, by generations yet to come.

INNKEEPER

It is perhaps in this role—as proprietor of several guesthouses over a period of some forty years—that Clarie was best and most widely known, not only locally, but internationally.

Even before her foray into photography, mentored by R.M. Anderson, Clarie seems to have been reared by her parents to be very comfortable traveling along what were, for her time and place, nontraditional paths for a woman. Years before she was a business owner, she was a landowner: In 1928, acting as their attorney, Robert Paynter purchased land in St. James Place in the names of Clarie (Nesta) and two of her sisters. In 1947, Clarie purchased the property outright from them. She also owned land in Edinboro and Ratho Mill.

While Clarie used those early real estate acquisitions primarily to provide single-family dwellings for herself and family members, within a few years she would venture into the more commercial aspect of real estate by owning multi-unit guesthouses. Her first guesthouse was located on Halifax Street, across from the marketplace. Later she moved the location to Sharpe Street, where Windermere Guest House began, and eventually, in 1956, to Kingstown Park, where she operated under the name of the Kingstown Park Guest House.

Clarie's guesthouses were well known and highly regarded among islanders and international visitors alike, especially for their hospitality, economical rates, and, by no means least of all, outstanding Caribbean cuisine. In effect, Clarie became one of the island's goodwill ambassadors, as guests from throughout the Caribbean and beyond, particularly the United States, Canada, and Europe, made return visits and referred family, friends, and associates. Locally, Clarie and her staff, including her loyal guesthouse manager, Olga Simon, also often catered Government House functions and local events.

Her guesthouses were often filled with sports teams who were traveling for inter-island tournaments. Cricketers, netball players, and footballers were frequent residents at these lodgings, especially in the 1940s, '50s, and '60s. There, too, over the years, temporarily resided many Boys' Grammar School Headmasters, teachers, and students (including a future Prime Minister, namely, Sir James Mitchell), as well as clergy members, and government employees and their families.

Kingstown Park Guest House was accurately described in its advertising brochures as "unequalled for the scenic grandeur it affords" because of "its prominence and central position." Perched on a hill, and in comfortable walking distance of the downtown area, the guesthouse gave its residents unobstructed daytime views of the harbor, with Bequia silhouetted in the background, and glorious tropical sunsets at day's end.

In the late 1960s, the facility's rates were $160 BWI monthly for an individual reservation, $8 BWI daily for groups of twelve persons or more, and $10 US daily for double occupancy. Three daily meals were included in all of those rates. (The authors of this tribute, remember four meals, but perhaps that was just a family bonus!)

As Clarie advanced in years, she began scaling back the scope of the facility's operation, and in 1997 she sold Kingstown Park Guest House. Said to be St. Vincent's oldest guesthouse, having been built in 1765 and originally serving as home to St. Vincent's first French governor, the property was then given a more contemporary appearance as well as a new name: Camelot Inn.

VOLUNTEER

Clarie was active in numerous community organizations. She was a founding member of the Red Cross, the Mental Health Association, the Civil Service Association, the National Trust, the Girl Guides Association, the Netball Association, the St. Vincent Cultural Club and Band, the Garden Club, and the Music Council, assisting this last group in the formation of the Royal St. Vincent Police Band.

She also belonged to the Child Welfare Association, the Save the Children's Fund, the St. Vincent Credit Union, and the British Legion, as well as the Edinboro Castle Club and the Harbour Club, and was registered as a "lady" member of the St. Vincent Cricket Association. For some of these organizations in which she was active, Clarie used her stenographic skills to preserve the official records of their meetings.

Over the years, at her guesthouses Clarie sometimes hosted fundraising teas and dinners at no cost to the charity. She held Christmas parties for children in the community, including those served by the Save the Children's Fund.

In 1969, Clarie was presented with the St. Vincent Certificate and Badge of Honour by Administrator Hywell George. In acceptance of this honour Clarie responded by writing, "I assure Your Honour that the very little that I have done...was for the good of St. Vincent and my fellowmen. I have always enjoyed being of service to others, and it is indeed gratifying to see that my work has been appreciated."

In 1991 Clarie was again acknowledged for her services when she was awarded the M.B.E. (Member of the British Empire). With her inclusion now among the country's unsung heroes, were Clarie still alive today, she would undoubtedly repeat the sentiments of gratitude that she had expressed in 1969.

PRIVATE CITIZEN

Nesta "Clarie" Paynter never married nor had any children of her own, but over the decades she was no less than a foster parent to multiple generations of younger family members. We would be remiss in making this public tribute to the lady we knew fondly as "Tantie Clarie" or "Aunty Clarie," if we did not also share at least a glimpse into her private side, including some of the qualities that inspired our affection for her and motivated this tribute.

Numerous children of Clarie's siblings and *their* children—including the authors—lived in Clarie's guesthouses under her care while their parents were away. Some of those absences lasted for not only short periods, such as during vacations, but years, while the children waited to join parents who had migrated to other countries or were otherwise absent from their lives.

By virtue of being chief executive officer of her own businesses, and even before that, as the eldest surviving child in her family, older by almost two decades than her youngest sibling, Clarie was used to wielding authority. Someone wielding the kind of authority that she did for much of her life—indeed, a female born less than a decade after the end of the Victorian era—almost inevitably ruffles a few feathers along the way, intentionally or not. And Clarie was not without her detractors. But for family members and others who were subject to her authority over the years, the feathers were invariably soon unruffled by the caring and compassionate nature they recognized in her.

Clarie readily shared with others—related or not—her material resources, her skills, her talents, her knowledge—and herself. For example, if she was aware of persons in the community who might be experiencing difficulty providing for themselves, she might have food or other provisions delivered to them from supplies at the guesthouse. And from her, one or more of us received our first lessons in music, art, Spanish, cooking, housekeeping, accounting, and etiquette, among other subjects.

And we must not forget dancing. She shared that with us, too. It was a favorite pastime of hers. For while it might seem surprising to those who knew only "Miss Paynter, businesswoman," Clarie did not lack for invitations to the social events of her day—nor for eligible suitors to escort her to those events. As attested to by stories told by older family members— as well as by mementos shared by Clarie herself—there was no absence of romance from her life.

One relationship that seemed to have had particular significance for her was with an American soldier named Jerry, who was stationed in St. Vincent as well as Trinidad during the 1940s. (Did that perhaps inspire her to want to join the military? We can only wonder.) From his letters to Clarie that she preserved, Jerry seemed to have established a close relationship with other members of her family as well, particularly with her sister May, her husband Alfred Samuel, and their young son. One letter also inquires about May's pregnancy with the couple's second child—Joan, one of the authors of this tribute.

What brought the relationship to an end, we do not know, but it was heartening to us to know that she had once had someone so special with whom to share her burgeoning multigenerational family, however briefly.

And now we are especially heartened to have had this opportunity to share with a wider community a more intimate look at Nesta Lucy "Clarie" Paynter, a hero no longer unsung.

* * *

A legacy she has left us of photos that show
Places, people, events we may never know.
Through her eyes we can see a St. Vincent of old.
It's fitting that now her own story be told.

Written jointly by nieces Joan and Anne, with invaluable input from great-niece Sara (Williams) Toyloy, niece Annelle (Paynter) Thomas, and numerous other relatives and friends.

Poem, *Clarie (Nesta) Paynter, St. Vincent's First Female Photo Historian* by Joan Samuel Simien, previously published in April 2006 on Tony's Oldies website.

Anne Samuel lives in Calfornia, USA. Joan Samuel Simien lives in Hawaii, USA

8. PHYLLIS JOYCE McCLEAN CHILD PUNNETT
(1917-2004)
By
Andrea Punnett Boos

[Phyllis Punnett is the author of the words to the National Anthem of St. Vincent and The Grenadines]

The date was March 17th, 1917. Czar Nicholas II of Russia had just abdicated his throne. Leonard Oliver Child was serving in World War I on the battlefields of Europe. Across the Atlantic Ocean, on the island of St. Vincent in the West Indies, Leonard's niece, Phyllis Joyce McClean Child was born. Her father was Francis (Frank) Child. Her mother was Lillian Liddelow Child. At the time of her birth, Phyllis' father was manager of a large estate called Orange Hill, on the far north-windward coast of the island, and it was there that Phyllis spent her early years. The usual mode of travel on the island in those days was by horse-drawn buggy, so for Phyllis' parents, social interactions with friends and family were rare and treasured events. Two years after Phyllis was born, she was joined at Orange Hill by a baby brother, Ian. As the children grew, they depended on each other for companionship and entertainment.

Living in this remote area of the island presented Frank and Lilly Child with a problem regarding the primary education of their children. When La Soufriere, the volcano in the north of St. Vincent, erupted in 1902, a pyroclastic flow of fluidized solid fragments and hot expanding gases poured down the eastern side of the mountain, destroying vegetation and carving a deep chasm all the way to the coast and into the Atlantic Ocean. At the point where the flow crossed the road leading to the north of the island, the chasm was about a quarter-mile wide. This chasm, just south of Orange Hill, became known as the Dry River because during the "dry" season no water flows down the mountain. Crossing from one side to the other is easily done on foot or by vehicle. However, in the "wet" season, a roaring torrent sometimes fills the chasm, making it impossible to cross from one side to the other and completely cutting off Orange Hill Estate and all points north – sometimes for extended periods of time. This situation, as well as the fact that the nearest school was hours away by horse-drawn buggy, made it necessary for Lilly Child to educate her children on the Estate. For a shy, quiet child like Phyllis, it was sometimes lonely and dull, but as often as possible, Lilly took the children to visit their family in Trinidad. Phyllis was especially fond of her cousin Jocelyn who lived there, the daughter of Charles and Marguerite Child. Jocelyn was the same age as Phyllis, and the two cousins maintained a close friendship for all of their lives.

The original member of the Child family in Trinidad was Arthur Child. He was Phyllis' paternal grandfather. Arthur's parents, Henry Child and Ruth Bates Child, were born and lived in London, England, where Henry was a Solicitor. Arthur was born on November 20, 1853. When he was 28 years old, his father died. That same year, Arthur Child emigrated to the West Indies and settled in Trinidad, where he became Stipendiary Magistrate. In 1884, Arthur married Ida Blanche McClean, a descendant of William McClean, who had come out to Barbados from Scotland around 1715. Ida's father, Charles Daniel McClean, was born in Barbados in 1830. As a young man, he became manager of Tourama Estate in St. Vincent and, on January 31st, 1857, in the Anglican Cathedral in Kingstown, he married Clarissa Weslyanna Free, daughter of Robert Free, an Irishman, and his wife, Rachel Maria DeMoree. Ida was born on the estate around 1866. Charles and Clarissa McClean, along with their children, later moved to Trinidad where he managed Cedar Hill Estate. It was in Trinidad that Ida and Arthur Child were married.

Arthur and Ida's first son, Charles, was born in Port-of-Spain, Trinidad, in 1885. Soon after their son's birth, they moved to St. Lucia where their second son, Francis (Frank) was born in 1887. Arthur Child became Chief Justice of St. Lucia in 1890. He and Ida had three more sons, Walter, Gerald and Leonard. Walter died in 1890 at age two and, twelve years later, on August 24, 1902, Arthur Child died in St. Lucia. About three years after her husband's death, Ida married Walter Barnard, a merchant and businessman who had been born in St. Lucia. In 1905, on Ida's recommendation, Walter bought five estates that had come up for sale in St. Vincent and created Orange Hill. Walter and Ida continued to live in St. Lucia and employed managers for their land interests in St. Vincent, which they visited from time to time. In 1907 Gerald Child died at the age of 14, and in 1922, at the age of 26, Leonard died from wounds sustained in WWI. Frank Child became the manager of Orange Hill Estate around 1916. Later (around 1935), he acquired and managed his own estate at Grand Sable, on the north-east coast of the island, in the area around Georgetown.

Walter and Ida Barnard had three sons, Bertie, Cyril and Dennis. The family left St. Lucia to live in Barbados in 1917 so that the boys could attend school there. However, on his doctor's recommendation for treatment of diabetes, Walter decided to move to England. In 1920 he and Ida sailed for London. Records indicate that soon after arriving, Ida and Walter both succumbed to the terrible Spanish influenza of 1919/1920 and died at St. George's in Hanover Square, London, within a very short time of each other.

Phyllis' maternal grandfather was George Liddelow. He was born in 1850 in West Dereham, Norfolk, England. His parents were Robert Liddelow and Harriet Atkins Liddelow. It is believed that Robert Liddelow died around 1862 and a few years later, in 1870, his son George emigrated to

Trinidad to work for the Colonial Company. He married Laura Augusta McClean in 1881. George was described as a very successful planter, and in 1884 he left the company to acquire Craignish Estate. He eventually sold the estate to his eldest son and retired to Port-of-Spain, living at Errol Park in St. Anns. Lillian Amy Liddelow was one of George and Laura Liddelow's nine children. She married Frank Child on April 26, 1916, in Trinidad, then they settled in St. Vincent at Orange Hill Estate, making a home for their two children, Phyllis and Ian.

As the children grew older, Frank and Lilly decided that they should complete their secondary education in Barbados. Around 1926, the family left the country to live in Kingstown for a few years in order that Phyllis and Ian might get a more extensive academic foundation prior to this next step. They moved to a house on Victoria Park, and in 1927 Phyllis became one of the approximately 100 students at the Girls' High School (GHS). GHS was then located at the end of Back Street, almost opposite the turning into the Park, so it was a short walk for Phyllis to and from school. At the age of thirteen, she left for Codrington High School in Barbados. Traveling to and from Barbados to school had to be undertaken by boat, and Phyllis hated it. She came to dread the long trips, often accompanied by sea-sickness, back and forth between the islands. It was a tremendous relief when she finally finished her high school education and was able to come home for good in 1935. She was offered a job at the Girls' High School, which had moved by then to its current location, and which at that time accepted very young students as well as the older ones. She took the job of teaching reading, writing and arithmetic to the younger children and Art and French to the older students. It was during this time in Phyllis' life that she and her future husband, Kenneth Punnett, began seriously talking about getting married.

Ken was the son of James (Jim) Deary Punnett and Sybil Turpin Punnett. Jim had met Sybil while visiting Tobago as a young man. The Turpins owned an estate in Tobago, and Ken spent some time working there with his mother's family during his teenage years. Ken was the oldest of Jim and Sybil's three children. His sister, Valerie and her husband Clive Williams had no children. His brother Ernest and wife Theresa had two children, Alison and Ralph, before moving to England around 1961, where they had another daughter, Suzette. Sybil Turpin Punnett died in 1947. After Sybil's death, Jim married Hilda Richards, a widow, and they lived at Prospect, on the east coast of St. Vincent, until Jim's death in 1955 while on a visit to Canada.

Phyllis and Ken were married on December 18, 1939. Their first home was a rented house at Villa, in the south of the island. Phyllis had left her teaching job and was looking forward very much to starting a family. Ken worked in Kingstown at Abbot & Sons, and later was a Director at Hadley Brothers & Company for many years. It was in Ken and Phyllis' third year of marriage that the incident which brought them the most heartbreak occurred – Phyllis lost their first child, a girl. She was a full-term pregnancy, but the birth was *placenta previa*. Despite the valiant efforts of the doctor and nurses at the hospital in Kingstown, the baby could not be saved. Phyllis never was able to speak about this without tears. By the end of 1943, however, their son Kenneth Patrick (Paddy) was born and, just a little more than one year later, they welcomed a daughter, Andrea Joyce.

An important event in the lives of Ken and Phyllis began in 1946. They started to build the home where they would live for the next thirty years. The house was built on the west side of Villa Bay in an area known as Rose Cottage, on a hill overlooking Young Island. The house itself was always referred to as "Rose Cottage", even though that was really the name of the area in which it was built. Phyllis was an avid housekeeper, making a comfortable home for her husband and children. She loved to bake, and often would take orders for cakes from friends and family members. The house always seemed to be full of the children's cousins and friends. Phyllis' young nephew inexplicably gave her the name "Gou", and this is what she was called by most of the young people for the rest of her life. Later on, another very frequent visitor to the house was the resident doctor in Bequia, a Canadian named Percy Corbett. Bequia, the most northerly of the Grenadine islands, is seven miles south of St. Vincent and, on his frequent visits, Ken and Phyllis' home became Dr. Corbett's "home away from home". He was like a member of the family until his death in Bequia many years later. There was a piano in the home at Rose Cottage, and Phyllis often would entertain friends and family with her gift of music, which she had cultivated while at school in Barbados.

During their children's early childhood, along with the enjoyable and happy times, there had been anxious times as well for Phyllis and Ken, with some serious childhood illnesses. Both children had whooping cough at young ages. At the age of nine, Andrea contracted typhoid fever and had to be hospitalized. Not too long after her recovery, very bad tonsils caused her to develop a kidney infection, which was followed by a tonsillectomy. This was an especially draining period of time for her parents and a great source of strength to Phyllis was her mother, Lilly. It would seem that these times of medical stress exacerbated Phyllis' tendency to worry about her children's health. She always had concerns, sometimes seemingly irrational, about their well-being. It was to no avail to ask her not to worry, as this was just a part of her protective personality. Fortunately, the children's health steadily improved as they grew older.

Phyllis' brother, Ian, after leaving high school in Barbados, had spent some time in Canada. He returned to St. Vincent to assist his father Frank in running Grand Sable Estate. Ian married Yvonne Richards in 1942 and they lived at Montague House on the estate. Their three children, Barbara, Lester and Elizabeth, were frequent visitors to their Aunt Phyllis and Uncle Ken's home at Villa, and Paddy and Andrea were frequent visitors to their uncle and aunt's home in the country. These visits to family in the country were always enjoyable for the two children. Even though they found the approximately twenty-mile trip along the winding windward coast road to be long and somewhat boring, it was worth the tedious drive. The sights of large fields of arrowroot and sugarcane, and the coconut groves along the far-north coast were a very different experience from the surroundings where they lived. Phyllis and Ken regularly took them to visit their grandfather Frank until his death in the mid 1950s. On the occasions when Paddy and Andrea stayed with their uncle, aunt and cousins, the children's favorite activities were visits to one of the many small rivers that flowed down from the northern range of mountains. A packed lunch of sandwiches with bottles of Ju-C soft drinks would be prepared and, in addition, their uncle Ian would sometimes take along a large breadfruit. He would find a flat rock beside the river and make a small fire of stones, dry sticks and twigs, on which the breadfruit would roast while the children splashed and swam in the river and shouted loudly about how cold the water was. Other favorite activities were taking donkey rides along the narrow dirt roads that bordered the sugarcane fields planted just inland from Georgetown, and trips in the jeep to buy delicious "penny loaves" of bread from the small bakery located in the town. Around the early 1960s, a movie theatre was opened in Georgetown and this provided welcome diversions and entertainment for its many patrons. When Ian and Yvonne Child divorced in 1953, Ian remained at Montague House and Yvonne went to live in Barbados, where the three children completed their high school education.

Paddy and Andrea went to the Kingstown Preparatory School, and later to the Boys' Grammar School and Girls' High School respectively. Phyllis was active during these years, not only with her children's school and extra-curricular activities, such as the Brownies and Cub Scouts, but also with several charitable organizations. One of these was the St. Vincent chapter of the British Red Cross, and Phyllis was one of its many volunteers. Two of the most hard-working members of the Red Cross at this time were Dr. Sydney Gun-Munro and his wife, Joan. In the earlier years, before there was a blood bank, Mrs. Gun-Munro was the Blood Transfusion Officer and was responsible for the quality and safety of transfusions in both the transfusion service and in the hospital. Once a year, in support of the many services performed by the Red Cross, the most successful source of fund raising took place through the sale of poppies. Just before "poppy day", the many volunteers would bring home large boxes of the red artificial flowers, and then the marathon sale of poppies would begin. On "poppy day", it was unusual to see even one person, in or outside of Kingstown, without a bright red poppy pinned to his or her shirt or dress. During this time, Phyllis was also very active in the Altar Society at St. Paul's Anglican Church in Calliaqua. In addition, for many years during the Christmas season, Phyllis and her mother had a tradition of delivering treats, cake and gifts to the sick children at the hospital in Kingstown.

By the late 1930s, Lilly Child had found living in the north of the island to be too cut off from family and friends. She and Frank owned a small house in Bequia and Lilly loved it there. She would spend a month every year at Easter time. Phyllis, and in later years all of Lilly's grandchildren, would accompany her for at least part of the time. At other times of the year, Lilly would go as often as she could. Living in the south of St. Vincent made trips to Bequia and the Grenadines much more accessible, so Frank bought a house for Lilly at Ratho Mill. This home became the center of many family gatherings and often extended visits from grandchildren, such as in the summer of 1954, when she took care of Paddy and Andrea while Ken and Phyllis were on a visit to England. On their return journey home by ship, Ken and Phyllis met a young Englishwoman who was also traveling to St. Vincent and the Grenadines. Her name was Dr. Vivian Usbourne. She had been posted to the islands by the British Colonial Service after working in Africa for two years. Vivian became good friends with the family and, in December of that same year, at a party in Lilly's house at Ratho Mill, the engagement of Vivian to Phyllis' brother, Ian Child, was announced. Vivian and Ian were married the following May.

A few years later, Lilly sold the house to her niece Mavis and husband, Errol Rooks. They converted the home into a small, but very attractive and successful hotel called "The Blue Lagoon". Lilly moved to Villa, into a house that was built on the hill just above Ken and Phyllis' home. She lived there until her death in 1958. Frank Child had died in 1955, leaving the sole management of Grand Sable Estate to his son, Ian, who continued to live with his new wife, Vivian, at Montague House, near Georgetown. After their marriage, Vivian had been posted as the resident doctor to Georgetown and the surrounding areas. Because many of the patients lived in remote and inaccessible areas of the countryside, with only a footpath leading to and from their homes, it was virtually impossible for any of these sick people to make the arduous trip for medical attention to the clinic in Georgetown. The doctor would make house calls to these patients, driving as far as she could in the jeep and then walking the rest of the way, carrying her bag of medical equipment. In many instances, the home to be visited was located far up on the side of a hill and the trek might take her along the banks of a river, through uneven fields of grass and scrub, across stepping stones in the middle of a stream, and finally a climb up the hill to her final destination. When as a young doctor with the British Colonial Service in 1951, Vivian had arrived at her first overseas post on Ukara Island in Lake Victoria, Tanzania, she found that the island had no electricity, no running water, no telephones and no roads – only footpaths. She walked everywhere, several miles daily, to visit patients and to take samples for research on certain diseases. Who could have guessed that her service in Africa would physically prepare her so well for her next job in the far-north areas of St. Vincent, West Indies! To this day, now at the age of 89, "Dr. Child" is a very well-known personality in St. Vincent society.

After completing his high school education at the Boys' Grammar School, Paddy left for England in 1962 to study at the Royal Agricultural College in Gloustershire, and to get some hands-on training in the business while living and working on a local farm. Early in 1963, after Andrea had completed her studies at the Girls' High School the previous year, Phyllis took her and her cousin Barbara to England, where they enrolled in a Secretarial and Business College. It was the following Christmas of 1963, while staying in a small hotel in London which was owned by friends of Ken and Phyllis, that Paddy, Andrea and Barbara met and befriended a young man from Trinidad named Roger Boos. He had spent the last five years at boarding school near Reading, and was completing his A-level studies in London. Roger's parents were Pat and Elsie (Dolly) Boos, who had moved from Trinidad to Venezuela in 1958. They had five sons, Roger being the oldest, and a daughter born in Venezuela. Not wanting the change in languages to negatively impact their two older sons' education, Pat and Dolly sent Roger and his brother David to school in England. Two years after they met in London, Roger and Andrea were married in St. Vincent.

In the meantime, with her children away from home and her motherly duties greatly diminished, Phyllis found time for a more social life outside the home and more time for her volunteer work. She belonged to a group of ladies who met once a week to play "Bridge" and to discuss their various community projects. It was around this time that Mrs. Gladys Webb, wife of the Senior Medical Officer, began the planning stages for a Children's Daycare Center in the town of Calliaqua. Mrs. Webb provided the funds for a building constructed specially for the project. This building consisted of one common room with a toilet/bathroom, a small area for breakfast and lunch preparation for the children, a place for them to eat, and cots set up in the same area for them to rest or sleep. After the building was completed, a Committee to oversee the operation of the Center was organized by Mrs. Beryl Stephens, a prominent member of the Calliaqua community. Mrs. Stephens was the Committee Chairperson and, in addition to Phyllis, the other members were Lucy Ann Cato, Mrs. Edgar Adams, Shirley Abbott Squire, Peggy Hughes, Sheila Regis, Gladys Hadley and Father Michael Odlum, pastor of St. Paul's Anglican Church. The mothers of the children contributed a small monthly amount, as did each Committee member, and frequent fund-raising events were held, such as teas, sponsored walks, fairs, jumble sales, etc. The Calliaqua Daycare Center opened around 1965 and was a great success. For the next forty years, it provided an invaluable service to the women of Calliaqua and the surrounding areas.

By the mid 1960s, Paddy and Andrea were back in St. Vincent. Andrea worked at the Grand View Hotel until her marriage to Roger in December 1965. They left St. Vincent right after Christmas for the United States, where Roger was enrolled at Texas A&M University. Saying goodbye to their daughter was difficult for Phyllis and Ken, as they had no idea when she would be able to return for a visit. However, after graduating in 1969, Roger got a job in St. Lucia, where they lived for almost two years before returning to the University for post-graduate studies. In 1973, they went to Maracaibo, Venezuela, and were there for six years, finally settling back in Texas in 1979. During these years, Andrea was fortunately able to take her children, Nicole, Patrick and Philip to visit their grandparents fairly often during the summer vacations. Ken and Phyllis also paid visits to them in Venezuela and Texas on a few occasions.

One of Phyllis' most endearing qualities was her wonderful sense of humor. She had a ready wit and just loved a good joke. Once when she was visiting her son-in-law Roger's parents in Maracaibo, she was introduced to an old friend of the family affectionately known as "Uncle Cecil". Cecil spent a lot of time in the jungles of Venezuela hunting for diamonds and emeralds – not very successfully. Some people might say that he spent way too much alone-time in the jungle. He was quite eccentric. When Cecil found himself from time to time back in civilization, he was a tremendous fan of the horse races called the "5 and 6", which were run every weekend in Caracas and televised all over the country. The lineup of horses for each race was published in the newspapers every Saturday, and people all over Venezuela would place bets on the races prior to their start on Sunday afternoon. Cecil proceeded to tell Phyllis a story about the time he had gone to a *bruha* (witch) so she could put a "spell" on him which would enable him to pick all the winning horses. He recounted how the *bruha* had wrapped his head in cobwebs, sprinkled him with various liquids, and put a frog on his foot. Phyllis, who had been listening intently and politely throughout, interrupted at the point about the frog, and informed Cecil that if the *bruha* had put a frog on HER foot, she (Phyllis) would have won the race!

In 1973, Phyllis once more found herself in the role of caregiver to two small children when Paddy and his wife Rita separated. She willingly stepped in to help care for two-year old James and four-year-old Michelle. Two years later, when Paddy married Frances (Tipi) Dillon, Ken and Phyllis felt that Rose Cottage would be much more suited to the young couple and the two children (later joined by Paddy and Tipi's daughters, Sophie and Kate). They decided to build a smaller house for themselves, and settled on a spot in the Buccament Valley on the Leeward (west) coast of St. Vincent. In 1976, they moved into their new home, and it was in this house, when she was 61 years old, that Phyllis wrote the words to St. Vincent's National Anthem.

In 1978, in anticipation of the island's coming independence the following year, the St. Vincent public had been invited to submit entries to be considered for the National Anthem. Each entry could consist of just the words, just the music, or both words and music. The word-entry that Phyllis submitted is titled "St. Vincent, Land So Beautiful" and consists of three verses and a refrain. It turned out, as Phyllis was later told, that her entry was the only one which mentioned the Grenadine islands, and this was a big consideration in its selection as the winner of the competition. Her words fit very well with a musical composition submitted by a young music teacher named Joel Miguel of Mesopotamia, and this also was chosen. Phyllis' family and friends were delighted that her entry for the words of the St. Vincent National Anthem had been chosen, and very proud of her success. In 1979, she was presented with a medal for her contribution by the Administrator of St. Vincent and the Grenadines, Mr. Hywell George. On October 27, 1979, St. Vincent and the Grenadines celebrated their independence from Great Britain. The islands are members of the British Commonwealth, and the St. Vincent government system is based on the British Westminster style of government.

By 1981, Phyllis and Ken realized that they missed living in the area of St. Vincent where they had spent the first 36 years of their marriage. In addition, a few years before moving from Villa, Ken had formed a partnership with Paddy in a business called "St. Vincent Sales and Services", with offices located in Kingstown. Ken was finding the daily commute from the Valley to the office to be quite tiring. He and Phyllis decided to sell the house in the Buccament Valley and build another, very similar in size and design, on a hill overlooking Villa and, to the east, Ratho Mill. It was a spot with a beautiful view, and they moved into the house in 1982. They lived there until Ken's death in 2001, when Phyllis moved to a residential center at Arnos Vale.

The years following their move back to Villa from the Buccament Valley were busy for Phyllis with home, family and community activities. In addition to her continued involvement in the operation of the Calliaqua Daycare Center, another of her volunteer projects was at the Lewis Punnett Home for the Elderly, located at Glen. Among other services to the Home, the volunteers, once or twice a month, would organize and serve a "high-tea" to the elderly residents. Music was provided and visitors were always welcome. These were very social events and thoroughly enjoyed by all. Phyllis also continued writing poetry, which she had begun several years earlier and, a few years later in 1990, one of her poems was included in a publication titled "Creation Fire: A CAFRA Anthology of Caribbean Women's Poetry".

In December 1989, Paddy and Tipi arranged a grand celebration for Phyllis and Ken's 50th wedding anniversary. Andrea made a surprise visit to St. Vincent, and some friends and family members came from Barbados for the occasion. On the morning of their anniversary, Phyllis and Ken, along with family and friends, took part in a Communion Service, with a renewal of wedding vows, at St. Paul's Anglican Church in Calliaqua. In the evening, Paddy and Tipi hosted a dinner party at Rose Cottage. It was a wonderful and joyous acknowledgement of two people celebrating fifty years of love and commitment to each other and to their family.

The next few years for Phyllis and Ken were filled with visits to and from family and friends. Four great-grandchildren were born; Michelle's Kai and Anya, and James' Emily and Rebecca. In December 1995, Roger and Andrea brought their children to St. Vincent for a rare Christmas and New Year visit with their family and grandparents. Phyllis continued to be involved with her community projects and took part in the "Tea and Bridge" get-togethers with her friends. Ken was still spending half-days at the office in Kingstown. He and Phyllis especially enjoyed watching movies on the VCR, and Ken had an arrangement with his friend Dr. Sydney Gun-Munro, who had retired in Bequia, to send over any good movies he thought Dr. Sydney might enjoy. The two men often talked on the phone, discussing the movies they had seen and current events.

By his mid-seventies, Ken began having problems with his feet due to nerve damage, secondary to adult-onset diabetes. He was having difficulty walking, especially up the stairs to the office and, by his late seventies, had to employ the assistance of a wheelchair. He became, in effect, homebound. Around this time, Phyllis was showing signs of forgetfulness and of losing her short-term memory. On a visit to St. Vincent in 1998, when Andrea came to stay with her parents while Paddy and Tipi were on holiday in England, Phyllis did not recognize her daughter. It was obvious to Andrea that her mother's memory had seriously deteriorated. As they sat together on the porch overlooking Villa and Ratho Mill, Phyllis pointed to the building in the distance that had been Lilly's home so long ago and explained to Andrea, as if speaking to a stranger, that this "used to be my mother's home". She mentioned the fact that she had lived at Orange Hill as a very young child, and also talked about her trips by sea to school in Barbados and how she had disliked the traveling. Her very long-term memory appeared to be still reasonably intact and active, but the previous fifty-plus years had faded. On Paddy's return from England, it was his sad task to explain to his mother that her brother, Ian, had died in Bristol a short time earlier. Within a couple of years, Phyllis no longer recognized Ken, and when he died in December 2001, at age 83, she had no idea that her husband of sixty-two years was gone. One of God's promises to us is that we will never be given more than we can bear, and that loss may have been more than Phyllis could have borne if she had understood it. Kenneth Oscar Punnett was buried at St. Paul's Anglican Church in Calliaqua, St. Vincent, on December 30, 2001.

A few months after Ken died, Phyllis went to live at Dr. Debnath's Riverside Residential Center at Arnos Vale. Around the middle of 2003, Paddy suggested to his sister that she come to St. Vincent, as Phyllis' health was deteriorating and it would be a good idea to spend some time with their mother. In October of that year, Andrea spent three weeks with Paddy and Tipi, visiting her mother often. Phyllis did not recognize her, but appeared to be content and comfortable in her surroundings. Exactly one year later, on October 12, 2004 – two weeks before St. Vincent and the Grenadines celebrated their 25th anniversary of Independence – Phyllis Punnett died of pneumonia, a complication of her Alzheimer's disease. She was 87 years old.

Phyllis' funeral was held at St. Paul's Anglican Church in Calliaqua, St. Vincent, on October 18, 2004. Officiating were Canon Hoskins Huggins and Arch-Deacon Sylvanus H.A. Regisford. Organist Mrs. Anita Nanton and the St.Paul's Church Choir provided the music and led the singing. In addition to a very large representation of friends and family, several members of the St. Vincent Government were in attendance. A wonderful tribute to Phyllis was given by the Deputy Prime Minister, Mr. Louis Straker, and the eulogy was given by Roger Boos. At the end of the funeral service, the St. Vincent Police Band played and the Choir sang The National Anthem, then the Police Band went to the gravesite and played hymns throughout the internment.

The eulogy of Phyllis, given by her son-in-law Roger, speaks volumes in tribute to a woman whose life was an example of love and dedication to her family and to her country. To those who knew her, and even to those who did not, no other explanation of this special lady's life is necessary. The following says it all:

Eulogy for Phyllis Joyce McClean Punnett (1917-2004)
Given by Roger Boos

"Phyllis Joyce McClean Child Punnett" – an impressive name for an impressive lady! Fifty years ago, however, when a little boy named Lester, her nephew, came to live with Ken and Phyllis and go to school in Kingstown, he gave his aunt a strange and inexplicable name that stayed with her forever – "Gou". We never knew where he got it or why he gave it to his aunt, but this is what her nieces and nephews and many of her children's friends have called her since then. This letter is addressed to:

Dear Gou,

Now that you have gone to be with your beloved husband, Ken, I feel glad for you, but there is so much we are going to miss. When I first met you at the Arnos Vale Airport, just before Christmas 1964, I knew you only as Mrs. Phyllis Punnett. I had written you and Ken to say that I wanted to marry your daughter, although I had never met either of you. You had written a friendly, but carefully-worded invitation to visit, but I was not too sure what my reception was going to be like. By lunchtime, I already knew that I would be calling you "Gou", and that you had accepted me into your home as if I had always belonged there. The two shirt-jacks you had put on my bed as a welcoming present touched me deeper than you ever could have known.

I quickly learned that your husband and your children were the center of your existence. You were a protective force, determined to ensure their absolute safety and well-being at all times. You were always there for them, and for all their cousins and friends when the need arose.

We remember your devotion to keeping an orderly home – your routine Thursday morning shopping in the supermarket, and having everything ready for the weekend. One day, when you were very rushed getting home from town, and hurrying to get everything put away in the kitchen before lunch, you discovered your car keys were missing. We looked EVERYWHERE, but they were nowhere to be found. Finally, someone asked, "Gou, have you looked in the freezer?" – and sure enough, there were the car keys, in the freezer, nestled right next to the frozen chicken. You were so frustrated, and so amused at the same time.

Your niece, Elizabeth, sent Andrea an e-mail soon after we heard that you had left us. She said:

"I will remember the oh so happy times at your home.... the jokes and the laughter, the music, and of course the food ...... the desserts!!! Sitting around that table for ages just talking, long after the meal was over. Oh heavens! Gou was so patient and so sweet to us ....through all the teenage dramas ..... What a precious mother you had. We will remember her with great affection."

Yes. Loving, affectionate, caring, devoted, protective and generous – all terms that can be appropriately applied to you, but you were so much more than that You were a teacher, and taught math at the Girls' High School. You had such a great love for poetry and music, and gave such enjoyment to others when you played the piano. You were a poppy-seller for the Red Cross. You helped with flowers for the church altar, and you were very involved with the Children's Daycare Center in Calliaqua. You had a masterful command of the English language. I remember once at dinner when Ken asked if you had had enough to eat. You replied, "Yes, thank you, I am replete." I had to look up what it meant and have never forgotten it!

Of course, you also wrote the words for St. Vincent's National Anthem. You were so engrossed with getting it just right, so proud you were of your "Hairoun" and your heritage. Ken jokingly suggested "Ta Ra Ra Boom De Ay, Today is Independence Day!" Thankfully, you declined to accept his contribution, and we were very proud of you when your words were chosen.

Jesus said that we would know a tree by its fruit. Good fruit comes from a good tree. Ever since I came into your family, I have been surrounded by good fruit: your children, Paddy and Andrea, of course. Your grandchildren, Michelle, James, Sophie and Kate on Paddy's side; Nicole, Patrick and Philip on Andrea's side. Then there are your great-grandchildren, Michelle's Kai and little Anya, who sadly left us even before you did. James' girls, Emily and Rebecca, and Nicole's little Gabriel. And I am sure there will be more. The seeds planted by you and Ken have borne a good crop, amply watered many times over by your generosity and love.

I was particularly touched by the relationship you had with your husband. Your attention to his needs, your caring for him, were examples of love that I take strength from to this day. When he came home from work, you immediately would make sure he had a cup of tea. You would sit with him and talk. We would join in. Even when you had begun to lose the sense of years and dates, you were so attentive to Ken. I remember one evening, after the sun was down and we were sitting all together at home in the patio, Ken in his wheelchair and you by his side, you obviously went way back to an earlier time. You said to him, your husband of almost 60 years then, "Ken, it's getting late. How are you going to get back home?" He looked at you with great understanding and compassion and said, "Don't worry, Phyl, I'll take the bus." You were perfectly satisfied with the answer.

Over the last few years, we have missed your conversation, your letters, your wit, your wonderful poetry, and we have had to make do with your quiet presence instead. It was sad seeing you gradually slip away, but even so you gave us time to adjust and to say goodbye. We were not really prepared when you left, but no one ever is. So many memories remain – wisps of conversation, expressions, laughter, things we would like to have with us still, but which are now yours alone, until we meet again.

May God bless you and keep you, and your beloved husband, in the arms of Jesus, in that eternal Kingdom of Peace and Love, into which you surely will fit. Confident in our faith in the saving power of God, we look forward to the time when we'll be together again and be able to sit and laugh as before.

We love you, we thank you for loving us, and we'll miss you.

NATIONAL ANTHEM OF ST. VINCENT & THE GRENADINES

St. Vincent, land so beautiful,
With joyful hearts we pledge to thee
Our loyalty and love, and vow
To keep you ever free!

REFRAIN:
Whate'er the future brings,
Our faith will see us through
May peace reign from shore to shore
And God bless and keep us true.

Hairoun! Our fair and blessed Isle;
Your mountains high so clear and green
Are home to me, though I may stray,
A haven, calm, serene.

Our little sister-islands are
Those gems, the lovely Grenadines
Upon their seas and golden sands
The sunshine ever beams!

Andrea Punnett Boos lives in Carrollton, Texas, USA.

9.   ALBAN RADIX
By
Hazeldene Phills Hercules and Cheryl Phills King

Alban Radix, or "Uncle" as he was affectionately called was the Founder and Fearless Leader of the Calliaqua Boys Scouts, a very successful movement in the community.

Alban was born in 1916. He was one of 14 children born to Thomas Radix and Catherine (nee Polite). His mother Catherine, to her friends in the village of Vicennes, St. David's Grenada, she was known as Cousin Angie. To her children, grandchildren and other relatives, she was known as Nennen: Nen, for short. A godchild gave her that nickname. It was the usual name given to godparents in those days.

Alban was the second youngest boy. Ivan was the first; Clarice and Iris were next. They were twins. Iris died as a toddler. Then followed John, Lloyd, O'Hanley, Matthias, David who died at ten, Rosey, Lincoln, Daniel, Alban, Eileen and Thomas. The last boy was named after his father. "Uncle's aunt (his mother's sister) also married a Radix, and Nen also raised the cousins after her sister died. They were Brighton, Helen, Veronica, Florence, and another John.

Alban was a man of few words. Nen delivered Alban by herself and went back to work in her garden. By that time, she was skilled at delivering babies. She called this son Alban because she thought that he would be the last child – "All born" (In the Grenadian vernacular, Alban would be a corruption of the English words: all born.) Alban was a teacher. He adopted Lloyd's habit of quizzing his young nieces and nephews in an effort to get them to spell words correctly.

He was born in Vincennes, in the parish of St. David's where his parents lived for many years. Alban was quite gifted and very popular as a young boy. He was an acolyte in the church and at one time some thought he might become a priest. He also traveled to many Caribbean countries as a boy scout. He was quite bright at school and was made a teacher at age 14 years at the St. David's Roman Catholic school in Grenada. Later he left the post when he was criticized for not wearing a tie in the very hot weather.

He then taught in Trinidad for sometime before going to the United States to join his older brothers who attended Howard University in Washington D.C. His oldest brother Ivan remained in Grenada and ran the family shop. However John, who was the first to travel to the USA studied Medicine and encouraged the other brothers to join him. The oldest girl Clarice Radix Ross was the second to move to the USA with her children. Lincoln also studied Medicine, Lloyd studied Dentistry and Daniel studied Optometry. The other sisters Rosey and Eileen moved to England.

Two brothers who went to South America nicknamed "Hanley and Tokes" did not fare as well as the brothers who went to North America. They returned to Grenada somewhat disappointed. The last of the boys named Thomas after his father, also dropped out of college in Washington D.C. and disappeared for many years.

"Uncle's father Thomas traveled the islands and traded kola nuts and other items. When trading was not good, he traveled to Cuba to cut sugarcane. Nen was very much influential in shaping the children's studies and careers. She was a strong disciplinarian.

The family lived in St. David's until sometime after Thomas Sr. died in 1926 of what was probably diabetes. After her husband died, Nen fought to keep things together and later moved to St. Georges where she opened a small business and took in boarders. Nen was left to raise 14 children on her own. She was a Catholic and very religious. She woke the family at five o'clock in the morning to pray. Generally she said the rosary and prayed for everyone. Nen was respected and admired by all. After all, she was the mother of a doctor John, another doctor, Lincoln, a dentist Lloyd, and after a while, a lawyer Alban.

Alban traveled to Washington, DC. He studied at Howard University then he proceeded to London to study law. He passed the bar in London and returned to Grenada.

When Alban returned to Grenada as a lawyer, he practiced for a while before going on to Carriacou where his brothers John and Lincoln also spent some time. While in Carriacou, he had a brief spell in politics but was not very successful.

Nen was always overweight and suffered from high blood pressure. When returning from her brother's house, Nen had a stroke on the road. She suffered paralysis on the left side. Her speech was slurred. Her doctor son John was called. He confirmed that Nen had suffered a stroke.

The next few days were very difficult. Nen and her spirit insisted on getting out of bed. She fell and went into a coma. She died on a Monday at 5:00 am, nine days after the stroke. Nen was born on October 25, 1884. She was 65 when she died. The day before her death, many of her sisters and children converged on the home. It was crowded. People slept on floors. When it seemed clear that her breath was labored and death was imminent, all gathered by her bedside and prayed. There were screams and tears. This noble matriarch had gone to meet her God, whom she loved and served faithfully, and her husband Thomas.

Nen's funeral was one of the wonders of Grenada. In those days, the dead person was prepared in the house for burial. The funeral service was held in the church a few doors away. School children from the nearby Convent and Boys' College were there. Ten busloads of people and fifty cars with their occupants led the procession to Macala, St. David's where Nen was buried near her beloved Thomas. Her sons, Lloyd, John, Daniel, Ivan and Alban were pallbearers.

While the funeral was taking place, drama was occurring in the sky. Her son Lincoln was a new doctor. On hearing of his mother's illness, he was hurrying home from the USA to help her. The island of Grenada was overcast with clouds and his plane was unable to land. On t he Wednesday, he surprised everyone with his presence; but his mother had died and was already buried.

As the coffin was lowered into the ground, it opened just for a minute or so and she was gone forever. The priest who presided over the burial ceremony remarked that one day her children and grandchildren would rise and call her "Blessed".

Here are the Obituaries of Catherine "Nen" Radix that appeared in the *Grenada Newspaper "The West Indian"* that Asquith Phills, got from Dr. Edward Cox of Rice University, Texas.

Catherine Radix Laid To Rest

Falling ill less than two weeks ago, Catherine Radix, aged 65, mother of a large and well-known family died at her home in St. Johns' Street early yesterday morning.

The funeral took place at the St. George's Roman Catholic Church at 4 pm yesterday and the corpse was then taken for burial to Windsor Forest Cemetery St. David's in which parish she lived until her change of abode to St. George's eight years ago.

Among relatives left to mourn their loss are nine sons: Dr. J.C. Radix and Dentist L.C. Radix well known here; Dr. Lincoln Radix, Florida, USA; Alban Radix. LL B. England; Ivan G. Radix, St. David's; Thomas and Daniel, students at Howard University, USA; O'Hanley and Mathias, South America; three daughters Mrs. Clarice Ross, Brooklyn; Eileen and Rosey Radix who lived with her until her death, numerous brothers and sisters.

Catherine Radix – A Tribute By J.V. RedHead

The death of Catherine Radix on the night of Sunday last after a brief illness removed from the community one of the GREATEST Mothers in the island. Born in St. David's sixty-five years ago she lived almost all her life in that parish. Her gallant husband Thomas W. Radix pre-deceased her several years ago and she was left with the great responsibility of educating and bringing up twelve children --- nine boys and three girls. How this beloved, devoted, indefatigable mother accomplished this task with complete success can easily be seen by the prominent positions held by most of her children not only here but abroad.

Believing firmly in the great value of home training, her principal concern was to develop her children's character. Being possessed herself with a strong character, she did not find it very difficult to inculcate the virtues and good qualities of a good character.

Her religious fervor pervaded her home and influenced her children greatly. In the face of adverse circumstances sometimes, she strove to give her children the best education. They were all educated at the St. David's Roman Catholic School where they all made good until they were able to pursue higher studies.

Three adorned the Teaching Profession for some time but looked further afield and now pursue more lucrative professions – Dr. John C. Radix, Dentist Lloyd Radix and Attorney at Law Alban Radix, LL.B.

Her good sense, assiduity, tenderness, industry and vigilance enabled her to overcome all obstacles and as the richest reward of her solicitude and toil, she had the happiness and satisfaction of her children distinguishing themselves as leaders and useful citizens in their different spheres.

The very large and representative gathering present at her funeral on Monday attested in no uncertain terms the popularity of this devoted mother and her family. They should have great consolation in the fact that she lived a most useful life. May the Angels lead her into Paradise to hear the joyful words of our Heavenly Father, Well done thou good and faithful servant, possess ye the kingdom prepared for you.

"Uncle" eventually moved to St. Vincent and practiced law there. Two of "Uncle's" brothers had married women named "Eileen" and he had a sister named Eileen. Alban married another Eileen, Eileen Walker from Glen whose parents were James and Millicent Walker. Father Walker, a well-known educator in St. Vincent and his wife, a seamstress raised nine children. "Uncle's" wife Eileen was fondly called "Teen" by her nieces and nephews. She was the youngest of the Walker family. "Uncle" and Teen have one child, a son named Denver. Teen was a headmistress at the Calliaqua Anglican School and retired as a teacher. The Radix family lived in Rathomill.

Alban was a true family man. He never lost touch with his family in Grenada.

Every year, "Uncle" and members of his family would take the boat and travel to Grenada and Carriacou to visit his relatives. Likewise, his relatives from Grenada would always visit him and his family in St. Vincent. He never believed that children should be seen and not heard. He encouraged and valued everyone's input. He believed in empowerment and building one's self confidence.

"Uncle" was a humanitarian. We cannot forget his godliness and his being the poor people's lawyer. If his clients did not have the money to pay for his legal services, that did not stop him from providing justice for the poor people. It wasn't about the money, or about him, it was about justice for the poor people. People rallied around him and called him "Uncle". Dubbed the "poor people's lawyer", since he did not charge for his court services, indebted people however did not hesitate to drop off ground provisions, fruits, animals on his porch to show their gratitude.

"Uncle" was a man way ahead of his times. He was a maverick and a trailblazer. "Uncle" wanted to plant trees and flowers and have animals all over. He felt that with so much land, people should not have to suffer. His remarkable contribution both individually and collectively will always be remembered. There is a small island about 200 yards off the mainland of St. Vincent known as Young Island. About 80 yards beyond Young Island is a small elevated rocky islet known as Rock Fort. It is extremely high and difficult to climb from the base to the top. "Uncle" had the brilliant idea to purchase a few goats and let them free on the Fort. The Fort had enough vegetation for the goats, but who would have thought about such a brilliant idea but "Uncle".

"Uncle" started a Scout Troop in Calliaqua and the scouts led an extraordinary life of travel and adventure. There was an emphasis on outdoor activities – camping, woodcraft, aquatics, hiking, backpacking and sports. He empowered the young men in the community to learn the skills and knowledge to become leaders. He made character building his goal.

The Scout Movement, supported young people in their physical, mental and spiritual development, so that they may play constructive roles in the society. The Scout uniform consisted of a khaki button-up shirt, shorts, and a broad-brimmed campaign hat, and a neckerchief which was chosen as it could easily be used as a sling or triangular bandage by a Scout in need. Distinctive uniform insignia included the fleur-de-lis and the trefoil, as well as merit badges and other patches to further develop a scout's skills and interests.

Alban Radix, "Uncle", was the scoutmaster of #1 Calliaqua Boys Scout Troop. He took over the leadership of the Troop from Israel Sayers who migrated to Trinidad in the 1950's. Boys were recruited from the Southern-most part of the island including; Calliaqua, Arnos Vale, Villa, Rathomill, Prospect, Brighton, Diamond, Glen, Golden Vale, Fair Hall, Choppins, Ribishi, Belmont and surrounding villages.

The boys ranged in ages from approximately 12 years to 20+ and were organized into three Patrols with a leader. The boys under the age of 12 years were organized in the Cup Pack and graduated to the Scout Troop when they reached approximately 12.

The troop began most of its activities with this Yell:

Leader: Number 1 Calliaqua.
Troop response: Number 1 Calliaqua.
Leader: Number 1 Calliaqua.
Troop Response: Number 1 Calliaqua.
All with gusto: C, A, L. L, I, A. Q, U, A.
Tis a pleasant place to stay
Fresh sea bathing in the East
Fresh fish and black eye peas
They will tell you down the Quays. (Pronounced Keys)
Rarrrr...Rarrr.
Calliaqua Scouts!

The Troop ended the day's activities with the Taps:

The day is done
Gone the sun
from the sea, from the hills, from the skies
All is well
Safely rest
God is nigh

"Uncle" emphasized "learning by doing" as a method of learning and building <u>self-confidence</u>. Activities and games provided an enjoyable way to develop skills such as <u>dexterity</u>. Outdoor settings provided contact with the natural environment. The scouts built unity, camaraderie, and a closely-knit bond and fraternal atmosphere. These experiences, along with an emphasis on trustworthiness and personal honor, helped to develop character, <u>responsibility</u>, independence, self-confidence, reliability, and <u>readiness</u>; which eventually lead to <u>collaboration</u> and <u>leadership</u>.

Under "Uncle's" leadership, the scout troop hiked around the island of St. Vincent in about five days. During this adventure, the scout troop pitched camps in burial grounds and slept in schools along the way. "Uncle" took a lot of risks that appeared to be second nature to him. The troop benefited a great deal from camping abroad in such places as Union Island (St. Vincent Grenadines), Grenada, St. Lucia and Barbados. A wealth of memories resulted from these trips, and the scouts and cubs owed them all to "Uncle's" trust and confidence in the scouts and his passion for scouting.

"Uncle" took the scouts on jamborees throughout the Caribbean, using the Morse code. The scouts mastered different knots, enjoyed campfires, and went Christmas caroling. "Uncle" was a very religious man. The first

Sunday of each month, the scout troop went to Calliaqua St. Paul's Church and would march down from church to Calliaqua Bay side.

The scouts also participated during the Lenten season by keeping watch in the St, Paul's Calliaqua Anglican Church, just before Christ crucifixion. Affiliated with the church was the Parish Hall, in which the scouts performed several plays under "Uncle's direction.

The Calliaqua Scout Troop was very famous in St. Vincent. The troop participated in every parade at Victoria Park, Kingstown (The Capital of St. Vincent and the Grenadines). Other participants in these parades included the St. Vincent Police Band, the Boys Grammar School Cadets and the scout troops. The Commissioner of Scouts always depended upon the contributions from "Uncle" and his scout troop.

"Uncle" was a revered figure and well known for his famous saying: "I say, boy, I say".

The legacy that he left was that most of his scouts went on to have successful careers and lives. "Uncle" contributed to the development of young people in achieving their full physical, intellectual, social and spiritual potential as responsible individuals of their local and international communities.

Apart from *"I say, I say boy"*, "Uncle" had many other wise sayings which always made you laugh. For example, he argued Court cases in the Layou and Barroullie Court Houses, and when he was driven on the Leeward roads he would say to the driver, *"Boy, if you miss the road, look for a lamppost"*.

You cannot talk about "Uncle" without talking about his wife, Eileen who was fondly known as Teen. This name she derived from her nephew. She was a wonderful, caring mother, sister, aunt, friend. She was one of the Walker sisters, the others being Beryl Walker Stephens, Edna Walker Dougan, Eloise Walker Phills. She was the youngest of the Walkers. She was a teacher for years and was once the headmistress of the Calliaqua Anglican School. She was in the first class to attend the newly built Teachers College in St. Vincent. We recall Teen paying particular attention to students who were struggling to learn and finding various innovative ways to teach them after school ended. Her passion for teaching and education was outstanding. Several of her students who have since become successful in their careers, still pay her homage that they would not be where they are today, if it weren't for her. Teen was committed to everyone learning the basics to be successful. Teen was also the leader of the Rangers, her sister Edna was the leader of the Girl Guides and her sister Beryl was part of the Mothers Union and the Children's Creche. Teen was quite an entrepreneur. After she retired from teaching, she opened a clothing store in Calliaqua and started her own business. Teen was not afraid of trying new adventures. She went to the United States of America and attended Columbia College where she studied square dancing. She came back home and taught the Girl Guides the dance moves she learned. "Uncle" and Teen loved their only child and son Denver unconditionally. "Uncle" particularly had pet names for Denver, namely Pudoo, Corby, and Gagay.

"Uncle" and Teen valued family. The Phills family, Artie, Cheryl, Vincent, Asquith and Hazeldene lived with Teen and "Uncle" until they graduated from secondary school and immigrated to the United States to meet their mother and to pursue their college education. "Uncle"was a disciplinarian and taught how to take responsibility for one's mistakes. He owned a piece of land on the beach in Villa and would take the family there for swims and picnics. He owned a house in Kingstown next to the Girls' High School and would go there for lunch instead of having to travel all the way to Rathomill. He would also stop for lunch at Simeon Cumberbatch's shop in Calliaqua.

Teen and "Uncle" valued education. There was every type of encyclopedia and book in the bookcases at home. Doing homework first was a prerequisite before playing. Beryl Stephens, Eloise Phills and Edna Dougan were sisters of Teen, so the Radix family, the George Stephens family, the Eloise Phills family and the George Dougan Family were tightly knit and lived close to each other in Rathomill. Not only were the sisters very close to each other, but the first cousins were equally close. They played together, ate together, partied together, hung out together. That bond among the Walker Family is still very close today. " Uncle" believed in preserving the family history. He would gather all the family members together for family picture taking days.

"Uncle" always brought treats home with him when he came home from work in the evenings and as youth we looked forward to his coming home to indulge in the fudge, chocolate bars, tarts, bodyline, Ju-C, lollypops, choc-ice, rocks, heavy bread, sandwich loaves, even blocks of ice to make shave ice. Uncle was a risk-taker. There is no meat in St. Vincent that he did not eat, including iguana. He loved cooking.

"Uncle" believed in youth being held accountable for their actions. One incident involved a motorcycle cop who caught a youngster, hardly a teenager, driving "Uncle's" car. As the youngster parked the car in front of "Uncle's" house and ran in, the motorcycle cop called on "Uncle" to report the incident. "Uncle" did not have tolerance for the nature of this business, so "Uncle" called the youngster and told him to talk to the motorcycle cop while he went inside the house. The motorcycle cop was scolding the youngster. After five minutes, "Uncle" came out and said, "**Boy, Get in here, that's enough**". **"All right, he has heard you now"**, **he said,** and left the motorcycle cop standing there, without any satisfaction.

There was another incident with Uncle, a nephew who was visiting with him from Grenada and the police. They went to Kingstown one morning.

There was no parking space near Uncle's office and he drove around for a while before finding a space, a little distance away. As he parked in the space, a police inspector came up and said "Mr. Radix you can't park here". Uncle then asked "where should I park then?" The policeman looked around and realized there was no parking space around, and answered "well, I don't know'' By this time Uncle had closed up the car and signaled his nephew to follow him towards his office leaving a perplexed officer standing there. Uncle's parting words to him were, "If you are an Inspector of Police and you don't know where I should park, how would I know?"

This behavior was not entirely strange to Uncle's nephew. On another occasion in Grenada, he recalled when he went with Uncle Lincoln (Uncle's brother) to the horse races in Seamoon. Uncle Lincoln parked his car and a policeman came up to him and said he could not park there. Uncle Lincoln ignored the young officer and closed up his car. The officer took out his little book and started writing. Uncle Lincoln then took out some paper and also started writing. "What is your name, Officer?" Uncle Lincoln asked in a stern voice looking straight into the young officer's eyes. The Officer was taken by surprise. He hesitated for a few seconds then stopped writing, put the book back in his pocket and walked away. Uncle Lincoln and his nephew continued to the race stand.

"Uncle" the husband, man, father, lawyer was a very caring, compassionate, gentle, generous, unruffled individual. "Uncle" was an unselfish individual. He is known for giving rides in his cars to individuals walking to and from Kingstown. "Uncle" always wanted to help others. He brought three disadvantaged children - Ridley, Patsy and Rosie - to live with the family to care for them and give them a better life. He and Teen would pay for them to attend Secondary Schools.

Even though "Uncle" was a Catholic, he faithfully attended the St. Pauls' Calliaqua Anglican Church. The Walker Girls were faithful members of the church, and were involved in the Mother's Union, Altar Guild. "Uncle" never wavered from his Catholic faith, Every Saturday evening, he will still do the rosary with the family.

Over the years, "Uncle" had several brand new cars and the younger generation who lived with him enjoyed these speed cars. "Uncle" provided the opportunity for the young people to learn to drive his cars and get their licenses. At first, he had a six cyclinder Zephyr, (P134). The Zephyr was probably the fastest car in St. Vincent and the Grenadines at that time. Then he invested in a Consul (P1234), a beautiful maroon and grey car. Two color cars were sports cars in those days. Later, "Uncle" invested in other models, such as the Opel. His cars were always clean.

In St. Vincent, Uncle Alban unsuccessfully ran for the seat of the St. George constituency as an independent candidate (which included the area of Ratho-Mill where we lived) on September 1956. He was also perceived as a maverick for always wearing sandals without socks and was devoted to scouting and his boy scouts. Today we can see the success of his efforts as many of his boy scouts have attained leadership roles in their various undertakings not just in SVG, but world-wide. Such was his influence.

"Uncle" was quite a writer about a topic he felt passionately about - "Education". The following are several articles written by Alban Radix, B.A. LL.B, entitled "Education" written to *"The West Indian Newspaper"*, Grenada in 1946. These articles truly depict "Uncle's" philosophy and who he was as a man.

Education (III) By ALBAN RADIX, B.A., LL.B – March 9, 1946

What kind of education should our children receive? Surely the strongest ray of happiness is health. I think children should be taught first about the functioning, the care and healing of their bodies. One hour of every day spent in school should be devoted to the subject.

Diet too should be taught. First aid is important.

Having sought a sound foundation for the body I should ask for the formation of character. Our schools should select teachers not merely for their technical ability but also for the influence their character and personality might have upon the children.

I should ask for such moral institutions as would help the individual student in some degree to see his neighbor as his brother and his countrymen as his family.

The ability to use experience-even of others-to attain one's ends is true intelligence. Science serves to train the intelligence for it proceeds from the careful sifting of evidence. It distinguishes between wishes and facts. Science teaches us to believe according to the evidence and to weigh all evidence skeptically. Such a habit of mind might bring to an end the age of propaganda.

I would not bother children with foreign languages at all. One never really learns even modern languages from books. There is but one decent thing to do with a dead language - bury it.

Health, Character and Intelligence constitute the bases of free personality and the primary goals of education. In short, the purpose of education is not to make Scholars but men.

Education (IV) By ALBAN RADIX, B.A., LL.B – April 2, 1946

Training in manual skills should receive more emphasis in our schools. The youngster won't need much encouragement. They have the natural creative impulse. Just give them the hint and the opportunity and they will be building useful things of their own accord. They will test theory in actual practice.

In the years from say, 12-16, when the creative urge ought to be developing, most of a youngster's energy is devoted to cramming theories out of books. He has no trade, no practical skill, no useful art. He must later devote several of his finest productive years fitting himself into a working world. Skills such as weaving, carving, carpentry, mechanics, painting, etc. give one a useful line or sideline involving manual skill. Teaches one to think, to do.

Even if a youngster is to be a preacher, a doctor or a lawyer, let him spend time at manual training and mechanics. He will have more practical sense if he has also had this training. Book learning is all very well, but if I knew what I know now I wouldn't let that interfere with my manual training at all.

Hand training is an essential part of brain training. The best man is the one who combines the learning of books with the learning which comes from doing things with the hands. The young man or woman who has that combination need not worry about getting along in the world today or at any time. There is nothing wrong with this island which brains, energy and good will cannot cure.

Education (VI) By ALBAN RADIX, B.A., LL.B – April 7, 1946

Teaching children to think, to think logically, for themselves is a most important part of home and school training. Information by stuffing a child with facts is no way to make him think for himself, or think at all. Youngsters naturally have exploring minds. Parents and teachers must keep them exploring. Every incident of the day should be an expedition into the familiar unknown. A bicycle breaks down. What makes it do that? How can one prevent it from happening again? Boys and girls who through quest and questions and thought, find out these things for themselves are acquiring a habit worth more than a thousand bicycles.

Children must be permitted to do creative things on their own accord rather than ours. There is almost always another perfectly good way of doing everything. Suggestions, guidance, and praise rather than ridicule is the secret of teaching. Then it is fun, not school or work.

Youngsters must be encouraged to probe for the cause and effect for everything that happens around them. They should at times be given difficult (though not discouraging) tasks to work under pressure to test their reasoning power at work. The going will be slow at first, but every time a fellow faces a first class difficulty and masters it, he becomes that much stronger. He takes on renewed courage and confidence in himself. He heads into the future with no fear nor fumbling.

Teaching children to think, to weigh arguments and to discover flaws, fallacies, weaknesses, errors and inconsistencies would bring to an end this age of corruption of propaganda and of superstition.

Education (VII) By ALBAN RADIX, B.A., LL.B – NY, May 18, 1946

"Sports too and Physical Training should receive more attention in our schools. Not only for boys, but girls. I say this because sports help with problems of temper and shyness, builds up confidence and poise, teaches cooperation, muscular coordination, draws one out of his shell. These qualities carry over into business and social situations. Sometimes children are too inclined to be individualists. Unless they possess the genius of an Einstein or Edison, they will be not only unpopular but unproductive. Any teamwork sport teaches the child that unless he subordinates his interests to that of the group he will enjoy the open dislike of his teammates or forfeit his place on the team. He thereby learns the importance of cooperation.

An alarming temper is often a stumbling block in the way of a child's progress. Certain sports are deemed to correct temper tantrums. The more infuriated the young player, the lower will be his degree of skill. In time he will discover that self control is the way to success.

Boys and girls who participate in Sports or Physical Culturists or Scouts or Guides usually enjoy better health and make better men and women. They are not afraid of being laughed at. They develop a well rounded personality through sports. Their fears are eradicated while they are young.

Too often children meet situations where shyness is a handicap. They can help overcome that early by sports where the participant is in the spotlight. If he is self conscious, the game suffers. Gradually, determination to overcome this problem plus playing experience will build up his self-confidence and poise. Boys and girls who take no part in sports are usually physically weak and enjoy poor health. They are clumsy and respond slowly and are prone to injury and late to recognize danger. While young, they need the training that sports will give them. As they speed up their game, they speed up their reflexes.

There was another article entitled: **Mr. Alban Radix speaks at St. David's – March 9, 1946**

Mr. Alban Radix on Wedesday, February 27th, 1946 delivered a very educative and inspiring address on "Adult Education" to the members of the St. David's Adult Evening Institute. The speaker who was introduced by Mr. M.A. Guillame, showed among other things the pleasure that surely must be derived during the learning process by the members of an Institute with ample equipments and a well balanced curriculum. A vote of thanks was voted my Messrs Eric Emily and Subdeo Bhagwan repsectively.

Education (9) By ALBAN RADIX, B.A., LL.B – June 1946

Too often a child's academic difficulties are due to a lack of emotional and mental well being. A sense of security, therefore is amongst the child's fundamental needs. One simple way in which the school can contribute to the pupils' security and well being is to make the school surroundings attractive. But under our present system students are assigned to uncomfortable seats in a crowded bench row and impressed with the three school commandments: sit still, keep quiet and do what the teacher says.

The child finds himself cowed into submission by a well intentioned, usually kind but impersonal strange and distant teacher who knows the job depends on keeping discipline and forcing a certain amount of abstract learning on the poor children. Could anything be further from giving a child a sense of at-homeness, of confidence and of security?

In the progressive schools of today, on the other hand, the student comes into a pleasant, sanitary, cheerful and comfortable room where he finds more things planned for his interests and activities where the teacher is concerned with understanding him and making him happy. The teacher relationship to the pupil in the progressive type of school is that of guide, counselor and friend rather than taskmaster. They must. it is true at times, be firm. This is as necessary to the child's security as is the teacher's interests and understanding. But there is a great difference between being guided by an understanding friend and being forced by a disciplinarian to do things which are neither desirable nor meaningful. In order to maintain this wholesome kind of relationship to pupil, the teacher must be secure.

Education (10) By ALBAN RADIX, B.A., LL.B – July 1946

An interesting topic in the field of education is that of a planned curriculum vs. the emergent curriculum. The first position is by far more widely held and much need not be said about it. Advocates of the emergent or spontaneous curriculum hold that there should be no adult attempt to determine in advance what subject matter the children should learn, but instead the curriculum should emerge each day from the interest and activities of the learners to be determined by the teachers on the spirit of the moment. The advocates see too clearly the evils that result by a detailed planning of school life, a planning that has usually been so complete and detailed that the range of the child experience in school has been sharply limited, and the response in school to experiences outside has been inhibited.

An interest expressed by a child resulting from a chance experience would be capitalized upon and would result in discussion and investigation. Sometimes the ramifications would be very wide and far reaching and a single incident might lead to hours or even weeks of work.

Actually, there are weaknesses in each of the positions and each has value. The positions are not incompatible, and the conflict can be resolved. One need not go to the extreme of an eagerly unplanned curriculum in order to avoid the manifest evils of the over- planned and intrusive curriculum which admits no deviation. We are effectively combining the values of the opposing positions while eliminating their evils.

Alban or "Uncle" was a dynamic, profound individual. It was on a Sunday New Year's Day, January 1, 1967 at a family picnic at Sand Bay that "Uncle" drowned. Many of "Uncle's" relatives and long time scout members were residing abroad when the news circulated. Needless to say that it was a time of sadness and reflection of the wonderful shared experiences. Everyone indicated that scouting would never be the same in St. Vincent and the Grenadines. His funeral was huge, and attended by many. The Boys Scouts and the Girl Guides from all over the country were in attendance. His individual and collective contributions will never be forgotten.

We want to acknowledge and thank Evelyn A. Henry, Uncle's niece for all the information about Uncle's life in Grenada; Uncle's nephew Roger Radix and Roger's daughter Cathy-Ann for their assistance, as well as Dr. Edward Cox for the newspaper articles. We also want to thank Denver Radix (Uncle's son), Henry (Artie) Phills,, Vincent Phills and Asquith Phills for their contributions.

Hazeldene Phills Hercules is Executive Staff Assistant to the Mayor of Rochester, New York, USA and lives in Henrietta, New York.

Cheryl Phills King is a political scientist. She lives in Madison, New Jersey, USA.

10. **THOMAS MOWBRAY SAUNDERS**
By
Adrian Saunders

Thomas Mowbray Saunders was born at North Union in St. Vincent on 7th August, 1910 to a humble family. He was the second of seven children. There were four girls (Gladys, Joyce, Lyn and Margaret) and three boys (Roy, Thomas and John). His father, Mowbray McKenzie Saunders, was the overseer of the Hadley estate and his mother did the laundry for the family. Roy, the first child, died when Thomas was still a young lad and so, from an early age, he assumed a great deal of family responsibilities as the oldest living child.

EARLY LIFE

Thomas attended the Union Methodist School. He was a bright boy but school work alone did not occupy his attention. He had many chores to perform both before and after attending school. It was his job to get up early in the morning to tie out the family's livestock, a cow and a few pigs, and in the evenings he would bring them back to the home. Thomas also helped to work on the small vegetable garden that the family cultivated. On Sundays he was responsible for cleaning all the shoes in the house.

Thomas's mother, Eglantine Saunders nee Adams, was a gentle, deeply religious woman who loved her children dearly. Thomas said that as a child, it was expected that before he left for school each morning, he would kiss his mother and greet her again in similar fashion when he returned from school in the afternoon. His mother conducted Sunday morning prayers with the family from 5.00 o'clock until day break. Hymns were sung, portions of scripture read, and each of the children took turns to pray. Their father always said the closing prayer.

Thomas was heavily influenced by the outstanding Methodist preachers of the day such as the late Wilberforce Roberts and Benjamin Nathaniel Bacchus. So impressed was he that, in his very early teens, he gave very serious thought to offering himself as a candidate for the Methodist Ministry. But this never materialised. However he began preaching the Word of God in 1930 and continued this vocation for over sixty years. His early life of Methodism, discipline, hard work and the positive influences of his family played a critical role in preparing Thomas for the life ahead of him.

THE TEACHER

After he had completed his primary school education, he was appointed a Pupil Teacher on the 10th November, 1924. He was barely 14 years old, younger than some still attending school. He was to remain in the teaching profession for well over 30 years. He first taught at the school he had attended and, while teaching there, he sat and passed all the Pupil Teachers' Examinations. Based on the results of his third year Pupil Teachers' Examination, he was awarded a scholarship in 1931 to attend the Rawle Training College in Barbados for a two year course. Upon successful completion of that course he was awarded a second class Teacher's Certificate.

On his return to St. Vincent in 1933, he was appointed to act as Head teacher at his old School for a brief period before he was transferred as Assistant Master to the then prestigious Glen Community School. This school, situated on the site of the present Lewis Punnett home, was very much ahead of its time. The students undertook academic studies in the morning and in the afternoon, engaged in practical subjects such as carpentry, sewing, cooking, gardening, broom-making, mat-making and clay modeling. The late Milton Mayers, who constructed many impressive buildings in St. Vincent and the Grenadines, including the Arnos Vale airport, was one of the persons who attended the Glen Community School when Thomas Saunders taught there.

Mr. Saunders spent two and a half years teaching at the Glen Community School and on 20th September, 1937, he was transferred to the Gomea Methodist School. It was while he was at that school that he met and married Theodora Alves in December 1940. Their happy union produced five children – Chesley, Keith, Camille, Ronnie and Adrian all of whom are still alive save for Ronnie who was cut down by cancer in 1978 shortly after he had completed his studies as a medical doctor.

Mr. Tommy Saunders' teaching career saw him appointed as Headmaster of schools in Union Island, Marriaqua, Questelles and Kingstown. As Principal, he always strove to imbue his students with a well rounded education. He went out of his way to develop their musical, sporting and other cultural talents. In Union Island for example, he introduced the game of netball to the girls at the school and later brought up a team to play against the girls on the mainland. He also organized the Union Island Cultural League which, among other activities, held meetings twice monthly at which debates, lectures and dramatic presentations took place.

As headmaster, Mr. Saunders always sought to encourage and to develop the musical talents of his students. While at Marriaqua he organized a school music band of 25 pieces consisting of drums, tambourines, triangles, castanets, recorders and banjos. The children took great delight in playing these instruments and eagerly looked forward to music time.

In 1951 he was asked to be the first Headmaster of the brand new Richmond Hill School (which was sited in the same building that now houses the Thomas Saunders Secondary School). At that school, he organised to raise funds to outfit a harmonica band among the students. Sebastian "Bassy" Alexander and Alexis Jeffers (the Mighty Sheller), both noted Vincentian musicians, were students of the school at this time and they credit Tommy Saunders, their Headmaster, as one of the key persons who inspired them to develop their musical talents. He himself played the violin, not very well, and only at his home, much to the amusement of his wife and children.

Mr. Saunders did not just teach and inspire his students. He also played a leading role in helping to secure better conditions for teachers throughout the State. So influential and respected among teachers was he that he was elected President of the St. Vincent Teachers' Association (as it was then called). Under his leadership the Association set about to secure better conditions of service for teachers. In 1954, as Head of the Association, he led a three day strike in order to pressure the colonial authorities to provide greater benefits to teachers. As a result of his firm stance and outspokenness in defence of teachers he was transferred by the colonial authorities from the Richmond Hill School, which was at the time regarded as a prized appointment, to a school in Questelles. This was a punitive measure that worked hardship on him. Commuting every day on his ARIEL motor cycle between Questelles and Murray's Road, Kingstown, where his wife and young family lived, was nowhere near as easy as it is today. This punishment did not however deter him from continuing his work on behalf of the Association.

THE CREDIT UNION MOVEMENT

Mr. Saunders read very widely. As a result of his reading and research, he became deeply interested in the Co-operative Self help philosophy. In the mid 1940s some civil servants had organized a credit union in Kingstown but it had failed miserably because of poor management. Credit Unionism in St. Vincent thereby gained a poor reputation among those Vincentians who had heard about the concept. It was Tommy Saunders who single-handedly turned that around. It was he who was responsible for the re-introduction of Credit Unionism in St. Vincent and the Grenadines. How did he do it?

In 1957, while on his way to British Guiana (now Guyana) to spend some of his vacation, Mr. Saunders spent two days in Trinidad where he went out of his way to visit the Co-operative department in that country. He obtained from them useful literature on Credit Unions and Co-operative Societies. On arrival in Guyana, he also spent a considerable amount of his vacation visiting the Co-operative Department and several Co-operative Societies. His discussions with the various persons he met convinced him that the Co-operative Movement held the answer to many of the social and economic problems of the people of St. Vincent and the Grenadines.

At that time in St. Vincent's history, the banks did not extend credit to the vast majority of the people. Few people on the mainland had title to land. The arable land in the country was consolidated in large estates owned by a handful of families. The banks felt that the ordinary people were not good creditors because they could provide little by way of collateral. They neither owned land nor were they in a position to guarantee repayments on a loan. The banks therefore catered to the planter class and to wealthy merchants in Kingstown. The banks and the colonial authorities were generally unsympathetic to the plight of the vast majority of people. With no access to credit facilities, it was extremely difficult for the underprivileged to obtain loans and so acquire land, make investments or generally to improve themselves.

On his return to St. Vincent from Guyana, Mr. Saunders set about, in his own words, "to preach the gospel" of Co-operatives. He used his positions as Headmaster and Lay Preacher to avail himself of every conceivable opportunity to persuade Vincentians of the benefits of the Co-operative Movement. He spoke to several influential leaders in Government and Church. He gave radio addresses which reached the wider community. He visited all the tailoring establishments where several young men worked and he spoke to them about the benefits of Co-operatives. He also wrote articles on Credit Unions for the local newspaper.

At the same time he enriched his own knowledge of the subject. He corresponded with the Credit Union National Association (CUNA) in the United States and they provided him with literature and materials which assisted him in his campaign and in his writings. In order to further his knowledge in Co-operatives, he enrolled in a correspondence course with Co-operative College in Loughborough, England. He successfully completed that course and obtained the College Certification. Amazingly, he did all this entirely on his own, without hope of personal reward, while pursuing a full time job as a Headmaster and caring for his family.

To culminate all of this preparatory work he convened a public meeting at the Memorial Hall in Kingstown in early 1958 to discuss the establishment of a Credit Union. The meeting was a monumental success. All the groundwork for it had been carefully and painstakingly laid by him in the previous months and the time was ripe for initiatives that were geared to promoting the economic advancement of a people who, in town and country alike, yearned for access to credit facilities.

Several influential persons in the community attended the meeting. They heard Mr. Saunders give an impassioned presentation on how a Credit Union works and the many advantages its members could derive from it. Following his presentation, a very lively discussion ensued and then a Steering Committee was elected as a precursor to what is now known today as the Kingstown Cooperative Credit Union. Naturally, the gathering wished to elect him President but he declined. He preferred to have that honour and responsibility bestowed on one of his converts. He had other work to do. Thus it was that Jerome Burke, a tailor, was elected President although Mr. Saunders did take up a position on the first Executive so that he could offer his knowledge and enthusiasm to the young Credit Union. Mr. Burke led the Kingstown Cooperative Credit Union for several years and his son, Jerome junior, also played a long and active role in it. The Credit Union began in 1958 with 51 members and a share capital of $253.98. At the time of Mr. Saunders' death it had a membership of several thousand and a share capital of millions of dollars. It also owns an impressive building at Granby Street.

After the formation of the Kingstown Cooperative Credit Union, Mr. Saunders also organized the Barrouallie Credit Union and the Carriere Credit Union both in 1958. In 1959 he published a pamphlet entitled, "A Brief History of the Credit Union Movement in St. Vincent" which he updated again shortly before his death.

In response to his persistent and vigorous promotion of Co-operatives, the Government of St. Vincent created a Division of Co-operatives within the Department of Agriculture. The Division was headed by a Registrar recruited from Jamaica, Mr. Smart, while Mr. Saunders was sent for training at the Institute of Cooperatives, Puerto Rico, to prepare him to take over from Mr. Smart. He also pursued further training at Western Cooperative College and at the Coady International Institute, both in Canada.

On his return from Canada, first as Co-operative field officer and then as Registrar of Cooperatives, Tommy Saunders worked tirelessly to develop the Co-operative Movement in St. Vincent and the Grenadines. Several evenings each week he would drive out to the rural areas with a projector and films on the Credit Union movement. There was no television in those days nor was there much else in the form of public entertainment. The villagers would therefore come out in droves to see the films. After the film show he would engage them in discussion and convince them of the benefits of belonging to a credit union. He organized and registered the South Rivers Credit Union in 1963, the Government Employees Credit Union in 1964 and the St. Vincent and the Grenadines Co-operative Credit Union League in 1964. His contribution to the early development of the Co-operative Movement of St. Vincent and the Grenadines is invaluable and unequalled.

A HUMBLE DECENT MAN

Tommy Saunders was a humble, pleasant, dignified human being. He had no airs about him. He lived a simple life. He enjoyed local food. He especially relished bananas, scuttle mangos, Dominic yams, corned pork and "cocoa tea". Whether it was this earthy diet or his passionate love of walking, he was a fit, healthy, sprightly person. Well into his 80s he could be seen gently strolling up and down the streets of Kingstown chatting amiably with the many persons who knew and respected him.

He and his wife were a couple that truly organized ecumenism because his wife, Theo, was as equally a staunch Roman Catholic as he was a Methodist. The couple never allowed religion or religious differences to get in the way of their loving relationship. They were both involved in the Red Cross Movement and Mr. Saunders was President of the Red Cross Society for some years. He was also very active in the Foresters' Lodge.

His children recall fondly that he used to own a small hand operated printing press. It was a messy, labour intensive hobby that he engaged in mostly at Christmas time. He found the time personally to format the material, set every single letter, then crank down on the Press with all his might to make one print at a time. With his Press he made and sold truly beautiful Christmas cards and invitations that were sometimes embossed in gold or red. He sold the Press in the mid 1960s to Mr. Alexander who owned Model Printery.

He had a very curious mind and loved to converse with people from all walks of life. No one was too big or too small to escape his attention. In the early 1960s he acquired a motor car, a flaming red Morris Oxford that carried the registration number P- 320. It was his habit then to offer a ride to all and sundry. As soon as they got into the car he would strike up a conversation. If he did not know the person, almost always his first questions were "What's your name?", "Where are you from?", "Who is your family?" He seemed to know an enormous amount of persons and so invariably was always able to establish some connection with the person irrespective of the village from which they hailed.

After he retired from the public service, not one to be idle, Tommy Saunders set about re-inventing himself. He bought himself a typewriter, learned to type and embarked on establishing a sole Commission Agency. He went around Kingstown inquiring from merchants what their needs were. Then he would research the manufacturers of those items and write off letters to them offering to represent them in distributing the product in St. Vincent and the Grenadines. The business was a huge success and he operated it right up to the time of his demise. He was the agent for several very reputable companies including Uncle Ben's Rice, Mercury outboard engines, and American Standard Sanitary Ware.

He also became more actively involved in the Methodist Church. He preached in all the Methodist Churches on the mainland from Georgetown to Chateaubelair. In 1974, when there was a shortage of ordained Ministers, he accepted the offer to become a Lay Agent and he was given a dispensation to administer the Sacraments of Baptism and Holy Communion. He was actually placed in charge of five churches – Evesham, Richland Park,

Marriaqua, Mt. Hope and Belmont – and the Methodist communities of those areas still remember him with great affection.

In 1999, not long before he died, Thomas Saunders was honoured by the country issuing a stamp with his photograph on it to mark the year of the Elderly. Dr. Ian Earle Kirby, Sir Sydney Gun-Munro and Mother Sarah Baptiste were also similarly honoured. He was saluted as a senior citizen who had inspired the people for over a half a century. The National Commercial Bank sponsored a documentary on his life as a Nation Builder.

After a brief illness, Thomas M. Saunders passed away quietly on the evening of 21st November, 1999 at his home at Cane Garden surrounded by family members. Earlier that afternoon he had been visited by, and he had chatted with, the Methodist Superintendent, Rev. Edwards and a group of friends from that church. He was survived by his wife of almost 59 years (now deceased) and four children.

It can truly be said of Tommy Saunders that he served the people of St. Vincent and the Grenadines educationally, spiritually and financially. He did all this selflessly, honestly, gladly giving of his time and his energy, never at any time seeking the limelight or desiring personal advantage of any sort. Indeed, his efforts and sacrifice for his fellow-human beings yielded no material reward to him although the high esteem in which he was universally held must have been a source of contentment for him. A local newspaper summed up his life in this way:

Mr. Thomas Saunders, a Nation Builder, lived an active and full life, contributed much to the welfare of his fellowmen and has earned a place in Vincentian history. He however never took personal credit. His frequent comment was "Whatever contribution I have made, whatever my success, whatever my achievements I owe to God and my wife, Theo".

A Vincentian Icon, he succeeded in giving Vincentians an easier option to a better life...

Letter to the Headmistress of the Thomas Saunders Secondary School (TSSS)

Dear Ms Harry:

I channeled your request to me and my siblings and it immediately prompted us to begin reviewing the life and accomplishments of our father. Fortunately for us, before he died, he himself wrote several short, unpublished pieces about his life story and so we have used these together with our own knowledge of him to put together the attached biographical profile. I suspect it is longer than you intended but that was quite deliberate.

While we were at it we felt that we should put down as much as we could now on the basis that it is always possible for one to paraphrase it. We have certainly not exhausted the subject and it may well be that in due course we shall strive to update and expand what is here set out.

Thomas M. Saunders was a remarkable man as a cursory reading of the attached profile will show. I believe the TSSS staff and students should know this and be proud to be associated with a school that bears his name. They will not be filled with that pride, however, unless they are provided with information on him, on what he stood for and what his accomplishments were.

I often bemoan the fact that we, Vincentians, do not sufficiently cherish our heroes. There are many reasons for this. Part of it is undoubtedly the fact that in their lifetime, unless they happen to wear the right political stripes, their work sometimes goes unrecognized by the State. Regrettably, many people believe that we have a warped set of criteria for bestowing national honours. This belief has persisted from time immemorial. An even more significant reason lies in the fact that we write so little about our heroes and, what is written is not very well preserved and handed down. As a result, their glorious accomplishments, their struggles and trials, the manner in which they overcame adversity, all these are lost to the generations who succeed them.

This is more than just an absolute disservice to the memory of our noble daughters and sons. It is a critical loss to us as an entire nation as we are robbed of a vital source of the strength of any civilization – a history of the struggles of its people. Each Vincentian generation blithely takes for granted the institutions, benefits and rights that it currently enjoys, blissfully unaware or uncaring of the fact that these are legacies, the fruit of the sweat and sacrifice and struggles of preceding generations.

I sincerely apologise if you detect an edge in the above. Such as there might be, it is of course not directed at you. I suppose what I really want is to beseech you, and through you, the Thomas Saunders Secondary School, to do whatever you can to have the students of the School know who was Thomas Saunders, what he stood for and what were his accomplishments. If you will permit me, perhaps I can make a few humble suggestions. For a start, if the attached biographical profile is too long (it is over 3,000 words), you can organize a competition among the students to see who can best reduce it to a length that is appropriate for the newsletter. If you did this I am sure that my siblings and I would be prepared to offer an attractive surprise to the winner. Perhaps the entirety of the attached profile can be printed into a little booklet and made available to every student as and when he or she enters the school. Perhaps the English, Civics and history teachers can use the profile or aspects of it as an integral part of their teaching courses. There are many other ways in which the material can be made available to the students and it is my fervent hope that the Principal and staff will consider them. It would certainly be a shame for a TSSS student to graduate that school and not be able, confidently and proudly, to tell someone something meaningful and true about the man whose name adorns the school they attended.

Thank you for prompting us to put together the attached and I wish you and the School all the best. If you do take up our suggestion about the competition please let me know so that we can quickly make appropriate arrangements.

Sincerely,

Adrian Saunders

Adrian Saunders is a Justice of the Caribbean Court of Justice in Trinidad and Tobago.

Caribbean Trailblazers: St. Vincent and the Grenadines

11.   **FRANKLYN ELLISON SEALES**
                              By
                       Jean M. Dorsinville

CURTAIN CALL

His final curtain call came on 14 May 1990 shortly before the midnight hour amidst sustained thunderous applause from an audience that had grown to celebrate a gifted Shakespearean actor at work. Only after the lights had begun to dim one by one that they filed out of the theater completely enthralled by another brilliant performance…One can only imagine.

He was at the family home in Brooklyn surrounded by his mother Olive, Sisters Joy and Deborah when this heartthrob thespian took his last bow to enter eternity: The applause had faded...his stentorian voice permanently silenced...like a flickering glow of a candle in the wind, his fire was extinguished. He was only 37, much too young one will say, for anyone to pass into the beyond, yet in these compressed years, he had amassed considerable living that may inspire many young Vincentians yearning to reach the stars. His was not a scripted journey drafted by a Hollywood writer, a world of make believe designed to transport the audience to another dimension, to escape its sometimes troubled world or dreary existence. His was by contrast a product of humble beginnings, the natural born son of Francis Seales, a merchant seaman and government employee of Portuguese, English ancestry and Olive Seales, nee Allen, a homemaker of Portuguese and native Carib Indian stock. He was born on 15 July, 1952 and was the youngest of that family of five (three girls and two boys) born in the small village of Calliaqua.

Franklyn, unlike his other siblings, was uncommonly precocious disclosing an accelerated maturity: dreaming of dreams that came deep within a fertile imagination that others found too challenging, and so left him to explore his singular world. Listening to his older brother describe Franklyn, one has to come to an indisputable conclusion that Franklyn always felt special in an almost ethereal way. He acted from his own unique perspective yet invited all to come along on the journey he envisaged. He exhibited a self-confidence and stubborn determination that carried a price that could either inspire you or become your worst nightmare. What mattered was his opinion in all conversations that made him the center of attention. The onus was always on those who wished to listen to what he had to offer. One might say his hubris carried a perceived insensitivity toward his listeners. To him, you had to maintain the same pace he was on because he wasted no time nurturing you along the way. One had to keep up on this unknown destination his mind's eyes were visualizing.

Very early on, as a young boy not yet in his teens, he showed a keen interest in the arts nurtured by his imaginary flights of fancy that he described to his listeners captivated by the images he painted. Whether they understood him or not did not matter. He had an audience that was willing to come along on that imaginary ride. He loved the Church, the old Anglican Church on that hill in the center of Calliaqua. The lives of the residents revolved around the Church and all the children were welcomed to serve. As his older brother retreated from the Church, Franklyn by contrast drew closer. He became an altar boy that seemingly gave him an audience where he fantasized drawing their attention. *"He was not what I would consider religious,"* his brother would say, *"but he became a fixture that none of his peers could miss."* Years later, in retrospect, his brother concluded that Franklyn began to answer the call to acting from his involvement at the Calliaqua Anglican Church.

His older brother Lennox, more familiarly known as Mike, reminisced about his childhood friend Syl who had given him a "broken down bicycle," as he called it. To get it on the road he "saved and scrimped every dime" until he finally had it running. *"I taught Franklyn to ride... "* he told me, *"It didn't take him long to gain control and very soon was showing off, pulling some stunts that I tried to discourage. At times, Franklyn however would steal the bike to satisfy an inner compulsion; showing off to everyone what a good rider he was... It truly did not matter what we were dealing with, he had a need to be right. Generally, we had our fair share of disagreements around these frequent episodes where I knew he did not know what he was talking about, yet acted as if he knew. The performer in him was always at play."* Mike evoked these memories while holding back tears from the emotions his childhood brought.

"When it came to clothes, he would choose one garment that he liked and wear it practically every day until it was completely worn. It was as if he got energy and comfort from his clothes. He would rather have one good sweater. He would wear it out, but to him it was all good... I guess his philosophy was, less is more " There was much to learn from him in that regard. His attitude and philosophy of less being more was carried right on into his adult life. Case in point, *"Instead of buying three sweaters for $100.00, Franklyn would rather buy one for $100.00...He had very little clothing for this reason. He would buy the best of everything: from food to clothes. He never wanted more. He was a minimalist before most folks knew what the word meant."*

Franklyn possessed an innate appreciation and love for music as well. According to his brother:

"He would befriend all of the women in and around Calliaqua who had pianos. First we would go to Ms. Pemberton who eventually became his piano teacher, then he would become friendly with Elsa Stephens who would show him a little more, then he turned to my Godmother, Ms Eloise Gonsalves Phills. Franklyn took her over from me. Truth be told, it was her daughter Barbara who was one of his tight friends. He loved to go hang out with them at Villa. When Franklyn was not home in Calliaqua, he was at Uncle John Phills and Nennie....Franklyn made an impression on everyone and he got attention. He was a magnet for attention....He forced people to remember him when they met him... As a young boy, friends, neighbors and teachers were always fascinated and intrigued.....Young girls loved and adored him. He had the girls hanging around him always.....Truly funny looking back at how it was...."

His brother Reggie recalls,

"He would always bring his art supplies: "drawing-book," colouring pencils and painting set and proudly proceeded to demonstrate his skills. It was fascinating to watch him sketch pictures of mutual friends and replicate some of St. Vincent's indigenous Carib art. His talent was compelling, and all of his friends respected and embraced him for his natural artistic ability..."

Another friend who shared his company was Antoinette who says:

"He was a brother and very best friend to me ... I shared my secrets and dreams with him. An entertainer from the early years ... always ready to dance, sing, play the piano or try any instrument that was within his reach. He knew that he would be famous, he had plans and dreams, very confident at age 14 that they would become real when he went to America. Designing fabulous gowns that he thought would be perfect for my then skinny little body. Great at telling stories and would have the family laughing at the little shows he would put on. He was able to make me laugh even when I was sad--Once we went to a dance at Crows Nest--he was dressed as a witch, of course he had the crowd laughing all night. He knew how to have a good time and was capable of holding every one's attention. When he wasn't sketching outfits for me, he was composing a song or writing a story...trying a new dance. He was always working at something. Franklyn was a multi-talented guy and very comfortable in his own skin...We sure had a lot of laughs Jean and my mother loved him so very much."

His sister Jennifer shared similar sentiments:

"Franklyn's early life in St. Vincent and the Grenadines spent with friends and family, we gave him a variety of titles: Actor, comedian, artist, dancer, hairdresser, make-up artist, fashion designer, scholar and teacher. I often wondered which title he liked best, for indeed he was multitalented. They all belonged to him. As a young boy, Franklyn loved the beach. He always maintained a great tanned complexion because he spent his holidays and weekends at his godmother's house at Villa Beach. He was an avid reader who always had one or two books in his possession most of the time. He loved reading romance and mystery novels. Going to the movies was one of his favorite hobbies. He enjoyed musicals, comedies and romantic stories. After seeing a special movie, he often returned home and dramatized the key parts with such great skill and accuracy that family and friends who viewed his performances often felt that they had seen these movies themselves. His favorite festivals were Carnival and Christmas. Carnival was a magical time for him. He spent many long hours at his friends' tents decorating costumes. He enjoyed participating in Old Mas. He always designed and wore one of his own comical creations. I recall that he kept a special notebook in which he drew designs of beautiful, extravagant evening gowns and costumes. He also attended the carnival queen and king of the bands shows, and the Carnival queen shows.

He also loved the Christmas season. The highlights for him were caroling, nine mornings, and the Old Year's Nights fetes he attended at his friends' homes in Villa. Though at times he had many struggles and challenges with asthma and bronchitis, he remained a good scholar at the Boys Grammar school. Franklyn loved to laugh. Hence he kept friends and family laughing too, with either his witty jokes or his comedic actions. His laughter at times was very boisterous and happy. Franklyn often advised those around him about hair, make-up and fashion. He taught us how to coordinate colors. I remember him teaching me to put on my make-up and styling my hair. At an early age, Franklyn was wise and talented beyond his years. We are all grateful for the many lessons we learned from him."

The year was 1968 when this young 16 year old handsome young lad landed in the promised land of milk and honey. To West Indians growing up in the developing world, America's streets could well have been paved in gold: Every child had access to decent schools...Everyone worked...All families lived in houses with white picket fences. After all, this was the story told in American magazines we had access to and the movies that were shown further accentuated the wonderful American way of life. One could well say we nurtured a certain naiveté. Franklyn, however, thought outside the box. He was a dreamer whose destiny he would control and prove to his contemporaries that all things are possible even for a boy who spent his childhood sharing a bed with his other siblings.

He landed on American soil on July 8, 1068 at approximately 9 PM, accompanied by his father, to join his older siblings. Leslie was the first to leave Calliaqua in 1961 and Mike in 1964 to join their mother in NY. I had married Leslie in 1965. I recall meeting him at the airport accompanied by my wife and our daughter who was eleven months old. He was a handsome lad bearing a golden tan of the tropics, his soft wavy hair (what we termed "good hair") looked disheveled following a five hour flight. I noticed the deepness in his eyes under arched bushy eyebrows. I extended my hand to him trying to catch his eyes more fully but he looked distracted. It could have been the excitement of arriving in the new world he fancied. I could not read his thoughts. A gentle hello from him sufficed that accompanied a faint smile. I guess. I noticed the joy he exhibited picking up his niece Natasha and planting a big kiss on each cheek as our daughter encircled his neck with both of her tiny arms. This eleven month child felt secure in her uncle's arms. Francis Adolphus Seales, the patriarch of the Seales family, was my father-in-law. We finally met face to face on that early July summer night. Three years before, I had written him a letter asking for the hands of his beloved daughter, Leslie. His letter of approval followed shortly.

12 July 1968 marked our daughter's first birthday. Since Franklyn's fell on the 15th, we held a double celebration for his 16th. As he entered our home to join the other guests, Natasha spontaneously flashed a smile. Leslie said, "Look, she recognized Franklyn..." Our daughter opened her arms as Franklyn lifted her in a wild embrace twirling around sending her into a shrieking giggle.

This is Uncle Franklyn, Natasha. Say uncle...u-n-c-l-e.
"on...kol."
Franklyn...Frank...lyn.
"Phan---kin."
That's close enough.

Franklyn dropped to his knees to be at eye level with his niece and the other kids who quickly surrounded him. Some stroking his head, his face. Others jumping on his back. Pretty soon, Franklyn was lying on the floor giddy as can be. Like a kid, he entertained them for hours.

At one point, he approached me and began to open up by asking:

"How did you and Leslie meet?"

"Glad you asked. I was a student at NYU and active in the West Indian Students Association that gathered students from various Caribbean islands..." I told him..."I was one of the organizers of our annual dance that took place at the Loeb student center located on the campus downtown

Washington Square. I was at the door welcoming our guests when in walks this tall rather attractive girl accompanied by a student with whom I was acquainted on campus. He introduced Leslie as his cousin. Before walking away, I told her a line that came out of nowhere: 'I hope you save the last dance for me.' Sure enough, she bought it, saved me the dance and the rest, as they say, is history."

"How long after did you get married?"

"A year and a half later we tied the knots...not quite two years later Natasha was born, three days before your birthday..."

This was one of the very rare occasions Franklyn found time to hold a conversation with me or anyone else because his life from then on became a whirlwind of activities, new discoveries in a world filled with possibilities.
    As Mike candidly explained:

"When we reunited in Brooklyn, we would have fights over the television. Franklyn dominated the one TV we had. Back in the day, everyone had one TV. He would sit on the sofa in the same spot daily. He painted, ate lots of fruits, drank juice, ate sandwiches, and stared at the TV. No one was able to get to see anything other than what he wanted. Funny, he thought that was ok. The sofa finally had a permanent sink hole where he would sit and lay daily. He would wear his sweater in the house in the winter time all day long... Later if he went out, he wore the sweater again and again. It was as if it was nailed to his body... Franklyn had what we would call "attitude," the kind of attitude that allowed him to rise above everything and everyone around him. I saw this early on even in High School in Brooklyn. Franklyn was enrolled in Abraham Lincoln High School. It was at Lincoln High that he became more vested in his Art and Drama...."

While the family would gather in front of the TV like millions of household in America on a Sunday night to watch the much anticipated Ed Sullivan show, Franklyn had a better idea and tuned to PBS on channel 13 in New York to the chagrin of everyone. He had the final say. Television had become a teaching tool for him. He watched performance by actors that one day he dreamed of meeting. He learned proper enunciation of words, critiqued their performance and memorized their parts.
    The Seales family occupied the upper floor of a two-family brick house located at 1661 Carroll Street, at the intersection of Utica Ave, a hub of activity, stores of all kinds lining both sides of the street and leading to what some like to call the heart of Brooklyn, Eastern Parkway. He had enrolled as a Junior at Lincoln High located 30 minutes away by bus, where his

assimilation of the American culture was surprisingly gaining ground. He grew his hair out sporting a huge afro-type hairstyle, very common in those days. He was a quick learner who befriended everyone, soon turning into the typical American teenager while shedding some traits of his upbringing. It did not take long for his house to become a gathering place to study not only the lessons of the day but also to develop his acting skills along with fellow "actors" in the making. The girls in school were attracted to this transplanted West Indian with the exotic look, product of miscegenation so prevalent in the islands. He soon experienced his first winter. One day, he and his friends took the subway to Rockefeller Center where he dared to ice skate. Did he know anything about ice skating? No, but that did not stop Franklyn who loved a challenge. He didn't do too well. He broke his leg on his first try and for days limped around in a cast. Speaking of one who takes his role seriously: "Break a leg." He took this idiom used among actors before they go on stage, quite literally. Nothing slowed him down though. He had enrolled in art classes where he could give full expression to his creativity as a young man in pursuit of a dream that heretofore was not taken seriously or perhaps misunderstood by the family. At the end of his first school year, we were invited to a school production of Shakespeare's Romeo and Juliet that gave him full expression of his budding talent. The stage was his calling and he was off running.

Though the theatre was his preoccupation, he also kept a drawing pad close to him wherever he went. When we dared ask him to show us, he would display the work he guarded jealously. Describing his sketches and painting was not a task that fell to the amateur. It was obvious to me that he was a student of the master, one of the most dynamic and influential artists of our century, Pablo Picasso. Some of Franklyn's paintings captured the mood of melancholy and isolation with his choice of somber colors, while others were draped with vibrant hues of the rainbow inspired no doubt by his Caribbean heritage. Asked to describe his paintings:

"I would like you to perceive my art as something of nature that can heal with its color, its movement and its simplicity".
"I love color. I also love the radiograph. I found that pen and really fell in love with it. It creates those lines that I want that segments the body...to treat the body not as an inhuman thing, but see if I could make something human out of something that was sort of angular. But mostly, I'm interested in a lot of color, a lot of vibrancy: nature! And, I'm not very interested in painting reality, per se. I'm representing reality, in color, in form, in line: in black and white and in color..."
"This is my dream. To get better, buy an old cottage or something...somewhere, have some dogs, paint and live out the rest of my days happy..."

By his second year, Franklyn had become an indomitable force in his school productions headlining all school productions where he expressed his acting versatility, delivering his lines with perfect erudition, and could also dance and sing with equal dexterity. At graduation time, he was cast to play Don Quixote from the Broadway play, Man of La Mancha. A month or two before graduation, a school friend from his group of actors asked him to accompany her to the famed Juilliard School for the Performing Arts in Manhattan to help with her audition. Franklyn casually tagged along totally oblivious of the destiny that awaited him. Upon their arrival, they were greeted by none other than the legendary director, producer, actor, John Houseman who asked him if he was auditioning also. Franklyn naively almost grudgingly responded that he was simply here to help his friend with a sketch they had rehearsed and was only here for the ride. However, Mr. Houseman insisted that he try out as well. Franklyn's performance so mesmerized the director that he offered him a full scholarship to Juilliard on the spot. His friend regrettably did not make it and went on to other pursuits. Someone defined destiny as a "concept based on the belief that there is a fixed natural order to the cosmos...a fixed sequence of events that is inevitable and unchangeable." Franklyn had met his on that day. Some on the other hand might also call it "luck" which is "a matter of preparation meeting opportunity." His brother had a more probable theory.

"My brother was born with a third eye: People who appear to know why they are here in this physical life. They come equipped...they know the path. Most of us will stumble, get lucky or be forever lost. Franklyn came with a knowingness that is beyond the consciousness of most. It is very uncommon and unless you have been exposed to these special people, one will never know what I am talking about."

September of 1970 marked a new beginning for Franklyn. With help from his brother Mike, content to lend him a hand, he moved out of his parents' home to an apartment on the Upper West side of Manhattan along with fellow actors from Juilliard, among them was an unknown Robin Williams who everyone with a pulse recognizes as a household name on Television and movies. As Franklyn honed his craft at Juilliard appearing in plays with a young unknown classmate, Christine Baranski who later went on to achieve enormous success on Broadway, in Television and movies. Franklyn and Christine were both cast in **'Tis Pity She's A Whore** at the Goodman Theatre in 1975 . A critic wrote:

"As the two lovers, Christine Baranski and Franklyn Seales display considerably more than just their handsome young bodies. They perform

with poise and passion that do credit to their training as recent graduates of the Juilliard School of Drama in New York City."

He began to appear regularly in Off-Broadway productions where he soon captured the attention of the celebrated American theatrical producer and director Joseph Papp who cast him in his Shakespeare in the Park productions. By that time, Franklyn Seales of Calliaqua had morphed into an authentic Shakespearian actor speaking in a stiff British accent, performing in Papp's Romeo and Juliet, Othello, King Lear and many others. The uncanny transformation was complete and baffled his relatives who grew up with him never anticipating success would come knocking at his door so quickly at the age of 23. He counted among his friends the great actor of stage, television and movies, the man gifted with an easily recognizable mellifluous voice, James Earl Jones who he called simply "Jimmy." As Mike summed it up, *"I knew then that he was not looking back."* Attending Juilliard was the epitome, the dream of every budding actor of consequence. Among the graduates, we can count Robin Williams, Christine Baranski, William Hurt, Kevin Kline, Mandy Patankin, Kevin Spacey, Kelly McGillis, Ving Rhames, who went on to achieve national recognition, and the list goes on and on and to be added was Franklyn Ellison Seales. Wow, from Calliaqua to Juilliard was a straight line for this son of St Vincent. It bears repeating: "Preparation meeting opportunity."

The question is: Should we act so surprised at his almost meteoric rise to national notoriety? He would be the first to answer, "I knew it all along..." If there were any doubts about his future success, listening to him would quell one's trepidation. He was not unlike Muhammad Ali who challenged our imagination with his nom de guerre: "I'm the greatest!!!" Franklyn, I would say, came from the same mindset that exudes supreme confidence in his God given gift that transcends the mundane.

Studying Franklyn's metamorphosis from his childhood days to the theatre stage became fodder for those competing for his attention and wondering why he seemed always on the go. The poem by Robert Frost comes to mind which may perhaps shed some light: "The woods are lovely, dark and deep, But I have promised to keep, And miles to go before I sleep..." Franklyn was only on the threshold of a promising career in showbiz that is reserved only for the select. But he had a long road ahead strewn with twists and turns and pitfalls that will discourage lesser mortals, nevertheless, he followed it with total abandonment and self-assurance.

Franklyn pursued his career appearing in a series of Shakespearian plays under the aegis of Joseph Papp. playing in Macbeth, The Taming of the Shrew, King Lear. His roles were garnering recognition among the glitterati, the habitués of Broadway productions. The family began to see less and less of Franklyn, unless for an occasional call to his mother to reaffirm his love for her and to say hello to everyone. King Lear was made for TV in 1974 and he played a minor role as the servant of Cornwall. In 1977 he appeared in a play, **A Very Private Life**, starring Celeste Holm, the seasoned actress of film, television and the stage. A theatre critic wrote,

"The only other character in the play is the houseboy. Franklyn Seales plays this important part, wearing Gucci shoes and forty dollar shirts. According to this play he walked in one day in need of work and food and just stayed. His duties include those of servant, secretary, and bartender. It's a good thing that he decided to stay when he did. He is a plus to this strong but small cast."

In 1974, Franklyn was cast in **The Tempest**. He received more glorious reviews:

*"Franklyn Seales is a soaring Ariel. He is particularly good vocally, and since Ariel has some of the play's most glorious language, this is a great asset. Visually he owes a lot to modern dance. His costume seemed to have been borrowed from one of Martha Graham's Greek gods, a web of ropes barely covering his nakedness. His makeup and movements are reminiscent of Nijinsky as the faun in "**Afternoon of a Faun**."*

It was however in 1978 that he was introduced to the nation when he clinched the lead role in **Trial of the Moke** based on the real life story of the humiliation and anguish suffered by Lt. Henry Ossian Flipper, the first black graduate of West Point. Assigned to serve at Fort Davis, Texas in 1881, Flipper became the object of a conspiracy to rid the base of its only black graduate. Flipper, portrayed by Franklyn Seales, was framed by white officers who accused him of embezzling government funds. Ninety-four years later, Flipper was vindicated only a week after **"The Trial of the Moke"** ended its world premiere run at the Milwaukee Repertory Theater in 1976. A military reburial with honors followed in 1978.

The fact that Franklyn was selected to play the role of Lt Henry Flipper, the principal character of the play, was no accident. Notwithstanding the physical resemblance between him and Lt Flipper that was uncanny, but far more importantly was the confidence he had generated for the producers to select him. One critic wrote:

" Seales carries the weight of the play's message, but he keeps the drama under control, resisting the temptation to push the message by "emoting" for dramatic effect. Instead, he portrays Henry Flipper with the dignity and self-respect which were his due."

His appearance on national television sent thrills through the family gathered to watch Franklyn deliver a masterful performance.

Franklyn's brilliant performance must have sent shockwaves in Hollywood. It was not long after his televised **Trial of the Moke** that we heard Franklyn was packing his clothes and heading West, to tinsel town, to the land of make believe, where stars are born and dreams crushed. The year was 1979 when the movie, The Onion Field was released, an adaptation of the book by Joseph Wambaugh. "It's the in-depth analysis of the true story of a 1963 event in Los Angeles. Two cops pull over two crooks in an otherwise routine traffic stop. But the desperate crooks get the drop on the cops, get their guns, kidnap them, drive them out to an onion field in the countryside, and murder one of them. One of the cops escapes death, but is haunted by guilt over the death of his partner and his inability to help. The murderers are captured, tried, convicted, and then retried over and over again on appeal." Here we have Franklyn playing the role of Jimmy Lee Smith aka Jimmy Youngblood, a petty thief along with his companion Gregory Ulas Powell played by James Woods, another talented actor on the rise.

By that time, Franklyn had taken permanent residence in California. He was beginning to live the life of a movie star; he bought himself a house and a car and helped himself to the finest. Why not? To paraphrase his mentor John Houseman, "he made his money the old fashioned way...he earned it." To say to someone, "you've gone Hollywood" is not exactly a pejorative but a term that may lead to conjecture. In Franklyn's case, I had observed a certain flair, others may call it arrogance, in his demeanor when he flew back to Brooklyn for a brief visit. The tone of his voice had changed, reminiscent of a character he might be playing on stage. He was definitely not the Franklyn I knew. I wondered if the actor in him is permanently set on the ON mode or perhaps did he forget he was talking to family. He didn't stay at his mother's home but at friends in Manhattan. We caught up with him long enough to query him about life in the rarified air he was breathing in Hollywood. He was gracious and as usual in a hurry to go his way. I could at least say I shook hands with a celebrity. "Franco" as his father affectionately called him was a man on the go whose childhood dreams had "metastasized" from the stage to television and now onto the silver screen.   He may not have had time for me or his sister but he was keeping a steady correspondence with our daughter Natasha, we learned much later. She had reached her early teens and like the other cousins of her age group, Uncle Franklyn had become a demigod, someone she proudly discussed with her school friends. For those who had reached that age group, parents had suddenly become "old fashioned" for not keeping up with the latest craze of the early 80's. The teen years were a time of discovery for them. Drawing from our West Indian background, we knew our values did not parallel those of the first generation born in America. We found no rationale however to abandon what we cherished, so told Natasha what we expected of her. It was a trying period that challenged our patience after discovering that her uncle Franklyn was advising her to stand up for herself. I decided to write Franklyn a letter disapproving of his interference and to inform him that his good intentions were not welcomed. Movie star or not, we were calling the shots in our house. We knew better how to raise a child.

Our little confrontation was not isolated as I discovered a few years later speaking with his brother Mike who had gotten married to a neighbor, a native of Savannah, Georgia. Their first child Liane was born in 1979 while still living in Brooklyn but they decided to relocate to Savannah a year later. Mike recalled Franklyn's reaction:

"He truly did not like the fact that I moved down South. He knew that we were after different things. He would tell me that I have the Karma to expand the family and he would help me. Truly, I never thought that he would ever come south to visit. However after he moved to California and was doing television, he would call me and write to me. I was more than shocked when he wanted to come visit. Sure enough, Franklyn showed up in Savannah. He loved playing with Liane and Gabriel who was a baby. He would come and hang out with us. Get down on the floor and play with the kids. He never traveled without his camera. He was constantly taking pictures. It is amazing the same childhood fights would continue between us. He was never married, but there he was telling me about marriage. He never had children, there he was telling me about children. It was funny as hell to me. I remembered Gabe being a wild little boy running and pulling away from me at the beach, Franklyn would tell me to let him run. Mean time, Gabe was running into the sea fully dressed at two years old. However, in Franklyn's mind it was ok. Let him have his freedom. All I could see is my going to jail for endangering the life of a child. We went to the river a couple of times, and he insisted that I do the same for Gabe, let him play...My being responsible, reminded Franklyn of our mother being nervous. I then had to defend myself not only as a person, but in every way possible. I would be pissed and hoped that he would never come visit. However, much to my disbelief, he would get back to California only to call me up telling me what a glorious time he had with me and the kids. It floored me when he would plan to come for another visit."

The eleven month old baby that Franklyn held in his arms upon his arrival in America and counseled during her teenage years had become a wife and mother of twins born in 2005. She reminisced:

"When I think of my uncle during the few stages of my life until he passed, my earliest memory is of the several paint tubes in his room, the

paint easel with various dried paint colors on it and worn brushes. He would sit in front of his easel focused, creating, expressing himself in beautiful ways. I appreciated his ability to focus and express himself in the form of a painting, in the form of his acting. He lost himself in that room in front of his piece of unfolding art as well as in his performance roles. I realized that he put forth the same focus and love toward me in so many ways.

He was present from the beginning of my life to the end of his. His expression of love came in many forms - calls, letters, gifts, visits. I even knew that his questions about what I was feeling, thinking and doing was his love for me no matter how probing they seemed at the time. He wanted to make sure that I was happy, smiling and laughing which he always made sure you did with him. I have now surpassed his age at death and know that his lessons are with me. He left the example that there are no limits in life, only the ones you self impose. And most importantly, he left me with the ability to know that I should live the life I love and love the life I live!"

This was the quintessential Franklyn, the vulnerable man/boy imbued with a "Je ne sais quoi" dealing with life as very few can. He possessed an air of sophistication, an elegance, a refinement that will charm a listener yet at times he will project a tackiness that will wear out your welcome. It is this dichotomy that set him so far apart from the common man. He was an artist carved from the Hairoun rocks of his ancestry into a shining star.

By 1981, Franklyn appeared in his second motion picture, **Southern Comfort** where he was teamed with Bowers Booth and Keith Carradine who were established movie stars in their own right. I recall Franklyn talking about the shooting of this movie in the Louisiana swamps, "cold and damp and fighting mosquitoes." This was undoubtedly the unglamorous side of movie making. In any event, Franklyn's star continued its ascent.

More acclaims would come to Franklyn when he was cast in the American sitcom, **Silver Spoons** which featured the main character, young Ricky Schroeder. Franklyn played the role of Dexter Stuffins, the erudite uncle of break dancing nephew Alfonso Spears (Alfonso Ribeiro.) Between 1983 and 1987 Franklyn became a fixture on that show brought to us every week into our living rooms in living color. One episode featured a very special guest, a mega star in the pop music world, Whitney Huston. She was Franklyn's love interest in a scene when the two are shown in a passionate, soulful kiss that left nothing to the imagination. When their lips finally parted, Whitney lowered her face and let out a cooing sound signaling total satisfaction. Franklyn's expression however was one that characterized the mindset of a man exhibiting supreme confidence in his charm. He kept his head slightly tilted upward while giving Whitney a smiling look that seemed to say, I have conquered you my Diva. With his subtle head fake I could see the consummate Calliaqua native son, Franklyn Ellison Seales.

For Christmas 1986, in the midst of his busy schedule, he found time to fly to New York to spend Christmas with the family. As was the custom for several years, we had gathered at my house. Between the Dorsinville, the Seales and the Richardsons, we had a nice crowd pregnant with anticipation for his arrival. I had my video camera ready to record the grand entrance with his entourage. He didn't disappoint me. As he walked into the room, he immediately spotted my camera and with mocked shyness shielded his face with a box bearing a Christmas gift. He flashed a huge smile. He sported a California tan, sans makeup. He wore a grey jacket with matching pants and shirt. He had a scarf around his neck with one end flung across his left shoulder a la Hollywood style. We were all excited to see him and to hear the stories we all wanted to know about the world of make believe. He spoke without pause, contented to perform before an audience of sort. This was the last Christmas we had him at our house. Twenty years later we can still review that video to remind us that Franklyn had indeed fulfilled his dreams as he always believed he would once he set foot on American soil.

In Fall of 1989, we received an urgent telephone call from Franklyn telling us he wanted to "return home." We were living in Somerset, N.J. at the time. He inquired if he could come to stay at our house. "Of course, you're welcome to do so." He had sold his house and much of his furniture. He had shipped his car to Savannah for his brother Mike, at the same time shipped us an antique armoire and several of his paintings that were eventually given to his sister Debbie. Leslie and I picked him up at JFK airport in the afternoon of September. He was a shadow of himself, no longer the gregarious Franklyn we knew and loved. For the next two weeks, Leslie fed him well and remained close by to provide any help to ease the passing of time. The change of environment seemed to be suited for him. He had time to rest while emptying his mind of the high pressure world he left behind. He was sunning himself every day on the deck. He had finally distanced himself from Hollywood for now. Day after day, we began to notice a perceived rejuvenation. He began to gain weight and his old spirit was coming back. He walked with greater assurance and flair that signaled he was feeling better. He was well enough to return to his mother's home in Brooklyn.. Sadly though, on the 14 May 1990, Franklyn passed away.

In the final analysis, whether by luck, destiny or Divine order, whatever we make of ourselves in this mortal flesh will be measured by the imprints we leave in the sands of time. Franklyn's prints were immense

Franklyn Seales' body of work:

-Wiseguy .... Paco Bazos (1 episode, 1988)
- Fascination for the Flame (1988) TV Episode .... Paco Bazos
-Growing Pains .... Dr. Jerry Marquez (1 episode, 1987)
- This Is Your Life (1987) TV Episode .... Dr. Jerry Marquez
-Amen .... Lorenzo Hollingsworth (3 episodes, 1986-1987)
- Casting the First Stone (1987) TV Episode .... Lorenzo Hollingsworth
- Your Christmas Show of Shows (1986) TV Episode ..Lorenzo   ------------
--Hollingsworth
- Pilo t (1986) TV Episode .... Lorenzo Hollingsworth
- Silver Spoons .... Dexter Stuffins (14 episodes, 1982-1983)
- Won't You Go Home, Bob Danish (1983) TV Episode .... Dexter Stuffins
- The Empire Strikes Out (1983) TV Episode .... Dexter Stuffins
- Three's a Crowd (1983) TV Episode .... Dexter Stuffins
- Junior Businessman (1983) TV Episode .... Dexter Stuffins
- The Toy Wonder (1983) TV Episode .... Dexter Stuffins
(9 more)
-The Taming of the Shrew (1983) (V) .... Petruchio
-Hill Street Blues .... Crawford (3 episodes, 1982)
- No Body's Perfect (1982) TV Episode .... Crawford
- Phantom of the Hill (1982) TV Episode .... Crawford
- A Hair of the Dog (1982) TV Episode .... Crawford
-Southern Comfort (1981) .... Pfc. Simms
-Macbeth (1981) (V) .... Lennox
-Beulah Land (1980) (mini) TV Series .... Roman
-Star Trek: The Motion Picture (1979) .... Crew Member
 -Star Trek: The Motion Picture - The Director's Edition (USA: DVD title)
-The Onion Field (1979) .... Jimmy Lee 'Youngblood' Smith
-The Trial of the Moke (1978) (TV) .... Lt. Henry O. Flipper
-King Lear (1974) (TV) .... Servant to Cornwall

Jean Dorsinville is a retired financial analyst and lives in Pooler, Georgia, USA.

12.   SHIRLEY RICHARDS ABBOTT SQUIRE
By
Elizabeth Punnett

Shirley Richards Abbott Squire is a truly charitable woman. It is one of the defining characteristics of this Vincentian patriot.

She is perhaps best known for her long and dedicated involvement with the Calliaqua Day Nursery, beginning a few years after its inception in the early 1960s, when she was married to William Jackson Abbott and living at Ratho Mill. Shirley served on the board chaired by Beryl Stephens for close to twenty years and, after a respite, returned to active service with the Nursery, chairing the board from 1986 to 1992. Although officially retired, her commitment to the Nursery continued until its demise, a well-considered and orchestrated end to an institution that had provided decades of invaluable support to its community. Shirley's tireless fund-raising efforts and fiscal prudence helped to leave the Nursery with a small bank balance which funds the board distributed to select charities after its closure in the mid 1990s. It is hard to capture the depth of Shirley's dedication to this endeavour. Her unabashed solicitations of practical and financial aid for the Nursery were largely successful because of the breadth and enthusiasm of her own contribution. Her way was hands-on and personal. She persuaded friends to help her take the children to the beach on bright days, she read to them, she loved them, and she followed their subsequent careers with pride. Hearing one young man on the radio years after he had graduated from the nursery, she called him up to congratulate him on his accomplishments. No sooner had she said, "Shane?" than he was exclaiming, "Granny Squires!" Such was the bond she had formed with these children that Identification was quite unnecessary despite the years that had passed since they had last met.

Here's what Bassy Alexander wrote about Shirley in his inimitable style in a June 05, 2009 Searchlight column: -

"Needless to say dat de Calliaqua Day Nursery is de second oldest of its kind in SVG, and would have provided an opportunity foh hundreds ah mothers in and around Calliaqua, enabling dem to go to work fully assured dat dey kids were well taken of, breakfast, lunch and afternoon snack. But Granny Squires originally belonged to de Planter Class. Her father was manager at de Mount Bentick Estate, and as she explains in one of her sketches in her book entitled 'Vincy Sketches' she was privileged growing up in SVG; she lived in the Great House where dey had maids and house-keepers, lots to eat and drink and who knows to throw away too. But living in all dat luxury in ah Great House did not prevent her, den in her early

teens, from seeing and feeling foh de poor, hungry kids running around de estate. No doubt she was powerless to correct what was happening then, but deep in her lickle heart she would have vowed dat one day she would do something to mek life better foh poor and needy kids. She did dat and much more."

Examples of Shirley's social conscience and compassion are tangibly evidenced in the public sphere, but are most abundant and typical in the private arena. I write this from an intensely personal perspective. Shirley is my godmother and has provided me with a second home all my life. For periods during both junior and secondary school, I lived with her at Indian Bay on weekdays, returning to be with my parents in the Buccament Valley at weekends. Taking responsibility for a rebellious teenager seemed not to cause her any pause, and it remains a time of happy memories for me – a time punctuated by spontaneous outings – drives to Argyle to walk on the beach, picnics and strolls in the Gardens, and regular swims and walks at Indian Bay both day and night.

Shirley was extraordinarily kind and generous to me, sharing whatever she had, always accessible, concerned, loving, non-judgmental. I saw her charity first-hand – to me, and to her community. By that time (the 1960s and 1970s), Shirley had divested herself of the greater part of her inheritance, mostly through generous, and sometimes foolhardy, gifts. She supported herself by working full time, and by renting out the main house on her property, while living in a small house on the grounds. We still laugh about the cheese sandwich variations we often ate, always beautifully presented on antique family china, and always, always, with flowers on the table. But I remember, too, that we usually had a stop between the grocery and the house, to share some of what she had been able to buy with friends less fortunate.

In her book, **Letter to My Daughter,** Maya Angelou describes the nature of charity thus:

"Philanthropists often are represented by committees and delegations. They are disconnected from the recipients of their generosity. I am not a member of that gathering. Rather I like to think of myself as charitable. The charitable say in effect, "I seem to have more than I need and you seem to have less than you need. I would like to share my excess with you." Fine, if my excess is tangible, money or goods, and fine if not, for I learned that to be charitable with gestures and words can bring enormous joy and repair injured feelings....

...I learned that I could be a giver by simply bringing a smile to another person. The ensuing years have taught me that a kind word, a vote of support is a charitable gift. I can move over and make another place for

someone. I can turn my music up if it pleases, or down if it is annoying. I may never be known as a philanthropist, but I certainly am a lover of mankind, and I will give freely of my resources. I am happy to describe myself as charitable."

Shirley is charitable in just this way; it is an essential part of her, as natural as drawing breath. It is the way she inhabits her world.

Several years ago when Sr. Patricia Ann Douglas was in the process of creating **Our** *Lady of Guadalupe* **Home for Girls**, Shirley was regularly bemoaning the fact that she didn't have the resources to do something significant to help Sr. Pat make this dream a reality. And then one evening she called me at my home in Nova Scotia to announce that she had found a way to help. She would publish a little book of her stories, seduce her granddaughter, the artist Caroline 'Bops' Sardine, to illustrate it, and it could be sold to raise funds. She threw herself into this project as completely and energetically as always, from the production of the book to its marketing, and also made every effort to arouse financial and practical support from all quarters. I was present in 2009 at a luncheon at the home of friends when she asked permission of the host to solicit the guests for assistance for the Home, made a speech, and was able to deliver cash and pledges of further assistance!

Of Shirley's "nameless, unremembered acts of kindness and of love", her friend and step-daughter, Margaret, wrote in a recent e-mail to me:

*"Of course Shirley did a lot for all sorts of people, going back to old Willie the groom at Prospect when he couldn't work, each Saturday he came for money. Then Dorcas, another Prospect person, and anybody she knew who was in need, she is a universal giver, the young man on the beach who paints well, is in drugs, she visited him in prison, has now given up on him. Daniel who brings coconuts when he needs money and something to eat, **she is never influenced by other people telling her bad things about those she has decided to help, because she knows their needs**."*

(The emphasis is mine). I believe this to be a crucial key to understanding the inclusiveness of Shirley's attentions and kindnesses.

Long-time friend, Tony Hadley, emailed about "Grannie":

"My memories are personal but even on my last trip she is consistent with her support for the underdog and the less privileged; a strong sense of fairplay. "

Another striking characteristic of Shirley's is her indefatigable nature. She needed every ounce of her prodigious energy in April 1979 when she found herself taking responsibility for the support of three generations of a Sandy Bay family displaced by the eruption of Mt. Soufrière. A political ally, Comrade Charles, offered the use of the ground floor of his house, and for three months Shirley rallied friends, acquaintances, government agencies and businesses to assist in obtaining funds for food, clothing and discretionary spending. She arranged for spiritual counseling, and for diversions in the form of games, and for beach excursions. There were twenty-eight people and baby Shirley, born during the evacuation period and named in honour of the woman who had done everything she could to make their upheaval bearable.

And this is at the heart of Shirley's gift to the world, her *raison d'être*: to make more bearable the lives of those she touches. She continues to go out on a limb for friends and, as always, to encourage them in pursuit of their dreams. She delights in creating bridges, making telephone calls to connect people who can be of service to each other, and unhesitatingly asking people to share their blessings, and to give of their best. Tell Shirley your problem and her mind immediately and unrelentingly goes into motion to find a resolution!

Born in 1927 to Hilda Simmons and Douglas Alan Richards, perhaps above all else, Shirley embodies and reflects a sea-change in the nature of the Caribbean identity.

Douglas Alan Richards's parents, May Hazell and Edwin Richards, had raised their family in Kingstown, at Granby House, opposite the Scotch kirk on Back Street. Hilda's parents, Mabel Richards and Charles James Simmons, QC, had their elegant home at what is now the Grand View Hotel, owned by the Sardine family. Early records show the Simmons men among the most prominent of the Saba sea captains, going back to the early 1700s. The family moved to Barbados, residing at the Eyrie, now the Barbados Community College, and on to St. Vincent by 1820.

Douglas Alan Richards attended the Boys Grammar School, then proceeded to Eton and to Sandhurst, joining the Royal Engineers and fighting in World War 1. After the war, he returned home and was tasked with setting up the first 'modern' sugar factory, at Mt. Bentick, and running the operation, which was to be his life's work.

Shortly after her birth, Shirley's parents had built a lovely home on their cotton estate at Prospect, since sold to the McIntosh family and operated now as the Prospect Racquet Club. Shirley remembers an idyllic childhood as the adored younger daughter of a gracious, genteel, tolerant mother and a fun-loving, charming father. Shirley was his shadow, going about with him on horseback from infancy, and very young riding out with him to his estate at Owia for overnight visits. Apparently he was held in high regard by the people who worked for him, as when the Directors of Mount Bentick sought to remove him from his position the workers apparently went on strike until he was reinstated!

Shirley went to school in Barbados when she was eleven, and because of the limits on shipping during *World War II, she* spent much of the next five years there, boarding at Codrington High School, and spending vacations with her mother's sister, Dorothy Hazell, who was at that time living in Barbados with her two sons, Ian and Robin. Ian and Shirley formed a close attachment that has survived years and distance, and he really was like the brother she did not have. Her beloved father, Alan Richards, died in 1943. Her mother, Hilda, later married James Punnett, who also predeceased her.

By 1945, Shirley had fallen in love with, and married, W J (William Jackson) Abbott. They had three children together, Alan, Tony and Heather. Their family included Jackson's four children from a previous marriage, Barney, David, Elizabeth and Margaret. Although they had a great deal in common and enjoyed a lively companionship, the marriage ended in divorce. They maintained a respect and admiration for each other, and were able to re-establish a rewarding friendship in later years. Shirley's ties with her step-children have also been enduring.

Newly single, and with her parents deceased, Shirley set about creating an independent life. She became an executive member of the St. Vincent Labour Party, and was a leading light in the Labour Party's Women's League. During the 1960s and early 1970s Shirley was actively involved in the political process, campaigning for her party and speaking at public meetings. In the years following her marriage to Canadian Jim Squire, she was often off-island, sailing the Caribbean, and was obliged to withdraw from active political participation. Today, Shirley continues to follow closely developments in her island, and to make her voice heard when she feels she has a contribution to make.

In the Foreword to **VINCY SKETCHES**, the booklet produced to raise funds for the Our **Lady of Guadalupe** Home for Girls, the venerable editor of "the Vincentian" newspaper, Nora Peacocke, captured much of the essence of Shirley.

"Caribbean history is sadly lacking in stories of human relationships that surmounted race and privilege, and demonstrated that love and tenderness have no barriers. We know all about the ruthlessness of slavery, the despotism of masters over servants, the cruelty of discrimination, and the injustice of segregation.

However, other things evidenced under that horrible old colonial system. The goodness and kindness of people, the lessons of nature, the determination and struggles in the cause of freedom, the courage and friendship that showed up in the combating of the natural disasters in the absence of the scientific facilities that now exist.

Only a few people remain who, through personal experience, can help us have a glimpse of some of the beautiful personal relationships that emerged in those days of tyranny. Shirley Squire is one of those few. The recording of a few of the past incidents of her life is a service to West Indians. We need to know that our cosmopolitan background has produced proof that humanity is greater than race."

Shirley's life has embraced a society that, in the words which Professor Rex Nettleford used to describe the typical West Indian was, *"...part-African, part-European, part-Asian, part-Native American but totally Caribbean".* She is to this day moved by her memory of the celebration of St. Vincent's independence in 1979. True to form, she was deeply involved in the preparations, including spending weeks collecting and preparing guavas for stewing! As she has described it to me on several occasions, she shared with her countrymen a unifying sense of optimism for the possibilities of her country as it stepped into the future as an independent nation, and a freedom from the shedding of an unjust past. I don't believe that Shirley has ever indulged in any sense of responsibility for the past, but she has clearly been guided by a sense of personal responsibility to play her part fully in the present, as a citizen, and as a humanitarian. To paraphrase Ted Kennedy, it is true to say of her too that she has been *"a good and decent person ...who saw wrong and tried to right it, saw suffering and tried to heal it..."*

Shirley was honoured to be appointed a Justice of the Peace and served for several years. When she believed herself unable to continue to serve adequately, she asked to be relieved of duty. She has always insisted on giving her all to any undertaking, and has never ever looked for the easy road.

While material needs inevitably came to her attention, her spiritual life has always been important to Shirley. She made a decision to convert to Catholicism, the religion of her three grandchildren, and was dedicated to the point of becoming a Eucharistic minister, and of giving Catholic instruction. For some years before age and infirmity intruded, Shirley was part of a group of devout women who met weekly to pray together. They formed a tightly-knit community who shared concerns for loved ones, for their country, and for the well-being of people near and far.

Sr. Reina Loe Sack Sioe, whom many of us originally knew as Sr. Cabrini when she was Principal of the St. Joseph's Convent in Kingstown back in the 1960s, had this to say about Shirley:

"Throughout the years...first as a parent then friend...Shirley has proved herself open to 'life to the full' (Jn.10:10) and was undeterred in her characteristic generosity of response to both God and neighbour.

She breathes and lives the beauty of nature as revealed in God's works of creation. She sees beauty in each and all...and so for her life is an on-going process of discovery and of hope."

Of the many contributions made by Shirley Squire, it is my contention that her greatest gift has been her personal characteristics, the democracy of her vision, and the example of her life. In every field of endeavour, she has given unstintingly of her best. She has been a person of action, resilience, unbounded optimism, and good cheer. Her embrace of life has been close to fearless; certainly courageous.

"For God hath not given us the spirit of fear; but of power, and of love, and of a sound mind."
(2 Timothy 1: 6 and 7)

Shirley thoroughly enjoys the simplest of pleasures – her garden, the evening sky, and most especially her beloved dogs. She is a humble person with absolutely no pretensions. Material possessions, social status, and all the other frills of success have mattered not a bean to her. In fact, over the years, Shirley has gradually given away anything of monetary value, and now her home is decorated, floor to ceiling, with photographs and artwork from dearly loved family and friends, like an ever-open photograph album!

Shirley is a loyal friend who keeps the people she loves always in her thoughts, and never overlooks an opportunity to make a difference, to lend a helping hand, to offer her guidance. Her service to her country, her wonderful friendships and her family have been the source of her greatest joys. She has loved her friends faithfully and truly, and I know that she has reflected back to them their best selves because she insists in seeing in us our possibilities rather than our limitations. In return, she has been blessed with the love and support of a wide and varied circle of friends and neighbours of all ages.

"In my mind, if you've changed one life, you've changed the world."
Barton Brooks, who founded and runs Global Colors – an international volunteer organization working to bring about change through specific and unique volunteer projects.

In 2005, I created a book for my godmother as a Valentine's gift. It was a collection of favourite verses, quotations and artwork, with a letter to her in dedication. I'd like to close with a portion of that letter, in representation of what Shirley Richards Abbott Squire has meant to me, and to many others:

"You opened my eyes, taught me to tackle the challenge of life with energy, to milk each day for everything it was worth, and heightened my enthusiasm for being fully alive.

You taught me to really look at the world around me, to enjoy every small moment, and never ever to ignore the bounty with which we were so richly blessed.

I learnt from you that elegance was not circumscribed by financial ability. I savoured every one of those memorable cheese sandwiches - only you could elevate that lowly standby into a delicacy!

I saw first-hand your generosity – your giving much when you had little, and your unabashed fund raising for the good causes that inevitably found their way into your heart...

I never knew you to be less than forthright and sincere. You refused to compromise yourself and lived always by your principles. Utterly without artifice or airs, you've been fiercely loyal to friends, chosen without regard to limits of age, class, colour or creed.

You never backed down from pointing out the wrong and praising the good, always in the best interests of our country and people. The rotten tomatoes of politics did not deter you; neither did the raised eyebrows of your peers.

Independent, passionate, imperfect, joyful and spirited, you live your life fully, honestly and with an abundance of love.

And it has been my privilege to see it firsthand, and my failure not to have better emulated your example."

Elizabeth Punnett is the daughter of Ruth and Chris Punnett. She resides in the oldest town in Canada - Annapolis Royal, Nova Scotia (established in 1605).

13.   GEORGE CALVIN HAMILTON THOMAS
By
Monica Thomas Woodley

"All one can do is to achieve nakedness,
to be what one is
with all one's faculties and perceptions,
strengthened by all the skill which one can acquire,
And then to stand before the judgment of time."
Stephen Spender

GCH Thomas, Tompo, Teacher George was a people's man. Why else, as he approached his twilight years, would he stop in the middle of Kingstown any where in his well-worn 1966 Singer Vogue and have a conversation with somebody, totally oblivious to the automobiles lined up behind him?   A Vincentian to the core - this was indeed his territory! His life and work were dedicated to the betterment of his country.

George Thomas was well-known, generally well-loved and well-respected by Vincentians. However, at his passing on the 19th December 1994, tributes suggested that his true value was much understated.

Sir Fred Phillips wrote:

"With his passing St. Vincent has suffered a great and irreparable loss – much greater than many people realize." (The Vincentian, 30th December 1994).

Dr. Ken John in his tribute entitled *'A Little Giant Departs' (The Vincentian, 23rd December 1994)* writes

"St. Vincent and the Grenadines will be the poorer by the loss of G.C.H. Thomas, a man of so many parts who had been taken for granted for so long."

It must be said that this self-effacing, unsung hero was indeed the being of GCH Thomas! Recognition was neither his motivator nor enabler.   A man of great humility although imbued with great confidence, George Thomas was quite unassuming with a delightful ability to laugh at himself as easily as he enjoyed poking fun at his friends.

The above writers' sentiments echo the sum total of a man small in stature; a cherished husband, father and friend; a man with a big heart; an infectious laugh; a hilarious sense of humour. He was enormously talented in a wide variety of disciplines and interests; committed to the education of self and others; with a love and devotion of country which saw him faithful to excellence and fearless to truth and integrity which often brought him both fans and foes; commendation and censure. He was also a man of deep faith and faithful to his God and his Church. George was indeed a man of many talents, plying each one with exceptionality and utilizing all for the building up of his country and its citizens, often with little recognition of the true depth or breadth of his contributions or his individual worth.

Born in the small town of Keartons in Barrouallie, on August 12, 1911, GCH Thomas was raised in Chateaubelair as an only child by his aunt, Nurse Madeline Thomas, a proficient, no-nonsense midwife of the surrounding communities. He attended the Troumaca government school under the headmaster tutelage of the renowned T. Webster Clarke. George barely fell short of gaining the single scholarship of the time to attend the Grammar School in the capital Kingstown. It would have been the only financial means for his family to give him a secondary education. So at a still tender age he became a teacher at his Alma Mater – the Troumaca Government School. This was the beginning of many endeavours in which he distinguished himself.

Even then, music was a part of young George and it was with fiddle or banjo in hand that he wooed Mildred McKenzie of Rose Bank, who eventually became his wife and bore him five children – Margaret, Dietrich, Monica, Nigel and Jacinta.

George Thomas was obviously fashioned for teaching and in due course was sent off to the Rawle Teacher Training College in Barbados in preparation for taking on the headmastership of the Troumaca Government School. Head teachers at that time, were community leaders who were expected to fulfill a litany of tasks which covered every aspect of life including legal (e.g. filling out forms, witnessing documents); and spiritual (e.g. Sunday school teaching, preaching); counselor and mediator. George Thomas handled himself and his roles in community service with love and distinction. It was therefore not long before he was sent to the Kingstown Anglican School as headmaster of one of the premier primary schools in the country, a tremendous responsibility while still in his twenties.

George was a serious disciplinarian, and as educators of his time (1940-50's) used the strap liberally. As Head teacher of the Kingstown Anglican School GCH moulded the lives of many youngsters, instilling in them the love and value of parsing, parts of speech, numbers and formulas, and the love of his own life – music!

To this day, many, many of his former students, dispersed in every corner of the globe, speak of their gratitude for that strap which seemed to enable them to be ultimately rewarded with a rounded, disciplined education that propelled them to much success in life. Not only were the three Rs – Reading 'Riting, 'Rithmetic taught with an approach of expected appreciation of the basic foundations which stuck, but music and poetry were a very important element of a child's education and "solpha tonic" was a vital part of the curriculum, all packaged within a good dose of spiritual and moral values. It was at this school that George Thomas made probably his largest contribution to the development of St. Vincent and the Grenadines as he shaped mind and spirit with indelible character traits for living and for life.

During this period, George Thomas was developing and teaching his musical talent on piano and violin. He played the organ at the Kingstown St. George's Anglican Cathedral, with his friend, the legendary musician, Weston Lewis. He always claimed that music was his real love and wished he had the finances to have pursued an academic career in this area. Up to shortly before his death in 1994, George was still contributing to spiritual upliftment through music by playing the organ and leading the choir at St. John's Anglican Church in Belair. It is noteworthy to recall that his musical talent was successfully passed on to his children. Older Vincentians will well remember the national pride when young Dietrich Thomas, violinist of about 12 or 13 years topped his competitors by receiving a first prize at a Music Festival in Trinidad in 1950.

Although unable to pursue higher studies in music, George had the opportunity to participate in studies in education and administration in Denmark and in England. Distinguishing himself as he was wont to do, George Thomas was one of the first West Indians to be interviewed on the BBC (British Broadcasting Corporation) while a student in the UK.

Following his foray at formal education as a school head master, he was boosted to the general public service. Service was his watchword as he carried out his duties always with distinction, and endeavouring to teach and to train all those persons in his work environment. George Thomas was a true role model to many – older and younger than himself. George Thomas served as Controller of Supplies; he served as a senior public servant, latterly as Principal Secretary in several ministries. As many senior public servants of that time Thomas was admired for his sense of fairness, work ethic, intelligence and general commitment to his responsibilities.

GCH was to further his national and regional contributions by serving in the Leeward Islands. However, before doing so, he again left his mark when he spent a few years in Union Island as District Officer and Magistrate of the Southern Grenadines. Again, even today persons in Union Island remember and speak of the Magistrate with great fondness. I guess one of his gifts is that people never forget him. Whether or not he is recognized officially by the authorities – the locals always remember him indelibly with much affection – and of course the anecdotes of the little giant who loved a good laugh!

In the late 1950s even as talks of West Indian Federation were brewing, he was seconded to Anguilla – then one of the three-island colony of St.

Kitts, Nevis and Anguilla. As Warden or Queen's representative on the island, the likes of Chief Ministers Bradshaw and Southwell would have been rattled and challenged by the fearless and outspoken GCH as he fought for an equal place for Anguilla in the scheme of colonial and national things. Is it a co-incidence that his successor as Warden, Mr. Vincent Byron faced many an uprising of the Anguillans, whose determination eventually resulted in the separation of Anguilla from the other two islands of the State?

GCH Thomas' next stop was Montserrat. In Sir Fred Phillips' tribute on the death of his close friend, George, Sir Fred reminisces that around 1961-62, he was instrumental in recommending GCH for Chief Minister William Bramble's request of a "good and experienced man" to serve as his Permanent Secretary. Sir Phillips continues "Mr. Bramble never ceased to thank me for so singular a choice". *(The Vincentian, 30th December 1994).*

Without doubt Montserratians would remember the eight years GCH Thomas spent there as Permanent Secretary and Chairman of the Legislative Council. He also acted as Administrator in Montserrat on several occasions. His influence on the political, social and economic lives of the people is legendary. It is interesting to note that here was yet another small island in which GCH provided leadership that did not embrace the attractive, popular trend of statehood and the release of colonial apron strings. It would appear – and is definitely brought out in his best-seller novel "Ruler in Hiroona" – that GCH Thomas was uneasy about the ability of Caribbean politicians to handle "power", and to negate 'self' for love of country. More on this later.

During his stay in Montserrat, GCH Thomas was awarded the Order of the British Empire (OBE). He was further privileged to have been presented this award by Her Majesty Queen Elizabeth II herself on her naval ship, the Royal Brittanica. The ceremony was witnessed by his wife, Mildred and daughter, Jacinta. Of course for months following, all and sundry were regaled by stories of his presumed conversations with HM the Queen!! The truth is that George was easily able to "walk with Kings and not lose the common touch" - as memorialized by Rudyard Kipling's "If".

GCH always had a hankering to publish something big. He wrote a great deal in his spare time. He was well known for his short stories and his journalistic incursions in various print media. Obviously a story based on his many political experiences working within Caribbean Civil Services, and the political turmoil at play in the Caribbean and the world in the 1950s to 1960's was brewing in his mind. As he tells it, it was on a Mediterranean cruise with wife Mildred before he completed his term in Montserrat, that "Ruler" began to take form.

Sir Fred Phillips tells it thus:

"Early in George's career I recall him telling me that he felt called to be a writer and would fail in his mission in life if he did not publish at least

one book. "Ruler in Hiroona" was that book and readers from many countries which I have visited have asked me if I knew the writer of "the tour de force" of a political novel". (The Vincentian 30th December, 1994).

GCH Thomas returned to his native St. Vincent in 1970, a learned man with a wealth of experience and a variety of talent. He became involved in such a wide and diverse number of national occupations, that this writer may not be able to keep them in sequence. For example, sketchy correspondence has surfaced and family members recall him serving on some major regional Inquiry organized by The Judicial and Legal Services Commission in 1976.

One of his early contributions on return to St. Vincent in 1970 was being appointed as Chair of the Public Service Commission. He again distinguished himself by performing with fairness, justice and objectivity.

George had a habit of scribbling thoughts on bits of paper – any paper, and presumably later using them in his writings, or just for clarifying his own thinking on certain issues. The following such scribble found on a torn airmail envelope, among his writings and papers suggests one of the philosophical underpinnings of his own work ethic and what was expected of others.

"All honest work is humanity's dance under the daylight lamps of social responsibility. But when the work is not honest, then it isn't work, it is plotting under a covered conscience of diabolical commitment."

As recently as in March 2010 Vincentian 'Bassy' Alexander recalls in his weekly article in the Searchlight Newspaper of George's candid approach, when he Bassy was almost fired for his writings while he was a Civil Servant. Bassy was brought before the Chair of the Public Service Commission. GCH Thomas told him that he actually admired his writing. He apprised him of the laws within which Civil Servants were obliged to operate. However, operating within his Human Rights he could continue. His serious caution however, was that he must write with integrity and truth. If he ever crossed the line of truth he would be in deep trouble!! Bassy never forgot this episode and credits George Thomas with his mentorship in Bassy's own journalistic offerings.

Further evidence of the regard in which GCH was held by Civil Servants comes in a letter dated November 9, 1981 from the St. Vincent Civil Service Association that reads:

Dear Sir and brother,

I have been instructed by my Executive to thank you for your invaluable contribution to our Public Service Union Week.

I am to express the hope that you would be willing to assist us with our workers education programme in the future.

Signed R. Irving Samuel ..Ex. Secretary

As previously indicated, GCH had a penchant for teaching and mentoring. Bassy Alexander is one such who still speaks of the tremendous impact George Thomas had on his life, and of the depth of things he learned from him. Bassy tells that he really got to know George well when they both sat on the Christian Council. They were two of the four lay persons and four clergy which comprised the then Christian Council. They were both members of the Social Action Commission.

Bassy recalls when as Council members they were sent to Barbados for a regional Conference. Bassy tells that it was there that he learnt so much from his mentor and roommate, GCH Thomas, of how things were done in such environments. GCH showed him how to work the room to gather information; how to meet and greet persons of all persuasions; how to buy a bottle of brandy or such and invite persons to their room and to engage them in heated and enlightening political discussions. "Ruler" was recently published and GCH was the political authority on all issues within the Caribbean and outside. He speaks of how persons literally absorbed his word like a great guru, and how privileged Bassy as a young man felt to be in the presence of such intelligentsia.

Politics was definitely in George's blood. That he never ran for elected office may not be surprising because of his candidness, integrity and deep sense of justice. He was a known supporter of the St. Vincent Labour Party, and even had a short stint as Senator. However, he would have been the first to speak out even when those whom he supported departed from what he perceived to be justice and truth. Speak out he did – especially in his journalistic writings, sometimes with a rigour that would send fear, tremour or applause depending on the reader's own view point.

GCH had a regular newspaper column in the Vincentian newspaper, and indeed served as acting editor on several occasions. He is noted as the person who brought improved physical changes to the Newspaper in terms of layout and presentation. He also brought a readership, as in the still-remembered infamous "Quo Vadis" saga:

In the Vincentian of Friday 1st May 1987, an article appeared entitled "Where are we going? By Quo Vadis. (Later it was believed to have been a *nom de plume* of GCH, although only a private disclosure of the identity had accompanied the eventual apology of Quo Vadis and the editor of the Vincentian.)

The article grew out of a statement seen in another newspaper which caused the writer, Quo Vadis, to *"read the statement several times with the knitted brows of unbelief and a puzzled mein."* Such a wonderful inimitable way of expression!!

The article went on to question the apparent issue:

"no longer, in fact, the separation of the judiciary and the executive government, which formerly gave the free citizen confidence in the administration of justice."

The Quo Vadis issue became huge in St. Vincent. In one of the reams of stories and articles by government and people that followed the initial article, Quo Vadis referred to the debacle as a "cause célèbre". The government did not take kindly to the original statements made by "Quo Vadis" and demanded the disclosure of his/her identity. This story seemed to have entertained and even enraged the Vincentian populace as much as it irritated those in authority. The saga took on an air of humour as signs, articles and even bumper stickers sprung up claiming "I am Quo Vadis"; "Leave Quo Vadis alone!". In addition debates on the Freedom of Speech raged.

If GCH was indeed Quo Vadis – of which the Vincentian populace was confident, he may have done well to heed the cautions of his wife. Jacinta, the daughter who spent most time living in the same country and close to the parents, shares how Mildred always kept him somewhat contained with the threat that his writings may encourage the authorities to victimize his children, who may wish one day to return and integrate into the St. Vincent and the Grenadines community. However, following Mildred's passing in 1985, George's pen seemed loosened. No Party affiliation prevented him from criticizing publicly "where wrong was wrong".

Following is a sample from a *1989 Vincentian Newspaper* editorial found among his memorabilia:

" The real astonishment is the utter lack of character, sensitivity, dignity and decency of all of us who make up the electorate of this place, to be able to allow this ... It is becoming increasingly clear that nobody in St. Vincent and the Grenadines really loves or cares a fig for St. Vincent and the Grenadines. Our Society, despite our schools-talk and achievements in so-called "higher education", and our religious pretentions, continues to remain a selfish, greedy, low-life, money worshipping tribe of negroes who still cherish the Mas'rBoss mentality of the slavery days. There is not even an alternative political party or group that is demanding our respect, confidence and trust."

Such were the mutterings of his political anguish when from his perception things were not as they should have been.

In Dr. Ken John's article on the passing of GCH Thomas he observed that twice GCH Thomas' name surfaced and was passed over, .for the post of Governor General of St. Vincent and the Grenadines. *(The Vincentian, 23rd December 1994)* It would not be at all surprising if George was the one who ensured that he was passed over for such a position.

In all of this, George Thomas was a first-rate family man. He and Mildred devoted themselves to ensure that their children were extraordinarily well looked after. Throughout the parents' lives they remained very close to and extremely supportive of all the children and grandchildren, including George's eldest child, Cauldric Debique, who sadly left this earth before his father. Despite living in different parts of the globe, children and grandchildren visited 'home' frequently much to the delight of GCH.

In addition to Mildred's artistic skills, love for children and general saintliness, it is very evident that many of George's attributes and talents were passed on to his offspring. Both Dietrich and Nigel continue to be outstanding musicians in Europe. Margaret has recently published a novel, and continues to write. Monica and Jacinta made important contributions overseas – particularly in Toronto and Montreal in areas of religion, education, drama, administration and politics and at present continue to play active roles in the national development of St. Vincent and the Grenadines.

This story of GCH Thomas would not be complete without more than a passing mention of what he and his family felt to be one of his most important life achievements: the publication of his novel "Ruler in Hiroona".

The original was published by Columbus Publishers Ltd., Trinidad in 1972; republished by Macmillan Publishers Limited, UK in 1989 and a third edition also by Macmillan Publishers in 2003. The salient factor of "Ruler in Hiroona" is its continuous relevance to Caribbean life and politics, and its timeless timeliness as time goes by. It is instructive to look at some of the reviews of the novel:

"The reappearance of George Thomas' novel, Ruler in Hiroona, is a welcome event for the many who have been unable to obtain a personal copy since its first publication in 1972. In some respects the book is even more timely than when it first appeared, and it has proven to be more prophetic than we might have wished." (An appraisal of the second edition 1989, by Professor Douglas Midgett –newspaper source & date are illegible. However Midgett's writings may be found on the internet).

***Ruler in Hiroona** was and is still acclaimed as a Caribbean Classic. Earlier editions were promptly consumed as a tale purportedly located on* *the fictional island of Hiroona, but which every Caribbean reader would recognize as that of their own island home. Such was, and is, the value and beauty of **Ruler in Hiroona** as it ever so ingeniously reflects the genre of every country and territory of the Caribbean Region – historically, socially and politically. Author, the late G.C.H. Thomas, brings to this infectious tale of Caribbean life and politics his disarming sense of humour; his inimitable writing style; and a bold analysis of Caribbean political leadership familiar to the 1950's as the Region's "territories" shook off the shackles of colonialism and endeavoured to determine their own destinies. (From the Preface of the third edition, 2003)*

Thus we see GCH Thomas' novel embodying the essence of the man of whom we have been writing, Here we grasp and take in his wealth of wisdom and experiences in many walks of life, his understanding of the nuances, foibles and eccentricities of Caribbean people, life and politics. Here we interact with his infectious wit and his amazing way with words and indeed of the English language. Here we drink up his skill at political analysis, and his obsession with justice and truth. It is indeed telling that the story around his main character Jerry Mole - aspiring politician and ultimately the first Chief Minister of Hiroona - is all about truth and begins …

" I am committed to tell the stark truth in this autobiography……. I have to write what may be regarded as some incredible stories about the West Indian islands ... There is something cathartic about telling the truth, ridding yourself of the burden of not doing so, freeing yourself of the choke of it in the throat of your conscience..." (Ruler in Hiroona, Chapter 1 page 1)

St. Vincent and the Grenadines has indeed been blessed by the journeying of George Calvin Hamilton Thomas in this land and indeed the Caribbean.

Time and space has not allowed detail on the spiritual and religious contributions of GCH Thomas. Sufficient to say that it was these elements which drove his life and made him the man he was. It is therefore quite fitting to end with a Biblical word:

LORD, you have assigned me my portion and my cup; you have made my lot secure. The boundary lines have fallen for me in pleasant places; surely I have a delightful inheritance.

I will praise the LORD, who counsels me; even at night my heart instructs me.

I have set the LORD always before me. Because he is at my right hand, I will not be shaken. Therefore my heart is glad and my tongue rejoices; my body also will rest secure, because you will not abandon me to the grave, nor will you let your Holy One see decay.

You have made known to me the path of life; you will fill me with joy in your presence, with eternal pleasures at your right hand.

Ps 16:5-11 (NIV)

We pray that our beloved GCH Thomas is indeed basking in the eternal pleasures from the right hand of his God.

Special thanks for the input of Jacinta Thomas Elliott.

Monica Thomas Woodley is a management consultant. She lives in Cane Garden, St. Vincent and the Grenadines.

14.   **HENRY HARVEY WILLIAMS**
By
Sir Fred Phillips

In writing a profile on the life of this citizen of St. Vincent and the Grenadines who was born in 1917 and who died in 2004, I must begin by acquainting my readers of the uncanny way in which our individual lives touched each other's.

I first met Henry in about June of 1930 when we were both competing for the only annual scholarship given by the Government for boys in the primary schools who wished to attend the only secondary school in the island for boys. Henry won the scholarship that year. In 1931 I again competed and that time I was the winner. By that time he had completed his first year at the Boys Grammar School (BGS): so that when I arrived there my only acquaintance was able to take me under his wing and "teach me the ropes" in what was a new and sophisticated environment.

Primary school buildings in those days were barn-like structures-without partitions; they were drab and dreary. The grades in the school were referred to as Classes; but peculiarly you were said to be in Standard I or Standard II and so on – not Class I or 2. The classes were all so close to each other that each teacher was rivalling with the other to be heard. This was also the case in the Gomea Methodist School which Henry attended before winning the Scholarship. His revered father Darnley Williams was the Head Teacher.

Henry's scholastic career at the Grammar School was outstanding. During the first year at this school I was amazed at his knowledge and the clarity with which he expressed himself; and if my own performance was good he was largely responsible for making it so, for he spared no pains to help me in the new subjects I was facing – Latin, French, Botany, Chemistry, Algebra and Geometry.

Eventually, in our last year at the school we caught up in Form V where we faced another competition with seven or eight others this time for an Island Scholarship of which only one was awarded every two years for a student to proceed to a university abroad for tertiary education. This was in 1936 – twelve years before a university college was established in the Caribbean under the aegis of London University. The winner of the Scholarship in that year was Landreth Cummings but Henry, who with Cummings, obtained a Grade I in the London Matriculation Exam, was placed second. Cummings went off to Edinburgh University to study medicine and qualified six years later. On the other hand it was nineteen years after that scholarship effort that Henry could reach the United Kingdom on his own steam to qualify as a lawyer (as explained below).

In those days, all Island Scholars would go to English, Scottish or Canadian universities to study either medicine, law or engineering.

Not being able to go abroad for tertiary education, Henry had to find some way of making a living. He chose the then only avenue, namely teaching. And by the opening of the new school year (September 1936) he was appointed as an Assistant Teacher in the Westwood Methodist School. The salary was $20 per month and he was to remain there for four years. In 1940 he joined the civil service as a junior clerk at an increased salary of (I think) $22 per month. But by this time he had become interested in professional studies. Soon after, he secured a Bachelor of Arts Degree externally from London University, a herculean feat in those days.

After a few years' stint as a laboratory technician in an oil refinery in the Dutch Caribbean Island of Curacao he returned to St. Vincent to rejoin the civil service as a master in his Alma Mater. From there he served first in the Administrator's Secretariat (succeeding me) and then as District Officer in Carriacou – a dependency of Grenada (again succeeding me). It was after all these moves that he decided to read law and joined the Middle Temple in London where in the mid-fifties he was called to the Bar. He later served as Assistant Administrator of Grenada (for the third time succeeding me) and he retired from the Service while holding a similar appointment in St. Vincent and the Grenadines After serving the University of the West Indies as a Resident Representative in St. Vincent and the Grenadines, he went into private law practice.

It was at that time that he was asked to serve as Governor- General – but for some incomprehensible reason, even though the office was then vacant his appointment was made an acting one although the entire population of St. Vincent wanted and expected it to be made permanent. To the great disappointment of the entire community after he had acted competently and with dignity for 18 months, a candidate of lesser calibre was permanently appointed. It was characteristic of this great citizen that he accepted this reverse with dignity and good grace – although he felt he had been hard done by.

But we must now examine the character of this gentle-man. A man of outstanding gifts and sincerity, he dearly loved his family and went to all lengths to maintain and train them in the way they should go. He was unassuming, humble and considerate – always ready to see the good rather than the bad in his fellow-man.

Having had a ring-side view of Henry from his earliest days, I hope I can be forgiven for sharing a number of personal recollections of him as we together travelled the same road and reached similar goals.

At the Grammar School he shone like a bright star – always at the head of his class – never boastful, never arrogant, ever pleasant, always calm.

And that was a characteric he was to carry with him for the rest of his life. I saw in full force the beauty of his personality when for two years in London while studying law we shared a room and studied together. We encountered many difficulties in the new environment but Henry was always able calmly to surmount them and to encourage me to follow suit. He was a classic case of being able to exhibit grace under stress. After living for sometime in a Students Hostel we decided that we would try and find alternative "digs". We were rebuffed time and again but he was never bitter. We found people patronising and he would always restrain me when I attempted to take some rash action. One day we saw in an advertisement that a room was vacant in an area that was near to the Inns and I telephoned to enquire about it. The landlady confirmed that it was vacant, informed us what the price would be and invited us to visit. She said we should take our time but that she would be there whenever we called. Later that same day we went. The lady looked at us and said "The room had been let since last week. You are too late." I was ready to attack her verbally but Henry simply thanked her for her kindness!

I thought I understood what a good student he was in our St. Vincent Grammar School days. But during our study periods for the Bar in England I saw a new, more determined and more focused Henry. He would instantly absorb the most abstruse points in Real Property or Conveyancing or Trust. An example in Conveyancing would illustrate this. Before I left Grenada for England in 1954, for a period of two years I had been studying the subject – reading as many books and articles as I could obtain. When I arrived in England in 1954 Henry had never done the subject at all, and I told him that for the Finals in May of 1955 I would put all my books and courses at his disposal and give him whatever personal help I could – thinking I had mastered the subject to the extent I could be his tutor in it. When we both went into the examination room I thought the paper was difficult but in his normal cool manner he said he thought "it was OK." There was one question that troubled me and I asked him if he had selected it among the five questions he had answered. He said he had done that question which he thought was "a gift." I told him it had taken me a whole page to answer it, to which he replied that he had covered the answer in three lines! When the result of the examination was released, he had gained a Distinction (an A) in the Conveyancing paper while I (his supposed teacher) came off with a bare "P"- the lowest grade! He was however characteristically polite and remarked that it was the extent of my knowledge that caused my downfall – a comment I readily accepted.

He and I had quite a time-table under which we would study for a given number of hours per night. Sometimes I would ask to vary the time table but he would veto my idea. There was one proviso that we agreed on; every night after 1½ hours of study we would take a half-hour's break during

151

which I would go and take a walk around Harrod's (since we lived next door) and he would take a <u>25 minute</u> nap. He never on these occasions ever overslept; but one night I thought I could follow his example and at midnight take a similar nap, only to find myself sleeping until 5am next morning!

We had great fun together. A few weeks after my arrival in England to join him, I woke him up about 3am (after we had retired only an hour before) to tell him that I had had a dream that I saw the Criminal Law Paper I was to write for the LLB Exam at 9am that same day. In the paper I could answer well most of the other questions but one that floored me was this:

Discuss, by reference to decided cases, the differences between burglary, house-breaking and sacrilege

He seemed more amused than convinced about my request that we should get out the Criminal Law Case book and go through the cases. But in his accustomed calm and unflappable manner he went through the answer with me for more than an hour. He could not believe his weary eyes when later in the day I returned to our lodgings and showed him that our labours had been rewarded because the question we had revised was in fact the first question on the Criminal Law Paper. Later as we took many other Bar Exams together he would frequently tease me to ask why my dreaming ability had deserted me at those later critical moments. We both took the Finals of the Bar Exams in May 1955 and were successful at the first effort. It was unusual in those days for a student to pass the examination on the first occasion – there were very many students then who would try five, six, seven times before achieving success. Quite honestly, I doubt if I would have made it if it were not for the organisation and study-planning to which Henry introduced me. For this I will remain eternally grateful.

Henry was a person of extraordinary gifts. He had a brilliant mind but was not given to boasting or ostentation. On the contrary, he was inclined to speak of his own abilities in a self-deprecatory manner – being modest to a fault.

He helped many people during his career in St. Vincent, Grenada, and Montserrat.

He was a most sincere and loyal friend always ready with a quiet word of wisdom. I recall with gratitude the advice he gave me when, as Governor of St. Kitts/Nevis/Anguilla, I was facing near-intractable problems with the Anguilla situation. He was then the University Representative in Montserrat and he came over to Basseterre to spend a week-end with me at Government House and to tender what turned out to be extremely useful advice as to how I should deal with the impasse.

The longest period I spent with Henry in the last forty years of his life was a stretch of nearly a month in 1986. The authorities in the People's Republic of China had invited me to select a team of Caribbean dignitaries to visit the People's Republic and I nominated Henry as a member of the group. In that four-week period we were able to look back and exchange thoughts on many vital issues and his presence on the team as we travelled the length and breadth of the People's Republic added greatly to the contribution the mission was able to make. He gave many addresses which were well received and he made quite an impression.

I last saw him in the flesh when I paid a 4-day visit to St. Vincent in November 2002. I spent more than two hours with him and although his health was declining, I could still capture glimpses of the old Henry, as he told me of the methodical way he tended his garden and attended his plants.

He and his lovely wife Elene produced a wonderful family and this appreciation would not be complete without reference to them. Nor would it be adequate without reference to Henry's parents and family whom I knew well.

His parents were wonderful, kind and gentle people who were model parents and who lovingly nurtured their offspring. They saw to it that all the children lived Christian lives and they brought them up in a way that would ensure they did not waste their lives. They paid particular attention to their education. The result was that the siblings showed great devotion and diligence in their studies at secondary school. I remember being particularly impressed in my earlier years at the Grammar School by the brilliance of Frank, Henry's elder brother, and I particularly recall how delighted his younger admirers (including of course myself) were when the results of this Cambridge Examinations were announced and we saw the number of distinctions he obtained in the various subjects.

When a couple of years later Henry's results from the same examination arrived, they were no less impressive. But Henry never let such achievements go to his head – a characteristic. I noticed with all his brothers and sisters. All the members of the family were great singers and musicians serving on the choir of the Kingstown Methodist Church where they regularly attended worship. Henry was one of the founders of the Kingstown Male Choir which also included Frank and Moulton; and this choir brought joy and cheer to many at Christmas during the years we performed that service. I also remember with what delight we listened to Doris's lovely voice when she sang a solo at any of our church services. I was to see a great deal of her when her husband Richard Robinson, also an old friend of mine, served with me in the Federal Government of the West Indies in Trinidad and was a senior executive in the Caribbean Development Bank in Barbados later.

Frank was to distinguish himself as Accountant General and Financial Secretary of St. Vincent while Moulton subsequently served as my Chief Revenue Officer when I was the District Officer and Magistrate of the St. Vincent Grenadines, and later as Accountant General and a distinguished Permanent Secretary in the Civil Service as well as a United Nations expert.

Henry passed on to his children the same principles his parents had instilled in him – excellence in whatever they did. His five children did not let him down.

Jeanne my god-daughter was a teacher for 33 years, having served with distinction in St. Lucia, Barbados and Bermuda before returning to St. Vincent where she retired as Headmistress of the Girls High School and was awarded an MBE for her contribution to education in St. Vincent. **Harvey** (deceased) first served in the Royal Bank and then as Henry's assistant in his law firm. **Cheryl** obtained a Ph.D in Education and is now a retired lecturer in Science Education in St. Lucia and co-author of a science text-book for secondary schools. As I write, one of Cheryl's daughters is serving as a surgeon in the Mount St. John's Medical Centre in Antigua where I now live. **Erlene** is a social worker by profession and presently serves the New York Consulate of the country. She too is well-known for her beautiful singing voice. **Dougal** has studied Accountancy and has since 1978 been working in the health care accounting field, being at present the Manager of Reporting and Budget in a hospital in Toronto, Canada.

It was my great privilege to give the main Eulogy at my dear friend's funeral in 2004. The number of people who crowded into the Kingstown Methodist Church for the occasion was a clear indication of the esteem in which he was held. The audience included the Governor-General, the Prime Minister, other members of the Cabinet and people from every walk of life. It was truly a wonderful service. I wish to repeat here what I said when interviewed on the radio at the time, namely., that Henry Williams was a man who, in Eleanor Roosevelt's apt words, "would rather light a candle than curse the darkness." Indeed, as we think of his life we must always be reminded of the great poetic verse:

"Full many a gem of purest ray serene
The dark unfathomed caves of ocean bear
    Full many a flower is born to blush unseen
    And waste its sweetness in the desert air"

Sir Fred Phillips is a former Governor of St. Kitts–Nevis. He presently resides in Antigua and Barbuda.

15.   EARL "OLD GEORGE" DANIEL
By
Bertram A. John

The day was March 14th , 2005, the day celebrated in St. Vincent and the Grenadines as National Heroes Day. The people who lined the route into Kingstown, and the thousands gathered in Heritage Square where the event was to come to a grand climax, were lifted by the air of expectation and pride that the event generated. At the end of it all, Earl, "Old George" Daniel and his walking companion, Joel Butcher, had completed a feat of endurance that was unmatched across the whole world. They had walked for six consecutive days without sleep through the towns and villages of the mountainous terrain of St. Vincent and the Grenadines. Vincentians were enthusiastic in their support of Old George and Joel. The spirit of unity in celebration of their achievement and, by extension, in the achievement of the people of St. Vincent and the Grenadines was exhilarating. And this spirit is central to understanding the life purpose of Earl Daniel.

Earl was born on July 6th 1963 in Murray's Village in Kingstown. This village has always been a close knit community of hard working, deeply spiritual people. He spent the first seven years of his life there. His father was Robert McDonald Daniel from Union Island and his mother was Greta Providence from Troumaca. When he was seven, he was sent to live with his great uncle, Minton Providence in Troumaca, where he completed his primary school education. He was deeply influenced by Minton's strong religious values. He virtually "grew up in the church". His uncle was a strict disciplinarian, who did not allow Earl to stray from the religious values he had instilled in him. On returning to Murray's Village at age thirteen, he was enrolled in the Intermediate High School, where he blossomed socially and academically.

At the Intermediate School, Earl held several positions of leadership. He was class prefect in the earlier forms. He became head prefect in the fifth form. He was given responsibility for running the school's cafeteria and was captain of both the athletics and cricket teams. He was the goal keeper on the soccer team and he founded and edited the school magazine, called the *Five A Times*. In addition to all of this, Earl was the organizer of the Intermediate High School's first graduation, and was the student leader who advocated on behalf of students for this graduation ceremony. He later on designed the school's graduation ring. This advocacy for fellow students helped Earl significantly in his development as a mediator. It is from this experience that his role as a mediator emerged. Or as Earl himself puts it, he considered school "as a spring board to the real world."

ABOUT OLD GEORGE

In 1976 Alex Haley published a book, **Roots**. It was an autobiographical epic that traced his family from its roots in Africa, through slavery, through emancipation and reconciliation. "Chicken George," later "Old George" was the enslaved grandson of Haley's iconic ancestor, Kunta Kinte. Two things stand out about the Old George of **Roots**. The first is his flexibility, his ability to adapt to the situation that life presented to him. He became an expert with fighting cocks, because that expertise provided a vehicle and a path to freedom. Old George was committed to buying his own freedom and the freedom of his family, from whom he had been separated. The second attribute of Old George, then, was an absolute commitment to freedom.

When Earl was in third form, he was assigned the role of Old George in a skit that was staged by his school. The passion with which he portrayed George earned him the nickname, "Old George" which his classmates bestowed on him. Earl adopted the nick name eagerly.

AN EARLY CRISIS

When Earl was five, he witnessed an argument between his father and his mother's only brother. He saw his father pack his bags and leave. He never saw his father again until he was twenty. At that time, Earl was a ticket agent for the Leeward Islands Transport, (LIAT). His father was on the ticket line, waiting to have his ticket confirmed. "I heard him proudly pointing at me and telling someone in the line, 'That's my son there!'" The crisis shaped by this paternal abandonment is not uncommon in the Caribbean. It generates deeply felt but seldom acknowledged emotions.

Earl acknowledges that he was deeply hurt by his father's actions (leaving the family), so much so in fact, that he developed a "hatred and deeply rooted anger" toward his father. One day, when he was an adolescent, his mother told him that his father was coming to stay with them for a period of time while he was visiting St Vincent. Earl strenuously objected. He told her that if his father "put foot in the yard" that he would kill him. Earl admits that he was absolutely serious in his threat, so deep was the hurt. His mother's response was "Don't do that, heap coals of fire on his head instead." In other words his mother encouraged him to express himself verbally. But his mother was a credible exponent of this approach. She herself never spoke ill of Earl's father to him or to any of her children. Earl recognized that his task was to forgive. But in order to forgive, he had to acknowledge his own feelings. He gained an understanding that his father's abandonment of him was his father's personal weakness. It was not directed at him, and was not caused by any failure on his part. It did not mean that Earl was a bad person or unworthy of a father. In order to learn this, he had to learn to express his fears and his hurt to others who were in a position to empathize with him and support his effort. His mother is such a person. He also had to learn to accept that life is not necessarily fair, but it is meaningful.

TURNING POINT

Earl later discovered that his love and his need for his father were what compounded his sense of abandonment. "I found out that I really loved him, and that was why I responded so strongly to being abandoned by him. I really looked up to him as a child." This story of abandonment had a relatively happy ending. Earl migrated to Canada in 1988. He went to live in Montreal. Sometime thereafter, he traveled to New York, in search of his father, and found him living in pathetic circumstances. Earl arranged for him to move to Montreal, where he reunited with Earl's mother and lived until his death.

Earl had a lot of questions for his father. "I asked him why he left, and he gave me his reasons. I understood why he never came back, even though I didn't agree with him. I forgave him, and that was the important thing. It was then that I really learned to forgive." Sadly, Earl's father died two years later, and Earl, in his usual role, arranged the entire funeral from beginning to end and buried his father. "He wanted that." Earl is particularly proud that his first child, his oldest son, now eighteen, got the opportunity to know his grandfather.

FORGIVING

The abandonment that Earl went through is not unfamiliar to our people in St Vincent and the Grenadines, throughout the Caribbean, and for that matter, in any part of the world with our shared heritage of enslavement, colonialism and neo-colonialism. In fact, his namesake, Old George, was separated from his family and became a seeker of freedom and family reintegration because of that experience. The abandonment of children always leaves deep scars, deep hurts, and we all defend our hurt through angry acting out, or building walls around our true feelings. So how do we forgive? And whom do we forgive? The healing process ultimately requires that we forgive ourselves. This essentially means that we have to acknowledge the pain, recognize what it means and through acknowledgement and acceptance, give ourselves the opportunity to change.

Forgiveness is ultimately a gift we give to ourselves. Mahatma Gandhi, Earl's hero, puts it this way, "The weak can never forgive. Forgiveness is the attribute of the strong." Forgiveness is really something that's within our own control. It's really not something that we do for someone else, so it affords us very important choices about the way we live our lives. The great thing about forgiveness is that it gives us the opportunity to create the kind of world that brings us peace of mind and happiness. Sometimes, the hurt is so great that we think that the only way out is to strike out at someone or something over which we have control, or to bury the hurt so deep within ourselves that it controls us in ways we never quite understand. Aggression and denial lessen the quality of life for us as well as for those around us, and build walls that make communication very difficult. Earl's experience demonstrates the possibilities that emerge from the strength of forgiveness.

MIGRATION

Earl resigned from his job at LIAT in 1988 and left St. Vincent and the Grenadines for Canada. The immediate reason for migrating was to get medical attention for a brain condition. He decided to remain in Canada because he knew that he would need follow-up care. He was also cognizant of the opportunity for professional growth that Canada represented. "I also took into account that I wanted more out of life than just being a ticketing agent for LIAT." Leonard "Charlo" Charles a colleague and friend to Earl urged him to pursue academic credentials. Earl took the advice to heart. He matriculated at Mc Gill University in Montreal and completed a degree in social work.

Leaving St. Vincent and the Grenadines was difficult. Earl has always felt a "passion" for his homeland. He is troubled that the country does not always live up to its designation of "Land of the Blessed". Love, humility, peacefulness, and contentment are the virtues that he believes must be cherished if the country is to prosper. His walks are designed to highlight and stimulate interest in these virtues.

While in Canada, Earl worked at several jobs. He was at one point a sales agent for the Kirby vacuum company. This is a company that sells vacuum cleaners door-to-door. As you can imagine, Earl is an excellent salesperson. His quick and winning smile and willingness to engage people from all walks of life give him a distinct advantage in this type of endeavor. Professionally though, he sees himself as a "social walker." This is Earl's unique blend of social work and client advocacy in which walking becomes both a challenge and a commitment. Earl brought this skill to his work as a social worker in hospitals in Canada and perfected it during the 1990's when he worked in St Vincent and the Grenadines as a welfare officer in the prison system. Yes! He did indeed return to St. Vincent with the goal of applying his training in social work. He worked with the inmates for five years before returning to Canada. He was and remains a strong advocate for rehabilitation of prisoners, and he used walking as a challenge to get both inmates and the prison administration to commit to a program of rehabilitation. To demonstrate to the inmates how important and also how demanding the rehabilitative process is, he challenged himself to walk for three days without sleep. The offer he made to the inmates and administrators was that should he complete the task successfully, something he had never done before, he would expect them to make a commitment to a rehabilitation project. It was this effort that got Earl started on challenging himself through walking.

While Earl truly enjoys his life in Canada, he maintains an abiding, unshakable love for his homeland. To this day, he continues to seek opportunities to make a difference there.

THE WALKS

"I am very serious about the god-given talent I have and I know God has given me the energy to serve my people, which involves all of humanity. I will forever walk, for any cause that is just and worth dying for."

To appreciate the walks that Earl, "Old George," and Joel Butcher have undertaken, it is important to understand the frame of mind that shaped the enterprise. Earl is deeply influenced by Mahatma Gandhi's life and philosophy. Gandhi too was a walker. Gandhi's assessment of happiness fairly well sums up the approach to life that Earl takes. "Happiness is when what you think, what you say and what you do are in perfect harmony."

Earl discovered that walking is a gift. He accepted the gift with gratitude, then he used that gift as an organizing principle in his life. His life, one of service, is a blend of walking, reaching out to people and helping. Each component reinforces the others in an energizing, integrated symphony. No wonder he is perceived by so many as an approachable, loving, respected father, husband and friend. He is a man with a big heart, big smile, generous spirit and infectious laughter. He clearly loves being around people. He has qualities once highly valued in Vincentian life, and he reminds us that those values are eternal. He lives by the simple creed that we should always endeavor to give our very best to each relationship and to each other. It is that principle that truly ennobles all of us.

GOING WHERE NONE HAVE GONE BEFORE . . .

Walking was important to Earl as a child. In rural St Vincent, where he lived, he walked to take messages for his family, to run errands and just to get around. He started walking formally, though, in 1999, a walk that took him from Georgetown to Rosebank. In that year, he walked as well from Richmond to Fancy, an almost complete circumnavigation of St Vincent. And then, to satisfy his curiosity, he did the same walk, but in the opposite direction. Between the years 1999 and 2005, he conducted several of these challenge walks throughout the island. Joel Butcher introduced himself to Earl in 2001, and the two of them have walked as a team ever since. In 2005, they decided on a six day walk without sleep. Earl learned of someone who had walked for five days. He decided to establish a new record. In 2005 then, the walk was done with a culmination on March 14th, which in St Vincent is known as National Heroes Day. Though they subsequently walked for more days, Earl still considers this walk his most demanding. In 2006, they extended the walkathon to seven days, with a walk in Jamaica around Emancipation Park in the city of Kingston. In 2007, they extended the mark to seven days and one hour, this time again in St Vincent. In 2008, they walked for an amazing eight days around Prospect Park in New York's Brooklyn. More recently, in September 2009, Earl walked in the Arctic. In sum, these walks have been physically taxing, but even more so, they've been psychologically taxing. What does it take to push yourself forward against the effects of the elements, rain, snow, sun, heat, cold, difficult terrain, blistered feet, exhaustion? Earl says that, like his hero, Gandhi, it is a question of drawing on the indomitable will to succeed.

HOW EARL PREPARES FOR WALKING

Earl has always been physically fit. He's also emotionally fit. He exercises regularly and he is very conscious of his nutrition and dietary habits. He loves fruit of all kinds, and enjoys seafood and vegetables. He's maintained his weight and his conditioning routinely. His earlier walks did not involve extensive preparation, particularly because they were personal challenges, but as his fame grew, the walks took on a different purpose. Many of his walks were sponsored and were designed to facilitate the work of charities or individuals in need. Ultimately, Earl recognized that his walking represents a legacy. With increased responsibility then, he has become more meticulous in preparation. He gets himself medically checked before and after, and moderates his diet to maximize his performance weeks prior to his walk. Very importantly, before each walk, Earl goes through a process of meditation and prayer. His point is that he must feel that he is walking for a purpose, a purpose worth dying for. And he takes the time to decompress after each one. He believes he has one major event left, another walk in St. Vincent and the Grenadines. Even now, he is praying about it.

Earl gives great credit to his team-mate, Joel Butcher. Joel introduced himself to Earl after one of his very early walks, and has been a steady companion on all the walks that followed. Joel failed to complete the walk in Jamaica because of injury.

This incredible Vincentian team has gone beyond the usual and find themselves at the very fringe of human achievement. For Earl Daniel, the task is far from over. For him, the journey will continue as he intends to impact Vincentian culture at its very foundation. He's walking, he says, to re-awaken the spirit of harmony that he thinks too many Vincentians have lost.

FAMILY

On July 5th 2003, Earl married Gweneth John. They parent four children. His greatest success so far, is that his children are in school and church and are doing well despite the hardships that children confront daily. He is pleased that they are willing to be guided appropriately, that they live in a happy home. He is grateful for the love of his wife, Gweneth, and the love they share, that is a precious example for the children.

Finally, Earl would like to be remembered as the man who dared to go the extra mile to discover new horizons, the man who challenges the status quo, who was never satisfied with accepting things as they are, as one who always looked to find ways to improve himself and his world. He's a man who believes in the power of the mind and the need to be mentally strong, a man who wants to be the change he wishes to see in the world.

Dr. Bertram John is a clinical psychologist. He resides in Queens, New York, USA.

PUBLISHED BY

KINGS-SVG PUBLISHERS

CARIBBEAN TRAILBLAZERS:
ST. VINCENT AND THE GRENADINES

VOLUME II

COPYRIGHT 2011 BY KINGS-SVG

ISBN: 0-9778981-8-0

PUBLICATION DATE: OCTOBER 2011

Dedication

To all the trailblazers of St. Vincent and the Grenadines, sung and unsung, dead and alive, on whose backs the country was built.

CONTENTS

CONTRIBUTORS

Yvonne Walker Andrew

Roy Austin

Rudolph Baynes, Jr.

George E. Daisley

Hayden Duncan

John Horne

Kenneth John

Baldwin King

Carleen Marshall

Philip Nanton

Nan Peacocke

Fred Prescod

Gwendoline Russell

PREFACE

It has been over a year since the first volume of *Caribbean Trailblazers-St. Vincent and the Grenadines* (June 2010, KINGS-SVG Publishers) was published as a successor volume to Sir Rupert John's *Pioneers in Nation-Building in a Caribbean Mini-State* (May, 2009, KINGS-SVG Publishers). We promised a second volume if we could find writers. And so here we are.

This volume profiles eighteen remarkable individuals (fourteen men and four women) who, by dint of intellect, hard work and perseverance, have succeeded in moving the beautiful island of St. Vincent and the Grenadines (SVG) a little further along, either directly or indirectly. Included are the biographies of five politicians, two diplomats, a medical doctor, an engineer, two poets, two journalists, two civil servants, a teacher, a feminist and a political scientist/sportsman.

As in the earlier volume, we have tried, as far as possible, to chart the history of SVG through the stories of the people mentioned herein. There are still many more inspiring stories to be told and we hope we can continue to tell them in the future.

As usual, we would like to thank profusely the eighteen contributors to this volume who took the time out of their busy schedules to pen these biographies, especially in view of the fact they did so not because of monetary gain but because they recognize that it is a worthwhile and important cause to chronicle the history of SVG and its people.

Also, thanks again to our children for their technological help in putting this volume together.

Baldwin King   October, 2011
Cheryl Phills King
(Editors)

1.   **ROY L. AUSTIN**
By
John C. Horne

How does one write immodestly about a lifelong role model, the shy retiring type who prefers to remain in the background, except when duty calls him to perform for his school or country, a highly successful man whose life has epitomized modesty? In keeping with this lifestyle, Roy Austin would probably not have chosen to include many aspects of the story that will unfold herein; but then much that could inspire stellar accomplishment would have been lost by concealing the extent of his accomplishments. He certainly would not want that to happen. Instead, this man who had spent most of his working life as a teacher, preparing young people to attain secure futures, will be happy to know that his life-story has actually motivated others to excel. And the main reason is likely to lie in developing an awareness that we can achieve, regardless of where we start in life and the size of the obstacles to progress we encounter.

The chasms mentioned in the title of this piece are obstacles to progress. Whether they are viewed as 'Everests' to climb or Grand Canyons to straddle, obstacles are magnified when they face people with limited financial means. But they become manageable if those persons are provided with literal and figurative bridges, physical and mental fortitude, ambition, tenacity and an early taste of even minor success. Caring family members and teachers who interact closely with young people are the ones who can help the youth to surmount obstacles. Also, location in suitable communities may provide ready access to facilities that make a difference. Notable experiences in Roy's life exemplify the truth of these claims.

Roy Leslie Austin was born in 1939 and grew up in the unpretentious western end of the capital city, Kingstown, in St. Vincent and the Grenadines, West Indies. This community was known to many as Bottom-town and in the 1970s, it was sometimes called "The Ghetto" because of the high percentage of underprivileged people residing there and the deteriorating housing stock. From the 1970s also, many young people applied the name of the lowest portion, Rose Place, to the entire area because they regarded the name Bottom-town as having a negative connotation. However, this community was also the location of a highly reputable private Primary School which stood only two houses from Roy's home; and the home of the owner and headmistress, Miss Louie John, was attached to the school. This is where Roy's formal education began.

Miss John, a deeply religious woman who would unblushingly accept the designation of being a "born again Christian," was respected by probably everybody in that generally lower-class community; men and women, accustomed to using foul language, would restrain themselves if they knew she was within earshot. In the obviously class-stratified society that was St. Vincent, the class and racial composition of her school's student-body suggested that admission was unaffected by such considerations; and to those whose parents had limited financial means, she was generous to a fault. Roy and a sister two years his senior who passed away at age eight, benefited from this generosity, their parents paying one-half the advertised monthly fee.

Sometimes when Miss John launched into one of her relatively frequent sermons, she seemed to be trying to make all of her students comfortable with their circumstances in life, once they developed decent habits within their reach. Thus, she often reminded students that "The cottage was a thatched one/ The outside old and mean/ Yet everything within that cot/ was wondrous neat and clean." Furthermore, her teaching philosophy seemed to embody the words from Proverbs 22:6 which she often quoted: "Train up a child in the way he should go, and when he is old he will not depart from it."

Miss John expected all of her students to develop middle-class mores and to achieve middle-class success, regardless of their social origin. She insisted that students speak "proper" English, not the "broken" English so common throughout the island. Boys had to tip their hats when greeting adults or clearly bow their heads. In almost daily sessions of reading aloud in front of classmates and a teacher, students were expected to "read with expression." And teachers did not hesitate to correct errors. Also, she wanted her students to aim for admission to secondary school, preferably by obtaining one of the few Government or Kingstown Board scholarships available at that time.

In 1950 and 1951, Miss John felt that Roy had a chance to obtain one of the scholarships for the Grammar School and advised him to take the examination. He did not obtain a scholarship and, unlike the custom, he did not sit the separate Entrance Exam because his parents did not believe that they could afford the fees they would have to pay to keep him in the Grammar School

For his final year in primary school, Roy moved to the Kingstown Methodist School. In officially organized competitions among the four primary schools in Kingstown at the time, he represented this school in cricket and football (soccer). He was one of the opening fast bowlers in the former sport as he was at Miss John's when her school played informal games against the three government primary schools in Kingstown. In soccer, he played at inside right. Roy's display of interest and some ability in these two sports is not surprising. He was growing up within easy walking distance of Victoria Park, for many years the only suitable playing field for cricket and football at the highest levels. At this field, he also gained exposure to some of the island's most accomplished players of these sports.

Furthermore, he spent many out-of school hours playing these sports on "the Park" with neighborhood youths.

Towards the end of 1952, an aunt who was working in Curacao promised to pay Roy's fees if he passed the Entrance Exam and was accepted by the Boys' Grammar School, one of only two boys' secondary schools in St. Vincent. He entered this school in January 1953 but it was his parents who paid the fee of $14.88 for the first and subsequent terms, his aunt being unable to keep her promise. Yet he credits her with playing a major role in his entry into secondary school because being well aware of his parents' limited financial means he had no intention of sitting the Entrance Exam before she offered financial assistance. However, his exceptional academic performance that first year and later apparently convinced his parents that any financial sacrifice was worthwhile. For instance, he was first in his form after the first term and second at the end of the first year. This performance earned him and two other students a double skip at the end of this year. In the promotion exam at the end of his second year, he was fourth but only three students received skips. In promotion exams at the end of the other two years before he took the Cambridge exams, he attained first on both occasions. He was then successful at both the Cambridge School Certificate and Higher School Certificate examinations (equivalent today to "O" and "A" levels) thereby qualifying for admission to British and Canadian universities.

Perhaps, Roy's stellar academic performance in secondary school should not surprise those persons aware of his home life. Parental encouragement was obvious in his parents' willingness to pay for a private school education. He also had a half-brother, George, about 13 years older who lived in the home. This brother was a voracious reader of all kinds of literature. He often borrowed serious books from the Public Library in the capital; but comic books and a wide variety of American magazines also found their way into the home through him. Roy became an avid reader of the many available books. Additionally, he often availed himself of the loan facility at the Public Library.

In secondary school, Roy also established an outstanding record of achievement in extracurricular activities. In the sixth form, he was appointed Head Prefect and attained the rank of Company Sergeant Major in the Cadet Corp, thus having the honor of holding the two highest positions available to students. He, also, served as editor of the handwritten sixth form newsletter, *The News and Views,* and was an officer in the debating society. One editorial he wrote alerted the headmaster to the existence of a somewhat unfair situation at the school in which students who entered at a late age had a diminished chance of winning an internal scholarship. Thus, the internal scholarship based on the results of the 1957 School Certificate results was given to a student who was age-eligible while a student with an undoubtedly better performance and fewer years in school but slightly older was ineligible by age. The former student, also, could not qualify if financial need were used as a criterion while the latter student would have easily qualified. The headmaster obtained a special scholarship for the needy, high-performing student.

Like most youths in St. Vincent in those days, Roy was born to parents of severely limited financial means. His father and mother, Clarence Austin and Florence Ferris (Miss Florie as she was called), were proprietors of a parlor, the name given to small establishments that primarily sold refreshments. The return from many of the items sold in the shop should have been greater than it probably was because they put many hours of hard labor into the production of those goods. This was the case for mauby, cakes, cocoa, coffee, sugar cakes, bread pudding, fried fish, "tree-tree" (tiri-tiri) cakes, black pudding, souse, "long bread," and vinegar. When he resided in Trinidad relatively recently, he decided that his parents should have been rich when he saw the price of a coconut drop; but they sold this cake for next to nothing. Other items such as mangoes, bananas, plums, "soft drinks," milk, water coconuts, and bread required little or no preparation on the premises. Since no value was added by the proprietors, the profit must have been rather small. In any event, competition and the financial status of most customers demanded that prices be kept reasonable.

With so many items to be prepared daily, Roy's parents worked hard to provide him with the opportunity for an education they lacked. They succeeded in covering the fees for primary and secondary school, but in the latter he often did not have required textbooks. Therefore, from his first year, he had to borrow the Algebra text and the Arithmetic text. He owned the Geometry text but that disappeared before the end of his first year, and he depended on borrowing the three mathematics texts right through to the end of the School Certificate examination.

In his third year in secondary school, textbook ownership became even more difficult for Roy. The Biology and Chemistry teacher held his classes in the laboratory and sent students without these textbooks back to the form room. Roy owned neither book and, therefore, spent an inordinate amount of time sitting in his form room while his classmates were learning these subjects. As might be expected, in his promotion exams that year, his unfortunate situation was reflected in his poor performance in these subjects. However, he had the best overall performance in the form, but not good enough to obtain the skip that he desired.

In the sixth form, only with the mathematics teacher's approval were students allowed to take this subject. The teacher had sufficient confidence in Roy's ability to select him to study mathematics. But now the required mathematics textbooks were used only in this form and few students were taking mathematics. Borrowing mathematics textbooks became virtually impossible because the students who owned them were likely to be using them just when Roy most needed them. After one term, he dropped the subject, a decision that made sense then but which limited his options for the rest of his academic life.

Less than a week after taking his last Higher School Certificate exam, Roy was employed with the Customs and Excise Department in the government service. With his eyes fixed firmly on university, Roy felt that the ideal job would be one in teaching that would allow him to maintain familiarity with academic information he had already acquired. Until a suitable teaching job was available, he was content to work at the Customs where he felt he was being exposed to information on importation and exportation of goods that could be useful if his further educational goal did not materialize. At the same time, he disliked being responsible for the government's money as he was during a relatively short period as the cashier at the Customs.

The impending resignation of a junior Customs officer opened up the opportunity to become the Customs Airport Officer, but he needed to be confirmed in order to obtain a uniform. At the confirmation hearing before the Public Service Commission, in response to a question from a Commissioner, he stated that he did not care to work at the Treasury. Immediately, the secretary to the Commission disapprovingly opined that Roy's response was determined solely by his desire to earn overtime fees at the Customs. Of course, Roy had an interest in earning as much as possible in order to hasten the day when he could use his savings to pay for a university education. The Commission, however, chose to punish him for his honesty and recommended that he be placed on a further probationary period. More negative experiences with working for the government would come later.

After twenty-one months at the Customs Department, Roy was appointed a non-graduate master at his Alma Mater at a salary of $143.50 per month. About one year earlier, without Roy's knowledge, an acting headmaster had requested of the government authorities that Roy be transferred to the Grammar School to fill a teaching vacancy. The authorities rejected the request claiming that he was needed more at the Customs. This information was relayed to Roy by a senior government employee several months after the decision was made. His monthly salary at the time of the decision was $72.00. Had he received the transfer when the request was originally made, he would have started with a salary of $160.00 per month. But in the interim, Mr. Grossmith, the head of a team of consultants appointed to review the structure and levels of remuneration in the Public Service, had recommended revised salaries, and, arguing that starting secondary school teachers were overpaid, he reduced their salaries to $143.50. At the same time, secondary teachers who had started when the original request for Roy's service was rejected received an increase to $184.00 per month. These were all people who obtained their Higher School Certificate at the same time as Roy.

As fate would have it, in 1964, Roy received notice from Yale University that he was accepted for admission in September of that year and would receive a specified amount of financial aid estimated to be sufficient to meet his needs. The University's decision was based on his performance on the Scholastic Aptitude Test, two Achievement Tests, a writing sample and his record of extracurricular activities in secondary school and beyond. One must wonder whether his performance on the required tests would have reached the level that brought him acceptance, if he had been kept at the Customs.

It was fate also that made him receive the acceptance letter barely in time to matriculate that year, the letter having found its way to him only after being sent first to Jamaica.

A few weeks earlier, he had been notified by McGill University in Montreal, Canada, that his application for admission to that institution was approved for that year too. He had applied to McGill because he believed that he had savings that were sufficient to convince the Canadian immigration authorities that he could pay for one year of study at that university. The information he had on these matters indicated that these authorities would then allow him to work to meet later expenses while attending school.

As Roy prepared to leave St. Vincent, he sought to straighten out his leave situation. Teachers at the Grammar School and Girls' High School were regarded in General Orders (the document containing the rules applicable to the conditions of government service) as civil servants with the same long-leave rights. As late as the year prior to Roy's intended departure, the teachers who resigned to study abroad received monetary payments appropriate to the time they had spent teaching. Now a government official, probably the Financial Secretary, informed the then President of the Secondary School Teachers' Association that teachers obtained long periods of vacation and were entitled to no more when they left the job. General Orders had not undergone any change of the rules governing long leave; and this official had no authority to institute any change, certainly not so precipitously. Nevertheless, the government paid Roy for the leave he had accumulated over 21 months at the Customs, but denied him payment for the leave he had accumulated over three years of teaching. For the third time in his years of service to the government, he suffered costly victimization at the hands of autocratic government officials.

Roy L. Austin

THE SPORTSMAN

Like the average youth in Bottom-town, Roy was well grounded in certain activities within his community. In addition to playing both Cricket and Football (Soccer), he was an excellent swimmer, not surprisingly, as he lived only a stone's throw from the beach. His prowess in sport was revealed in every discipline in which he participated. In the second of two years that the Grammar School held Aquatic Sports meets, he placed first in the younger age group in the two dives and the breast stroke. He played soccer for his school and reached the pinnacle of secondary school football in 1958 in Dominica when he represented St. Vincent in the Windward Islands Inter-Schools Tournament. Playing at right wing, Roy scored three of the four goals scored by St. Vincent to win the competition, two against St. Lucia and the lone goal that beat Grenada. Most of the members of this team also played for the school in 1959 when they won the DaSilva Cup in a knock-out competition in local club football, probably the only time that a secondary school placed first in an open competition in local football. Again, Roy was one of the most prolific scorers for the Grammar School.

The transition from Secondary School soccer player to after-school community/club player was smooth for Roy. He was now cast in the roles of a founder and President of, as well as a player for, the Eagles Club, a Sports and Cultural organization to which many like-minded young men gravitated and found tremendous satisfaction. For Eagles, he mostly played at left-midfield, and this is the position in which he represented the national squad in the January 1962 Windward Island Tournament in St. Vincent. In this tournament, he scored an important goal with a hard shot from outside the penalty area against Dominica, helping St. Vincent to take the coveted Popham Cup, symbol of Windward Islands Football supremacy.

In December of that year, another Windward Islands Football Tournament was held, this time in Grenada. This came about because the islands' football associations agreed that games would improve if the tournament were moved to a time closer to the end of the football season in the islands and prior to the festive Christmas season. For this tournament, Roy was elected captain of the St, Vincent national team and continued in this position until he left for the USA in September 1964. He switched to play sweeper (then called stopper), a position he had occasionally played for Eagles when a dangerous forward such as Lawrence "Babs" Jones was presenting too great a threat to the Eagles goalkeeper.

Throughout undergraduate school at Yale and graduate school at the University of Washington in Seattle, Roy continued to find time to participate in soccer. At Yale, regardless of your soccer prowess, first-year students were limited to playing on the freshman team, and Roy was a starter. Later, he started for the Yale varsity during his three remaining years of eligibility, occasionally scoring a goal when he played in the midfield. However, his greatest contribution in his sophomore year was to convince his teammates that Coach Jack Marshall's change to a 3-3-4 system was consistent with changes in international soccer. Early in his junior year, he was switched to stopper and goal-scoring became less frequent. He was elected captain for his senior year and, continuing in the position of stopper, he scarcely ever got close to the opponent's goal in the regular flow of the game; but he was the team's designated penalty kicker and got some goals while missing none of his penalty kicks.

During the spring of his freshman year at Yale, Roy's mother passed away a few weeks before the beginning of final   exams. He wondered why he should continue his studies when his mother would not be around to enjoy the satisfaction of an achievement for which she had sacrificed so much. He still feels that her hard work to help pay for his primary and secondary education may have brought on the hypertension that caused her death. He remembers that the hypertension first manifested itself one night when he was in the middle of sitting his Higher School certificate exams. However, he was able to remind himself that she would want him to obtain his degree. The Yale students in his Hall and an adjacent one as well as his freshman Counselor made every effort to console him. One of these students was George W. Bush, future President of the United States. Grief clouded some of what was occurring around Roy, but he was told that this is the student who obtained signatures of other students on a sympathy card which he received.

Roy arrived at the University of Washington in fall 1968 with a left knee injury sustained about the middle of his senior year at Yale. After a period of leg extensions and leg curls with weights, he returned to soccer but was always concerned that the knee would collapse if subjected to much strain. He joined the University's club team called "Internationals" which comprised students from various countries, including two Trinidadians. Although he tore a quadriceps muscle in a game and was forced to miss several, he had the pleasure of scoring four goals against "Olympia," a team named for the capital of the state of Washington.

THE SOCCER COACH

It was not until 1995 that Roy's close association with soccer ended. While teaching at Penn State, when his older son, Roy Jr., reached the fourth grade, Roy volunteered to coach his son's team in the fall competition sponsored by the community's Parks and Recreation Department.   He continued through the sophomore high school year of this group of kids, although Roy Jr. and some other players from this team that had chosen the name Cosmos had started playing for the high school's Junior Varsity team in their freshman year. The Cosmos had been very successful over the years; and at the end of their two last seasons in Parks and Recreation, with the addition of a few players from other Parks and Recreation teams, they defeated their age- and class-mates on the Junior Varsity. Roy was the coach of the victorious select team.

By about 1986, Roy joined other parents who felt that the Parks and Recreation program's limits on competition were limiting development of the full soccer potential of local kids. They formed the State College Soccer Club (later Centre Soccer Association), organized a spring competition, and entered the Central Pennsylvania Soccer League that involved traveling up to about two hours from their local community. Roy became Secretary of this group and, after the first year, agreed to coach the Under-16 team, Sting, on which Roy Jr. played. He had the opportunity to coach the team in its first year; but he accepted only an assistant coaching position because he believed that he would find the relatively long trips to away games too burdensome.

Meanwhile, his second son, Roger, started playing in the fall Parks and Recreation program and Roy started coaching this team too. Roy Jr. left for college just in time for Roy to start an Under-12 team in The State College Soccer Club and he continued with this team, Sparks, until Roger graduated from high school in 1995. This team traveled to more tournaments than the Sting and played in the North Central Pennsylvania League (NorCenPen) which Roy had a hand in organizing. The success of Sparks in this League also made him the coach for some select NorCenPen select age-group teams for the Eastern Pennsylvania youth tournaments at the end of the season.

THE CRICKETER

In that most English of games, the conservative Roy should have excelled. Although his performance in this sport did not quite match that in soccer he gave a pretty decent account of himself as a bowler , being able to lift the ball from a good length and with sufficient pace to keep even wicket keeper, Michael Findlay, a respectable distance behind the wicket. Findlay later represented the world-class West Indies team as wicket-keeper.

Roy was not regarded as a batsman or batter, the newer gender-neutral term. However, in the 1958 Windward Islands Inter-schools Tournament in Dominica, he made the top score of 39 runs for St. Vincent. Later, when he represented the Eagles club in local competition, he had an even more remarkable performance in 1964. On this occasion, Hairoun had Eagles reeling with an embarrassing score of 28 for eight wickets. Then Roy joined Alfred "Jack" Dear at the wicket, and they rescued Eagles from the predicament of perhaps a record low score in an innings. Here is Jack's written account to Roy of the end of that Eagles innings:

"With my turn at the crease, I made two big swings at the ball after which you approached me and told me to take it easy 'we can pull the team out of the rut.'... The first over (a turn to bowl six consecutive balls allowed each bowler)you faced, you also took a big swing and missed and I came down the wicket and assured you that we can make it. That same over, in the last two balls, you had the pace bowler (I think Clouden) in the Annexe for two sixes. After that, we went on to punish all the bowlers — Speedy Anthony, Brisbane, Ladd Winsborrow, Bendix Dopwell, Leonard Sandy, Clouden and others -- ... We both took the score to 218 before I was stumped ... for 97 ... Your score was 75."

Jack concluded that he believed that the partnership of 190 runs for the ninth wicket must still be standing as a record in St. Vincent and the Grenadines local cricket .

That same year, Roy was called to trials as a potential opening fast bowler for the national team. In the first game, he turned in a creditable performance in his specialty of bowling and made more runs than other fast bowlers. Jack Dear was also being considered for selection to the national team as a batsman at this time. But he felt that Cecil Clarke (not his real name) was being pushed by two influential persons for selection ahead of him. In recent correspondence with Roy, he wrote about this experience in a manner that paints a picture complimentary of Roy's sometimes intimidating bowling:

"You were bowling from the hospital end at Clarke, and you had bowled him for duck. When he was halfway to the pavilion, he was asked to return to the wicket to bat again. I then ran on the field and told you that my pick depended on him and to dismiss him as soon as possible. The first ball from you after his return was a bouncer which almost decapitated him. The next ball was a Yorker and his stumps cart-wheeled towards the palm trees. ... and in another trial game, as I tried to flick an in-swinger from Rodway Fraser, the ball hit the bat and then the left pad which was defective at the knees, thus fracturing my knee cap."

Roy did not show up for the second trial match; and neither he nor Jack was selected. Roy's decision was based on his expectation that his teaching responsibilities would prevent him from obtaining time to travel abroad for the tournament. After all, in 1962, the Headmaster had reluctantly allowed him to travel to Grenada to play soccer with the national team "only because you are the captain." He had also been persuaded only after Mr. Vivian Hadley, an older well-respected teacher, told him that it is customary to allow time-off to represent the island in sports competitions.

With respect to the cricket tournament in 1964, Roy was mindful that he was teaching Chemistry in the fifth form and Organic Chemistry in the sixth form to students at the Grammar School. These students would have been taking the Cambridge "O" and "A" levels, respectively, during the first administration of these exams under this new name. He was also teaching "O-Level" Biology to a small group of female students from the nearby Girls' High School. The tournament was scheduled for June in Dominica, shortly before the start of these examinations that are so important for students' future.

Few if any friends understood that Roy's low batting scores in most games may have resulted from an unpleasant interaction with a teacher in his second year in the Grammar School. In his first year, he had scored 43 in a junior house match and was selected to represent the School's junior team to play against a select primary school squad. It may have been rain that prevented that game from being played. In his second year, he was elected as captain of his house's junior team but had no exceptional batting score. The new Games Master named him the 13th man for the match against the primary school representative team, but Roy informed him that he could not get his white clothes ready in time. Shortly thereafter, Roy agreed to play for his third form team against the other third form. When the captain of Roy's team took the list of players to the Games Master to obtain his permission to use the School's ground and cricket equipment, the Games Master removed Roy's name from the list. After the morning break, the Games Master entered Roy's form room and announced to all of the students that he was not allowing Roy to play because "Austin does not like to play unless he is captain." The falsity of this statement is clear since Roy was prepared to play under another student when the Games Master denied him the opportunity.

In response to the Games Master's outrageous statement, Roy decided that he would no longer take cricket seriously. And he never again played a cricket house match, but time has erased from his memory other actions he may have taken. In the event that the Games Master was considering prolonged vindictive behavior toward him, Roy's decision would have been effective in lessening the chances of further conflict between them over this sport. Yet Roy could also have chosen to work harder to show that he was a good batsman as well as a bowler. Success in batting would then have left him more satisfied about the outcome of the series of unfortunate incidents. In any event, some of Roy's closest friends often teased him over his approach to batting, playing a confident defensive shot to the first delivery to him, then jumping down the wicket and swinging at the next ball only to lose his wicket. He never let on to what led him to adopt this style of batting.

ATHLETICS, BASKETBALL AND WEIGHTLIFTING

In Track and Field, Roy had no success in the track events, but he sometimes placed first in the pole vault and shot put in the annual house competition. Additionally, he played Basketball with some distinction for the Grammar School, the Eagles Club and the national team. And Eagles even won the first national championship with him on the team. But his performance in this sport must be placed in context. Few people played the game in St. Vincent; and he had never seen it played before he started playing at about age 16, not even on television because that technology had not yet arrived in the island. Basketball games were also not carried on radio. To develop some knowledge of the game, he and others at the Grammar School relied on a "Know the Game" booklet published in England. Then they tried to play on a bumpy grass court in a corner of the Grammar School field. Especially after exposure to the game in the U.S., he readily admits that his basketball skills were rudimentary when he left St. Vincent, and they remain poor.

As for weightlifting, St. Vincent had a relatively large group of youths interested in building strength for competition in the three (now two) Olympic lifts. Roy was one of these, but he often faced a conflict between the time he could devote to this pursuit and to other athletic activities. He had started weightlifting with the DaSilva brothers in 1955 and then joined Maurice "Chuck" King when Nigel DaSilva, the older brother, left St. Vincent. Maurice and Nigel went on to represent the Federation of the West Indies in weightlifting in the 1959 PanAm Games, Maurice winning a silver medal.

Sometime after Inter-schools tournament in 1958, Roy decided to quit soccer and devote that time to weightlifting. He had also worn out his soccer cleats and saw no means of replacing them. After all, he could not even buy the required sixth form mathematics texts. When the Headmaster learnt that Roy and Winston Roberts were no longer with the School team, he called them into his office and informed them that he expected them to turn out for the team. Additionally, he told Roy that if he lacked cleats, he could play in tennis shoes. Bernard Hewitt who was Roy's longtime friend came to Roy's aid, lending him a pair of cleats that his cousin Clement Hewitt had left behind when he migrated to America.

Roy has no idea how strong he could have become if he had spent more time in the gym. One year after he left secondary school, he was slated to represent St. Vincent in the Middle-heavyweight (198 pounds upper limit) class in a meet against the Vikings Barbell Club of Barbados. But Vikings did not bring a representative in that weight-class and competition in the class was cancelled. In hindsight, Roy believes that he benefited from continuing with soccer. At the same time, he continued to lift weights when

Roy L. Austin

time allowed. Contrary to the relatively widespread belief in those days that weightlifting made you muscle-bound and interfered with your performance in sports like soccer, Roy believes that the strength he gained in weightlifting improved his performance in soccer.

CULTURAL PURSUITS

The earliest indication of where this man was headed in respect of interest in the Arts was when the tiny living room in his small home became the hub of music-appreciation for his friends and colleagues in the informal group called "The Bridgeboys." Night after night, members met to listen to and discuss the merits of music (on vinyl discs) of various vocal and instrumental artistes and of different genres—The music of Dave Brubeck with Paul Desmond as featured in the "Time Out" Album, the rich beautiful voice of Miriam Makeba, "Chopin by Starlight"—The Philadelphia Philharmonic Orchestra with guest pianist Leonard Penario, Elgar's "Pomp and Circumstance," the Norman Luboff Choir, and many more. Certainly, calypsos, especially the "Mighty Sparrow," and Latin music such as the mambo and cha cha were among our favorites, but most of these may have been heard on radio.

Our musical listening motivated Roy, using the pen name "Ralla," to write a skit he entitled "Seek We Ever." It was based especially on one of Miriam Makeba's songs and a song from West Side Story. Several of his colleagues in the Bridgeboys and/or The Eagles Club were involved in amateur theatre and provided support for his effort. One of these colleagues subsequently graduated from the National Theatre School of Canada and has made a career of acting. Tim Daisy, a member of Eagles and one of those with some theatrical experience liked the skit sufficiently to offer to direct it while the Club became the producer. The author of this essay and Pat Clouden were lead actors.

During his stint at the University of Washington, Roy joined a group of other West Indians living in Seattle to found a steel band which they named "Tropical Rainstorm". The band was able to share with students, the community and sometimes a local television audience the pulsating rhythm of this unique musical group. They played for social functions such as birthday parties, concerts for senior citizens, and dances sponsored by the West Indian Association of Washington to which many band members belonged. The band also organized their own dances to raise funds that helped to repay the original outlay of money by members. Roy played the triple cello set of instruments.

West Indian students also formed a separate organization called the West Indian Students Association. Roy was one of the founders and won election as the first President. With the turmoil amidst the Black Power and

183

Student Movements at the time, Caribbean students felt that they needed an organization to represent their interests, should events warrant it.

One thing led to another in the field of cultural activity. There was something deeper within Roy that was yet to manifest itself but the yearning intensified. Soon it would be revealed to all and sundry.......Enter.... the Mas'Man or Carnival Band Leader...... ! Undoubtedly, as a secondary school student and as a secondary school teacher, Roy's academic interest lay primarily in the Natural Sciences. He, however, pursued Sociology in undergraduate and graduate school. Where then did history come into play? He must have had a secret love for History; and his sound knowledge and understanding of the subject as well as a willingness to conduct research combined to form his launching pad for successive annual Bridgeboys' Carnival productions, the names of which tell a story:

1961	Peoples of Palestine	
1962	Barbaric Splendour	1st Place
1963	Portrait of Ancient Egypt	Band of the Year
1964	From the Story of Western Colonization.	
1965	Invassores Britanniae—Invaders of Britain 55BC—1066AD	
1966	Journey through the Orient	1st Place and Band of the Year
1968-	Africa- The Dark Continent.	

The impact of Roy's legacy is borne out by the fact that 1964 was his last year of direct involvement in Carnival in St. Vincent. Yet, the band's banner in 1965 carried his name in recognition of his years of contribution to an excellent product. Undoubtedly, his involvement with Carnival was also influenced by the many hours he spent drawing human figures, buildings and other subjects. This pastime sometimes eventuated in informal competitions with Carlyle "Carka" Duncan, who later made some money painting signs, Winston Roberts and others. Roy was also handy with tools, being able, for instance, to use a pair of pliers and wire to build the frame for parts of costumes.

Roy's artistic bent also became useful for the Eagles Club of which he was the President from its inception to his departure from the island. He designed and painted the two banners employed by the Club at opening ceremonies of sports competitions. And when Eagles added a Netball team, the girls benefited from the existence of these banners and two crests designed and painted for them by Roy. Moreover, his advice on the design of their second uniform won them recognition one year as The Best Dressed Team. Members of at least one opposing team complained that the uniforms were made with a cheap fabric.

A measure of this man's inner strength and determination to succeed can be exemplified by his exploits on the clarinet. No one knows what motivated him but he set about to teach himself with no one around to guide him. On many a night as colleagues got closer to his home, questionable strains of music akin to that of a wind or reed instrument could be heard with increasing intensity. So too were the off-notes or missing notes as Roy labored on undeterred by the off-hand comments or heckle proffered by the first "guests" entering the door. Nothing seemed to faze this man in pursuance of mastery. Even after he had begun to achieve a measure of "domestic success" his friends took great delight in reminding him that more wind than sound seemed to be coming through the instrument. Roy has probably had the last laugh!

UNCLE SAM—HERE I COME!

As was said earlier Roy's alma mater, The St. Vincent Boys Grammar School, had prepared him to some extent for his pursuit of further and higher education. While nothing can prepare a Caribbean person for the cultural shock, social relocation and sheer awe of a big country, Roy's natural conservatism and reserve combined with his perceptiveness and resourcefulness would easily have cushioned the adverse effects.

In 1968, Roy Austin graduated from Yale University with a BA in Sociology and was a classmate of the future U.S. President George W Bush. He then attended the University of Washington (Seattle, Washington) and obtained a Master's (1970) and PhD (1973) degrees in Sociology. Through the years, Roy accumulated an impressive occupational record:-

2001-The Pennsylvania State University: Associate Professor of Sociology, Justice and African-American Studies. Also Director of the Africana Research Center

1994-1998 The Pennsylvania State University: Program Director of Crime, Law and Justice.

1972-2001 The Pennsylvania State University: Sociology Department-Assistant to Associate Professor

1968-1972 The University of Washington: Teaching Assistant/Research Assistant

Sept. 1961- Sept 1964 Secondary School Teacher

Dec. 1959- Aug. 1961 Customs Officer

Roy Austin is the author of numerous publications (some based on Caribbean Research), has delivered addresses and similarly participated in countless symposia, discussion sessions, service activities related to official positions held including Radio and Television appearances; and he has received various awards in the course of these events. At Penn State University, he continued his contributions to the Caribbean, becoming a founder of The Caribbean Students Association (CSA) and remaining as faculty adviser of this organization for nearly 20 years. He was one of the originators of a Cultural event entitled the Caribbean Experience which was passed on to the CSA after its founding. Before the University's mammoth pots, large ovens and other kitchen utensils were made available to the Association, the large number of tickets that were sold for this spring celebration caused his wife, Glynis Sutherland Austin, to have to cook many pots of Caribbean-flavored meats. And Roy baked several batches of bread pudding, sweet potato pudding or coconut-pineapple cake, surprising many with their delightful taste. He had learnt well the baking techniques and recipes of his parents.

Roy is also a foundation and lifetime member of the Caribbean Studies Association which began with a contentious meeting in Puerto Rico. He has attended meetings of this organization, presenting papers or organizing sessions in Jamaica, Martinique, St, Lucia, Barbados, and Belize.

In the late 1980s, Roy's father passed away. After he had suffered a bout of typhoid in the early 1970s, Roy assured him that he could take care of his future financial needs and he closed the shop. This dutiful son kept his word, perhaps remembering the sacrifices made by both parents to help him obtain the education that allowed him to earn a decent living. He regrets that he was never able to give his mother a similar few years without her having to rise early and labor all day while worrying about paying bills.

To have so distinguished himself in his field as an educator and to have been awarded Emeritus status upon retirement from Penn State is in itself highly commendable. But to be elevated to the Diplomatic Corps and in particular to be appointed Ambassador of the United States of America to the Republic of Trinidad and Tobago must have been undoubtedly the highlight of his career. Roy was sworn in on October 19, 2001, as United States Ambassador Extraordinary and Plenipotentiary having been nominated by U.S. President George W. Bush on August 31, 2001.He arrived in Port of Spain on November 27, 2001 to assume duties. His tour of duty ended on January 20, 2009, the day President Barak Obama was sworn in.

A SIGNIFICANT POINT

President George W Bush, in his new book,"Decision Points," recalls the following experience:

"Leaving Andover was like ridding myself of a straight jacket. My philosophy in College was the old cliché: work hard, play hard. I upheld the former and excelled at the latter. I joined the Delta Kappa Epsilon fraternity,

played rugby and intramural sports, took road trips to girls' colleges and spent a lot of time hanging out with friends.

My boisterous spirit carried me away at times. During my senior year we were at Princeton for a football game. Inspired by the Yale win-and more than a little booze-I led a group onto the field to tear down the goalposts. The Princeton faithful were not amused. I was sitting atop the crossbar when a security guard pulled me down. I was then marched the length of the field and put in a police car. Yale friends started rocking the car and shouting, "Free Bush!"

Sensing disaster, my friend Roy Austin---a big guy from the island of St. Vincent who was captain of the Yale soccer team---yelled at the crowd to move. Then he jumped into the car with me. When we made it to the police station we were told to leave campus and never return. All these years later, I still haven't been back to Princeton. As for Roy, he continued to hone his diplomatic skills. Four decades later, I appointed him Ambassador to Trinidad and Tobago"

.

The incident discussed by President Bush does not constitute the only occasion on which Roy intervened with the police to the benefit of friends. He had done similarly before he left St. Vincent to help the Bridge Boys regain acceptance to continue hanging out on The Bridge. His letter to the Deputy Chief of Police and a discussion he and another Bridge Boy held with this Deputy convinced the Deputy that the group presented no threat to law and order in Kingstown. Nor were raised voices during discussions on the Bridge deliberate attempts to disturb the peaceful pursuits of the residents of nearby homes. Therefore, he asked the Bridge Boys to give him some time to discuss the matter with the Assistant Chief who had issued the order to remove them from The Bridge. He allowed them to return to the Bridge after the passage of about a month.

It would have been difficult for President Bush to find a better Ambassador to Trinidad and Tobago than Roy. Although he had been physically removed from the Caribbean for 37 years, he had extended his knowledge of Caribbean affairs through Caribbean newspapers, scholarly works and web sites. At Yale, he took two courses with professors who had conducted research in and published about the Caribbean. He obtained an A in a drawing course for which his final project was based on a tradition of predicting the future from the shape taken by the white of an egg placed in a glass of water in the sun on Good Friday. At Penn State, he developed and taught a course entitled Caribbean Social Structures and conducted research on Caribbean issues.

Every spring at Yale, he played cricket with the Yale Club which later joined with the New Haven Club that had primarily Jamaican players. The opponents of these clubs were Caribbean teams from Boston, Springfield,

Hartford, New Rochelle, New York City and Newark, NJ. One league in which he played was named for Alexander Bustamante, Jamaica's first Prime Minister after the country's achievement of independence in 1962.

During his posting in Trinidad and Tobago from November 2001 to January 2009, he easily fit into the society, befriending people of all classes, races, ethnic groups, religions, and political persuasions. His acceptance is reflected in some of his accomplishments. For example, he worked with a group of Trinidadians to establish the Endowment for National Advancement through Indigenous Song (ENAIS) with the goal identified in the name. For seven consecutive years, he and the Minister of Education worked together to organize The Ambassador's Song and Verse Contest in which primary and secondary students from throughout the country utilized songs and dramatic presentations to assist in ameliorating various social problems. Based on the literature used in teaching a course in Juvenile Delinquency, he early realized that SERVOL'S (a community organization) Early Childhood Care and Education (ECCE) program was likely to succeed in helping to reduce the frequency of delinquency in Trinidad and Tobago. He developed a good relationship with Sister Montrichard (Program Director) and Father Gerry Pantin (Founder and first Director) who readily agreed that it would be worthwhile to have ECCE scientifically evaluated. Roy's belief about the efficacy of ECCE was supported by research the U.S Embassy commissioned. Earlier, he had influenced SERVOL's receipt of a grant from the Embassy to assist with their ECCE program.

It is understandable that Roy became associated with SERVOL and ENAIS. Both helped to narrow chasms or build bridges to reduce obstacles to human progress. So, too, did the Rotary Clubs to which he delivered several speeches, and the Cadet Force with which he developed a strong bond and attended many of their parades and other events. The volunteer work performed by the former was exemplary; and he formed close relationships with several members of the Princes Town Rotary Club. As for the Cadet Force, he regarded it as one avenue through which youths built character and discipline. He based this judgment on his experience with membership in this paramilitary organization in which he had attained the highest rank open to students at the St. Vincent Grammar School.

Youths almost always found a place in Roy's life. Secondary school teaching would have been his earliest occupation if he had sufficient control over his first job upon graduating from the Grammar School. He also spent many years as a volunteer youth soccer coach. Additionally, one course he taught almost every year for over 29 years at The Pennsylvania State University is the Sociology of Juvenile Delinquency. And his dissertation and later published research had juveniles as subjects. Likewise, some of his research on the Caribbean had youths as subjects.

During his tenure as Ambassador, Roy continued to devote attention to the welfare of youths, as readers may have realized from our discussion of SERVOL, The Ambassador's Song and Verse Contest, and the Cadet Force. But he led the Embassy in many other youth-oriented projects, sometimes being the primary mover behind the activities, sometimes attending and participating in opening ceremonies and handing over buildings and equipment. Often, however, projects were conceptualized by the U.S military and executed by U.S and local military personnel with the Military Liason Office (MLO) at the Embassy in Trinidad supplying valuable support or conceptualizing projects. Included are the construction and presentation of buildings to the St Mary's Home for Children, the Princess Elizabeth Home for the Handicapped, and renovation and painting of a Catholic home for young girls.

Other projects, sometimes aimed at "demand reduction," were developed by the Embassy's Political Section as part of its International Narcotics and Law Enforcement duties. Among these are the presentation of computers to the St. James Police Youth Club which serves youths from disadvantaged homes and high-risk areas; to the Pan Trinbago Youth Group; and presenting sports equipment to various sports clubs.

Additionally, Roy scarcely ever failed to attend Powergen's Special Children's Fun Day where he presented some prizes to the children and toured the tents to meet and converse with them. He influenced the financing of construction at the St. Clair Coaching School in Tobago and gave a motivational speech to the young footballers. He visited the Cyril Ross Nursery that houses HIV-infected youths and takes care of their other needs. Moreover, he gave many speeches, usually at graduation ceremonies to primary and secondary schools. In the case of the Youth of Tobago, he preached a sermon at the Scarborough Anglican church on their celebration of an anniversary and returned on another occasion to deepen their appreciation of efforts at political integration in the Commonwealth Caribbean.

Part of the credit for Roy's focus on uplifting youths probably belongs to the impression left on his young mind by Miss John's repetition of "Train up a child in the way he should go ...." However, his exposure to the delinquency literature and his preference for social control/self-control theory as an explanation of delinquency must have had an important influence on relevant activities in Trinidad and Tobago. This theory proposes that familial, educational and community institutions, in that order, are the key influences that keep youths on the straight and narrow path. Moreover, early education research projects such as the Ypsilanti, Michigan, Perry Pre-School Project and the University of North Carolina's Abecedarian have shown that early educational intervention yields long-lasting benefits. The findings support the propositions derived from control theory. It is instructive, too, that SERVOL's ECCE program is influenced by the Perry Pre-School project.

Undoubtedly, the mix of pleasant and unpleasant experiences throughout his lifetime must have contributed to his openness to people without regard to their social standing. As he grew up in St. Vincent, and especially during his Grammar School years, he realized that many students were not so subtly reminded of their lowly place in the class structure. He was one of these students, and he believes that the snobbery became more intense, or just more noticeable in the sixth form because the introduction of girls into the equation made students more sensitive to intimations of unworthiness. He believes that he withstood such suggestions without harm to his psyche because he excelled in sufficient areas to dismiss undesirable definitions of self by others.

Racial discrimination was also a feature of the social environment in which Roy was raised. While they recognized its existence, he and his close associates did not dwell on the limitations this aspect of life presented to Vincentians. Today, many West Indians might be accused of having been in denial about the amount of racial discrimination and disguised racial antagonism that restricted their life-chances. Perhaps, this is the reason some West Indians have been known to claim that, unlike its obvious presence in America, racial discrimination was absent in the islands.

When Roy started attending school in the U.S. in 1964, he had read enough American literature to realize that he was likely to experience racial discrimination and other racial indignities there. He was in the Yale Infirmary with a high fever during national elections in November of that year when he was exposed to an instance of this troubling phenomenon. There were some students and at least one nurse attending to the returns on television when he heard the nurse exclaim "that is the ignorant black vote." One or more of the students informed her that a black student was in the nearby room and she went no further. Lyndon Johnson was winning.

More surprisingly, perhaps, after all that he had read and heard, Roy developed remarkably congenial relationships with many Caucasian Americans in New Haven. The most memorable of these involves a family with whom he spent his first Thanksgiving weekend. Although he tried to cancel his acceptance of the invitation when he learned from the Foreign Student Office that someone in the family had asked if he is an Englishman, all members of that family quickly set him at ease once he showed up. They also showed their beneficence in many other ways, including inviting him back for Christmas. He still occasionally communicates with the matriarch in that family, the patriarch having passed on. It turned out, also, that the misunderstanding about his nationality occurred because at the time Vincentians were regarded as British citizens, and he had so stated on the form he had completed.

At the start of his final year at Yale, he tried to find an apartment in New Haven for his wife-to-be (Glynis). He phoned and inquired about one that was advertised. Upon being assured that it was available, he immediately went to look at it, a walk that took less than 10 minutes. When he arrived, he was informed that it had just been rented.

After soccer practice on another day, a Jewish teammate drove him to see another advertised apartment. The male Caucasian manager did his best to convince Roy that he would not find the apartment convenient. As they returned to the vehicle, Roy's teammate showed both embarrassment and anger and asked him whether he understood what was going on. Roy assured him that he did.

The next time that he saw an ad for a conveniently located apartment, Roy asked another Jewish friend to complete the transaction for him without letting on to his race. He had no difficulty obtaining the apartment and Glynis moved in. She soon started being harassed, a male voice calling her on the phone to threaten Roy's life, and even telling her correctly that Roy was the captain of the Yale soccer team. One night, a male also turned up at the door to the apartment insisting that she let him in. She phoned Roy in his room on campus and he advised her to keep talking while he used another phone to call the police. The man caught on to what was occurring and left before the police arrived. A male also turned up once while Roy was in the apartment with her and challenged Roy to come out and meet him. When Roy informed the landlord about these events, he advised Roy to fly the door open and shoot the offender.

Roy and Glynis obtained another apartment in a short time from a Jewish landlord, but lost their deposit on the previous one. They stayed nearly a year in this later apartment without any untoward incidents. Glynis also took good care of the apartment, even scrubbing the steps to their second floor with a hard broom and disinfectant to remove the strong scent of urine perhaps left by vagrants who apparently sometimes used the stairwell to sleep. When they were about to leave New Haven, the landlord told them that if they ever again needed an apartment in that city they should approach him.

Before they moved at the end of August 1968 to Seattle where Roy was about to enter graduate school, he took up the University of Washington's offer to request a host family. Suffice it to say that their Caucasian host family helped them overcome many difficulties that foreign students might face in a large city in which they are strangers. In Seattle, too, Roy and Glynis met with several instances of racial discrimination. The wife in their host family had told them that they were unlikely to suffer racial discrimination in Seattle. But after spending an entire day with them apartment hunting, she advised them the following morning to file a charge of racial discrimination with the city's (or state's) Human Relations

Commission. One landlady, after learning of Roy and Glynis' race from a neighbor who had shown the apartment in the landlady's absence, told her the previous evening that the apartment was already rented. By the next morning, the landlady said that she still had the apartment to rent, but when informed of the identity of the phone caller, again said that she had indeed rented the apartment the previous day.

When Roy and Glynis moved to State College, Pennsylvania, in 1972, they had similar experiences, some Caucasians going out of their way to help, and others making their life difficult by subjecting them to racial discrimination. The details are omitted here.

There can be no discounting the fact that this Ambassador's formative years were shaped by the British colonial influence but tempered by a Vincentian-Caribbean culture which sometimes was more pervasive. This strong-willed man recognized early that he was destined to become a mentor to many Vincentians and, therefore, had to forge a new and creative independent thinking in step with the evolving march towards national independence. It is not too much to assert that Roy's involvement with the Bridge Boys helped to shape his future.

Who were these Bridge Boys about whom President George W. Bush could confidently ask the present Prime Minister of St. Vincent and the Grenadines whether he was a member?

During the mid-fifties a group of young secondary school boys started hanging out; and over time, the group grew larger, they spent more and more time in one another's company, and the ideas they shared became more varied. They were mostly from the same area and found the best place to gather was on the North River Bridge in Kingstown which spanned a small stream. This bridge crossed the major thoroughfare where at nights fewer cars passed to and fro. The unusually wide concrete walkway between the bridge-rails and the road allowed as much movement as the boys needed without hindering pedestrian traffic. This became the meeting place, indeed the home, of the legendary Bridge Boys. But the group had started forming many years earlier near the Middle Street bridge one block closer to the sea.

Roy Austin's stoic personality and level-headedness made him the group's mentor. Bridge Boys will forever remember the revered organization that gave meaning and purpose to their lives, a warm and genuine brotherly relationship, fulfillment and satisfaction, the joy of doing things together, the ability to disagree and still live in harmony and love, to humour, nay heckle one another, with recrimination remaining an unknown thing, to enjoy the nightly 'lime' on the bridge without it interfering with schoolwork. Today, long after migration signaled the physical end of the organization, members remain closely in touch with each other across the world even as the reality of our own mortality has seen the "Bridge" bidding a final fond farewell to fallen brothers. This was the "Bridge"—a unique organization   that facilitated an unconscious cohesion among the people of the immediate environs through its outstanding contribution to the annual national Carnival celebrations.

In speeches in St. Vincent on two occasions in 2002, Roy drew on the acronym BRIDGE (Bottom-town Reading Institute for the Development of General Education) to recommend the creation of an institution that would tutor the youths of that community to make them better prepared for secondary education. He advised that the institution could also serve to train adults in the community in saleable skills. He felt that free tutoring could be obtained through student and adult volunteers. He knew from experience in that community that fewer youths would have failed to obtain a secondary education if only they had a little help with reading, English and primary school mathematics. As for adults, he assumed that some would be happy to spend some time trying to improve their circumstances. Such BRIDGES do not have to be limited to Bottom-town, but BRIDGES there must be to help optimize the accomplishments of unfortunate citizens.

Roy Leslie Austin can look back on his career with immense pride and satisfaction knowing that at several points in a long span of professional responsibility, official duty and philanthropic endeavour he represented faithfully and well both the country of his birth and that of his adoption and citizenship. Who could imagine that in his hectic round of official engagements as Ambassador, Roy would have found time to pursue a hobby of photography, taking some exquisite photographs on the grounds of his official residence? However commendable his achievements may be, let it not be said that like the proverbial Hercules he did it alone. Not so! Roy Austin has been married to Glynis Sutherland Austin since 1967.The bride's father-giver was the groom's friend, George Walker Bush! Mrs. Austin continues to be a fine complement to this busy husband. They have three grown children, one adopted, and five grandchildren.

The author acknowledges and greatly appreciates the considerable help given by Dr. Roy Austin in the preparation of this biography.

The Hon. John Horne was a former Minister of Government in St. Vincent and the Grenadines. He is presently a businessman and lives in St. Vincent and the Grenadines.

Caribbean Trailblazers: St. Vincent and the Grenadines

2.   **Eileen "Betty" King**
                                    By
                          Rudolph Baynes, Jr.

What are the odds of a native of Saint Vincent and the Grenadines (SVG) heading up a State agency in the USA? Or appointed Deputy Commissioner in the District of Columbia? Or confirmed by the United States Senate to be the United States Ambassador to the Economic and Social Council of the United Nations in New York? For that matter, what are the odds of being appointed to one of the highest positions at the US State Department in the Obama Administration? A job requiring extensive background checks that would take an FBI agent from as far away from the seat of government in Washington to Saint Vincent and the Grenadines to gather personal information. Information to be gleaned from local records, by conducting interviews with teachers and acquaintances of the nominee, reviewing current and former connections to ensure that nothing untoward arises at a grueling Senate confirmation hearing before the U S Senate Foreign Relation Committee, chaired by one of the most hawkish senators in US history (Jesse Helms), all this to certify the nominee's fitness to represent the USA in its foreign affairs?

The odds become progressively more remote as we sift through the breadth and depth of the responsibilities that come attached to each of these assignments. Beating the odds requires more than being the smartest in your graduating high school class or having impressive college grades, as is easy for some of us to conclude. But Betty King has done that and much more. She currently holds the office of the US representative to the United Nations and other International Organizations in Geneva, Switzerland where she oversees a staff of about two hundred professionals, and represents the United States at fifteen UN agencies on a wide range of issues including intellectual property, health, development, telecommunications, labor and humanitarian response.

Because of her background and prior experience, on October 22, 2009, President Obama nominated her to her current position, and she was confirmed by the US Senate on February 12, 2010. Her resume is broad as well as deep and although during our interview for this article, she tells me that this is her last assignment, there appears to be energy for more.

Betty's journey through the thickets of professional life in the US began in the mid seventies. While living and working in Little Rock, in the State of Arkansas where she and her husband, Dr. Errol King, whom she married in 1970, had moved in 1975, had a chance encounter with Bill Clinton, a then Presidential hopeful and at that time the Attorney General of the State of Arkansas. As has been told, the recently arrived couple was spotted at a bank by Bill, who, on noticing their unfamiliar presence, inquired of the bank manager as to who were these two strangers. The bank manager arranged a meeting in which Clinton, a then candidate for governor talked extensively about his vision for the State should he be elected and about his political future including his run for the presidency of the United States in 1990. They marveled at his erudition and confidence. He impressed them with his knowledge on virtually every topic in the universe. With Betty's sound education at one of Canada's leading Universities and Graduate work completed in the US including a National Humanities Fellowship at Harvard University, and her work experience in New York City, he too was also impressed by her potential to lead one of his agencies, should he be elected. He also spoke of Errol's training as a surgeon as vital to Arkansas where medical services were in short supply compared to other states. Clinton became the Governor that same year and offered her the job to be the director of his Administration's Office of Aging.

The appointment drew controversy among local politicians who thought that at 35, Clinton's candidate was too young to manage such a sprawling agency. Her first appearance before the Arkansas Legislature had the Governor's staff in a state of nervous anticipation. They feared the reaction of the legislators to the appointment to head an agency that loomed so large in the life of their constituents (at that time Arkansas had the second highest percentage of elderly persons in the US – second only to Florida). So the staff paced the back of the chamber as she laid out her agenda to an unusually silent audience of legislators. At the conclusion of the presentation, one of the legislators raised his hand and said "Hone (southern twang for Honey) where did you learn to speak English like that?" "Good schools". Came the response. This was followed by an uproar of laughter.

As the director, the office brought her in contact with the then Democratic Senator Dale Bumpers and his predecessor in office, J William Fulbright who had an extensive career in Washington. These contacts paved the way for her easy re-entry to her professional career when she returned from SVG in 1987 following Errol's desire to serve the government and people of SVG. A call from one or both of them landed her a job as deputy Commissioner for Mental Services in the District of Columbia. To Betty, the job had both a personal and professional significance since she had been out of the workforce for more than a year. So, returning to a job at that level was reaffirming. The professional significance was that it entailed the planning and implementation of the transfer of the historic St. Elizabeth hospital from Federal to District control – a potent symbol in the District's effort to become an independent self-governing entity. John Hinckley (Reagan's failed assassin) is still a patient there. Also, it is the place where the brain of the famous American poet and critic, Erza Pound, who was committed there in 1945, is still kept preserved in one of its laboratories.

Nothing in Betty's background prepared her for the career path she eventually took. She was the fifth of eight children, born to Althea and Sinclair Boyea in the town of Byrea Hill, just about eighteen miles outside the capital city of Kingstown. Members of her family always have demonstrated an aptitude for business, which seemed to have been passed on by an independent- minded father and a hard-working mother. Sinclair was, what was then called locally, a "small farmer" or a "grower", planting and harvesting mainly bananas which found an export market in the UK through the local Saint Vincent Banana Growers Association. He also supplemented the family income as a "shopkeeper". This streak of independence seem to have found its way into a number of her siblings: Stilly, her eldest brother, for many years during the sixties ran a successful night club in Toronto, Canada. Many would also recall the Aquatic Club at Villa, which he owned and operated in the eighties and nineties and which he eventually sold after a successful run. Ken, after a stint as Managing Director of the Eastern Caribbean Group of Companies, a number of subsidiary companies owned in part by Maple Leaf Mills of Canada, now owns and operates two supermarkets and franchises that include a Kentucky Fried Chicken and a Subway sandwich shop. Cally manages the Exxon Mobil operations throughout the Eastern Caribbean, Ann manages the local government-owned Cobble Stone hotel. Keith manages a number of business enterprises which he owns and operates under BMC Holdings.

But Betty decided to break convention by pursuing a different path. Not that it was her intention. Sometimes fate has a way of pulling in a direction one never intended but because of circumstances "stuff happens" according to former US Defense Secretary Donald Rumsfeld. That path was not visible at that time during her high school or college days.

At the Girls High School which she attended between 1956 and 1963, Betty, like some of her peers, was a known standout. However, lacking a clear sense of the career path she wanted to pursue, she gravitated to subjects she liked rather than those that led to the more recognized careers of the day,:science and law. She distinctly remembers a speech given by her former Form II teacher Fleur Byron Cox on the occasion of her admittance to the bar, in which all her classmates, including herself, thought about law as a career. She also remembers the many references by her high school teachers' comments in her report cards: "too talkative, dictatorial and argumentative"—traits that would have served her well in the practice of law.

After graduation, knowing that her stay in SVG would be short-lived, she joined the staff of the Bishop's College in the town of Georgetown. She also did a stint at the Convent High School in Kingstown where she taught Mathematics and English. One extra-curricular highlight of the period was being crowned Carnival Queen of St. Vincent in 1965. She left shortly thereafter to pursue a degree in Sociology at the University of Windsor in Ontario, Canada.

At Windsor, beginning in 1966, she was elected the first female President of the International Student Association and was elected every year up until 1969. This position gave her insight and access to the governing structures and workings of the university system.

After graduate studies at the State University of New York in Stony Brook, she responded to an ad in the New York Times and was accepted for a position at Consolidated Edison, a public utility power company that provided electrical services to customers in New York City and the outer boroughs. This turned out to be the first and last job Betty ever applied for. All the jobs that followed resulted from a network of contacts she made on her way up.

That first job entailed improving the Math and English skills of "blue collar" workers in the company. Studies had shown that the lack of proficiency in these critical subjects was hurting the company's bottom line resulting in millions of dollars being lost, causing a less than efficient rate charged to consumers. To Betty's surprise, the job was classified as management which entitled her to the use of the company's elevator. She vividly remembers her first day on the job when she stepped on the elevator at the Company's offices, and an employee informed her that she was using the wrong elevator. At that moment, she thought that the remark was directed at her because of the color of her skin, but quickly discovered that it was the dearth of women in management at the company that led to that unfortunate remark.

She still considers her work on the rights of women to be her major legacy at the company. One of the victories of which she is most proud was a change in its maternity policy. The company had lavished maternity benefits for male employees' spouses but never made similar benefits available to its female employees. Her recommendation (and protests) to upper management changed all that.

Sometime in 1990, Betty received a call from Douglas Nelson, someone she had met at a White House reception during the Carter years. They both were attending a conference on Aging. Nelson had served as Director of Aging in Wisconsin and they had known each other when she served as Director of Aging in Arkansas. He had just been offered the presidency of the Annie Casey Foundation and asked whether she would be interested in the job as the Vice President. Ever ready for a new challenge, she accepted, since this new assignment would have catapulted her career to a national level.

The Annie Casey Foundation was created by the founders of UPS with a multi-billion dollar asset base, so making decisions about how those resources were deployed to improve the lives of disadvantaged children and families was a significant opportunity that would have put her career on a new trajectory. It was in this capacity that she was asked to go with other philanthropists to the Republic of South Africa, before the election of Mandela to the presidency, to assess the health and socio-economic needs of the population that until then had been disenfranchised. One highlight of that visit was the presentation of a humanitarian award to Nelson Mandela who refused to cross picket lines in Miami to accept the award from the Council of Foundations. The vice presidency of the Casey foundation also afforded her opportunities to spent some time in France and other countries analyzing their exemplary health care for children with a view to replicating part of it in the US.

Much as she loved the job at the Casey Foundation, Betty could not resist the call from the Clinton Administration to accept an ambassadorial appointment to the UN in New York. This literally opened up a new world for her both literally and figuratively. One incident that took place at a General Assembly meeting she remembers quite vividly: following her response to a comment that was made at that meeting, a European diplomat came up to her and made the following remark: "only in America could someone with such an accent represent her adopted country at such a high level". Obviously, this diplomat had never listened to Dr. Henry Kissinger, a child of German refugees and Secretary of State under President Nixon..

Foreign policy giants like former Secretary of State, Madeline Albright and Ambassador Richard Holbrooke became mentors, colleagues and friends. The job also connected her to Susan Rice, the then Assistant Secretary for Africa. During the period the Democrats were out of office, both she and Rice became a part of the Global Women's Network that focused on improving the lives of children. For Betty, this social connection was an important link to the Obama campaign where she served on the multi-lateral foreign policy team that reported to Rice. She admits that, although Rice was supportive of her getting her current assignment, in the end it was Secretary of State Clinton who ensured her nomination.

Betty considers her current position to be the high point of her career. She treasures her role in the historic presidency of Barak Obama, and her close up view of the changing world order—she is amused by the many references to the G8 meeting when she was seen in the company of the Chinese ambassador. But the career achievement of which she is most proud is her successful negotiations with the G77 (the group of developing countries) in the final months of the Clinton Administration that resulted in the Millennium Development Goals. The UN recently celebrated the 10th anniversary of these goals, which have become the gold standard by which development achievements are measured. Her pride stems not only from the success of these goals—all but two are on track to be achieved by 2015— that have helped to spur improvements in the lives of disadvantaged people around the world, but from her successful efforts to convince the Clinton White House that this was the right thing to do. That achievement has given her some credibility in Geneva where she occasionally finds herself on the opposite side of the debate with countries that see development as the prism through which every issue is viewed. She will not accept any correlation between poverty and the abuse of women or between poverty and the violation of human rights. And yes, in these debates she does not hesitate to remind others of her intimate knowledge of these issues from her own childhood experiences in Byrea, St. Vincent and the Grenadines where this incredible journey began.

Rudolph Baynes Jr. hails originally from St. Vincent and the Grenadines. He is a Certified Accountant and lives in New Jersey, U.S.A.

3.   **Kerston M. Coombs**
                        By
                   Baldwin King

We have all heard about ethanol or "alcohol' which is present in beer and wine and other alcoholic drinks. However, there is another alcohol you may not have heard about and it is called methanol. Like ethanol, it is a colorless liquid at room temperature but is very toxic and is often used as a denaturant for ethanol; that is, adding methanol to ethanol makes ethanol unfit for drinking. More importantly, methanol is used as a fuel, like ethanol. It is also used in antifreeze and as a feedstock for the manufacture of many important chemicals like formaldehyde and acetic acid which in turn finds their way into the manufacture of plastics, explosives etc. The methanol industry is a multibillion dollar industry and one of the largest producers of methanol in the world is Trinidad and Tobago (T&T). One of the biggest players in the T&T methanol and energy industry over the past three decades or so has been a Vincentian by the name of Kerston M. Coombs.

Kerston Coombs was born in Georgetown, St. Vincent and the Grenadines on November 13, 1937. His father was Henry Coombs and his mother Bobsie Coombs nee Quashie. For many years, Henry operated a shop in Georgetown. He was also a farmer who grew crops of various kinds such as arrowroot, sugar cane, bananas, sweet potatoes, etc. Henry had several brothers, but most of them died fairly young. However, there are some Coombs family members in Trinidad who are the descendants of one of Henry's brothers. Kerston's mother Bobsie had far more relatives which include the Kings from Diamond Village and the Smarts from Park Hill. Bobsie was from the Byera area and most of the family lived in that area, as well as in New Grounds. Interestingly, there's a branch of Bobsie's family in Grenada, namely the Quashies. Bobsie was an accomplished dress designer and milliner.

Kerston had three siblings. Orde, who was a well-respected writer and journalist in New York died in September, 1984, at age 45. He held a B.A. in English from Yale University and an M.A. from New York University (NYU). Claerwen (Heather) lives in England and is a physiatrist counselor and management consultant. She is married with three children. Kerston's youngest sibling Kay died at the very young age of 18.

Kerston began his education at the Georgetown Government School, a primary school headed at that time by Ebenezer Duncan (the author of a Brief History of St. Vincent). Mr. Duncan was succeeded as headmaster by Melvyn Cuffy, father of a couple of Kerston's schoolmates in secondary school, Vin and Owen. However, the person who made the most impression on Kerston in primary school was a teacher, Rhona Liverpool. According to Kerston, Rhona Liverpool was an amazing person. She taught in

Georgetown and later taught in Langley Park. She was such a good teacher that she had offers to come and teach in the capital, Kingstown, but steadfastly refused to move, preferring to teach in the country. But, she was the first person, really, who taught Kerston how to read properly, what we now call speed reading. He was age 5 at the time.

For his secondary education, Kerston attended the Boys' Grammar School beginning in 1948. William M. Lopey (the Don) was Headmaster at the time. Kerston progressed through the various forms and successfully sat for the Cambridge School Certificate in 1954. Two years later, he sat for the Cambridge Higher School Certificate and read mainly science subjects because he had decided he wanted to be an engineer. He did Chemistry and Math but no Physics which was not offered at the school at that time. Later on, he would have to spend some time doing his physics at a polytechnic in England before proceeding on to his engineering degree.

At the Grammar School, Kerston played cricket at the inter-school level and football at the inter-house level. He was also a member of the Cadet Corps. Some of the masters with whom he interacted included his Math teacher, Fitz Gordon (a Guyanese) who later became Headmaster, Harley Moseley (a Barbadian who is still alive) who taught Latin, Philip Greaves (a Barbadian), A. Blackett (a Barbadian), Mark Mapp (a Trinidadian) who taught Chemistry and Ellsworth 'Shake" Keane who taught French. Some of his school mates at that time included Dr. Robert Sutton (a pediatrician in Toronto, Canada), Wallace Dear (a retired accountant in Toronto), Dr. Freddie Ballantyne (the present Governor General of St. Vincent and the Grenadines), Ken Boyea (a prominent businessman living in St. Vincent), Alphonso Roberts (deceased, an outstanding cricketer/batsman who made the West Indies team to Australia in 1956 and Dr. Kenneth John, a prominent barrister and political commentator in St. Vincent and the Grenadines.

Kerston left the Grammar School in 1956 with a Cambridge Higher School Certificate in hand and headed to England to further his education. Chemistry was his favorite subject in Grammar School and he thought vaguely that he might pursue a career in Industrial Chemistry since he was more interested in large scale chemical production than, for example, chemical research. However, as he investigated his options more closely, he realized that the subject closest to his aspirations was Chemical Engineering, so he settled on that course of study.

Chemical Engineering, like all other branches of engineering, is grounded in physics. However, Kerston had not done any physics in Grammar School so he had to spend the first 2 years after arriving in England in 1956, doing Physics to London GCE Advanced Level. To accomplish this objective, he entered a small technical college just outside London called Norwood Technical College. Some of these technical colleges offered courses from A level all the way to graduate level and Norwood was one of them. Norwood was particularly good in Electronics and offered a Master's degree in it.

In 1958/59, he transferred to Westham College of Technology, now the University of East London, to read for a degree in Chemical Engineering. At that time, Westham offered an internal degree of London University meaning that the faculty members were all approved and certified by London University, the courses were essentially London University courses and the degree obtained was a London University degree.

Kerston studied Chemical Engineering with an eye to returning to the Caribbean and especially St. Vincent to make his contribution. At that time, in St. Vincent the cotton ginnery and the arrowroot factory were functional so he thought he might be able to find employment in one of these industries but as fate would have it, the cotton ginnery burnt to the ground in the late 1950's and the demise of arrowroot was not far behind. Alternatively, there was a place like Trinidad and Tobago where there was an existing oil refinery and a budding petrochemical industry.

Life at Westham for Kerston was enjoyable but uneventful. Kerston played cricket for the college as part of the University of London colleges tournament. This was a time of much political activity; for example, on apartheid in South Africa; on several occasions, Kerston would join his fellow students in picketing South Africa House in Trafalgar Square. The racial climate at Westham, which was not a campus-type university, was also relatively quiet in spite of agitation by Oswald Moseley's 'Keep Britain White' group to repatriate all West Indians. In any case, Kerston graduated with a Bachelor of Science degree in Chemical Engineering in 1961.

After graduating, Kerston sought employment as an engineer in Britain in his attempt to get some experience before returning home. However, engineering jobs were hard to come by because of a downturn in the British economy, so instead he did some substitute teaching in a number of secondary schools in England for about six months before setting sail for St. Vincent to make his contribution.

Kerston spent the next year in St. Vincent looking for employment. Everywhere he turned, whether in the cotton industry or the arrowroot industry, he was told he was overqualified, that there was no place for a chemical engineer in a place like St. Vincent. The authorities were not willing to even give him a chance to see if he could have helped, for example, in saving the cotton industry which was on the brink of collapse. Regrettably, he was forced to seek employment elsewhere and was permanently lost to St. Vincent as a result.

Trinidad beckoned. It had always been the most industrialized of the English-speaking Caribbean countries especially because of its oil resources. There was an oil refinery churning out thousands of gallons of gasoline and other fuels per day. Also a number of US multinational companies like W. R. Grace were operating there. Kerston decided to apply for jobs at both the oil refinery and Federation Chemicals (FedChem), the first fertilizer plant in Trinidad and owned by W.R. Grace. He got job offers from both companies and chose to begin his illustrious career as an engineer with Federation Chemicals in 1964

Kerston began his work with FedChem as an Inspection Engineer which at first involved more mechanical engineering than chemical. Ever so often, he had to crawl into boilers, examine heat exchangers, etc. to ensure their proper functioning.. Doubtless, his chemical engineering background helped because during one's training as a chemical engineer, the curriculum does include aspects of other engineering disciplines.

In any case, after about a year and a half as Inspection Engineer, he was transferred to the production department as senior engineer where his chemical engineering skills were now being utilized. The production plants included those producing sulfuric acid, ammonium sulfate fertilizer and urea fertilizer. In addition, he had overall responsibility for the utility plants – the steam generators, the boilers, the water treatment plants. Shortly thereafter, Kerston was promoted to Assistant Manager and then Manager of the fertilizer section about 1967. Up to that time, all the managers were expatriates, mainly American, Canadian and English so it was a first that a Caribbean man like Kerston was made manager of an important section of the company. Later the company decided to set up a process engineering department and Kerston also managed that department . The department employed several chemical engineers who, on an ongoing basis, did studies on the plants with a view to optimizing the operations for better efficiencies.

The company continued to expand. Two new ammonia plants came on stream, the first one starting about 1974/75 and using brand new technology. Soon Kerston was made Manufacturing Manager, having responsibility for all the operating plants which now numbered four ammonia plants, a small sulfuric acid plant, a small urea plant and a urea bagging and loading facility.

The ammonia plants produced some 3,000 tons per day. The feedstocks for ammonia production are hydrogen and nitrogen. The hydrogen is made from natural gas (which contains mostly methane and which is plentiful in Trinidad and Tobago) by heating with steam in the presence of a catalyst like iron (III) oxide. The hydrogen is then heated with nitrogen (from air) at high pressures in the presence of a catalyst to produce ammonia. Urea is made by reacting ammonia with carbon dioxide which is itself a byproduct of the ammonia process. The sulfuric acid is made from imported sulfur which is first converted to sulfur dioxide by burning in air, then to sulfur trioxide by reacting with more air and finally dissolving the sulfur trioxide in water to form concentrated sulfuric acid.. Finally ammonium sulfate fertilizer is made by reacting sulfuric acid with ammonia. Note then that the only imported raw material was sulfur, making the whole manufacturing process a fairly tight and efficient operation.

In 1982, after spending eighteen years at FedChem, Kerston left to join the National Energy Corporation (NEC) of Trinidad and Tobago, subsequently a wholly owned subsidiary of the National Gas Company (NGC) of Trinidad and Tobago Trinidad and Tobago was flush with oil money at the time and wanted to develop a natural gas-based industry. Among the projects that were being considered were a methanol plant and a mega-size urea plant capable of producing some 1,600 tons per day (compared to the 250 tons per day at Federation Chemicals). The National Energy Corporation of Trinidad and Tobago was formed in 1979; its forerunner, the Coordinating Task Force on Energy was formed as early as 1976. The expressed mandate of the NEC was to develop, manage and operate all the required infrastructure that services the gas-based industries or the large industrial estates such *as the Point Lisas Industrial Estate.* When Kerston joined the NEC as Technical Engineering Manager in 1982, the first elements of the methanol plant, which was designed by a Japanese company, Toyo Engineering, were arriving on site. Under the leadership of Malcolm Jones, the team including Kerston set about building and commissioning Trinidad's first methanol plant.

The methanol plant started operations in 1984 after undergoing some minor alterations in the Japanese design. There were some teething problems but basically things got off to a fairly smooth start. One of the noteworthy things was that the plant was started up entirely by local people. In 1985, the first full year of operation, the methanol plant produced some 358,000 tons of methanol or 90% of capacity.. In fact, the plant turned a profit in its first full year of operation.

Kerston was also involved in the operation of the urea plant which was operated by another company, Fertrin (Fertlizers of Trinidad and Tobago). Fertrin was a joint venture between the Trinidad and Tobago government and Amoco Oil Company. The urea plant also came on stream in 1984 and in its first full year of operation in 1985, produced some 340,000 tons of urea or 60% of full capacity.

Kerston left the NEC in 1985 to start his own consulting business, Entech Ltd, something he had wanted to do for a long time. He thought the time was right to become an independent energy consultant because there were still several large gas-based government projects on the drawing board in 1985. Unfortunately, oil prices collapsed in 1986 and these projects were cancelled because of the changing economic climate. However the NEC turned around and hired Kerston as a consultant to work on specific problems with the existing plants. For example there were some inherent weaknesses in the Japanese design of the methanol plant; every time there was power failure, no matter how small, there was a plant shutdown. Kerston and his team were able to pinpoint the problems and Toyo Engineering was asked to implement the changes which they did successfully.

About 1986/87 the Trinidad government decided to remove the methanol plant from the authority of the NEC and set it up as a separate company, Trinidad and Tobago Methanol Ltd. Kerston managed the new entity for about eight months until a new Chief Executive Officer could be installed. From 1987-89, Kerston operated as a consultant, entirely on his own with no real connection to the NEC.

In 1989, Kerston met Mr. Lawrence Duprey of the Clico Group which started an association with that group that led to the formation of Caribbean Methanol Company. The Clico Group's major business was in insurance and based in Trinidad and Tobago. However, they were bold enough to become an equity player in the most ambitious, pioneering project ever undertaken by the private sector in Trinidad. They formed a joint venture with two German companies in which Clico owned some 60% of the shares. The rest of the financing came from a German government bank to the tune of US$170 million. The loan had to be approved by the Minister of Finance of Germany. Because it was a state bank, the interest rate on the loan was very reasonable. Kerston assembled a team of local engineers who became involved in all aspects of the design, construction, commissioning and operation of the new plant. In addition, as representative of the major shareholder, he played a major role in the negotiations of the main project and financing agreements.

Caribbean Methanol started operations in 1993 when methanol prices were actually depressed but prices rebounded in 1994 and in its first full year of operation, Caribbean Methanol actually made a profit. Caribbean Methanol now owns five methanol plants and two ammonia plants representing an investment of some US$1.6 billion. In 1999, Caribbean Methanol merged with Trinidad and Tobago Methanol and Methanol IV Company Ltd to form Methanol Holdings Trinidad Ltd, one of the largest methanol producers in the world with an annual capacity of some four million metric tons. Kerston was named Executive Director of the merged entity Today, the company is managed and operated entirely by nationals of Trinidad and Tobago.

Kerston retired officially from executive management in 2000 but remained active as a member of the boards of several companies. For example he remained on the Board of Methanol Holdings and CL Financial Group until 2004. He was Chairman of the Board of Trinidad Nitrogen Company (Tringen) which, with Yara Trinidad Ltd. (formerly Federation Chemicals), owns and operates three ammonia plants in Trinidad and Tobago with an annual capacity of some 800,000 tons. The presence of four other ammonia operating companies makes Trinidad and Tobago the largest exporter of ammonia in the world.

Kerston M. Coombs

Kerston was President of the Trinidad and Tobago Chamber of Industry and Commerce for two years (1999-2001) and continues his involvement with the Chamber as a member of the Energy Committee. He has been a Board Member and past Secretary of the Methanol Institute, a lobbying group for the global methanol industry, based in the U.S.A. He was also a member of the Commonwealth Business Council, a group of business people from several Commonwealth Countries based in London. He has also been Chairman of the Board of Caribbean Business Services Ltd which was set up in 1995 to provide managerial and technical help to small and medium-sized businesses in Trinidad and Tobago and was funded in part by the European Union. He was an original shareholder and Chairman of Ventrin Petroleum Co. Ltd which is engaged in the bunkering of ocean-going vessels with marine gas oil and fuel oil. It was formed in 2001 and is based in Point Lisas, Trinidad and Tobago. He was owner of Synchem Limited, a catalyst and chemical distributing company also based in Point Lisas.

Kerston received a Diploma in Management Studies from the University of the West Indies, (UWI), St. Augustine in 1972 and has been Chairman of the Board of UWI's Engineering Institute. In 2008, he was named an Honorary Distinguished Fellow of the University of Trinidad and Tobago for his long and distinguished career in the energy sector of Trinidad and Tobago. In 2009, he was honoured by the Ministry of Energy and Energy Enterprises of the Government of Trinidad and Tobago as an Energy Pioneer Hero during the commemoration of the country's one hundred years of commercial oil production. He has been a presenter and panelist on numerous conferences both locally and internationally. He was also a member of the Rotary Club of San Fernando and a founding member of the Rotary Club of San Fernando South, and is deeply involved in these Clubs' fundraising and charitable activities.

Kerston is married to the former Marlene Simmons of Bermuda. They have two children- a son Dane and a daughter Kelli. Marlene is a former mental health visitor who did her training in England where the two met. Dane is a veterinarian. He studied at UWI, Mount Hope, Trinidad and Tobago and University of Wisconsin,, USA. After practicing for a while in the USA, Dane returned to Trinidad and Tobago to lecture at his Alma Mater. He now has his own veterinary practice in Bermuda. Kerrston's daughter Kelli has a B.Sc. in biochemistry and a Master's in Leadership and Management and works in at-risk communities in Trinidad and Tobago.

It is safe to say that this Vincentian-born chemical engineer/entrepreneur has been a pioneer in the energy sector of Trinidad and Tobago, especially in the area of petrochemicals. He continues to play a part in the energy business through his consulting firm, Entech Ltd. We salute him as a true Caribbean Trailblazer.

Dr. Baldwin King is a chemical educator and researcher. He is Professor Emeritus and Research Professor of Chemistry at Drew University, New Jersey, U.S.A. He presently resides in Madison, New Jersey but spends a lot of time in his homeland of St. Vincent and the Grenadines.

4.   **Hubert E. A. Daisley**
By
G. Errol Daisley

Hubert E A Daisley was born on 24th November 1873 in the island of Barbados. He was the first of two sons of John Daisley and Phoebe Daisley (nee Smith) and was born just after the abolition of slavery.

His earliest memories were of playing with his brother on the large plantation where his father worked and the family lived. He remembered his home as a small chattel house set among many similar homes that were occupied by the workers on the estate. Although the homes were small, they were well kept, with flower gardens in the front and vegetable gardens in the back yards.

Hubert often saw the plantation owner, a Scotsman, riding on his horse, or traveling in a horse-driven carriage with his family. He said that Daisley, the surname of his family, was taken from that of the plantation owner which could have been Paisley, a popular Scottish name, and changed slightly to give the family its own identity.

The British always had a very strong influence on the culture of Barbados. Once it became a colony of Britain, it never changed hands like many of the neighboring islands, which were at various periods colonized by the French, Dutch, Spanish and Portuguese. Thus British traditions and institutions were well established when slavery was abolished. The British did not segregate the churches and the schools in Barbados, as was the case with the post-slavery era within the United States of America, so that the children of former slaves were exposed to an excellent education system as well as the influence of the Protestant Church. Some of the other islands were not as fortunate as Barbados. The wars and the changes in colonial powers, which ruled the islands, prevented the building of strong institutions and stable cultures.

The young Hubert's parents must have been very progressive and encouraged their children to take advantage of the opportunities that opened up for them. Not only did he excel academically but at an early age, he became an accomplished musician, playing both the piano and violin, as well as a trained secretary with several proficiency diplomas in book-keeping, typing and Pitman's Shorthand.

Hubert was able to pass the London Matriculation Examination of Durham University in England as an external student in Greek, Latin, English and Mathematics. He entered the teaching profession in Barbados and successfully completed the professional teacher training course offered by Durham University.

His progress as a teacher in the elementary school system was meteoric and he became a headmaster by the age of twenty two. The following year he met and married a music teacher, Eloise Adina Moore.

In 1898, the young Hubert was selected by the Colonial Office to assist with the training of teachers in the smaller Caribbean island of St Vincent. He and Eloise left Barbados to start their new life in neighboring St. Vincent.

Hubert was appointed headmaster of the Stubbs Government School, located in the rural area of Stubbs-Brighton. He developed the teaching curriculum and trained the teachers at the school. At the end of each year, these teachers took qualifying exams and if successful were transferred to various school districts.

The first year in St Vincent was difficult. A hurricane did considerable damage to the Stubbs home soon after Hubert and his wife had settled in. It was a difficult time for the young couple, particularly for Eloise, who even thought of returning to Barbados.

Hubert's faith was again tested when there was a volcanic eruption on the island in 1902. But by this time, he had settled in and was very involved with the settlement of refugees from the more affected areas.

Hubert was appalled at the low quality of education in St Vincent as compared with that of Barbados and with the conditions of the facilities provided for schooling. He was however impressed by the ambition of the villagers, who though illiterate, understood the importance of education for their children. He was equally appalled by the lack of concern and comments of the plantation owners, who thought that educating the children would deprive them of the pool of cheap labor to work the lands in the coming years.

He organized the villagers in groups and started adult education classes. In addition, he encouraged a practice where a family wanting to build a home or till a field would get free labor from the other villagers in exchange for meals. This practice continued in the village for several generations.

He also got the villagers to provide local lumber from trees to expand the capacity of schools. This effort was appreciated by the local Administrator, (Britain's representative on the island) who provided additional material and some skilled labor to complete the project.

Hubert, or Teacher Daisley as he was affectionately called, was a great community organizer and many of the activities and ideas he promoted must have been based on his experiences as a youth in Barbados. He encouraged the villagers to save a portion of their wages, but because their pay was so small, he organized "sou-sous" which enabled them to accumulate sizable amounts of cash. He organized debating societies in the schools and started debating competitions between schools. He started sports teams within his school and once a year would have a sports day during which competing teams from other schools would participate.

Hubert E. A. Daisley

He was very active in a village council where his typing and short-hand skills came in handy. He was a devout Christian who strongly adhered to the teachings of John Wesley. He was a strict disciplinarian, always orderly, punctual and a stickler for detail. He never drank alcohol, smoked or played cards.

He spent much time in the study of the Bible. His knowledge of Greek allowed him to read from the original text, and he was both a good student and teacher of the Word. He conducted a Bible study class and was a local preacher in the Methodist church.

The same Christian discipline was to be found in his home. He had six children: three boys, Duncan, Hubert and Mont, and three girls: Claire, Daisy and Myrtle, all of whom began their adult lives as teachers and as accomplished musicians. Duncan and Mont subsequently worked in the private sector.

The day began in the home at 5.00 a.m with family worship with Dear Pa, as he was affectionately called at home, on the piano playing the doxology:

Praise God from whom all blessings flow
Praise Him all creatures here below
Praise Him above, ye heavenly host
Praise Father, Son and Holy Ghost .

This was the wake up call and continued until every one in the household turned up for the morning devotion- the ladies having their heads covered. The devotion consisted of singing a hymn, reading a chapter of the Old Testament and prayer.

The day ended at around 9.00 p.m. in similar fashion with evening prayers, this time with Dear Ma on the piano and with the reading of a chapter from the New Testament and prayers of thanksgiving.

Dear Pa functioned as a village elder on whom the older villagers relied to settle family and neighborly disputes, make wills, counsel young couples before marriage and fill out official forms.

In addition the younger folk always came for lessons in English or mathematics, typing or shorthand, music or book-keeping. For these services Dear Pa never charged a fee. The villagers often showed their appreciation with gifts of eggs, chickens, fruit or vegetables. Very often he would receive a letter of gratitude from someone whom he had helped years before and who had migrated to North America, England or elsewhere, forging a better life with the help of the education they had received.

As the head teacher in the village his opinion was often sought, not only on personal and local affairs, but on national and international events. In the period 1930 to 1939, just before the Second World War, there was the period of the Great Depression. This resulted in social unrest throughout the Caribbean region. The people protested against the grave injustices in the society; the low wages, the poor working and housing conditions and the exploitation of the masses by the Plantocracy. Most of the arable land was owned by the large estate owners while little of it was being cultivated, so that the land owners sat on the engine of economic growth. The masses were liberated from physical slavery but were now bound by an economic form of slavery.

The social unrest reached St Vincent around 1935 when there was spontaneous rioting on most of the plantations and in the capital city, Kingstown. The colonial government dealt with the uprising ruthlessly and set about arresting perceived leaders throughout the island, including the labor leader George Mc Intosh. It would appear that villagers at Stubbs met at Teacher Daisley's home to discuss the gravity of the situation. A domestic worker in the home listened in on the discussions and told the Methodist minister that Teacher Daisley was inciting the people to riot. Immediately the minister, an Englishman, contacted the Administrator and the Police Chief and Teacher Daisley was arrested for sedition.

It was a critical time for Dear Pa as he was about to retire or had just retired and it would have meant, if found guilty, not only being incarcerated but the loss of his pension after so many years of hard work. Fortunately the case was dismissed and there was great jubilation in the village when he returned in the afternoon in the car of his attorney Mr. O W Forde. They were both lifted on the shoulders of the villagers and taken to his home. There were many tears of joy in the Daisley family on that eventful afternoon.

This experience made him much wiser and ended his relationship with the Methodist Church. He then became a member of the Gospel Hall Assembly and is well remembered for his evangelical work in many villages including Brighton, Enams, Calder, Akers and Stubbs. He eventually became one of the senior and most trusted members of that Assembly in St. Vincent.

After his retirement, Dear Pa settled on a small farm of some ten acres under the King's Hill forest reserve. His farming practices were very methodical. The lands were sectioned with different crops planted in each section. Ever so often, crops were rotated and periodically each section was left fallow for a certain number of years. These fallow sections were used for the tethering of animals.

Some sectional plots were used for traditional crops like cotton and arrowroot. Others were used for ground provisions, while others were used for the production of vegetables and corn. There was also an abundance of fruit trees like coconuts, mangoes, cocoa, plums, sour sop and sugar apples. Cows, goats and pigs and donkeys were also bred on the farm. Chickens roamed freely around the family home and beehives were also to be found under the trees which functioned as wind breakers around the home.

The family always had a good supply of fresh milk, vegetables, fruit, meat, eggs and honey.

He operated a small shop for the farm workers. Here he stocked the basic food-stuffs that the workers would need and gave them credit as was needed.

His days were fully occupied. After morning devotions, he went on the lands, tethered the animals and set out work for the workers. On completion he returned for breakfast and then he went to his office, either to study the Bible, to fulfill an appointment or to assist a student in private lessons.

After the election in 1952, one of the elected representatives, Mr. Rudolph Baynes, a businessman, was of the opinion that four pioneers of education in St. Vincent should be honored. To do so, he published 'exercise' books with the photographs of the four on the front cover, replacing the photograph of the Queen. The four were Darnley Williams, C. W. Prescod, H. E. A. Daisley and Webster Clarke. Most Vincentians thought this was a good tribute and supported the venture. Unfortunately the local Administrator, who was the British representative on the island and the Colonial Office, thought it was disrespectful to the Queen and the books were all withdrawn after the first issue.

As a grandson, I must pay tribute to his influence on my own life. He was my role model and I looked forward to the vacations when I would spend most of the time with him and my grandmother. During these times, I enjoyed accompanying him on Sunday evenings to open-air evangelical meetings in the neighboring villages as the lantern bearer on the dark and unpaved roads. He was extremely compassionate and had a great burden for taking the gospel message to as many as possible, an anointing which was passed on to many of his descendants.

His influence on my academic life was transformational. During the first two terms of my first year in the Grammar school, I was last in the class. During the August vacation he instructed me in Latin and Mathematics and enabled me to grasp the fundamental principles of these subjects. I never read much as a youth, but from my understanding of Latin grammar, I was able to appreciate the structure of the English language. From that time, I was always at the top of my class. Several of his grandchildren can similarly attest to his influence on their lives. Our family thanks God for him.

Teacher Daisley, Dear Pa, died in 1963 at the age of ninety. He had the pleasure of seeing many of his students and descendants excel in the medical and legal professions, in teaching, agriculture, engineering and in the Civil Service, not only in St. Vincent but throughout the Caribbean and in North America and Europe.

G. Errol Daisley is a retired Civil Engineer. He was born in St. Vincent and the Grenadines but presently resides in Trinidad and Tobago.

5. **L. JEANNETTE "JEAN" DUNCAN**
By
Hayden D. Duncan

Jean, as she is popularly known, was baptized Lyris Jeanette Duncan. The eldest child of Alphonse Donelan Duncan and Olive Elaine Duncan neé Porter of New Montrose, Jean was born and grew up in Kingstown, as did her siblings Julian, Greta, Lennox (deceased), Hayden and Hildred (deceased). Along with her sisters and brothers, Jean was nurtured under the watchful eye of her parents who instilled a strict discipline and strong Christian values in their children.

Jean's early education began at Miss Jennie Jacobs' school, which she attended until 1942 when Miss Jacobs closed her private school because she was about to begin her teaching career at the Girls' High School. Consequently, Jean enrolled in Miss Louie John's private school on Bay Street, and at the end of that year she entered the Girls" High School.

"LET US NOT BE WEARY IN WELL DOING"

The above-cited scripture verse (Galatians 6:9) is the tenet that has guided Jean's life. In the Preface to a booklet of hymns and meditations composed by Jean in 2001 and printed in 2004[15], by way of explaining what inspired one of the hymns, Jean wrote:

"When I was a child, I was fascinated with a certain picture that hung in one of our bedrooms. I sometimes ask myself why would a picture with very little colour, just a bunch of white lilies of the valley with green leaves and stalks, attract a child. Written in gold Old English lettering, the inscription on the picture read, "Let Us Not Be Weary in Well Doing" Galatians 6:9. I often read the words without ever seriously considering their meaning. Over the years, I extended kindness to a number of young people, both male and female, by sharing my home with them. Then at one stage, a situation arose which caused me to become disheartened, and I vowed that I would discontinue this act of kindness. However, as I reflected on the past, I realized that the number of those who showed love and appreciation for what I had done far overshadowed this one situation. Immediately, my favourite Bible verse, "Let us not be weary in well doing" came to mind. What followed—my thoughts and pen flowed. Thus, I penned "Never Be Weary."

---

[15] L. Jeanette Duncan. Inspiration Through Word and Song. (Printed in Minnesota, USA. 2004)

As I compiled information for this essay, I was humbled by Jean's record of involvement in various organizations, in some of which she held membership concurrently; her contributions to Vincentian culture and society; the range of her work experience; and the sense of dedication with which she committed herself to her responsibilities. Several opportunities, coupled with a strong sense of dedication set Jean on a trajectory that involved a life of service, as evidenced in her contributions to Guiding, the Red Cross, Broadcasting, Netball, Carnival, music and diverse cultural activities. Indeed, Jean's having witnessed several "beginnings", be it by dint of her own initiative or by consequence of her having been invited to be a part of something new, makes her a trailblazer in her own right. Over the past decades, Jean has received several awards from some of the organizations mentioned herein, in recognition of her contributions.

CONTRIBUTIONS TO GUIDING

Jean was a brownie, a girl guide and a ranger and ultimately, became a guider. As a ranger, she was attached to the No. I Ranger Company, which was led by Captain Kathleen Connell (subsequently Mrs. Kathleen Paul). In 1954, District Commissioner Audrey Broomes charged Jean with the responsibility of founding a Methodist brownie pack. The No. 4 Brownie Pack was thus established with Jean as the Brown Owl, and Kathleen Patterson (Mrs. Kathleen Mason) as the Tawny Owl. Jean did everything to ensure that the Pack was soon up to par with existing brownie packs. In order to stretch funds for the new pack, she economized by making their toadstool out of *papier maché* and painting it herself. On occasion, she would solicit the help of our mother, who was adept at making children's clothing, to sew a uniform or a tie for one of her brownies. No one who wanted to join the pack was bereft of the opportunity to do so. During her period as a guider, Jean served as Secretary of the Guiders' Council, setting a paradigm for her position in several of the organizations to which she would belong.

THE ST. VINCENT RED CROSS SOCIETY

Perceiving that there was a need for a Red Cross Society in St. Vincent, the aforementioned Mrs. Audrey Broomes decided to form one. She invited several dedicated women of the community, varying in age, to become a part of the new organization. Among the charter members were Jean, Mrs. Theo Saunders, Miss Pauline Correa (Mrs. Pauline Lung), Miss Nesta "Clarie" Paynter and Mrs. Gwendolyn Lewis, to name but a few. In preparation for their work, these ladies received appropriate training in First Aid through lecture series that culminated in examinations and the awarding of certificates that reflected the successive levels of achievement. This experience sparked Jean's interest and she elected to pursue a certificate in Home Nursing. Her work schedule afforded her "free time" on Wednesday mornings. At that time, she was working at the Kingstown Public Library, which opened at 1:00 p.m., on Wednesdays. Thus, Jean took advantage of the 7:00 a.m. through noon period to work toward her Home Nursing certificate. Preparation included a designated number of hours working on the various wards at the Kingstown General Hospital, as well as in what was then known as "Casualty" (today's "Accidents and Emergency"). Upon the completion of the requirement of the designated hours of work, Jean had to select the ward on which she would be stationed for a period of time before earning the certificate. Jean told me, "I chose Male Ward, as I noted that I would be able to encounter more health problems." Jean admitted that the experience that she undertook to achieve the Home Nursing certificate served her in good stead and added, "I don't know if this is why some of my friends refer to me as 'little doctor'. I believe this is based on advice or suggestions I am able to offer." Eventually, Jean was appointed Secretary of the St. Vincent Red Cross Society.

INVOLVEMENT IN NETBALL

A Girl Guide Thinking Day celebration would reaffirm for Jean the love that she had for netball. The programme for one particular Thinking Day included a netball match: Guides versus Rangers. In those days, Jean played "centre" for the team known as "Guides". The match ended in resounding victory for Guides, whose playing duly impressed Mr. Clyde McKell, a Trinidadian gentleman who worked at the same government office as the Guide Captain, Miss Connell, who later became the Ranger Captain. Seeing potential in the young players, Mr. McKell asked Captain Connell to allow him to coach the "Guides" team because he felt that they could do well in St. Vincent's Netball Competition. Her decision to comply with his request was well rewarded. The only schoolgirls who participated in that competition were those who comprised the Guides team. They made everyone proud as they defeated all but one team: the invincible KNBC (Kingstown Netball Club), captained by Miss Sylvia Wilson (the late Mrs. Sylvia DaSilva). Year after year, Guides tried in vain to defeat KNBC. Jean recalls that, in the position of centre, her KNBC marker was none other than one of her School Mistresses, Mrs. Sydney Morris. As the saying goes, "every puppy has its day" and so it was for the erstwhile Guides team. Some of the girls on the team became rangers, which meant that the team could no longer be called "Guides". Accordingly, they recruited new [additional] members and adopted the name "Dodgers". In 1950, Dodgers walked away with the tournament trophy. At last, the former members of Guides had achieved their long sought goal (no pun intended). Later that year, Jean took a break from playing netball. During an exhibition match against a visiting netball team from St. Lucia, the centre marker, who was much taller than Jean, collided with, and fell on top of her as she caught the ball. Jean sustained a couple of fractured ribs and was obliged to give up her beloved sport for a while. So eager was she to return to the field that, perhaps unwisely so, she decided to play in a match before she had completely healed. Needless to say, this decision did not sit well with our mother. Jean still vividly recalls the wonderful times that she spent playing netball, and a visual trip through her photograph album reveals souvenirs of her days with that special "Guides" team.

FROM EDUCATOR TO BROADCASTER

The role that Destiny seems to have played in shaping Jean's employment record was that of providing Jean with a wide range of work experiences that took her from teaching, to library work, to various posts as a civil servant and finally, into broadcasting. It must be noted that the seeds for what later became her major career – broadcasting – had been sown as early as the mid-50s, as will be explained further on.

After completing her secondary school education, Jean applied for a teaching job and was assigned to the Richmond Hill Government School, which had recently been established, with Mr. Thomas M. Saunders as its first Headmaster. At the end of the school year (December 1951) a diagnosis of fluid in the knee necessitated a period of sick leave for Jean whose entire leg had to be encased in a Plaster of Paris cast. When she returned to work, she was assigned to teach at the Kingstown Preparatory School, whose Headmistress was Miss Katie Wilson. Jean recalls that, after leaving school one Friday afternoon, as she made her way through what was called the Government Office yard, the Personnel Officer called to her, requesting that she come and see him. He was curious as to why she had never applied for job in the Civil Service. In reply, she explained that our father—himself a civil servant–had preferred his children to seek employment elsewhere. The Officer then revealed the reason for his curious question. While looking out of his office window at lunchtime, he had observed Prep School children standing by the "Iron Gate", i.e., the entrance to Prep School's compound, and noted how the students scuffled to get hold of Jean's hand as she approached. It had struck him that she related well to children and this gave him an idea that led Jean in a new direction, work wise.

It so happened that the Chief Librarian was abroad on Study Leave. Her temporary replacement, a librarian from Trinidad, had advocated creating a section of the Public Library, which would be dedicated exclusively to children's books. Convinced that Jean would be the ideal person to be in charge of what was to become the Children's Section, the Officer gave her an application form and encouraged her to discuss the prospects with our father. Having met with no opposition from that quarter, Jean forged ahead with the plan, and during the July-August school vacation, she transitioned to her new position at the library.

In Jean's own words, "This was very exciting. Although the Children's Section was my responsibility, I worked throughout the library." Many were the contributions that Jean made to the new Children's Section of the Library. She introduced a "Children's Story-Telling Session" which was held every Saturday from 9:00 to 10:00 a.m. (The regular library hours were 10:00 a.m. to 8:00 p.m., Monday through Saturday, except for Wednesdays when the Library opened at 1:00 p.m. and closed at 8:00 p.m.) At Christmas time, Jean arranged a party for the children who attended those Saturday morning sessions. She got one of the local firms to donate a tree (in those days evergreens were imported at Christmas time) and from others, she solicited a gift for each child.

Jean described to me how she was affected by a specific piece of news: "Disappointment came, when one day, the Chief Librarian called me and told me she had just received correspondence stating that I was to be borrowed at Head Office." She went on to explain that she had been recommended as a replacement for one of the typists at Head Office who had fallen ill. Thinking that this was a temporary arrangement, Jean was saddened upon learning later that she was to be retained as one of the clerks at Head Office, even after the return of the person she had replaced. Incidentally, as if her plate were not already full, Jean took typing, shorthand (Pittman) and bookkeeping from Mr. Wilby Prescod, who had his students take overseas exams.

To fast forward a bit, while still working at Head Office, in 1959, Jean was commissioned to sit the Efficiency Bar Examination. She was one of two successful candidates and as a result, she was assigned as Secretary to the first Chief Minister, the Honourable E. T. Joshua, effective January 1, 1960.

As mentioned earlier, Jean's foray into broadcasting began in the early 50s, albeit at an amateur level. In 1954, St. Vincent did not have its own radio station. The then Public Relations Officer, Mr. A. V. Sprott used to publish a weekly newsletter, which, as he soon came to realise, was not accessible to everyone. Some chose not to read, while others could not read. Thus, Mr. Sprott, conceiving the idea of an "on air" programme, approached Mr. Weston Lewis, who was an Amateur Radio Operator (HAM RADIO). With Mr. Lewis' cooperation, a weekly 4 o'clock Sunday afternoon programme was aired from a makeshift studio at Mr. Lewis' home. Jean was invited to read the News, which was followed by reports by sportscasters, and ended with a special feature. After a few months, Jean was asked to produce a programme for children and she designed and produced what she called "The Children's Quarter of an Hour." This was very much in the style of Radio Trinidad's "Aunty Kay" which usually aired at 2:00 p.m. on Sunday afternoons. "The Children's Quarter of an Hour" provided many children with an opportunity to share their talent on the air. They sang, played musical instruments and recited poetry. On the Sunday closest to Christmas, there would be a special programme of carols (both sacred and secular) accompanied by readings. The Christmas chorus of children usually comprised those who had performed throughout the year. Of course, there were rehearsals prior to the actual day of the programme's airing.

In 1955, when hurricane Janet was expected to hit St. Vincent, the team of Mr. Lewis, Mr. Sprott and Miss Jean Duncan was poised to provide incoming information to the public in the following manner: Jean was to have remained at the Public Relations Office to receive telegrams from the Cable Office, prepare them for airing and then send them by the Office Attendant to Mr. Sprott, who was at Mr. Lewis' home studio, ready to air the news. That was not to be. As the situation grew ominous, the "team" had to abandon the plan and in the case of Mr. Sprott and Jean, head to their respective homes. Jean recalls, "When I got home, I turned on to WIBS (Windward Islands Broadcasting Service) and heard Governor Deverell wishing St. Vincent 'a safe passage through the storm'. At that point the transmission was cut off. Janet had begun to strike Grenada." The twist of fate that caused Janet to wreak havoc on Grenada brought sighs of relief to Vincentians because the island was spared, experiencing nothing worse than high seas and ground swells.

In 1959, WIBS, which was stationed in Grenada, was expanded to include substations that operated on the medium wave Band in the other three Windward Islands: St. Vincent, St. Lucia and Dominica. It was at this time that Jean, intrigued by the "airwaves", decided to become a Licensed Amateur Radio Operator. This afforded her the opportunity to make contact with other "HAMs" from around the world. As the number of local HAMs grew, an Amateur Radio Operators organization was formed, with Jean as the Secretary.

In the absence of an Office of Meteorology, the HAMs assumed the responsibility of relaying local weather conditions to Puerto Rico every morning. The important service that local HAMs rendered to St. Vincent and the surrounding region is underscored by two incidents recounted here, in Jean's own words:

Two incidents I often recall. One Sunday, I was combing the Band and I picked up an SOS signal in Morse code. I responded and discovered that a ship, located to the North of [St. Vincent], was in distress. We did not have the Coast Guard then, so I rang the Police Headquarters and passed on the information. The other incident also took place on a Sunday morning. Someone was trying to contact St. Vincent. I responded. These were the days when migration to the United Kingdom was prevalent. The caller was from Grenada, and wanted to know whether I knew Mr. Hudson Soso, who was the agent for a particular steamship line. When I responded positively, I was told that the "SS Bianca C", which was scheduled to arrive in St. Vincent that day, had caught fire in St. George's.

THE AMATEUR RADIO OPERATOR MOVES ON TO BROADCASTING

When the substations of WIBS were established in St. Vincent, St. Lucia and Dominica in 1959, they were staffed with personnel from the Main Station. Nine years later, the decision to include a local person at the Vincentian substation prompted the advertisement of the position in question. One of the required qualifications was experience in Broadcasting. Several persons encouraged Jean to apply for the position. However, she was reluctant to consider it because at the time, she was a Public Servant working as an Executive Officer at the Magistrate's Court. Eventually, someone was able to convince her to submit an application, which she did, and the rest is history.

She embarked upon this new venture in October 1968 and seized the opportunity to introduce new local programmes in timeslots that were formerly filled with Network broadcasting. Among the new programmes that Jean introduced were "The Law and You", "You and Your Health ", "Farmers' Diary" and "Dancing Party".

On 31st October, 1971, one of Jean's WIBS colleagues in Grenada phoned her with the news that Mr. Gairy would be appropriating the Network, and that from the next day hence, the signature announcement, "This is the Windward Islands Broadcasting Service" would be replaced by "This is Radio Grenada." Jean communicated the information to the Permanent Secretary in the Premier's Office, explaining that she would be unable to air the station on the following day, since WIBS would no longer be in existence. Three days later, a meeting was convened in the Premier's Office. Among those present were Jean and Mr. Claude Theobalds, who was a member of staff in Grenada and at that time was in St. Vincent on a special assignment. The groundwork was laid for the launching of Radio St. Vincent and the Grenadines (RSVG). Mr. Claude Theobalds was appointed Station Manager and Jean, Programme Manager.

In 1974 Jean participated in a course of training in Radio Production at the BBC in London, England. Upon her return to St. Vincent and the Grenadines, she resumed her duties at RSVG. Jean recalls what she refers to as two of her most challenging experiences at the Radio Station. The first occurred in 1979 during the eruption of La Soufrière. At 4:00 a.m., on 13th April, she received a call from our Dad, who told her that the volcano was erupting. She quickly got dressed, got into her car, headed for the Station, and went on the air. RSVG became her "home" because the Ministry commissioned her to sleep at the Station (she was provided with a cot). The seismologists were instructed to relay information to her. This was important because misinformation, on the part of foreign reporters, was being disseminated, causing some individuals who were living abroad to be concerned about their relatives. For instance, one night, Jean received a call from someone in the British Virgin Islands, who wanted to know on what side of the island her family was because she had heard, on her local radio station, that the force of the eruption had caused the island to be split in two.

Similarly, in 1980, when hurricane Alan was expected, the Station Manager instructed Jean to be on the air from 10:00 p.m. because the hurricane was due to strike at midnight. Jean spent the night at the Station and drove home the following morning to a structure whose roof had been blown off, leaving extensive water damage to her personal property. The losses were substantial.

In 1982, when Mr. Claude Theobalds retired, Jean became Acting Manager of RSVG. The following year, she received a Commonwealth Scholarship to pursue studies in Media Management, and travelled to Sydney, Australia for this purpose. Upon her return home, she was appointed as Station Manager. Shortly thereafter, the Station was to become a Corporation. Jean was informed that the Minister whose portfolio included the Radio Station had opposed her continued appointment at the Station. Thus, she was relieved of her duties at the RSVG.

According to a well-known adage, when one door closes, another opens. And so it was, in Jean's case. She continued her work in Broadcasting, serving at FIRST FM, and subsequently, at CROSS COUNTRY. Regrettably, when Jean began to experience problems with her sight in 2006, she found it necessary to end what was obviously a brilliant career in Broadcasting.

CARNIVAL

Jean was still a schoolgirl when Mrs. Elou Cozier asked her to assist with what was then referred to as the Children's Carnival. In those days, a stage was erected specifically for this event, which was held on the lawn at the back of the Court House. Whether or not this had to do with Jean's subsequent involvement with Carnival is anybody's guess, but what followed were six successive years of high profile participation in this festival. From 1953 to 1958 Jean did not just play mas'; she organized and led her own carnival band. There was a perk to being her "little" sister—I was allowed to play carnival in four of those bands. Three of the bands were advertising bands. One of the local entrepreneurs would sponsor the band whose costumes depicted the product that the band advertised on behalf of the sponsor. The band would travel in a large "truck" enclosed on the sides and in the back. Upon arrival at Victoria Park, advertising bands would patiently await their turn to go on stage and render a song about the advertised product. (Advertising bands were usually listed at the end of the programme, following the Historical, Fancy Dress and Original categories).

Jean's 1953 band advertised "*O-So* Beverages", sponsored by the bottling company of that name and owned by Mr. Hillary DaSilva. In 1955, Mrs. Marie McMaster sponsored "Ilford Selochrome", and in 1957 and 1958, Mr. P. H. Veira was the sponsor of "Tennants Beer & Stout" and "Sisson Paints", respectively. The 1955, 1957 and 1958 bands placed first in their category.

In 1954 and 1956, Jean deviated from the "Advertising" mode by entering her "Dancers from the Ababu Cabaret" in the Fancy Dress category, in 1954. The band won the second prize that year. Her 1956 band was entered in the "Orginal" category.

In 1958, the long talked-of West Indies Federation became a reality. However, in 1956, Carnival spectators were afforded a glimpse into the future when Jean's band "West Indies Federation" presented a panorama of the ten islands that would comprise the federal union. Some of the players in the band depicted produce associated with the islands, for example, Barbados, the flying fish (depicted by Jean herself) and sugar cane; St. Lucia, coconuts and bananas; St. Vincent, Sea Island cotton and arrowroot; Dominica limes, etc. Other players depicted the workers who harvested the produce, for instance, the flying fish was accompanied by its fisherman (played by Mavis Hadaway, now Mrs. Mavis Williams); the sugar cane had its cane cutter, the cotton, its picker, and so on. But that was not all. To create a context for the birth of the Federation, there had to be a Great Britain. Great Britain's presence was evoked by the figure of Britannia (as seen on the back of penny coin), which was admirably depicted by the then Miss June Baynes. "West Indies Federation" walked away with the first prize in the "Original" category.

That was Jean's last production, but she continued to play mas', joining Miss Sylvia Wilson's band in 1960, and in subsequent years, she played with Mr. Winston Samuel (Samo) up until he emigrated to the United States.

Later on, Jean's involvement with Carnival evolved into helping Miss Sylvia Wilson prepare contestants for the Queen Show, soliciting sponsors for the contestants, and providing the stage commentary, i.e., describing the costumes and gowns on the night of the Show.

In the early seventies, at the invitation of Mr. Elliot Anthony, Jean began to train contestants for the Miss Leeward Show. Shortly thereafter, she received a similar request from the Mesopotamia Committee. In 1981, at the request of Mr. Peter Ballantyne, she travelled to Sandy Bay on evenings to assist with training contestants for a show that was initially called "Miss Carib". After a brief hiatus from this type of commitment, the Vincy Mas'committee asked her to assist contestants with their interviews, which she did until 2006 when, as mentioned earlier on, she began to experience problems with her sight. This interfered with her driving at night. That year, as it was too late to find a replacement for her, she agreed to work with the contestants, at her home.

Jean's early days as a Girl Guide provided her with another skill that she would later on be called upon to share with others. Guide Captain Kathleen Connell organised for her guides folk dancing and country dancing sessions. The instructor was an English woman by the name of Miss Forrest. In those days, concerts were very popular fund raising events, and were mostly held upstairs at the Court House. (Prior to the construction of the Peace Memorial Hall, concerts were held at the Court House and the upper level of the Library, both of which had small stages). Captain Connell's girls were in great demand and performed at many of these concerts, as well as at other events beyond Kingstown. Mr. Grafton Vanloo, the Agricultural Officer stationed at Barrouallie, knew of Jean's experience with the group and in the mid 1960s invited her to teach Folk Dancing to the members of a club that he had formed in Barrouallie. In her usual spirit, Jean accepted the invitation.

THE ST. VINCENT LIGHT OPERATIC GROUP

"Don't' be afraid to dream, for out of such fragile things come miracles". This anonymous quotation aptly describes the following situation. Jean recalls that, during the time that she was engaged with teaching folk dancing to the above-mentioned group, she had an idea. In Jean's own words,

I told myself, we have a great deal of talent in drama and music. Why not a merger? I approached Mr. Pat Prescod who said, 'You are thinking of opera" and I said, "Exactly". I followed it up; perhaps I should say, pestering. This resulted in the formation of the first ever operatic group in St. Vincent. I was selected as the Secretary.

The St. Vincent Light Operatic Group was founded in 1965. The group, largely made up of members of the renowned Kingstown Chorale, performed two operettas: Gilbert and Sullivan's THE MIKADO in the year of the group's inception, and in the following year, THE GONDOLIERS, another work of Gilbert and Sullivan. The group's third and final performance was a musical programme entitled "That Christmas Feeling", which was performed on 21st December, 1965, at the Peace Memorial Hall.

In the months leading up to the group's first operatic production, the Publicity Manager, Mr. Wilson McKeckney of the S.P.C.K. Bookstore devised a plan to promote the newly formed group and its upcoming production (THE MIKADO). He had a pamphlet printed with the profiles of the group's executive officers, accompanied by brief comments. Here is an excerpt from his comment about Jean: "Her unflinching efforts are mainly responsible for St. Vincent's first ever OPERATIC performance."

With each performance, Jean worked tirelessly, as did many others who were involved in the preparations, to ensure that the production would be a success. I offer two such examples of her dedication, each of a different nature. Choral rehearsals were usually held either in Grimble Hall, at the Girls High School or in the old building of the Boys Grammar School. Jean took it upon herself to drive around Montrose picking up members for practice (Loren Daisey, Jennifer Glasgow, Marcelle Alves, Theresa Jack, La Fleur John, yours truly). Reflecting upon those days, I marvel at how she managed to stuff so many of us into what was a medium size car.

Various seamstresses were engaged to sew costumes. Attention was given to the smallest detail. In the case of THE MIKADO, Jean undertook the task of preparing one of these details. This was the *kanzashi* (the chopstick-like adornment that geishas wore). There were at least forty women in the operatic group, and since each geisha needed two of these ornaments, at least 80 – 100 would be needed. What did Jean do? She bought boxes upon boxes of macaroni (the fragile nature of macaroni warranted having extras). In addition, she bought lots of perforated beads; yards of wire; and small cans of black, green, red and yellow enamel paint. For weeks, Jean rose way before dawn in order to paint each stick of macaroni, in one of the above-mentioned colours, and leave them in a "safe place" to dry. At the end of that phase of the project, the next step was that of cutting the wire to a suitable length and carefully threading it through each bead. Finally the two protruding ends of wire would be brought together and then deftly inserted into each painted macaroni stick. I doubt that anyone who had not witnessed this routine had any idea of the work and patience that went into those hair ornaments.

Productions of the magnitude of THE MIKADO and THE GONDOLIERS required a huge performance space. In the absence of an auditorium, the executive council of the St. Vincent Light Operatic Group (SVLOG) entered upon an agreement with Mr. R. Russell of Russell's Cinema. With a temporary extension built on to the existing stage in front of the projection screen, the cinema was transformed into a space that supported the above-mentioned productions. Understandably, SVLOG had to ensure that Russell's Cinema did not lose revenue by having to relinquish the cinema for a weekend. As a result, two successive years of grand scale productions proved to be a financial burden for the fledgling SVLOG. And the period of elaborate operatic productions came to an end. The group's final activity was a Christmas concert that was held at the Peace Memorial Hall, in 1967.

CHURCH AND MUSIC

Having parents who were two devout Christians made it easy for Jean to love going to church and Sunday School. Miss Veda Cropper, who was the Superintendent of the Kingstown Methodist Primary Sunday School, recruited Jean to be one of her Sunday School teachers. Jean, who had taken piano lessons from an early age, was also asked to accompany the singing as well. A couple of years later, the Reverend J. B. Broomes made Jean a Class Leader and gave her the responsibility of preparing the young members who were to be received (confirmed). The Reverend's reasoning was that, as a young leader. Jean would be a good model for the youth. Since she was a Class Leader, Jean had to attend Leaders' Meetings and as in the case of other organizations and groups to which Jean belonged, she was made the secretary.

Once again, she was called upon to use her aptitude for music. She was put in charge of the Junior Choir. They were the choir in attendance every third Sunday, and Jean was the accompanying organist. In 1968, the Reverend Errol Wiltshire organized a [competitive] Choir Festival of all Methodist Church Choirs. It was held at the Kingstown Methodist Church, on Easter Monday. The judges were Mr. Weston Lewis, Mrs. Sydney Morris and Mother Stanislaus of St. Joseph's Convent. The only junior choir that performed in the Festival was the one that earned first place: The Kingstown Methodist Junior Choir.

Mr. Patrick Prescod was the Organist of the Kingstown Methodist Church and when he left, in 1968, to pursue his studies in the United Kingdom, Jean became relief organist for the next six months. Two years later, she was engaged as the organist at the Chauncey Methodist Church, to replace their organist who had emigrated for North America. This was not new to Jean, who oftentimes travelled with our father throughout the years of his career as a Local Preacher. Whenever he was assigned to preach at a church on the Leeward or Windward side of the island, he would check the availability of an instrument and/or accompanist and as if there was a need for the latter, Jean was asked to do the honours.

Now that she has retired from the whirlwind of activity that is described in the foregoing paragraphs, Jean lives at a more relaxing pace in the company of her beloved pets. She still enjoys playing the piano and the harmonica; she likes to read; she stays in touch with friends and relatives; she is a regular attendant at the Calliaqua Methodist Church, where she worships on Sundays. To summarize, Jean is still the God-fearing, fun-loving person who continues to help others in whatever small way she can because she firmly believes that "[one should] never be weary in well doing."

Postscript: I consider it an honour to have been given this opportunity to write about someone whom I have long admired, not only because of our filial relationship, but also because of whom she has shown herself to be over the years. It is with pride that I have shared the foregoing insights and information, drawn from my experience, and conversations with Jean.

Dr. Hayden D. Duncan is a Professor of Spanish Language and Literature and chairs the Dept. of Modern Foreign Languages, Literatures and Cultures at Gustavus Adolphus College in St. Peter, Minnesota, USA where she resides.

Caribbean Trailblazers: St. Vincent and the Grenadines

6.   **EDWARD GREIG GRIFFITH**
By
Kenneth John

Edward "Eddie" Griffith was born on December 10, 1936 in St. Vincent and the Grenadines to Nathaniel J. Griffith and Althea Nanton. He died prematurely on December 16, 1986 at the tender age of fifty. At the funeral service, I had the distinct honor of giving the "sermon-eulogy". It was with a deep sense of humility, tinged with a strange mixture of joy and sadness, that I stood there to say a few words by way of a public farewell-or was it au revoir – to our beloved brother, Eddie Griffith.

For a few days or so after his passing, there was a general outpouring of grief that flowed from every stratum of society and percolated through every nook and cranny of our Village-State. There could not have been a more eloquent testimony of the public esteem in which Brother Griffith was held, no better demonstration that he had in fact reached out and touched the lives of many.

There was one common theme, a silken thread, running through every tribute that was paid to Eddie: it was his sincerity and simplicity; his lack of pomp and show; his possession in abundance of "the milk of human kindness"; his generosity and largeness of spirit. The folk whom our Lord has referred to as "the salt of the Earth" had remarked over radio call-in-programmes and interviews that Eddie was a man of the people who always greeted "with a smile, a nod and a wave". And the voice of the people is, indeed, the voice of God.

Before he left us, Eddie had completed arrangements with Bassy Alexander to ensure that the 1986 Christmas Party for the poor and needy of his constituency would come off without a hitch. Christmas cards from their representative had already been mailed to the constituency of East Kingstown. Plans for the New Year had been carefully laid. Then Eddie was suddenly snatched from centre stage. He, certainly, would have advised "business as usual". But I was persuaded to subscribe to the view of one caller to "Searchlight" who felt that Brother Griffith's death had been sweetly timed by Providence to give us pause during the hectic festive season so that we might take stock of our life and reflect on the true meaning of Christmas- a mere nine days away.

RELIGIOUS PHILOSOPHY

As little boys, Eddie, John Horne, Douglas Williams, James Pompey, Kerwyn Morris, others and myself attended Sunday school in the very building in which I spoke that day, under the tutorship of such pillars of the church as the Jacobs sisters, Laura Hendrickson, Priscilla Anderson-Williams and Alphonso Millington.

During adolescence, Eddie in his relentless search after an elusive truth, was swept off his feet by religious fundamentalists to whom he had given a temporary allegiance.

Later on, Eddie and many of our generation who had enjoyed the benefits of tertiary education became introspective and reflective on religious questions. Made wiser by age, we had come to learn that the bedrock of Christianity lies in Faith. And "what seems to be God's foolishness is wiser than human wisdom, and what seems to be God's weakness is stronger than human strength". (Cor1:23). Shakespeare's Horatio made much the same point to a skeptical fellow-student intoxicated with the erudition of university "studentese"; Hamlet, remarked the simple Horatio to the cerebral university under-graduate, "there are more things in Heaven and Earth than are dreamt of in all your philosophies".

And so, Eddie decided to eschew all theories, leaving them to the trained theologians, and lived the life of a Christian as he conceived it. He might not have been religious in narrow conventional terms, but he was deeply spiritual, always. He lived an exemplary family life. He was not a practicing communicant, but I verily believe that he was in constant communion with God. If the outward and visible signs were absent, Eddie moved with the inward and spiritual grace of the sacraments.

There was no self-righteous approach or pharisaic attitude in Eddie's life style. He was humble to a fault. In Luke 18.9-4 our Lord tells a beautiful story, the gist of which bears repeating. The Pharisee in prayer had stood apart by himself and said, among other things, "I thank you that I am not like the Tax collector over there. I fast two days a week, and I give you one-tenth of all my income". But the collector stood at a distance and would not even raise his face to Heaven, but beat on his breast and said "God, have pity on me, a sinner." "I tell you", said Jesus "The Tax Collector and not the Pharisee was in the right with God when he went home. "For everyone who makes himself great will be humbled, and everyone who humbles himself will be made great".

AT SCHOOL AND PLAY

I knew Edward Grieg Griffith for almost my entire life. He attended the Kingstown Anglican School from which he received a scholarship to attend the Boys' Grammar School (BGS). At the BGS, he was the very embodiment of that Latin phrase: Mens Sano in Corpore Sano- a healthy mind in a healthy body. His scholastic career was sound without being spectacular. He, however, distinguished himself in extra-curricular activities, especially sports. In 1952 at age 15, Eddie, together with 14-year old

Alphonso Roberts, were babies of the school team that took part in the Windward Islands Interschool tournament in Grenada. In one vintage year, 1955, Eddie was at once captain of football and athletics, vice-captain of cricket, N.C.O officer in the Cadet Corps, fine exponent of the art of boxing, skilled performer in dives and swimming during the school Aquatic Sports. When Eddie pursued a course in agriculture at what is now the St. Augustine Campus of the University of the West Indies (UWI) in Trinidad, he added hockey to his wide repertoire of sports.

I recall two incidents on the field of play. In Grenada in 1952, Opening Batsman Griffith was felled by an express delivery which caught him in "the tender spot". He never took the shine again. In St Lucia in 1954 when Skipper Vin Cuffy called on spinner Eddie, the field setting took an eternity while Eddie meticulously placed his fielders according to a sheet of paper withdrawn from his pocket!

The foregoing, of course, instilled into Eddie a sense of discipline and moulded him into "team-membership", a quality so essential to the art of Government and the practice of party politics. In these roles, Eddie played his part well, guided by the democratic belief in collective responsibility, the good sense of majority decisions, and the practical necessity of compromise as a settlement to issues of policy. But just about everybody must have heard of Brother Griffith's inflexibility on matters of principle which, like Nkrumah, he felt could not be compromised without being abandoned.

Eddie worked at the Agriculture department after leaving BGS. Later he studied Agriculture at UWI, Trinidad but did not graduate, preferring to switch to Pharmacy which he studied at the University of Calgary, Canada.

Eddie had been a teacher for the greater part of his life. It is noteworthy that he first chose the Emmanuel High School which needed help, and did not respond to the snob appeal of the more prestigious schools at the time. At age thirty, he and Stinson Campbell ran Adult Education classes free of charge.

GROWTH OF AN IDEA

Eddie's political development fell into definite stages. He was a foundation member of the Kingstown Study group which introduced a progressive intellectual current to the stilted social thought of St Vincent in the mid-1960's. With the publication of "Flambeau", literary life in St Vincent took a great leap forward. Norma Keizer, Clem Iton, the late Danny Williams and myself, among others, agitated for serious social change. One issue of the Forum magazine carried a pioneering article by Brother Griffith that exploded the myth of the so-called discovery of St Vincent by Europeans.

Eddie's persistence paid off when he won adherents to his cause, and 22nd January ceased to be recognized officially as our Discovery day as from 1976.

In later years Eddie recalled with nostalgia the times that he held the front line of a Forum demonstration, protesting human rights violations by a human chain-link, or the nights when in abysmal ignorance of the South African situation, local police tailed his car and harassed him for "harbouring" a member of the African National Congress, Joseph Assinini.

In 1974, the Education Forum of the People (E.F.P.) graduated into the Democratic Freedom Movement, whose abbreviation, D.F.M. was mischievously twisted to read "Damn Foolish Men." In the view of many, Eddie and I lived up to the nickname, in daring to challenge the combined forces of the People's Political Party (P.P.P.) and the St. Vincent Labour Party (SVLP) in the December elections. But we felt vindicated, that we had stood up to be counted, and made a point whatever the electoral result which had swamped the "Two men submarine". I had received 146 votes in West Kingstown, and Eddie had amassed a total of 78 votes in East Kingstown.

At the end of the 1970's, Eddie Griffith retreated from politics following the D.F.M.'s alliance with Left leaning groupings with which he had no truck. He had decided to concentrate on building up his bookshop and drug store, practicing the concept of self reliance which he preached. The early 1980's however, found Eddie back on the political trail with the New Democratic Party (N.D.P) to which he had given himself unsparingly by providing yeoman service at both the level of party and government up to the time of his sudden death. He had apparently found in "Son" Mitchell something of a kindred spirit.

In the seat of government, Eddie continued to flesh out his own philosophy of life: better to wear out than rust out. On several occasions he dropped broad hints to family and friends that he would not be tarrying here on Earth too long. He seemed to have had a mission to fulfill, an assignment to complete. So he performed as if he were driven, living on borrowed time and had a dead-line to meet in a rendezvous with destiny. Seemingly, he planned his own obsolescence in preparing his family for his absence.

The ephemeral nature of this transient life, a topic so dear to the heart of bible students, was a constant subject with Eddie. Often times he would seek to puncture man's self-importance and deflate his vaunted pride with the reminder that "Man is but a grain of sand, one little puff of wind, and he is gone" This kind of stoicism led him like Job, to an easy acceptance of the death of his two-year old infant son, Jose "Joe-Joe" Enrique, in 1967. Indeed, "the Lord giveth and the Lord taketh".

By the same token, Eddie did not set great store by material things. In 1964, he could take in stride the loss by fire of all his worldly possessions. Like the young Derek Walcott staring at Castries engulfed in flames, Eddie could pose the rhetorical question that bristles with religious significance: "why should a man wax tears when his wooden world crumbles."

In a similar vein, Brother Griffith believed in the functionality of things, not in their symbolism. Over the last eighteen years of his life, Eddie owned three vehicles:, one at a time: a baby fiat, a mini Austin, and a small van, all of which in turn doubled up as transport vehicles for his book store and pharmacy as well as served as a family car, even while he was Acting Prime Minister of this State. He was casual in the matter of clothing, provided the fit was comfortable. And the interior of all his vehicles betrayed his disbelief in the saying that "cleanliness is next to Godliness"!

Indeed, the story has been told that tailors had hurriedly to run up a few shirt-jac suits so that Minister Griffith could be appropriately attired on formal occasions where, in any event, he often felt uncomfortable and looked ill-at-ease. Unable to engage in small talk, participate in alcoholic drinking, or tolerate gossip, Eddie stayed as long at cocktails as was consistent with decency and the expectations of his office. I remember when Eddie was being persuaded to attend my Silver Wedding Anniversary. He turned up precisely at seven when it was supposed officially to begin and left promptly at eight when our friends started to gather.

This mode of behaviour was a far cry from that of adolescent days. I recall a lovely lass living in Frenches whom Eddie fancied. On a week-end night he would serenade her and she would open the window and light up the whole place with rays from her smile. There our troubadour, Eddie, will bang away on this Ukulele, Bassy –Alexander style.

On a more serious note, I recall a visit to Eddie in his later years. He motioned to me to a window and conspiratorially muttered in an under-"breath", as if silence would break the spell "Look at her, watch grace, see how she walks, man, with chest push forward: "I tell you, that Patsy De Freitas has to be my wife!" So said, so done. They were married in 1962.

Generally speaking, although Eddie could light up among a small group of friends, he was visibly embarrassed by the trappings of formal power which were thrust upon him. He was in his element during the "moonlight" celebrated by Forum at the Market Square when Anansi stories were told and ring games performed.

In deference to Eddie, I wore a light-brown shirt-jack suit to his funeral. Brother Griffith could never accept black – the colour of his race-as appropriate to occasions of mourning and sorrow, nor to its generally negative connotation. But Eddie would readily forgive those who were taught to think otherwise.

Edward Griffith was a most telling communicator with a convincing platform style. He got his message across not by spell-binding rhetoric but by the sheer force of his sincerity and the vitality of his conviction. I will always remember the wild criss-crossing arcs described by the microphone cord as Eddie warmed to his subject, the index figure stabbing the air as he emphasized his points, the twinkling, beady eyes that riveted on a representative member of the audience caught in their steely focus.

I understand that Eddie had kept back the best wine for the last. One of his most convincing speeches was made at his Grand Finale, before the final curtain was drawn and his dramatic exit made. He died as he lived, and, if he could, he would hardly have chosen a more appropriate mode of departure. Eddie lived a full life that must be judged by deeds rather than in years: a life: rich in quality, if not impressive in quantity.

His immediate family, wife Patricia "Patsy" DeFreitas Griffith and children Jillian, Yulu and Khary, are fortunate to be able to draw strength from the cherished memory of a life well spent in the welfare of man and the service of God. If at all necessary, I know that the in-laws as well as the extended family of supporters who had claimed Brother Griff as their own would chip in with solace and comfort and succour.

I want to end this capsuled life portrait of Eddie by reciting part of what had become his personal anthem during the good old Forum days. Eddie fairly thrilled to the singing of "Take Warning" which played at the opening and ending of public meetings.

"Take Warning, Take Warning, you better do good,
Let your light shine bright, let your light shine right
Respect your brotherman as you should
The evil that men do live after them
The evil today will blight your tomorrow
So do good today and avoid your sorrow,"

Edward Greig Griffith took warning. He always tried to do good. His light shone bright. He had no fears of tomorrow. And so should we, if we heed his warning.

Dr. Kenneth John is a lawyer and political scientist and resides in St. Vincent and the Grenadines. He also writes a weekly column in *The Vincentian* newspaper.

The Editor acknowledges some information about Eddie's family background from Dr. Paula Nanton.

7.   ELLSWORTH MCGRANAHAN 'SHAKE' KEANE
By
Philip Nanton

'When you're dead, you're famous'. This was one of Shake's more caustic observations about heroism that he offered his friend, Eric Bye, the Norwegian singer, television producer and journalist. The statement also suggests that well meaning biographers, like me, should be careful in their handling of his story. Keane, the jazz musician and poet, that is, the Keane I came to know through his writing and music and through one year's contact in St. Vincent in 1979, was a complex and sophisticated artist. Artists, who use their gift to hold up a critical mirror to their society, often do not make trailblazers or, by implication, heroes, sung or un-sung. Their work is unique. In the flesh they can be difficult people. So, why should society value their gift? Because they utter hard truths though they are often derided for their pains, until, of course, they're dead. My story of Shake Keane, then, will not fit comfortably in a St. Vincent story that implies a simple onward and upward narrative. It is precisely the contradictions and ambiguities that comprise an artist's work that ultimately distinguish art from linear history or hegemonic representation, whether colonial or post-colonial. Where, then, to begin this story of Shake Keane? One place is a poem of his that brings out a number of contradictions between him and Vincentian society.

In his seminal poem, 'Credential', also called 'Lesson Seven' from 'Thirteen Studies in Home Economics', Shake offered a commentary on his life story and his relationship with St. Vincent. Later, towards the end of his life, there were other poems like 'Angel Horn', which were much gentler. But 'Credential' came at an important and difficult time. It is an autobiographical tale of a boy raised by a music loving father who taught him to honour his trumpet and himself. The poem is also about his gift as a trumpeter – which his father gave him and how it is spurned when he attempts to return it 'home'.

Forty year ole
an' Ah touch back down 'pon me country
an' Ah like it
an' Ah cool it
an' Ah bring back all me farder trumpit
gie dem.
But de sweet fool-dem say
Boy What yo come home for
wheh yo big car
wheh yo snap-soul an' yo whiskey an' yo 'tankerousniss
All-we culture all-we potential

is definitely non-residential
all this trumpet is a famous load o' piss.
Hold on to dis

It will be remembered that in 1972 Shake returned to St. Vincent, not with any great wealth beyond his musicianship and world-wide experience, to become Director of the national Department of Culture under the 'Son' Mitchell-led government. This position lasted for only two years after which it was discarded with the infamous statement by the incoming Prime Minister, Milton Cato, 'We can't eat culture'. Of course, this casual discarding of talent could be interpreted as no more than the common tradition practiced by most incumbent political parties in the region, that of clearing out the old guard from the public sector, who are assumed to hold a bias against them. For Shake, on the receiving end of one such decision, it was a substantial blow. His friend Edgar Adams, who at that time ran the 'Fishnet Restaurant' in the middle of Kingstown and where Shake was a frequent visitor, has stated: 'He was completely shattered when he got the letter terminating his appointment'.

Many years later, when I interviewed Eric Bye, he told me how he often expressed an interest to visit St. Vincent with Shake, then he recalled Shake's rebuff: 'we can go somewhere in the Caribbean but I don't think I should go to St. Vincent'. Bye went on to observe: 'There was a wound there.' ('Angel Horn', BBC Radio Feature, 2002) Not surprisingly, with an abandoned international jazz career, quickly followed by the loss of an influential role in cultural development which had brought him back, his feelings were expressed in the final lines of the poem:

So Ah hice up me credential
same one wha' me farder show
how fe polish
how fe _espect'
how fe blow
an' Ah say to dem
fe arffffff (Keane, S. 2005, 91)

This is certainly no hero talk. The writing is spare, fragmented, satirical and angry. Harsh as the ending may be, the poem also reflects a turning point in Shake's life and in his relationship with St. Vincent society. Stylistically, the anger and frustration in the piece are played off against a story told with considerable humour. The ending suggests that he is left with no option but to go his own way and please himself – reflected ultimately in his departure for New York where he lived the last ten years of his life.

Ellsworth McG. "Shake" Keane

It is through the concept of 'turning points' that I want to chart this brief biography of Shake Keane. The notion suggests key moments or decisions which are sufficiently fundamental that they change a person's life's pattern irrevocably. But to begin at the beginning and to establish the patterns that were to be both built upon as well as changed.

Ellsworth McGranahan Keane was born on May 30th 1927 in Kingstown, the son of Charles and Dorcas Keane. Education was an important feature of the household into which he was born. He was educated at the Kingstown Methodist Primary School and the Boys Grammar School. At home, his father taught each of his seven children to read music at an early age and often Keane Senior organized singing evenings in neighbours' homes. Books and discussions on many subjects were an essential part of the Keane household. (C. Keane, Notes, n.d.)

'McGranahan' is an unusual middle name. Given his father's love of music, the name may have been borrowed from one James McGranahan, a famous nineteenth century American composer of hymns. Young Ellsworth was given the nick-name 'Shake' at an early age. It became a preferred name that remained with him all his life. There are at least two explanations for its origin. One suggests that it comes from his love of literature – and is a diminutive of 'Shakespeare'. The other apparently arises from his fondness for a particular Duke Ellington tune of the forties, Chocolate Shake, in which the trumpet features prominently. Which-ever may be the explanation, the nick-name is linked to one or more of his three passions: the trumpet, English Literature and the poetry of the Caribbean.

Conditions were difficult in the family household while he was growing up. His father, well read and self educated, held down various jobs to make ends meet – he was at one time a waterworks mechanic and for a time a policeman. However, when Shake was 13 years old, his father died and his mother had to work to bring up her seven children. (C. Keane, Notes, n.d.) The family investment in music and education had practical benefits. For example, Shake helped to pay for his school fees at the BGS from the money that he earned by playing music. At the end of his secondary schooling, he had become a 'pupil teacher', a position filled by the brightest pupils in the top form of secondary school. By then he had demonstrated an aptitude for the French language which he taught along with music in the St. Vincent Grammar School, then the island's leading secondary school for boys. During this time, he also completed the early stages of a Bachelor of Arts qualification.

Shake recounted his early musical career to the jazz historian, Val Wilmer. She recorded that: 'At the age of six, he made his playing debut in public, as a member of the brass section in a parade band at a Boy Scout jamboree. He had to run to keep up with those of longer stride, but he was already sufficiently competent to hold his own with the older musicians. At eleven, he joined Ted Lawrence and his Silvertone Orchestra and began to play dance music. The band dressed in Cuban shirts with frilled sleeves, but the trumpeter was still wearing short pants, a combination he recalled with some amusement.' (Wilmer, 1991,1) Shake also played in a family band called simply the 'Keane Brothers'. In 1940, when he was aged fourteen, an older brother abandoned music. This gave Shake the opportunity to lead the family band for some five years. His distinctive trumpet also featured regularly in St. Vincent's annual carnival celebrations.

His active interest in literature from his early years became a lifetime commitment that ran parallel to his developing musicianship. He had started writing poetry in childhood and been in demand to compose verses for the island's newspapers at times of festivals. As his writing matured, he extended his range to articles and individual poems which were published in the regional magazines Bim, based in Barbados under the editorship of Frank Collymore, and Kyk-over-al in Guyana, edited by A.J. Seymour.

But this process was not purely an individual one. During the late 1940's, Shake was part of a small flowering of talent that included Danny Williams and Owen Campbell. They became known regionally as a trio of versatile Vincentian poets whose writing was distinguished by a sense of local commitment. Their work was regularly published and broadcast over the BBC World Service programme, "Caribbean Voices". His writing at this early stage drew on a West Indian version of writers of the 1930's including W. H. Auden, Louis McNeice and Cecil Day-Lewis. Underlying all these influences was a growing awareness of contradiction in the whole colonial experience, out of which the poetry was also growing.

In 1950, at the age of 23, "L'Oubli: Poems", Shake's first collection of poetry, was published. The collection takes its name from a long meditative poem that offers six variations on the theme of human fallibility and the transitory nature of the age. As a first collection it showed great maturity:

Our time is of forgetting
and today's dreams – meteorite
come, and gone.
Scrawling nothing on our sole night.

For I who have invented death
Am your forgetting...

Give us time to reconfirm
The last illusion
To remember the last success

For of forgetting is our age

And we too are
Wished alive only at our setting. (Keane, 1950)

L'Oubli was followed in 1952 by a second collection, Ixion, which developed these themes with an economy of language that reflected a range of conflicts and moods.   This early work, along with two articles that he published in Bim, also in 1952, titled 'Some Religious Attitudes in West Indian Poetry' and 'Nature Poetry in the West Indies: Some Religious Aspects' reveal a particular interest in religious and contemplative themes. His articles illustrated how writers such as A. J. Seymour, J. E. Clare McFarlane, M.G. Smith and Derek Walcott all found the spiritual muse central to their writing. Some poets, he argued, borrowed ritual prayers and wove poems around them, others showed a preoccupation with love and charity.

His early poetry fluctuates between introspective philosophical musings that draw on biblical references, nature and environmental interests as well as a public focus that present creatively some of the folk traditions of St. Vincent. These come together in his often anthologized poem 'Shaker Funeral' in which he captures the emotional fervor and incantations of a burial procession for a leading 'shepherdess':

Sweet Mother gone
 to the bye and bye
 follow her to the brink of Zion. (Keane, 1950, 17)

In 1970, in a discussion about his early poetry, he summarized the contradictory focus of his writing which stemmed from 'typical West Indian consciousness [with themes of] self-realization through nature, nationalism, sense of the unreality of colonial life; therefore, social protest on one hand, and on the other [an] obsession with identity (after death since present life seems unreal). On the positive side an attempt to understand and restructure poetically the tragedy, hope, conservatism and ecstasy of peasant and folk life.' (Contemporary Poets, 1970, 587)   Two themes combining jazz inflected patterns with a folk interest became important features of the poetry that he wrote in later years.

His first significant turning point came with the opportunity to go to England. There appear to have been two pressures behind this move. There was the push of the limitations of a small society and the other was the pull of wider opportunities abroad. In an interview with Cecil Cyrus, he recounted to me how he and Shake spent many evenings after school on the steps of his father's tailoring establishment in Kingstown hatching plans for further study abroad. Cecil's interest was to study medicine and Shake to attend university to read English Literature. (BBC Radio 3, 2002) The opportunity to travel was presented to Shake in 1952. He arrived in London, according to Christiane Keane (nee Ricard), his first wife, with a mere eleven pounds sterling in his pocket.(C. Keane,. Notes, n d)

London in the 1950's was, for a black West Indian migrant with little money, a difficult place. But if you were talented, it was also a place with potential. His teaching credentials were not valued in England and financially, money was tight. In 1954 he had married Christiane Keane and they were soon to start a family. She described vividly the circumstances of those early days that they spent together as students in London: 'In the 50's we lived in a sort of tenement house in Tufnell Park, ... A number of West Indian students lived there. Some of them were later to hold significant government posts.... At that time we were all penniless, sleeping in front of paraffin heaters or coal fires".

Discussions about Caribbean culture and politics were very frequent. It was also the time of racist tensions (e.g. Mosley and Notting Hill riots) (C. Keane, Notes, n.d.) But Shake was known to at least one person of influence in the capital city, Henry Swanzy. When the boat that he traveled on passed through Barbados on its way to London, Frank Collymore provided an introduction to Henry Swanzy, the legendary producer who had broadcast Shake's writing from St. Vincent. Swanzy edited a number of programmes for the BBC Overseas Service including Caribbean Voices. Shake became a regular freelance contributor to BBC radio arts programmes first as a reader and later, more formally, as a producer. His work with the BBC continued until 1965.

A second major turning point was his abandonment of his formal literature studies as his life as a musician increasingly dominated. At first this was as a jobbing musician and then as a creative trumpet and flugelhorn jazz player. It is not possible to offer a precise date when this happened. For a while, music and his study of literature rubbed along together. For example, although he was awarded a place to study literature at the University of Hull, he preferred to remain in London. In 1958 he registered to study English Literature at the University of London. In 1961, as a full time mature student and a part of the University of London Jazz Band, he won the award for the best instrumentalist in the Inter-University Jazz Contest. But the family needed a regular income to survive. And with the pressure of a young family to support (Christiane had given birth to two sons, Alan and Julian), music became his main focus and source of income. The question, however, was what sort of music?

His lifestyle became as gregarious as his art, as he freelanced in widely different forms of music of the day. Wilmer has noted that 'in appearance he was a fearsome six-foot-four, with full beard, dark shades and a constant supply of roll-up cigarettes always to hand. This fierce demeanor was offset by a playfulness and lyricism which permeated his style'. She has also described how these features combined with his music. 'His playing', she writes, 'combines two extremes: the fragile lyricism for which the wide-bored flugelhorn is particularly suited, and an almost brutal aggressiveness and unpredictability. It is this sound of surprise in his playing, and his ability to handle music of any kind, that put him at the forefront of his generation of trumpeters.' (Wilmer, 1997)

His range and adaptability was noticed also by jazz musicians. Michael Garrick, his one-time band leader in London, described Shake as a 'musical chameleon', remembering how different styles came to him easily. Horn playing for Shake, he said, was 'like breathing'. (Interview, BBC Radio. 2002) He became adept at a wide range of styles and as a jobbing musician he could not afford to be elitist. Wilmer notes that in the 1950's ' Britain was caught up in the grip of the latest Latin-American craze, the mambo, and it was not hard for any dark skinned musician to find work in the night-clubs of the West End.

But Shake was not an average musician. He was rarely out of work. Shake worked with a range of established black musicians including the Trinidad guitarist Fitzroy Coleman, the Guyanese pianist Mike McKenzie and on many of Lord Kitchener's singles'. (Wilmer, 1991, 1) He also played with the Nigerian drummer Ginger Johnson, he played sessions for Oh Boy, British TV's Top of the Pops of this era and he could be heard regularly at Sunday lunch-time London pub gigs, matching whoever brought an instrument in the saloon bar of his local.

By the late 1950's, Shake began to see himself more specifically as a creative jazz player. The next ten years were to represent perhaps the high point of his career if judged in terms of his high levels of music making and international recognition. This started when, as part of his work for the BBC, he went to interview the Jamaican born saxophonist, Joe Harriott. Along with Dizzy Reece, Harriott was developing a new 'free form' concept in music that paralleled the modern jazz developments in the USA. He was looking for a musician who could match his talent and interests.

With encouragement from Coleridge Goode, the bassist in Harriott's band, he found in Shake another artist with whose style he could interact. Wilmer describes the form of music Harriott developed as 'conversational' and notes that it 'demanded an alertness from each participant and the ability to follow the logic of what another might do, even if this meant departing from previously established harmonic or rhythmic patterns'.(Wilmer, 1989, 45) Steve Voce, the British jazz presenter and writer, noted that Harriott 'composed little themes, beautifully phrased, which served as a point of departure for his musicians to improvise solos' around which 'Keane was able to construct a mellow and imaginative flow of ideas that created its own form.' (Voce, The Independent, 1997). Shake's varied style was thus the ideal counterpoint to Harriott's playing. He suggested that his style was reflected in his personality, which he described as 'two-fold'. 'It's partly gentle and partly – well, vulgar and violent. I had never really thought of it before, but it hit me: how you could involve both these things, both extremes of personality, in any given set of jazz solos or any given series of tunes.' (Wilmer, 1989, 45)

By the 1960's in London, Shake's horn playing was in demand increasingly. In that decade he had become one of the most active instrumentalists of free form jazz. He can be heard on the recording of 'Indo-Jazz Fusions' with Ravi Shankar. He was invited to play in poetry and jazz events which had become very popular. As well as a regular member of the Joe Harriott Quintet, he played with bands led by Michael Garrick and Jeremy Robson. These performances included readings by established poets Laurie Lee, Danny Abse, Adrian Mitchell, Michael Horovitz.

The Joe Harriott Quintet disbanded in 1966 and in 1967 Shake returned to mainstream playing. He cut three albums of pop songs and ballads with Ivor Raymonde's Orchestra and the Keating sound. He then moved to Germany to play with Kurt Edelhagen's Radio Band, Europe's leading big band at that time. The band that he joined, one reviewer in The Times noted, was 'probably the most accomplished trumpet section in jazz' and included Benny Bailey, Idrees Sulieman and Jimmy Deuchar. Shake also freelanced with another legendary European big band led by the Belgian pianist Francy Boland and drummer Kenny Clarke. These years involved a large amount of touring and playing to audiences in countries as widely scattered as France, Switzerland, Denmark and Lebanon.

His next major turning point was his decision to return to St. Vincent. One can only speculate on the reason for this move. Perhaps many years of ceaseless playing and touring with the band had taken its toll – Voce claims that soon after returning from Germany, Shake told Michael Garrick 'I'm totally played out'; there may have been the call of 'home' and a sense of a developmental role in St. Vincent society; or the sense of a possible Caribbean stage to which he could contribute – the first CARIFESTA was being prepared for 1972 in Guyana, it appeared to hold much promise as a regional initiative and he was invited to be a part of the event. Whatever was the precise reason, soon after the festival, he was asked by James 'Son' Mitchell, the then Premier of St. Vincent, to lead the Department of Culture. I have summarized above the unfortunate outcome and the consequences of this decision when local politics intervened.

The experience of return was not a wasted one. The hardships endured were productive for his poetry. At the same time, a few secondary schools, local writers and musicians based in St. Vincent had access to a talent of intellectual authority, experience and depth. For example, Cecil Blazer Williams recorded that: "His criticisms of my work were invaluable. He gave great support and encouragement to myself and the New Artists

Movement and became a regular contributor to our literary magazine, 'NAM Speaks' (Williams, The News, 1997, 6). I retain in my possession from 1979 a scruffy piece of paper with Shake's penciled suggestions on how to improve a poem of mine that I showed him. The paper is stained with his roll-up cigarette ash and neat circles of Guinness bottle marks. The paper once rested on the counter of a long disappeared rum-shop located on the corner of Bay Street, diagonally across the street from Intermediate High School in Kingstown".

So, in the mid 1970's, Shake was once again employed as an official and unofficial teacher in St. Vincent. He held posts first as Principal at Bishop's College, Georgetown followed by a spell at the Intermediate High School in Kingstown. During his time in Georgetown, he wrote "One A Week With Water: Rhymes and Notes", which was completed 11th March 1976, as stated in the book's dedication. In 1979, Shake won the Cuban Casa de las Americas Poetry Prize for this collection. Only 500 copies were published. I doubt that the collection can easily be found.

However, it was probably here that Shake achieved his most imaginative commentary on Caribbean society in general and St. Vincent society in particular. Superficially, the book presents the reader with a simple calendar, offering observations for each of fifty-two weeks. These observations he described in the introduction to the collection as 'notes and rhymes'. The main text of this slim seventy-four page collection takes the form of a collage of verse, riddle, story, letters, spoof bureaucratic form, aphorisms, reportage and rhyme. Among the predominantly humorous pieces in the collection are distributed a number of poetic shards with flashes of anger, despair and loss. There is the sublime and the ridiculous. Regular patterns are avoided. Standard as well as local forms of English are tossed about for humor and with serious intent. I have suggested elsewhere that this collection is original in many ways. Shake manages to maintain a tension between the domain of order and continuity on one hand and on the other, nonsense and fragmentation. His improvisatory technique, close to jazz in its riffs and refrains, takes shape both in the fragmented arrangement of the text and in the flouting of conventional expectations.

The movement between playfulness and anger that has been noticed in his music also found expression in his writing. This was noticeable in the particular piece like his 'Credential' as much as throughout the entire collection 'One A Week'. In this collection he invites the reader to play with time, words, tradition and perceived social and cultural order. He utilizes creatively the long tradition of St. Vincent's 'nonsense talk' or 'nonsense making', a form of speech performance in public places where 'rudeness', which involves talking 'broad' or talking 'bad' also occurs. These displays are contrasted with the private yard where 'sense' and 'talking sweet' and structured order and behaviour are expected. (Abrahams, 1983).

In spite of the difficult circumstances in which 'One A Week' was composed, while Shake recognizes that St. Vincent 'deals perhaps less comfortably with situations of fact than with engagements of personality', for him, ultimately he suggests that hope comes out of creativity. Thus his optimistic comment towards the end of the collection: 'what we will create, and even a'ready done create, pon this scarred and hallowed mountain top, could blow yo mind.' (Keane, 1979, 73) What he seemed to be suggesting in this play with 'nonsense' and what he seemed to be saying to St. Vincent society is that social order is not a given, but needs to be worked for and revalidated. The route that he takes in this personal poetic journey is via techniques of linguistic improvisation which stretch language, credulity and startle the reader into laughter. In this way he pays tribute to a rural folk tradition while offering an oblique comment on the nature of order in Vincentian society as well as its obverse, chaos. (Nanton, 2003)

Shake published two more collections of writing, 'The Volcano Suite' in 1979, and 'Palm and Octopus' in 1994. In 2005, a selected collection 'The Angel Horn Shake Keane (1927 – 1997): Collected Poems' was published posthumously by his partner, Margaret Bynoe, who lived with him for the last ten years of his life in New York.

In 1981, Shake left St. Vincent once again, this time for New York where he settled and made his home with Margaret Bynoe till his death while on a lecture tour in Norway in 1997. The return to St. Vincent had taken its toll in various ways. Long before he left St. Vincent, his second marriage, to Lou Keane, with whom he returned to St. Vincent, had also dissolved. Before he returned to St. Vincent, a third son was born who maintains the musical tradition in England. In these latter years in New York, he turned his musical skill to arranging and he played less regularly. Though, in 1989, with Coleridge Goode and Bobby Orr, he did carry out a tour with the Joe Harriott Memorial Quintet.

While living in New York he experienced a mugging resulting in a loss of a tooth which compromised his own high standards of musicianship. He made his one and last CD in the early 1990's "Real Keen: Reggae into Jazz: Shake Keane" under the British LKJ label. During this time, he also traveled to carry out occasional teaching assignments on jazz in Oslo and Bergen. Bly recounts that he opened the first Oslo Jazz festival in 1986 and he was regularly invited back to perform. In 1991, in one of these visits, he obtained a role in a film 'The Search for Margas Coloradas'. In 1997, although suffering from lung cancer, he attempted to carry out a further gig in Norway, to meet a commitment that he promised his friend Bly. But he succumbed soon after arrival.

Shake had sometime previously (possibly at the 1981 CARIFESTA held in Barbados) made a connection with the British-based Jamaican dub poet Linton Kwasi Johnson. This contact developed further while he lived in New York. Johnson had become a prominent and popular presence on the British poetry scene. He had recently established a record label, LKJ Music Publishing, and the CD "Real Keen" was one of the first that his label had produced. The CD was the result of a collaboration between Dennis Bovell and Johnson and reflects Johnson's political concerns with tracks like 'Tianenmen Square', 'Prague 89', 'Yankie Invasion'. It contains also a reading with music backing of Shake's poem 'Credential'. Johnson also included Shake on poetry readings in England and there is at least one BBC recording of a poetry discussion in which they both participated.

During these years the poetry that he wrote appears to be more reflective, personal poetry as illustrated by 'Palm and Octopus', a collection of twelve love poems which he published independently in 1994. The poem 'Angel Horn' offers a vivid contrast to 'Credential' cited earlier. It was perhaps the last poem that he wrote. It offers a gentle interpretation of his musicianship and a lyrical summary of an older man's perspective on his art and his life:

> When I was born
> my father gave to me
> An angel horn
> with wings of melody.
> That angel placed her lips
> Upon my finger-tips
> and I became, became
> her secret name. (Keane, 1997)

In the context of a rich and varied artistic life, how is Shake's legacy of poetry and his musicianship to be assessed? A central theme that runs throughout much of Shake's work is that of 'play'. It provides a fundamental link to his life as poet and musician. Today we live in a world in which leisure time for most people is something distinct and separate from work. It's a freedom from the obligation to go to work, freedom to do as you want. Professional musicians are one of the few groups of people in the modern world for whom this is not the case; for them work and play remain combined. Playing is their work and vice versa. They continue a practice from ancient times before there was a formal separation between the worlds of work and play.

But this play is not a harmless thing; musicians, especially jazz musicians, and poets also play in another way. They take the familiar, like a familiar tune, tradition, story or even nursery rhyme and make them unfamiliar, reworking and changing them to create different effects. This is what Shake does with many of the folk traditions that he explores through the tea meeting, the kaiso and 'jumbie metaphysic', (see, for example, his posthumously published The Angel Horn, the section 'The Wisdom Keepers'). Play is also important to his writing in that it provides a freedom to create, invent, distort, change, say one thing and mean something else, to create an effect by the arrangement of words on a page. This was what his award winning collection 'One A Week' was also about. To this extent Shake was also a Rabelais of his time, unable to resist mocking the world of officialdom, common sense and good behavior. In addition, his fluency with more than one language helped him to hear Vincentian speech patterns as a linguist and so to capture them with precision in his writing.

Play also involves some element of being disorderly. By disorderliness I mean a questioning of established forms of order, rather than disorderliness for its own sake. Play as exploration affords the possibility of discovering something new. Disorderliness in this sense then is a zone of cultural creativity, which may challenge conventional ways of seeing the world. Thus, I return to my critique of the notion of 'hero' that I began with at the outset of this chapter. This is why artists are often seen as people who are out of time or somehow a threat to society's norms. By challenging the existing institutional or social order, they offer new and unfamiliar forms of interaction which may look at first like disorder. But this is an essential part of the artist's role. Shake's music, his writing and his life throw out such challenges.

But the last words of this brief biography go to Shake's friend, Coleridge Goode, the bassist from the Joe Harriott Quintet. One bright summer's morning in 2002, I interviewed him in his pent-house flat in West London for 'Angel Horn', the BBC radio programme I was making about Shake. As he played for me a Shake Keane solo, he remarked, in his quiet, cultured voice: 'I'm glad I've got recordings of his which I can play now-and-again, to remind myself of what we've lost'.

References

Abrahams, R.D., 1983, the Man-of-Words in the West Indies: Performance and the Emergence of Creole Culture, Baltimore, Johns Hopkins University Press.

Boulding, C., 1991, Boho Soho Revisited: The Poetry and Horn of Shake Keane, Straight, No Chaser 11, Spring,

British Broadcasting Corporation, BBC 2 TV., 4th July 1992, Rhythms of the World: Shake, Beat and Dub, London.

British Broadcasting Corporation, 2002, BBC Radio 3 Feature: Angel-Horn, 15:12:2002, London.
CARICOM Perspective, 46 – 47, 1990, Ellswoorth McG. Keane, Held Together With Rhythm and Rhymes: Shake Keane Talks With Perspective

Keane, C., n.d. Unpublished Notes, Mimeograph.

Keane, E. McG. 1950, L'Oubli: Poems, Advocate Co., Barbados

Keane, E. McG., 1952, Some Religious Attitudes to West Indian Poetry, Bim 4, no. 15.

Keane, E. McG., 1953, Nature Poetry in the West Indies: the Religious Aspects, Bim 5. no.16.

Keane E. McG, 1954, Ixion: Poems, Miniature Poets Series, 10, Georgetown, Guyana.

Keane, E. McG. 1970, Contemporary Poets of the English Language ed. Rosalie Murphy, St. James, London.

Keane, E. McG., 1979, One A Week With Water: Rhymes and Notes, Ediciones Casa de las Americas, Havana.

Keane, E. McG., 1979, The Volcano Suite: A Series of Five Poems, Fishnet Restaurant, Kingstown, St. Vincent.

Keane, E. McG., 2002, Brooklyn Themes: Poems, September 1981 – February 1983, A Selection of these poems is published in Poui: The Cave Hill Literary Annual no. 4, Department of Language, Linguistics and Literature, University of the West Indies, Cave Hill, Bridgetown, Barbados.

Keane, E. McG. 2005, The Angel Horne: Collected Poems (1927 – 1997), House of Nehesi, Phillipsburg, St. Martin.

Nanton, P., 2003, Shake Keane's Nonsense: An Alternative Approach to Folk Culture in the Caribbean, Small Axe, no. 14.

Voce, S., 1997, Shake Keane, The Independent, 14/11/1997.

Williams, C.B. Ellsworth McGranahan 'Shake' Keane, The News, 14:11: 1997. Kingstown.

Wilmer, V., 1989, Shake Keane: Burning Spear, Wire Magazine no. 69, 44 – 45.

Wilmer, V., 1991, Shake Keane: A Biography, Unpublished Notes, LKJ, London.

Wilmer, V., 1997, The Anger Behind a Free Form of Jazz, Guardian (13 November 1997), London.

Philip Nanton is a free lance writer. He lives in Barbados.

8.   **ERROL G. KING**
                              By
                        Roy L. Austin

During the 1950s, and most likely in other years, certain academically outstanding students at the St. Vincent Grammar School were referred to as "bright-boys." Usually, these students had turned in such stellar performances in Form 2B, the higher of two entrance forms, that at the end of the year they had been double-skipped past Forms 2A and 3B to Form 3A. At most, three students out of 30-plus were accorded this honor. However, in two cases of which I am aware, at the end of their second year, these students then skipped Form 4B and entered Form 4A. One of these exceptional students was my friend, Dr. Errol Gladstone "EG" King, son of Norma Hamilton and Fitzroy King, who departed this life on August 13, 2006.

My most vivid memory of EG is that he possessed a sharp mind that attended to and retained details that many other people had difficulty grasping and/or remembering. I am almost equally impressed with his super patriotism that kept him constantly seeking ways to engage in activities that benefited St. Vincent and Vincentians. His generosity in this regard, and in numerous other respects, knew no bounds. Admirably, too, he put a substantial amount of time into athletic activities and developed some prowess in this sphere. That is, despite his academic brilliance, he was not just a bookworm. It would be difficult to justify describing someone who "limed" with the Bridge Boys as such.

In correspondence with me, EG once attributed his concern for the well-being of Caribbean people, especially Vincentians, to his early experiences in Paul's Lot. According to him, this community on the periphery of Kingstown was derisively called "the slums." He did not say when this name came into being and I do not remember that it was called this during the years that he and I spent together in secondary school. But I suspect that the name may have come into being in the late 1960s as Vincentians became more familiar with the term as applying to poor inner-city communities in the USA. Undoubtedly, however, as far back as I can remember, this area was ridiculed, especially by persons affecting higher status, as possessing undesirable characteristics. In the relatively rigid class structure in which we were reared in the 1940s through the 1960s, people had a way of reminding some of us in subtle or obvious ways that we were "from nowhere." EG's ready admission of the denigration of his community of origin may be a way of saying to prospective detractors that he is already insulated from being hurt by such an intended insult.

In St. Vincent, as in other countries, stigmatized areas like Paul's Lot produce only a limited number of high-performing students. Indeed, there are people who have opined that "nothing good comes out of them". But EG's academic performance gave the lie to this latter opinion. Those who knew him in Paul's Lot and were familiar with his brilliant academic career must certainly have proudly claimed him as one of their own. Moreover, as I think of relevant characteristics of this community and former residents with whom I am familiar, I wonder whether objective indicators would qualify it as a slum. There was some substandard housing, but this was mixed with more acceptable housing. There were also many socially disadvantaged dwellers, but as far as I know, the area did not lack clean water, electricity or sanitation. Nor did it, as far as I know, produce a disproportionate number of criminals. Furthermore, many former residents live satisfying lives today.

EG entered the Boys Grammar School in 1954 on a Kingstown Town Board Scholarship, one of only three scholarships for which he was eligible. These scholarships paid school fees and provided books, a significant help for the fortunate few out of the many parents who had difficulty meeting these expenses. Throughout his years in this school, he showed that his winning of this scholarship was no fluke. There was only one end-of-year exam in which he did not take the first place, his Form 4A final. Although he placed second, a conversation I had with him in 2001 suggested that he had still not come to terms with what he may have perceived as a meaningful blot on his record. He clearly held such high expectations of himself that he did not regard being at least two years younger than almost all others in the form as an acceptable reason for not taking first place. Most of the other students had also entered school at least two years before he did.

Whatever may have been the depth of his feeling about that second-place finish, in later years, his performance left no doubt about his academic superiority over his competitors. In the 1957 Cambridge School Certificate Exam (later replaced by the London GCE "O-Level"), EG emerged as the top student. He obtained four distinctions, a number rarely achieved in St. Vincent at that time, and a similarly rare First-Grade Certificate. Two years later, he took the top spot in the Higher School Certificate Exam (later replaced by the GCE "A-Level") and earned the Island Scholarship, then awarded every other year.

Did EG take the first place so consistently and win the Island Scholarship because of the weakness of the students against whom he competed? The success at later educational pursuits of his secondary school classmates suggests otherwise. For instance, all but one of the thirteen boys who wrote the HSC in 1959 later obtained at least a baccalaureate. The group also counts at least two terminal Masters degrees, four Ph.Ds and two MDs.

You may marvel at such a remarkable record when you discover that five of the members of this class, including EG, were "Bridge Boys", then often regarded as spending too much time in idle pursuits on the "Back

Street" bridge over the North River in Kingstown. EG once sent me a copy of a letter that he may have sent to the *Searchlight* newspaper in June 1997 in which he tried to correct this negative image of the "Bridge Boys." He alluded to the seriousness of some of our discussions by pointing to our occasional half-joking declaration: "The Roman Senate is now in session."

We who hung out on The Bridge prefer to see the hours spent there as contributing to our educational success. This was a place to gain some respite from a rigorous study session, especially during the long vacations that preceded our School Certificate and Higher School Certificate exams. As importantly, we learnt who could faultlessly repeat the long speeches from our Shakespeare textbook and everybody endeavored to be up to this task the next time that we met. Also, chemistry students left knowing that they needed an extra effort to become proficient at balancing equations. Having a good student like EG in our midst inspired us to work harder; but he, too, was pushed toward stronger performances because he was not dealing with slouches.

Further evidence of EG's academic prowess is manifest in his performance in medical school at the University of the West Indies, Mona, Jamaica. Especially illustrative is that he won two of the three prizes awarded on the basis of 2nd MB (Bachelor of Medicine) results. His achievement is more remarkable when one realizes that the six (there was one girl from the Girls' High School who took botany) of us who wrote botany and the five who wrote chemistry exams for the H.S.C. in 1959 had no regular teacher during the year. Indeed, our Lower Sixth Form teachers in these subjects had us write out the exam syllabi before they left the country in 1958; and we studied these subjects with occasional assistance from Dr. Chaudhuri and Mr. Boss, botanist and chemist, respectively, employed in arrowroot research.

For most of our science periods in 1959, Winston Daisley, Cyril Lewis, Chris Stephens, EG and I ran metals tests, practiced titrations, sharpened our botanical section-cutting skills, or simply studied from our books. Even the dirt from outside the laboratory was a suitable medium for metals tests. (We always found iron but no precious metals). We also conversed about a wide variety of subjects.

Our activities in the laboratory strengthened our friendship. However, I assume that the presence of teachers provided EG's 2nd MB classmates from other islands, especially the "big-islanders," with a more supportive Upper Sixth Form educational environment; but he overcame this disadvantage and left them behind too.

On the basis of his 2nd MB accomplishment, EG was offered the opportunity to spend a year in England pursuing further studies in one of the subjects in which he had won a prize. He told me that he declined the offer because he did not wish to fall behind his classmates; but I suspect that we who are from relatively disadvantaged economic circumstances often try to hasten the day when we can feel a modicum of economic independence. Thus, I once felt that seven years of schooling to become a medical doctor was more than I could bear. However, my post-secondary education kept me in university for eight years.

After medical school in Jamaica, EG interned at Queen Elizabeth Hospital in Barbados. Then he completed a residency at Lenox Hill Hospital in New York City, specializing as a general surgeon and becoming board certified by the American Board of Surgery. While he was at Lenox Hill in the summer of 1968, he visited me and my wife, Glynis, in New Haven, our first meeting since I left St. Vincent in September 1964.

As many of us grew up in Kingstown, there was often a recreational location that we frequented. EG's residence in Paul's Lot placed him in close proximity to Guide Ground. Prior to entering the Grammar School, this was his primary playing field, and the place where he developed his love of sports and his athletic skills. He became a dependable football defender and often took the first place in the high jump in his age-group in the secondary school's annual track and field meet. In 1960, he represented St. Vincent Grammar School in the Windward Islands Inter-Schools Tournament held in Grenada. There, he won the high jump and played on the St. Vincent football team.

In 1960, too, the Eagles Club was reconstituted to include some classmates who were previously members of another youth club, other Grammar School alumni who were close in age to us, and age-mates who were alumni of other secondary schools. We fielded teams for local competitions in cricket, football, track and field and basketball; and EG became a member of the club, but was studying in Jamaica when most of our sporting events were occurring. However, he was available for a few of our football games.

In a letter to me dated October 10, 2000, EG recounted the joy he felt when he contributed to two of Eagles' victories. Interestingly, the vanquished teams were comprised largely of Grammar School alumni who were our contemporaries or nearly so in this school. The core members of one club, Olympiads, had left secondary school one or two years ahead of us and organized at that time. Several core members of the other club, Saints, were temporary teammates in Eagles who left us when a slightly younger cohort who had been their form mates graduated. These characteristics of the losing teams may have contributed to EG's elation over the outcome of these games.

At half-time of the game against Olympiad, EG says that the score was 1-0 in our favor. He said that he asked me to move him from defense to the forward line; and for the first time in his life, he had a hat-trick. Because it is so unusual, scoring three goals in a game is quite an achievement for any footballer. It was especially so for EG who had previously always played as a defender.

According to EG, his second memorable game had Saints as our opponents. On one occasion, he remembered overlapping down the left side, dribbling past a childhood friend from Paul's Lot, and was one-on-one with goalkeeper Mike Findlay who later became the national squad's goal keeper. His shot was weak, and failed to beat Mike. Later, he started his play in a similar manner but passed to Mike Bennett in front of the goal; and Bennett buried the ball in the net. That turned out to be the only goal in the game, and while he did not score it, he deserved great credit for successfully dribbling past the full-back, deciding to pass, and making an accurate pass. He expressed a similar opinion in his missive. Incidentally, in 2000, I had no such clear recollection of goals I scored or with which I assisted while playing for Eagles.

In 1975, after completing his residency at Lenox Hill Hospital in New York City, EG, his wife Betty, and his young son Erik moved to Arkansas where he set up a private practice. He now took advantage of the respite from intense studies to begin working on his interest in advancement of Caribbean people. He founded the West Indian Association of Arkansas, the first known organization devoted to the concerns of these nationals in the state. The Association sponsored cultural events at which they prepared and served foods reflecting members' culture, engaged in raising funds, and planned recreational and sporting events in parks. Also, EG took advantage of the opportunity to aid in recruiting tennis players to Harding University in Arkansas to improve their academic education and receive coaching in tennis. Recently, I learned from Dawn England that when she and her husband met EG in New Orleans, he told them that he and his family had driven to that city a few times for jazz festivals. Many "Bridge Boys" had an eclectic musical taste, jazz being just one musical genre that some of us favored.

Arkansas could not meet EG's strong desire to compensate his native land for the many opportunities his secondary school scholarship and the Island Scholarship had afforded him. Therefore, in 1984, he returned to St.Vincent to serve and show his appreciation. As might be expected, he soon experienced some of the difficulties of trying to provide first-class medical care in a developing country with a weak economy and an inefficient health care system. Nevertheless, outside of his medical practice, he threw himself with great vigor into activities that could make a difference in people's lives, including membership in the St.Vincent Tennis Association and the Grammar School alumni association.

Some readers who are familiar with tennis in St.Vincent around the 1960s and earlier may wonder at his choice of tennis as an area in which to devote time. An important part of the answer is that at U.W.I., Mona, EG began playing tennis, a sport that the economic and social circumstances of most of us put outside of our reach as we grew up in St. Vincent. He became an avid tennis player; and, in Arkansas, he was able to help Caribbean students obtain more education through tennis scholarships. It made sense that he should help to promote this sport when he moved his medical practice to St. Vincent.

The Tennis Association organized local junior and senior tennis tournaments, assisted in sending players overseas to tournaments, and staged tournaments involving overseas players in St.Vincent. In 1987, he managed a team of seven juniors who visited Trinidad for a competition. At some point, EG also began following international tennis closely, and when it was convenient, he was certain to attend some U.S. Open matches in New York. Every year, at the time of this tournament, my wife reminded me that EG was in attendance much more than in the distant past.

In 1988, a good job opportunity arose at Kings County Hospital in Brooklyn, New York, and EG accepted a position with that institution. In addition, however, he seemed more determined than ever, to continue to contribute to the country of his birth and to the wider Caribbean. He committed himself now to working individually and through Caribbean-linked organizations in the U.S. to achieve his patriotic goals. Unsurprisingly, one area that received his attention was better health care. With this in mind, he became involved with the health fair sponsored by Vincentian nurses in New York and furnished other assistance as discussed below.

EG became a member in good standing of several organizations with Caribbean interests. One of these was Friends of the St.Vincent Grammar School (FSVGS) which he served as president for several years. He also represented this organization on the Council of St.Vincent and the Grenadines Organizations, Inc. (COSAGO), was the Council's President for two years, and held other positions on its executive. These positions and his medical knowledge allowed him to influence the purchase of medical supplies to send as gifts for the main hospital in St.Vincent; and he used every convenient means to get such supplies to the island. For instance, Carlton Horne remembers performing the job of courier for some burn ointment EG asked him to deliver to the hospital. During his visit, Carlton's grandson turned over a lighted lamp and received some burns. The courier's grandson then became the first person to benefit from the gift of ointment. Certainly, EG richly deserved the award that COSAGO bestowed on him.

There are yet other organizations with Caribbean ties in which EG was an active member. One of these was the St.Vincent and the Grenadines American Medical Association. Another was the Guild of Graduates of the University of the West Indies which gave towards the improvement of education in the Commonwealth Caribbean. He also sat on the Editorial

Board of Carib-Beat Magazine which is published by the New York Daily News. Additionally, he represented the Vincentian community on the National Council of Caribbean Organizations, a group based in Washington, D.C. , and served as its Vice-Chairman.

The St. Vincent Grammar School was a major beneficiary of EG's commitment to service. He gave trophies to this school for Speech Night awardees, leading the drive to obtain trophies even after FSVGS in the U.S. started paying for them. And I have seen him in a photo with then Principal, Margaret Leacock in *The News* newspaper after handing over a television and VCR to the School in 2001. These were gifts from FSVGS while he served as president. Also, on one occasion, he used his own funds to purchase a set of track suits for the Grammar School's track and field team. Furthermore, he received the cooperation of companies that shipped "barrels" to St. Vincent to send many boxes of books to the School. Then in his typical meticulous fashion, on visiting St.Vincent, he sometimes traced the whereabouts of boxes that the Headmaster had not received. He knew that I would be interested because I sometimes sent him books by Penn State University Caribbean students traveling to New York. His acts of thoughtfulness and giving should be emulated by more among us

Here is some information from three letters of appreciation addressed to EG which further indicate the extent of his kindly disposition towards St. Vincent and the Grenadines. On June 13th, 1995, Lynette Glasgow wrote: "On behalf of the Ministry of Sport, I wish to thank you for your assistance in getting the St. Vincent Association to donate the sports equipment (stop watches, playground balls, and medicine balls) which the Division... will use in its sports program." On June 10th, 1996, Brenda Bibby, Principal of the Richmond Hill Government School wrote "to express our sincere gratitude to your organization for the donation of a television set." EG attended the Richmond Hill Primary School when he won his scholarship to the Boys Grammar School. And on October 1st, 1997, Noel Cooke, Permanent Secretary in the Ministry of Housing ... Sports ... etc., thanked him "for your contribution to Justin Haynes' participation in the World Athletic Games at Rhode Island University, and the Basketball Camp in New Jersey." It must have been particularly comforting to EG to learn from the Permanent Secretary that upon his return, Justin "has been sharing his expertise with the youths in the East St.George area."

Vincentian and wider Caribbean affairs seemed to fascinate EG. Whereas most of us are satisfied with others' reports, the scholar in EG led him to examine his environment himself. Thus, he shared with me systematic notes he took on various aspects of fruit trees that grow in St.Vincent, such as when flowers appear and the time of the year that they are ready to be eaten. In part of the introduction to these notes, he lamented the omission of a requirement in our Cambridge/GCE exam biology or botany syllabi that we obtain first-hand in-depth knowledge of these plants and their produce.

Sometimes EG supplemented the information he collected himself by sending me manuscripts produced by others. Among these are: Pauline Daniel's "A Tribute to Professor Orde Coombs," our friend who was in Upper Six when we were in Lower Six; the text of a speech by King JaJa of Opobo by Edward Cox; *Tropical Trees* and *Tropical Blossoms of the Caribbean* by Dorothy and Bob Hargreaves; and *The Trial of George McIntosh*, edited by Dr. Ralph Gonsalves and reprinted by EG and Norris Quow with permission. In their Acknowledgement, EG and Norris wrote: "We believe it is imperative that the generations today, and those yet unborn, be aware of this important epoch in the history of St.Vincent." This statement exemplifies the altruistic motivation underlying many of EG's actions.

Some of the reading materials that EG mailed to me show our joint interests and have become more valuable to me over time. One such consists of two pages of official weightlifting results from the 1959 Pan American Games. These games produced St. Vincent's first medal of any kind, silver, in a major international sports competition. The winner of that award was Maurice "Chuck" King, a friend of both of us and someone with whom I and many other friends had trained. I received the copy of these pages from EG in 2000, but I was surprised to discover from the pages about one month ago that Chuck had represented the West Indies Federation (1958-62). Among other notable results in those Pan American games were the Federation taking the three medals in the 400 meters in track and field, and gold in the 1600 meters relay.

Copies of articles from the *Trinidad Guardian* newspaper that he sent me have made me incredibly knowledgeable about some of the changes in the world of sport in Trinidad. For instance, a November 1996 *Guardian* article recalled that Rodney Wilkes was Trinidad and Tobago's first Olympic medalist, a silver in the 1948 Games. The *Guardian* article on Wilkes focused especially on his financial circumstances at the age of 72 which resulted in a government grant to him "to cover outstanding debts." In the article, Wilkes is said to have stated that after his return to Trinidad in 1948 he had received cocktails, medals and trophies, things with "no financial value." In a letter he enclosed with this article, EG's sensitivity to such situations led him to comment on how "athletes go from fame (1948) to old age and poverty in Trinidad." He also gave the names of some well-known Vincentian athletes he felt had been similarly treated. He would have been happy to learn that Wilkes now receives a regular stipend from Trinidad and Tobago's government.

I wonder whether it was his consideration of the plight of these athletes that prompted him to devote great effort to help Carlton Horne successfully organize a reunion of Vincentian footballers in St. Vincent. According to Carlton, someone who had originally promised to help had withdrawn at the last minute, claiming that it was too late to pull off the function. EG happened to be vacationing in St. Vincent at the time and with a determined effort he proved that person's pessimistic assessment wrong.

After our meeting in New Haven in 1968, EG and I were mostly separated by long distances. However, we occasionally had enjoyable face-to-face meetings in several different places. In the early 1970s, after I returned east from Seattle and joined the Penn State faculty, and shortly after the birth of Erik, we met in New York City. We also met in St.Vincent at carnival time in 1985; in East Brunswick, NJ, in 1990 at a youth soccer tournament at which I was coaching; at my older son's wedding in New Orleans; and in other places including my hometown for nearly 40 years, State College PA. This last deserves some elaboration because the circumstances were so unusual.

The Caribbean Students Association (CSA) of Penn State met every other Friday evening on campus. On one occasion, I invited the organization to meet at my home because a Vincentian, Gloria Regisford, was scheduled to make a presentation about St. Vincent. To create the right atmosphere, I planned to show a video with Vincentian scenery and carnival footage; and my wife, Glynis, offered Vincentian cuisine. About midway through the proceedings, I answered the doorbell and was pleasantly surprised to behold EG at the front door. He knew that our close friendship allowed and could only be strengthened by such amusing behaviors. Many years earlier, I had allayed any doubt about the esteem in which I held him by naming him my older son's godfather. With the focus of the CSA meeting being on St. Vincent, it was appropriate that EG who had given so much of his time, energy and money to help Vincentians should show up.

I have wondered whether EG's retirement to SVG in 2004 was his way of ensuring that he would draw his last breath in this land that he loved so dearly. I saw him twice in 2002 and on neither occasion was he in good health. I also heard about his weakened state from many friends; but he never once discussed with me the severity of his illness, telling me instead that he was returning home to spend some time with his aging mother. And his son, Erik, recently informed me that EG continued to repay Vincentians, this time by running a radio program every Thursday evening devoted to Vincentian history. Some pages he sent me in the 1990s from a manuscript about the centennial of our country's main library suggest that he may have been preparing for some time for just this opportunity to enlighten our people. Also, the discipline he chose for his broadcasts reminds me of his stated reason for reprinting the booklet about George McIntosh. Vincentians need to know their history. Furthermore, if he ever covered the Carnegie Library in the broadcasts, this is a place where he had spent many late afternoons reading and conversing with close friends while we attended the Grammar School and after.

EG had never been a complainer. Indeed, one Vincentian told me that EG in 2006 upbraided him for mentioning the hardships the friend had endured in his youth in St. Vincent. In a voice that seemed to hold some annoyance, he told this friend that he was not the only one who experienced such difficulty. Like EG, many of us who were his closest friends know firsthand of what he spoke.

Looking back now, our last set of contacts suggest that we were engaged in summarizing our relationship. Starting in 2002, we sauntered over familiar territory that we had often traveled together. In that year, he visited Glynis and me in Trinidad, and for the first time in many years we solved all of the world's problems. Later in the same year, we celebrated Vincy Mas on the streets of Kingstown, lingering near the Bridge to be introduced by Bridge Boy Spence to his niece. Then about two weeks before he died, we had our final phone conversation. He informed me of a 2006 Carnival band that included a repeat of an earlier Bridge Boys portrayal. Also, he mentioned a publication project intending to collect issues of the magazine *Flambeau* in three volumes. Interestingly, the first volume "Search For Identity", then already published, contained an article on The Bridge Boys, and we discussed its accuracy. Our conversation was a most fitting finale to our long friendship.

EG is survived by many people for whom he cared deeply. The day that I learnt of his death, I phoned his mother to offer some words of comfort. Her voice displayed the strength, composure and pride of a mother who knew that she had reared a special son who showed his gratitude in numerous ways. Yet the grief she felt at his passing may have hastened her own death about one year later. Then there is his son, Erik, on whom he lavished much attention. When surgery deprived EG of his voice for a while, we kept in touch through Erik; and I sensed in this son many of the decent traits of his father. Furthermore, as I discussed this essay with him, this son's rapid speech delivery marked him as an apple that has not fallen far from the paternal tree.

There are also many others with whom he had the kind of close relationship that should encourage them to honor his memory by continuously demonstrating in large or small ways his compassionate predisposition. I think of his former wife Betty, and of Margaret with whom he later formed a close friendship. I also know that he has a multitude of friends who will always remember the happy days we spent with EG in the Grammar School, in sessions on The Bridge, traipsing the streets of Kingstown, and sharing membership in The Eagles Club. We have every reason to understand the importance of always fighting against the propensity in stratified societies for one stratum to demonize another. We realize from personal observation that success in this dastardly enterprise may reduce the integrity of the society and increase the amount of retaliatory behaviors among the disadvantaged.

That some among the disadvantaged may prosper should not blind us to the hurt felt by perhaps a majority of the members of this group and the increased likelihood of negative consequences on the society. As importantly, undesirable treatment may prevent optimum development of many with inherent capacity to make significant contributions despite their less lofty origin. EG is a good example of someone who overcame the stigmatizing of his community of origin, and there are other Vincentians who have been able to rise above their humble origin. But there are yet others who were hampered by the societal reaction to their community of origin and to them as individuals. They, unfortunately, internalized the slurs thrown in their direction and fulfilled the prophecy that they "would amount to nothing."

I once received from EG a copy of Thomas Gray's "Elegy Written in a Country Churchyard." In my second year in the Grammar School, I had succeeded in memorizing all 32 verses as required by our English teacher. I do not now remember if EG told me why he sent it to me; but he might have found the following verse to have some relevance to his achievements, if only to remind us that failure may result from placing obstacles in a person's way rather than from a lack of potential and/or effort:

Full many a gem of purest ray serene
The dark unfathomed caves of ocean bear:
Full many a flower is born to blush unseen,
And waste its sweetness on the desert air.

Acknowledgement

I thank Arnold "Lydon" Charles, Betty King, Erik King, John Horne, Dawn England, and Carlton Horne for providing me with valuable information included in this essay. However, I alone am responsible for any weaknesses.

Dr. Roy Austin was US Ambassador to Trinidad and Tobago from 2001-08. He was also formerly a Professor of Sociology at Penn State University, Pennsylvania, USA for many years. He was born in St. Vincent and the Grenadines but is now retired and lives in Pennsylvania, USA.

Caribbean Trailblazers: St. Vincent and the Grenadines

,

9.   **CHRISTIAN I. "CIMS" MARTIN**
                         By
                   Roy. L Austin

A life of perseverance and reward

I am sure that many Vincentians have for many years known of "Cims" Martin. I am equally certain that with the exception of his contemporaries in the St. Vincent and the Grenadines Boys' Grammar School (BGS), few know that his full name is Christian Ivor Martin, his initials being the basis of the name by which he is widely known. It is his remarkable career in the civil service of his homeland that gave him such name recognition; and many of us who were his classmates at BGS are unsurprised by his copious contribution to the country, although most would probably have predicted during his secondary school days that he would be a legal luminary, an elected member of parliament or both. However, we knew that he possessed a brilliant mind and a determination to excel that did not waiver in the face of obstacles that would have proven insuperable to others. Instead, he always found a way to exert greater effort and emerge victorious.

This essay will reveal some of the awkward situations which Cims had to overcome on his way to leading the St. Vincent and the Grenadines civil service at an early age. A limited amount of the information that I shall provide derives from the days we spent together in BGS, sometimes as classmates, sometimes as friends hanging out on the Bridge and at the Carnegie Library or traipsing through Kingstown. Since our intense interactions ended after he left for the University College of the West Indies (UCWI) in the latter half of 1961, I depend primarily on his recollections. I may also have picked up tidbits over the years from conversations with mutual friends.

Cims was born to Mr. and Mrs. Bovell and Almena Martin (nee Boyea) on August 19, 1940 in Biabou, a rural town on the Windward side of St. Vincent and the Grenadines. In a short essay he published in the *Searchlight* newspaper about his early childhood, he says that he lived on Back Street in Kingstown in his maternal grandfather's home. At the time, before the migration of wealthier people to the suburbs, this was an ideal location of mostly middle- and upper middle-class homes. His home was one of the smaller homes in the block but was close to the three major churches and the primary schools associated with these churches. Furthermore, next door was the home of one of the well-known "white" families, the Sprotts, whose parties attracted persons of similarly high status, including the British Administrator. Cims recalls partaking of some of the excess food that remained after these social affairs.

Later, his parents moved to Sharpe Street, also sometimes referred to as the "last cross street," at the southern end of Kingstown. While this was a lower-class area, he seems to have been exposed to a greater variety of the cultural activities that occurred in Kingstown. He was now close to many of the colorful characters who were well-known in the city and who were teased to anger by adults and children alike. The Commandos steel band was next door, the beach was a block away; you could see the seines being thrown out of their boats and pulled onto the shore with their catch; large and smaller boats were built at nearby Carpenter's Yard; and a short walk took you to the "Pastures" where informal games of football and cricket took place. It was certainly a more exciting place than Back Street, although greater freedom to roam because of increased age may have brought more of the surroundings into reach.

Given the custom in Kingstown, one might expect that Cims would have learned to swim when he lived in this location. He did not. According to him, his parents strictly controlled his visits to the sea. Therefore, it was not until he was in the sixth form that he learned to swim after a few trips to the beach near the Anglican Primary School in Kingstown before he got ready for school in the morning. I am the person he asked to be present to save him from drowning, offer encouragement and a few tips on technique. He was a fast learner in this as in other instances when he set his mind on accomplishing a task.

When Cims was 10 years old, following his parents migration to Trinidad, he went to the rural town of Biabou on the Windward coast to live with his paternal grandmother, Dorcas Martin. He considers the primary school headed by Esau W. Ballah in that town to have been one of the best in the island. This headmaster, whom he regards as exceptional, ensured that students were drilled in Reading, Writing and Arithmetic. In this last subject, he opined that the level of instruction was such that he could have passed the School Certificate exam in Arithmetic by the time he left primary school. Also, Mr. Ballah expected students to know West's English grammar from cover to cover. This experience greatly aided Cims' excellent performance in Latin in secondary school.

Mr. Ballah's emphasis on rote learning extended to other subjects too. On Mondays, students read a chapter of their *Royal Reader* and were instructed to learn to spell the words listed at the end of the chapter. On Friday mornings, there was a written spelling test of 20 words; and on the afternoon of the same day, the headmaster strolled along a line of assembled students and allowed those with a maximum of three errors to sit. Other students received up to six lashes with the strap. The memorization of poems in this school allows Cims to be able to recite many lines of Thomas Gray's *Elegy Written in a Country Churchyard* even today. And he still remembers that the Turks captured Constantinople in 1453, but learned only in 1990 when he visited the city that Istanbul is the present name.

Undoubtedly, Cims' appraisal of Headmaster Ballah's merits as an educator is likely to be questioned by some readers. In support of Cims, I, too, attended a school where *Royal Readers* were used and feel that these books were superior to J. O. Cutteridge's *West Indian Readers* which served as the alternative readers. Also, an article in Trinidad's *Sunday Express* of August 27, 2000 covers some of the alleged weaknesses of *West Indian Readers* relative to the *Royal Readers*. Yet the former survived while the latter disappeared from Caribbean primary schools; and a favorable argument can be made for the Readers that reflected Caribbean culture rather than readers written for British children. Additionally, the extensive rote learning and harsh physical punishment that Cims regards as characterizing Headmaster Ballah will have few defenders among current educational experts. But it should be noted that most of the primary school headmasters with outstanding reputations were strict disciplinarians and rote learning was the order of the day.

Like the majority of youths in St. Vincent in the 1950s, the transfer to secondary school was not a foregone conclusion for Cims, despite the high quality of the education he received in Biabou. Even if Cims obtained acceptance into secondary school, someone had to pay the required fees and provide the financing to meet other needs such as clothing, food and textbooks. Fortunately, his paternal grandmother stepped in to ensure that he did not follow in the footsteps of her six sons, none of whom had attended secondary school. She blamed her husband, Samuel Martin, a primary school headmaster, for the failure of her sons and believed that God had placed Cims in her care to give her another chance to achieve a cherished goal. He realized that she could not afford the necessary financial outlay, but she insisted that he take the entrance exam, telling him that he was "not to reason why" because "God would provide."

The stubbornness evident in Grandma Martin's response suggests that she was responsible for a similar inclination that Cims would display in secondary school. She may have also reinforced a tendency that he had picked up in the Kingstown Methodist School earlier when Miss Nelcia John was headmistress of this primary institution. Cims has told me that this headmistress insisted that you courteously salute adults in appropriate situations. Her sister, Miss Louie John, my private primary school headmistress, imbued her students with similar politeness. The latter also frequently reminded us to "Try and try again boys/ and you'll succeed at last." It certainly would not be surprising to find that "Miss Nel" succeeded in imparting the same tenacity to some of her students.

Before Cims received the results of the Entrance Exam, he also displayed an uncommon boldness that must have aided his success later in life. He met Mr. Gordon, then Acting Headmaster of BGS, on the road and asked him if a C. I. Martin had passed the Exam. Mr. Gordon looked him over and answered in the affirmative. Cims saw that quizzical look and the response as indicating that he had performed well. Mr. Gordon later taught him mathematics in several forms, and according to Cims, his frequent comment communicated orally and in writing in his Report Book was that Cims "works too hurriedly so the quality of his work suffers." Some readers may regard this as a warning that overconfidence made Cims reckless and was hurting his performance.

The BGS headmaster when Cims entered was Mr. William Lopey, a person who generated both respect and fear in students. His constant reference to "my school" immediately made students aware of who was in charge in that school. And although at the time Mr. Lopey was close to retirement, Cims quickly developed a fear of rubbing him the wrong way. Imagine then the fear he instilled in Cims when he greeted his knock on the door with "Martin, come in, I'll cane you soundly." Cims managed to announce with quivering lips that he had not come for a caning but to register the five distinctions he had acquired in the promotion exam. Mr. Lopey took the papers and informed him that he had examined his grandfather when he was a teacher and found him to be very good at mathematics and English. He then asked Cims to convey his regards to his grandfather. Cims says that he was usually uncomfortable in Mr. Lopey's presence, never being certain whether he was due for a caning or about to be commended for the good work expected of him because of the good impression Mr. Lopey had of his grandfather.

The incident with Mr. Lopey occurred in Cims' second year in BGS when he was in Form 3B. Mr. Dacon, a teacher at the school was a regular visitor to Cyrus Emporium, a tailor shop that Cims also frequented. Mr. Dacon announced to the after-work assemblage at this shop that Cims was content to rank second in the form, helping students who bought him cakes at the Tuck Shop instead of attending to his own work. The laughter which erupted at his expense encouraged Cims to approach his work with greater seriousness; and that is how he earned the five distinctions. His reward was a double skip to Form 4A, a promotion hitherto unknown to me. Nor did I ever hear of such during the remainder of my years in BGS or thereafter. This skip also placed Cims again in the same form as his academically outstanding cousin Errol King who had been a classmate in their first year but had moved to a a higher form than Cims for his second year. He also became the classmate of several of us who had entered school at least one year before him.

Cyrus' Emporium played a very important role in Cims' academic life. Indeed, Cims acknowledges that, were it not for the many forms of assistance he received at that tailor shop, he may not have been able to complete his education at BGS. The proprietor was A.C. Cyrus who had risen from humble beginnings to become a successful businessman and serve as a nominated member of the island's legislature. One son who carried his name was arguably the most highly reputed surgeon in the country. At the time of writing this essay, his outstanding reputation remains intact although he has reduced the size of his practice.

After the workday ended, many employees of the tailor shop as well as others, all adults, gathered at the shop to discuss the issues of the day. Many, if not all, had the intellectual capacity to obtain a secondary school education. That they failed to do so is testament to the limited educational opportunities available at the time. And Cims, even when he was in his early teens, was a welcome presence in their midst. So, too, was C. St. C. Dacon, then a master at BGS.

Ironically, Cims suffered a major academic setback in form 4A in Mr Dacon's English exam at the end of the year. Mr. Dacon asked students to write an essay about "a memorable achievement or adventure." Cims wrote about Dr. Williams' election victory in 1956 in Trinidad and Tobago. Mr. Dacon said that Cims had chosen a subject that did not satisfy the stated requirement and failed him in English. Unfortunately, students failing English were not eligible to be promoted. Nevertheless, three teachers, including Mr. Millar the Headmaster, supported Cims; and in a compromise, he was promoted to the lower fifth form and could, therefore, take the Cambridge School Certificate Examination with other fifth formers whose pre-certificate exam results were acceptable.

During that year in the lower fifth form, Cims worked assiduously to show that he was as good a student as any other fifth former. I learnt only since I started working on this biography that he and two other students in the same form met frequently at one home to study mathematics together. They also acquired study-guides to help their preparation in other subjects. I am unaware that any other students were engaged in such activities, although it may have been occurring. Yet these three were full-fledged members of the Bridge-boys, a group that often congregated on the Tyrell Street bridge over the North River in Kingstown. Furthermore, those of us who were members usually took a time-out from our studies to relax on that bridge , discuss what we had studied during the day, challenge others to repeat a long speech from a Shakespeare play that was included in our exam syllabus, or answer questions from one of the subjects we were offering. I am, therefore, led to believe that they preferred that other members of the group remained ignorant of the extent of their studying or time has wiped this activity from my memory.

It may be at this time, also, that Cims told us that he often chose to sleep on the bare floor so that he could arise early in the morning to study for a few hours before school. He was clearly prepared to redeem himself after the embarrassing substandard ranking the previous year. This determination paid off handsomely, Cims being one of three BGS students to earn a Grade 1 School Certificate, the highest ranking possible on the examination.

An impressive result on the School Certificate exam was one criterion used for determining which student might be awarded an internal scholarship. I have no knowledge that Cims received even cursory consideration for this award because he had passed the upper age-limit set for this scholarship. The student who obtained the scholarship had obtained a Grade 3 certificate, had no apparent financial impediment, and had spent more years in the school than Cims; but he was sufficiently young to qualify.

I happen to have been the Editor of our Sixth Form newsletter which we named the *News and Views*. And my feeling that there was something unfair about the rules for awarding the internal scholarship led me to write an editorial expressing this opinion. It was Cims who told me that the Headmaster, Mr. Millar, felt that the matter should have been discussed with him, but he also remedied the situation. I have no recollection of being made privy to the manner in which he accomplished this until Cims provided the following details in the 2008 BGS Centenary magazine: "Of another of his pupils, he wrote to Cabinet saying that this particular boy was the poorest in the school and ought to be given a scholarship so that he could stay in the Sixth Form."

There were other boys in the Sixth Form who were known to belong to underprivileged families while many of the girls who joined us for certain subjects had middle-class origins. In the extremely class-conscious society in which we lived, some of us felt that these girls limited their interaction with the boys regarded as beneath them. I doubt that we openly discussed our feelings about this snobbery because our knowledge of social class relations in Vincentian society must have told us that these girls were simply following what their parents and peers expected of them. But we knew which boys received favorable treatment. Mostly, if not always, their parents' occupation and the appearance of the homes they occupied gave them, too, middle-class or near middle-class status.

If I am to believe the story that came from a girl who is likely to be knowledgeable about it, not even Cims' generosity in assisting some female classmates with Latin at the Kingstown Public Library saved him from being treated with condescension. Today, Cims bears no grudge towards any of these female classmates but admits that they were "standoffish." He also sees some redeeming attributes in some of the girls, describing one as kind and friendly and another as formal but wondering if we may have shown ourselves to be less than friendly to the girls.

I defer to Cims' perception of the behaviour of the Sixth Form girls and his claim that our unsociable demeanor may have contributed to the girls' aloofness. The subjects he took gave him a greater frequency and intensity of association with them than several of us had. Perhaps, familiarity in this instance bred greater understanding.

However, to show that our Sixth Form boys may not have misjudged our female counterparts, I exemplify the social class discrimination in male-female relationships with a student who migrated before reaching the Fifth Form. I had not seen this male student for more that 10 years when I ran into him in the United States. During the course of a long conversation between us, I inquired about his failure to ever return to the island. He forthrightly informed me of his strong feelings of having been a victim of class discrimination on the island, and stated that he had no intention of ever returning. He specifically mentioned the stuck-up behavior of some girls attending the nearby secondary school. But his response seems so extreme that some readers may argue that he was oversensitive.

At BGS, Cims put a considerable amount of time into playing cricket on the grass at the School ground. He went out of his way to borrow the School's cricket equipment, thereby ensuring that they were available for the informal competitions between teams selected at the vicinity. Not only did he replace Vannie Alexander as the "Grass King," but he also scored into the fifties for Lopey House seniors with his captain John Soso, a promising batsman and bowler, as his partner. He may not have become a star batsman but he had not wasted his time on the "Pastures" with the talented cricketers produced there. However, when Mr. Winston Baptiste was Games-master, he named Cims the captain of the School's second eleven in cricket. But Cims admits that Mr. Baptiste quickly realized that he was not suited to this task and rightly relieved him of it.

As a batsman, Cims showed no flash and made few big hits. He seemed unconcerned with how quickly his score mounted, being satisfied to defy bowlers to claim his wicket. It was an approach reminiscent of the way he lived his life, exerting maximum effort with his eyes firmly fixed on the prize and doggedness stamped on his face. If he were a Park-boy, as those of us who habituated Victoria Park were known, he may have defiantly declared that "one-one does fill basket."

As happens upon the death of close friends who pass away at an early age, Cims seems to have suffered unusual distress when John Soso suddenly passed away before he could fully realize his tremendous athletic potential. The two first met during the Entrance Exam, and the friendship that began then blossomed on the cricket field. During Cims' first term after leaving BGS, and shortly before the 1960 Windward Islands Interschools Tournament, John was on his way to the dentist when he and Cims' met near the latter's home. They chatted, John mentioning his hope for success in the tournament and Cims informing John that he was about to leave for Biabou. Hardly had Cims arrived at his destination when he heard that John had died of leukemia.

Cims' remarkable sadness, which I sensed from the detail he related to me, may have resulted from the relative recency of their strong bond. I knew John for many more years, having attended the same private primary school as he and three of his siblings did for several years. Also, until the year prior to his death, John and I were teammates on the BGS cricket and football first elevens. Furthermore, Cims was not known to show signs of emotion. Yet, I had no memory of specifics such as the cause of John's death. Now, I wonder whether the impassivity we saw in Cims was a carefully controlled cover intended to protect him from the injuries that might follow knowledge of known vulnerability.

However, sprinting was the area in which Cims displayed the greatest ability in sports; but his speed only manifested itself in the senior school. He believes that better nutrition provided by Mr. Cyrus and a spell of lifting weights, especially squatting, brought out his potential. By taking the sprint championship in Lower Six, he assured himself of selection to our School's 1958 Inter-schools team to compete in Dominica. But then he and four others missed the boat that picked up most of the Vincentian team when they were not notified of the proper time to return to the jetty to meet the late-arriving boat. These five made the trip to Dominica on a cargo boat and probably had a more luxurious ride that the remainder of the team

The Vincentian track and field team failed miserably, as did Cims. Whether he could have been more successful had he arrived earlier is open to speculation. His knowledge of sprinting and preparing for the same was rudimentary, as might be expected of a person who had suddenly burst on the track scene. But expressing himself verbally had never been a problem; and at the end of the tournament, the Headmaster selected him to give the vote of thanks. He must have made a good impression because many years later when he visited Dominica as a senior civil servant he was reminded of the speech. It should be noted that he was also BGS' sprint champion during his Upper Sixth Form year.

Other extracurricular activities in which Cims excelled in BGS include debating and essay writing. As a member of the Debating Society, he represented our school against teams from Trinidad and the Choate (now Choate Rosemarie Hall) School in Connecticut, USA. He became captain of his House, Lopey, and was elected a member of the student council shortly after this was established by Headmaster Millar. He also emerged as the top Vincentian essayist in the Lincoln Memorial Essay Competition sponsored by the U.S. State Department to honor the centenary year of President Lincoln's election.

In December 1959, Cims took the last of his Cambridge Higher School Certificate Exams, the equivalent of today's Advanced Level General Certificate of Education Examinations. Within a few days, he was working at a Christmas job at the General Post Office. And when the new BGS term started in January, he was a member of staff. He learned a few months later that he had successfully negotiated the perils of the Cambridge Exams and was qualified to enter just about any tertiary institution in the world.

During each of our two Sixth Form years, students from the Choate School in the U.S., a high status and expensive secondary institution (an American Prep school) that counts President John F. Kennedy among its alumni, visited BGS. For us, their most important activity was familiarizing us with the means of obtaining financial aid to enter American tertiary institutions. Prior to their visit, I doubt that any of us had given any thought to attending an American University since we had no idea of how this could be managed. Now, however, we were assured that acceptance especially to private Liberal Arts Colleges was possible, and so was the receipt of financial aid from the accepting college. But we needed to arrange for the establishment of a College Board examination center and register for the Scholastic Aptitude Test (SAT) and Achievement Tests.

By following the advice of the Choate School students, Cims gained acceptance by Carleton College in Minnesota, then ranked fifth among liberal arts colleges in the United States. At about the same time, the Ford Foundation gave the then Federal Government of the West Indies, 20 scholarships per year for two years specifically for the small islands and attendance at the University College of the West Indies (later University of the West Indies). Cims was awarded one of these latter and studied economics for his first degree in Jamaica. According to him, he chose UCWI because he wished to stay close to home and be with Vincentian students such as Leroy Mulraine, Kenneth John, Carlos Mulraine, Errol King, Baldwin King and Michael Joshua who had preceded him there.

I was not surprised by his choice but suspect that there were some additional considerations. Most of us who were Bridge Boys, his close membership group, must have known that Cims had a strong desire to work in St. Vincent at least partially for patriotic reasons. Indeed, a Barbadian student with whom he formed a close relationship at UCWI called him naïve for being obsessed with this desire. But as long as Cims maintained this inclination, attending Carleton would have seemed foolhardy. We had been sufficiently brainwashed into seeing an American education as inferior to a British education, and even a Canadian education. UCWI was affiliated with a British University (London), similarly organized and gave exams from that university. Therefore, a degree from UCWI would have been readily acceptable to Commonwealth Caribbean decision-makers. These same people may not even have heard of Carleton College. They would have been unlikely to regard even an Ivy League college in the USA as providing an education that was qualitatively equivalent to UCWI.

Another reason that Cims' choice made sense is that it is unlikely that he quite understood that he was likely to obtain financial aid for all of his undergraduate years rather than for just the first year alone. American private liberal arts colleges tend to inform students of their financial aid for only the upcoming year but do in fact fund the four undergraduate years, unless the student becomes academically ineligible. In the Commonwealth Caribbean, we had become accustomed to knowing that a scholarship would cover the years required to obtain a first degree.

During his years in Jamaica, Cims made time for physical exercise. He frequently jogged two miles to a pool, swam and then jogged back to the dormitory. Some evenings he played "softball" cricket , especially with the Guyanese students. He also joined other Vincentian students to play tennis, a sport that few Vincentians had the opportunity to enjoy when in St. Vincent, unless you had the good fortune to have an upper middle-class upbringing and the wealth that accompanies such status. Indeed, I do not remember a single boy in Cims' Sixth Form who played tennis during our years on the island. The cost of equipment and membership in the single club that would have accepted people of color was beyond what our pockets could afford. That so many Vincentian students in Jamaica turned to this sport when the opportunity arose probably reflects the strong but unstated feeling of deprivation concerning tennis, that existed during our youth.

I doubt that Cims won any tennis competitions in Jamaica, but he showed that his essay-writing skills remained intact. Every year, there happened to be an essay competition; and one year, he wrote an essay entitled *"The Two Cultures"*. Then he threw the pages in the waste basket after considering that students of English usually prevailed. A Trinidad neighbor who later became a Permanent Secretary condemned him for being stupid, retrieved the essay and entered it in the competition. That neighbor was kind enough to share the third place money with him.

At UCWI also, Cims benefited enormously from the subjects he studied and from some people with whom he came into contact. Among the subjects studied were Agricultural Economics, Accountancy, Applied Economics and Public Finance. He subsequently obtained a Masters of Science in Agricultural Economics. And in England some years later, he became an Associate of the Chartered Certified Accountants (ACCA). Given his goal to work in St. Vincent and the Grenadines, with an agricultural economy, and the jobs that he performed, he selected his subjects well. Or conversely, the subjects he studied fit him well for the occupational roles that he filled in later life.

As for important contacts, he entered UCWI at a time when the eminent economist Sir Arthur Lewis was Principal. With the aid of scholarships such as the 40 awarded by the Ford Foundation to the countries that later formed the Organization of Eastern Caribbean States (OECS), Sir Arthur was presiding over the rapid expansion of the institution. Guyana, too, then still a part of the University, had sent many former teachers to study social science.

And the PNM government in Trinidad had sent many mid-level civil servants to study Economics. Several of these students attained high government positions, some becoming Permanent Secretaries. Cims developed lifelong friendships with these persons of substance from throughout the Commonwealth Caribbean. These friendships proved to be particularly important when he later became involved in the founding of the Caribbean Community (CARICOM) and the Caribbean Development Bank (CDB). In negotiations for the establishment of these key Caribbean institutions, he and others were dealing with friends from university days or their colleagues. Among these friends was Edwin Carrington, the long serving Secretary General of CARICOM, with whom he went through the Economics faculty.

Two events that occurred when Cims returned to his homeland for vacation are worthy of recall. On one occasion, he took a date to the beach known as Breakers or Sand Bay on a Sunday afternoon. Theo Providence and his date were the only other persons there. Cims was alone in the sea when Theo and his friend began leaving. Suddenly, Cims heard Theo shouting from the top of the hill and saw him gesticulating furiously. Eventually, Cims realized that a large shark was swimming between him and the beach. He made a dash for the shore and got there before the shark could attack him. It happened that the Eagles Club in which Cims and almost all Bridge-boys held membership were playing a football match late that afternoon. When we reached the Bridge after the game, that life-threatening escapade made Cims the butt of much teasing. We told him, jokingly of course, that he almost lost his life because he neglected to be at the field to support his club. Members of the Bridge faced such harassment whenever they provided other members with the opportunity to try to irritate them.

The second incident was one that threatened the very existence of the Bridge-boys. One evening, a police officer whom we all knew well, ordered us in the sternest of tones to remove from the Bridge. This was surprising especially because he had usually been quite friendly and was often given a ride to his relatively distant home by a member who lived in the same area. I wrote a letter to the then Chief of Police explaining that we congregated on the Bridge because our homes were inconvenient for this activity. I also listed the alternatives as places where we could engage in drinking alcohol or gambling. The Chief was out of the island but his Deputy invited two of us to discuss the matter with him. Cims happened to be home on vacation, was known to the Deputy and was expected to be a good negotiator. Suffice it to say that the Deputy, a reasonable man who understood the limited recreational facilities available to young men like us, told us to continue to stay away from our haunt for about a month and gradually return. Meanwhile he promised to discuss our situation with the Assistant Chief who had given the order to remove us. It was a complaint from the owners of a nearby home that we were too loud that caused our removal. We kept our word to lower our voices.

At UCWI, Cims was befriended by a Welshman, Dr. David Edwards, Professor of Agricultural Economics. As soon as he completed his final examination, Dr. Edwards took him to Antigua for three months as his research assistant. There he met Dr. Lionel Thomas, an Antiguan of African descent who had studied Veterinary Medicine at Guelph University at the same time as St. Vincent's Dr. Earle Kirby. He was also a confidant of Vere C. Bird Sr. and contributed greatly to Antigua's development. Cims would meet him again at CARICOM and CDB meetings.

From Antigua, Dr. Edwards went to UWI, Trinidad to establish the Department of Agricultural Economics and Cims accompanied him. There Cims completed an M.Sc. in Agricultural Economics. His thesis, entitled *The Role of Government in the Agricultural Development of St. Vincent,* involved a review of all major initiatives by the Government between 1900 and 1960. Among these were the establishment of the Agriculture Department, the land reform of 1901, the Land Settlement Scheme of 1945, agricultural credit societies, a feeder roads program, The Banana Board, The Arrowroot Board, The Marketing Board, the Sugar Agreement and the Oils and Fats Agreement. Therefore, when Cims obtained employment at the Agriculture Department shortly thereafter, he was already familiar with important information about the place.

Trinidad was an ideal location to work on his thesis. The faculty of Agriculture in that island had succeeded the Imperial College of Tropical Agriculture (ICTA) which in turn had succeeded the Imperial Department of Agriculture that the British set up in 1901 with a branch in each Eastern Caribbean island. In St. Vincent, it was the predecessor of the Department of Agriculture.

For whatever reason, the Imperial Department of Agriculture had conducted considerable agricultural and economic experiments in St. Vincent, leaving reports that were unavailable elsewhere. As Cims used them, he realized that the paper on which the reports were written was already disintegrating and would probably be irretrievably lost. He completed his thesis in 1966 and published it in a limited edition. It has been extensively used by other researchers, often without attribution.

We cannot bring Cims' time in Trinidad to an end without recounting two especially noteworthy occurrences. Most importantly, for the first time in some years, he was afforded the opportunity to visit his mother on several occasions. She was then living in Diego Martin, a suburb not far removed from the capital city of Port of Spain. She later moved to the USA where she passed away many years later. Despite the closeness of our friendship and years of association on the Bridge, I do not remember hearing him ever mention her or his father. It is only recently in response to my question about how his years in BGS were financed that he stated that his mother tried to cover his expenses despite her marginal financial circumstances. But she was often late in meeting these obligations. At some time, he did come to understand that his father's irresponsible lifestyle was the major cause of the difficulties his mother faced. I resist the temptation to speculate upon the possible effects of parental absence at an important stage of his development.

The other occurrence involved obtaining a visa to the USA through the U.S. Embassy in Trinidad. He was one of three students chosen by the Embassy as most promising and likely to be high achievers. These students received a six-week tour of the U.S,, staying in tertiary institutions such as North Carolina State University in Raleigh where they met then Governor Sanford. At Florida State University they almost got arrested for drinking sherry on campus. They did not realize that students were prohibited from so doing.

Upon leaving the University, Cims was appointed to the very senior Civil Service post of Marketing Officer. He would have been in charge of the Marketing Corporation, but the then Administrator Hywell George, an Englishman, felt that he had insufficient experience and he was not allowed to take up the job. Also, the incumbent, for reasons on which Cims could only speculate, did not wish to retire. Like his father before him, this "white" person who had lived in the large house next to Cims for several years, had once held the position of Chief Secretary, the most senior position in the Civil service and outranked only by the Administrator. The small house in which Cims lived was owned by his maternal grandfather, James Boyea, who had been the messenger at Barclays Bank. Was the incumbent aghast at the idea that the little black boy from next door could grow up to take away his position?

The British Administrator's decision also requires a comment. A Master of Science degree was not a commonplace achievement in St. Vincent when Cims returned from the University. Even the Bachelor of Science degrees and Bachelor of Arts were held by few persons. Besides, the subjects that Cims had studied certainly suggest that he would have been a more competent Marketing Corporation Manager than the incumbent. The latter's educational qualifications were inferior and his many years of experience in the Civil Service were virtually irrelevant to the job he was performing.

It was Henry Williams, then Chief Secretary, who had appointed Cims to the Marketing Officer post. He, his brothers Frank and Moulton, brothers Norris and Saville Cummings, Hugh Hamlet, Dennis Crichton, G.F. "Jakey" Jack, and Earnest Laborde were the first of the island's descendants from enslaved Africans to have attended secondary school, BGS. They had performed well in secondary school but with only one scholarship given to enter university every three years, they had not realized their full academic potential. However, they joined the Civil Service and according to Cims "became one of the finest batch of Civil Servants the island would ever see. They embodied all the qualities of good Civil Servants: unfailing courtesy, mastery of the English language, encyclopedic knowledge of the Civil Service, its procedures, rules and regulations, analytic ability and thoroughness. It was my good fortune to have been apprenticed to these men, in particular Dennis Crichton and Moulton Williams."

Instead of going to the Marketing Board, Cims was sent to the Ministry of Agriculture where he became economic advisor to the new Minister James Mitchell, later Sir James Mitchell. That posting was "a blessing in disguise," helping greatly to rapidly advance his career. At the time, the Caribbean Free Trade Association (CARIFTA), the forerunner of CARICOM, was being organized. James Mitchell, as Minister of Trade, was St. Vincent's representative on the regional committee entrusted with the preparatory work, and Cims was his Civil Service advisor. The Civil Servants usually met first and prepared a report that would be examined and approved by the Ministers.

Minister Mitchell and Cims realized quite early that the small islands would receive little benefit from the CARIFTA/CARICOM agreement since, unlike the larger islands, they had little to sell to the region. One exception for St. Vincent is that it shipped sweet potatoes to Trinidad every week. The St. Vincent Marketing Board bought potatoes from small farmers and sold them through an agent, an American, who kept the Board waiting for unreasonably long periods of time before paying. Meanwhile, the Board was borrowing from the bank to pay the farmers cash on delivery; and bank charges were eating up most of the margins.

In one preparatory meeting, the St. Vincent representative requested that the CARIFTA/CARICOM agreement include a Protocol to facilitate the sale of agricultural produce by the small islands to the large ones. And Cims was asked to return to the next meeting with a draft Protocol. Guided by the agreement on marketing Oils and Fats, which Cims had evaluated as part of his thesis, he got the Protocol through the Preparatory Committee despite their rigorous examination. St. Vincent immediately started selling its sweet potatoes directly to the Trinidad Central Marketing Agency and receiving its money promptly. Trinidad, for its part realized that it had nothing to gain by late payment of a small sum of money to St. Vincent when it wanted to sell industrial goods to St. Vincent.

Next, St. Vincent discovered that it could profitably grow carrots and sell them to Guyana. This crop was now promoted among farmers and the government provided seeds and technical advice. The people of Rose Hall showed particular interest, and carrots were sold to Guyana's Central Marketing Agency. But carrots require careful rotation to prevent soil exhaustion and soil disease. Sadly, business was so good that the farmers failed to rotate the crop as advised and the boom did not last.

However, the Marketing Board thrived. It arranged to ship ginger, sweet potatoes and other root crops to England by the boats taking bananas to that country weekly. At the same time, it started retailing produce in St. Vincent and soon became a full supermarket. Eventually, it was one of the biggest businesses in the island.

By this time, the Administrator who thought that Cims was too inexperienced to be Marketing Officer realized that he had erred. Therefore, he recommended that Cims be appointed the head of the Civil Service, either as the Cabinet Secretary or Financial secretary since with the arrival of the Ministerial system, the post of Chief Secretary had been abolished. Cims was therefore appointed Cabinet Secretary and Permanent Secretary to the Prime Minister with a seat on the Marketing Board, eventually becoming its Chairman. He was quite pleased with this turn of events because the changes justified Henry Williams' judgment and his faith in him. He continues to show his appreciation to Mr. Williams' eldest child, Ms. Jeanne Horne, former Headmistress of the Girls' High School, in an unusual way. When she inquires about his action, he never gives her a straight answer.

The success of the Marketing Corporation so pleased St. Vincent's major aid Donor, the UK Ministry of Overseas development, that they gave the island the building which now houses Food City. Cims gives credit for the success of the Corporation at its zenith to the then General Manager, Clinton Antrobus, and his staff. This staff included Baldwin Johnson, Rufus Pemberton, "Parson" Thomas and Howard. He also mentions an Indian national, Indar Pardasani, who served as accounting advisor. Cims says that the Organization went downhill after these employees moved on.

Another aspect of Cims' contribution to Caribbean integration was involvement in preparatory work for setting up the CDB, partly to help the small islands to benefit from integration. While large borrowers could deal directly with this bank, smaller borrowers required an intermediary organization in each island.. Therefore, he assisted the government with starting a new state-owned organization, the Development Corporation, and became its first general manager. This Corporation focused on founding the industrial estate at Camden Park and on making loans to small entrepreneurs. The Corporation lasted for about a quarter of a century. The industrial estate, however, continues to function and flourish. Several of the small entrepreneurs went on to bigger things.

The Development Corporation was involved in projects other than those financed by CDB. It undertook the disposal of land the Government had reclaimed on the Kingstown waterfront some years previously and in which Cims had been deeply involved. The Corporation also undertook the management of two farms totaling some 6,000 acres and known as the land settlement estates. These not only treated their workers and retirees well but for the first time in the island's history, both farms were profitable. The bigger farm, Richmond Vale, profited from the cultivation of traditional crops such as bananas and coconuts. The smaller one, Wallilabou, which is much nearer to Kingstown, grew many vegetables which were sold through the rapidly expanding Marketing Corporation.

The Board of the Development Corporation may have had the vision of what was possible, but the man who made it all happen on the estate was Vivian Delicia. Of Portuguese origin, he hailed from the Biabou area and had an innate managerial propensity. Equally important, he had attended the Glen School, an educational institution that in its earlier days prepared boys for practical pursuits. Later, it tended to try to turn at-risk boys into useful citizens. This school had a beneficial effect on many of its students and they went on to make significant contributions to St. Vincent.

In 1972, the Government changed hands, and the new Administration under James Mitchell showed no interest in having Cims' service. Therefore, with assistance from the British Aid Office, he went to the United Kingdom to complete his professional qualification in Accountancy, the ACCA. He returned to St. Vincent in 1974 following another change in Government. Now he was appointed Financial Secretary, a post subsequently renamed Director-General of Finance. One consequence of the appointment is that he became the liaison officer between the government of St. Vincent and its main aid donor, the British government.

Cims was quite happy to have landed this job. He readily describes himself as an Anglophile, an identification that owes a great deal to the assistance he received from Welch Professor David Edwards during his university days both in Jamaica and Trinidad. As importantly, in October 1968, he married a British national who is Caucasian. At this time, many Vincentians of obvious and not so obvious African descent who were influenced by the Black Power movement saw Caucasians from England as colonial oppressors and racists. Unsurprisingly, certainly to those familiar with the racial views and behaviors prevalent from the mid-1960s into the early 1980s in the Caribbean, several Vincentians whom Cims considered as friends or who were likely to become so, had his wife's race been otherwise, instead openly condemned him for his interracial marriage. One agricultural officer whom he barely knew was sufficiently emboldened to approach him and call him stupid. Cims rightly felt that his choice of a mate was his own business.

As might be expected, Vincentians were not all of one mind with respect to Cims' marriage. A few of his grammar school contemporaries and others with whom he had a longstanding relationship defended his prerogative to marry the woman of his choice. The Chief Minister, Mr. Milton Cato, and other Government Ministers respected his decision. So, too, did several senior public servants. Of course, the group of men at Cyrus' tailor shop fully supported his decision. Among other factors that reduced the burden of

Christian Ivor "Cims" Martin

the disapproval his marriage had stirred up is that his work kept him rather busy, especially the setting up of CARICOM and CDB. Additionally, he was also busy outside of his Government job since he lived in a rented house surrounded by five acres of land that he farmed and used to raise pigs.

After spending eleven years in the USA, I returned home early in 1975 and immediately learned of this distressing state of affairs. With careful thought, our friends and countrymen would have realized that their own behaviour bore all of the hallmarks of the racial discrimination and racism they so vociferously condemned in Caucasians. Also, I have never heard of any such racial animosity expressed toward other Vincentians who had made Caucasian foreigners their wives not long before Cims did this; and some of these couples were living in St. Vincent at the time. Furthermore, Cims' wife, Cathy, had left her homeland and, far from oppressing anyone, was making a contribution to the education of secondary students on our island.

Moreover, Vincentian culture possesses sufficient admonitions that should have aided avoidance of the egregious errors we made in this instance. We should have learnt to keep our mouths out of "husband and wife business." And we must have learnt to allow mature people to make their beds because they are the ones who would lie in it. In any event, judged by the longevity of the marriage under consideration, this couple may have made a more comfortable bed than some of their critics.

Sadly, prejudice and discrimination lack the rational thinking that results in treating people as individuals rather than as members of groups, defined negatively because they possess certain physical traits. People of African descent who have so often been placed in disadvantaged positions because of our color and other physical characteristics, should have used the opportunity of an interracial relationship to show moral superiority over the racists we abhor.

It is doubly ironic that the British Government's Ministry of Overseas Development in 1974 supplied Capital and Technical assistance to St. Vincent; and Cims was St. Vincent and the Grenadines' primary representative in negotiations with the British. That is, the people against whom virulent anti-racism activists in St. Vincent railed soon served as the cornerstones of St. Vincent's development program.

British aid was given through the British Development Division's (BDD) office in Barbados. School-building, low income housing and feeder road construction to facilitate growth of the banana industry were among the outstanding Capital projects. And significantly, the gift of a ferry and landing facilities in the major islands of the Grenadines had a remarkable demonstration effect. The ferry lasted a few years but local entrepreneurs caught on and started buying second hand ferries in Scandinavia. Today, there are some six ferries plying the waters between the islands constituting SVG.

Technical assistance was provided by experts in agriculture, education, engineering and finance who staffed the BDD and by short-term experts from the UK. The experts collaborated with local technical officers to design and implement development projects. In this era, SVG had realistic annual Capital Budgets, funds being provided by the UK, and projects being both ongoing and new.

However, the British disliked recurrent budgetary assistance, and this led to problems for the SVG Government almost from the first day of Cims' appointment as Director-General. In the first year, the Government experienced difficulty paying the salaries of the Public Service. To prevent a recurrence, the Government took three major steps. Firstly, in the recurrent budget, it increased the rates of existing taxes and introduced new ones. It also froze public sector wages and curtailed foreign travel. Secondly, since the existing commercial banks had refused to lend it money and it had no other mechanism for borrowing, the Government set up the National Commercial Bank with funds from the National Provident Fund (subsequently upgraded to the National Insurance Scheme) which it had established some years previously.

Thirdly, the Government sought to develop the economy by expanding the manufacturing sector. It had earlier reestablished the sugar industry and started a milk industry. It also promoted the development of other industries by the private sector, providing incentives including tax holidays, duty free imports, space on the industrial estate and loans. The domestic market was also expanded by becoming a part of the Eastern Caribbean Common Market.

Between 1975 and 1978, the economy grew at the rate of nine percent per annum. By 1976, recurrent revenues had increased by 61 percent and recurrent expenditure by only 21 percent. Therefore, for the first time in many years, SVG had a surplus on the recurrent budget; this, after being unable to pay salaries in 1974. Yet, the Labor Party's restoration of the sugar industry was not regarded as economically valuable by the National Democratic Party (NDP) that replaced Labor. Cims claims that sugar was on the verge of making a profit, a position that is consistent with Labor Party statements but at variance with the position of James Mitchell, the NDP leader who was about to become Prime Minister. I lack the knowledge to make a well-informed choice between these opposing views. But the NDP Government that followed the Labor Party Government that had reintroduced sugar dismantled this industry. Also, the Unity Labor Party Government, consisting of several members of the previous Labor Party, had supported the return of sugar during their successful campaign to replace the NDP in 2001. But after 10 years in power they show no interest in resurrecting a sugar industry.

The freeze on the salaries of public servants' wages was the main reason for the limited increase in expenditure. But they had not received an increase since 1970 despite rampant inflation. To compensate these employees, Government granted a salary increase of 30 percent, leading to a deficit of $5.4 million or about 16 percent of total expenditure. To make matters worse, the volcano erupted around this time. Cims realized that with a small disaster-prone economy SVG had a hard row to hoe. Besides, after five years as Director General, he now found that he had developed hypertension. Therefore, he tendered his resignation from the Civil Service.

In appreciation of his efforts, the Head of the British Aid Office in Barbados had arranged a three-month UN assignment concurrent with his Civil Service Job. Cims informed him that he could not accept his offer because he did not wish to be seen getting money from outside while imposing austerity on his colleagues. In any case, once he declared the UN earnings for tax purposes, he would receive little of it. The Deputy Head of the overall UK aid Ministry then visited and offered to help him obtain a UN job, reminding him to take care of his finances then, because when he aged no one would care about his contributions.

Cims now started another phase of his occupational career. He joined the Project Centre Planning (PPC) staff of the University of Bradford in Yorkshire, UK. The Centre, headed then by Professor David Edwards under whom he had studied at UWI, trained experienced graduates from developing countries in project preparation and evaluation. Its main offering was a three-month course but some students took a Masters degree. Cims ran mainly courses relating to agriculture as well as the finance component of other lecturers' courses. Since some of the training took place overseas, he was able to visit several developing countries, especially in Africa. The practical nature of the courses also had him taking participants to farms and agro-processing facilities in the UK.

Cims benefited greatly from his four years at Bradford, particularly with regard to Project-assessment, presentational issues, knowledge of the world and cricket. His knowledge was put to good use in authoring a monograph entitled *A Manual on Project Planning for Small Economies.* He also gained much knowledge simply by interacting with several able Englishmen and one Indian on the staff. Travel and the project-materials that students took to England from their countries provided added information.

As for cricketing knowledge, this derived from being in Yorkshire where the game is taken seriously and the time Cims spent watching the game at grounds and on television. He regrets not having this exposure in his youth and remembers an embarrassing incident that he experienced while living in Bradford. It involved English wicketkeeper David Barstow's comment about sharing a rather rough practice ground in St. Vincent with pigs. Cims vowed to correct this problem if he ever got the chance. In fact when he did return to St Vincent years later and became Chairman of the Authority responsible for garbage disposal, a proper landfill was established at Diamond and the facility next to the cricket pitch closed.

The United Nations Industrial Development Organization (UNIDO) in Vienna, Austria was Cims' next stop. This organization's mandate is to promote industrialization in developing countries by identifying projects and trying to get developed countries to fund them. He was assigned to Africa and visited eight countries in his twelve years in UNIDO: Gambia, Kenya, Sierra Leone, Somalia, Sudan, Swaziland, Tanzania and Uganda. Cims has some interesting memories from this posting, including an encounter with racism in Johannesburg, learning of the rapid death of some AIDS victims with whom he was acquainted and contracting Lyme disease.

The racism incident occurred in South Africa which he passed through on his way to Swaziland. On a train to Johannesburg he was advised to travel first class as he looked like a foreigner and could easily come to grief in any other class. He got to Johannesburg strolled around and even visited a township without any problems from his fellow blacks. On his return to his hotel, however, after preparing for departure, a white man approached him and said "I wonder where this 'kaffir', all dressed up, thinks he is going Another white man then came up, enquired who he was and suggested that he ignore the other man and issued him an invitation to visit him in Port Elizabeth the next time he was in South Africa.

. The country he favoured most was Uganda which he visited on several occasions. Unfortunately, this very beautiful land had not yet recovered from the ravages of the Amin years. Moreover, AIDS was rife. What troubled him most was how often he would deal with an official only to learn that the person had died by the time Cims was back in Vienna. The senior ranks of the civil service were being decimated. Particularly poignant was the case of three children for whom he used to take presents. One day he turned up and the children were not there. The official explained that they were his brother's children .Both parents had contracted AIDS while at university and the children now also had it.

Although he was not aware of any encounters that should give him AIDS, Cims was scared out of his wits when his right hand began withering and his doctor kept sending him for AIDS tests. A UN nurse sent him to a leading neurologist who relieved his anxiety by diagnosing his ailment as Lyme disease. He had been bitten by the tick which transmits the disease when he was hitting tennis balls against a wall at the back of the court by himself. The location, as everyone but he knew, was infested with the ticks. He was lucky to contract this disease shortly after a method of treatment had been developed. The neurologist prescribed this treatment and visits to a physiotherapist. A female colleague then advised him that he could reduce the visits to the physiotherapist once he became familiar with the exercises.

Soon, he was able to save some money by performing the exercises in a Jacuzzi and he recovered. He remains grateful to these three white women, including the physiotherapist, who played key roles in getting him through separate phases of this ordeal. But he had come to expect this kindness from Austrians, some being more willing to help a black than a white foreigner.

There were many things that Cims liked about Austria including the people's congeniality, their punctuality, their music and the suburban restaurants. There was also easy access to the rest of Europe and he took the opportunity to visit Czechoslovakia, Yugoslavia, France, Germany, Hungary, Italy, Poland, Spain, Switzerland and Turkey. These trips to Europe were not without their hilarious moments. The one which seems to have stuck most vividly in Cims' mind occurred on his first trip to Yugoslavia. On presenting his passport, the immigration officials did not know what to do as they had not seen a Vincentian passport before. Then one officer, homing in on the Grenadines bit of our country's name, shouted 'Grenadines! Grenada! Member of the Socialist block, let him in immediately'.

In the United Nations, Cims had also learnt much about bureaucracy and the behaviors of people from different nations. And he had faced the occasional ironic situation such as having a Japanese colleague complain that Cims' English was so poor he could not understand a memorandum Cims had written to him. The Indian secretary had to inform the Japanese that his rudimentary English was the real reason for his difficulty. Cims had ignored a warning from a Trinidadian friend that he should only write in basic English.

Since he had worked in Austria with the UN for more than ten years, Cims was entitled to permanent residence. Nevertheless, he took early retirement from UNIDO in 1996 and returned to SVG sometime afterwards. It was not long before the new Unity Labor Party, formed from the older St. Vincent Labor Party (SVLP) and another existing party (the MNU) requested that he join their administration in a consultant capacity as Fiscal Adviser. All of his Public Service work in SVG had been performed when the SVLP was in power, and he seems to have been deeply loyal to this party and its political leader and Prime Minister, Milton Cato. His feelings about this man and the party are obvious in the way he opens a sentence in a recent newspaper article as if he were talking about a revered religious personage: "In the days of Milton Cato, of blessed memory, ..." (*Searchlight, April 15, 2001, p.8)*. It is, therefore, not surprising that he acceded to the request and has continued to hold many important positions in this government.

From 2001 to early 2011, there is a multitude of the ways in which Cims has contributed to the governing ULP in SVG. He set up and ran the Cabinet Committee on the economy during a period when SVG experienced one of its strongest fiscal situations ever. At this time, he was associated with the construction of a new prison at Belle Isle which the Government offered to name after him. He firmly declined that honor. He served as Chairman of the SVG Development Bank and successfully campaigned to have it merged with the National Commercial Bank with the expectation that the larger entity would be more viable. He became Chairman of the International Financial Services Authority (IFSA) which licensed and regulated offshore entities such as banks and insurance companies. He was successful in reducing the number of registered banks from 40 to six to reduce the likelihood that these banks which are known to engage in Pyramid schemes would tarnish the country's reputation.

Next, Cims became Chairman of the Central Water and Sewerage Authority (CWSA). In this position, he oversaw the construction of a large catchment area in North Windward, ensured an increase in water rates and discouraged any talk of privatization. But his main interest was garbage disposal, CWSA's other main business, which had fascinated him after collecting compost from such a facility in Vienna. Now, with research having shown that 50 percent of the garbage from throughout the island could be composted, he concentrated on having compost produced at Diamond, one of two garbage collection sites. He expects compost production to have economic and environmental benefits, providing fertilizer for the vegetable production that has replaced bananas, and removing unsightly deposits of refuse.

'The Prime Minister normally represents SVG on the Board of the Mustique Company. However, on coming to Office he asked Cims to take his place. Mustique is a Grenadine island owned by wealthy foreigners, mainly from the UK, North America, France and Venezuela. The owners have built homes there. Through taxes, goods purchased and jobs created the Company brings in millions to SVG .It is the largest going concern outside the government itself. The Company elects its Board from the property owners and they run the island, seeing to land sales, public utilities, transport, villa rentals and physical planning. Cims says that the Company was so fastidious about its relationship with government that he spent most of his time on the board learning how these very successful businessmen go about things and trying to transfer what he learnt to boards on which he sat in SVG. He seems to have even managed to persuade a few of them to contribute their time and money to Vincentian causes.

Another chairmanship, that of National Properties (NP) fell into Cims' hands when the previous Chairman suddenly resigned. Here he renewed a long standing partnership with Harold (Hally) Dougan, NP's Chief Executive Officer. Hally and he, had many years previously worked together at the Development Corporation. Hally, according to Cims, is one of those Vincentians who served SVG in a totally selfless manner.

NP was established to manage some of Government's properties, and the previous Chairman's success with farming and real estate after a stint in the UK's military suggested that he was quite suited to the task. He was a BGS contemporary of Cims and this author, my cricket teammate on the BGS First Eleven, our Inter-schools Tournament teammate in Dominica in 1958, and a fellow camper with the Cadet Corps in Barbados in the same year. In 1958 also, prior to our Dominica visit, his father had organized a cricket match between our BGS team and one from his coconut estate and had served us a large and delightful meal. It is disturbing to learn that this genuinely amiable person was continuously attacked on the basis of his Caucasian race and descent from the planter class. Apparently, we make exceptions to doing "unto others as you would have them do unto you."

And what has National Properties accomplished? It has raised about $70 million EC for the construction of the international airport still underway. It has constructed four buildings, two of which have been sold. It is negotiating to redevelop the site formerly occupied by Bottlers Ltd. It manages the Campden Park and Diamond industrial estates, the Reclamation site, Ottley Hall and the Cobblestone property. Additionally, it is involved in a farming project at Peter's Hope although this estate and Mt. Wynn have been earmarked for tourist development. The farm project, comprising 10 green houses, a poultry unit and some arable acres is covering its direct costs but no part of management costs. But this last would be present even if the land had not been farmed. Presently, the plan is to expand the area farmed so that the project can become fully viable.

Furthermore, several years ago, Government acquired a 4,000-acre plantation and expended a sizeable amount of money on it with the intention of conducting major land reform. While awaiting evolution of a satisfactory plan, NP has obtained 80 acres with the intention of establishing a theme park and a farm in a phased development. Currently, 10-acre blocks have been planted in a variety of crops including soursop, plantains, breadfruit, mango, carambola and a variety of coconut that is easily harvested and suitable for drinking and coconut oil. The farm is to be the production nucleus of an agro-processing unit, Vincyfresh, another of NP's default projects.

Another NP project involves a building constructed by the Ministry of Agriculture in which food processing equipment was installed. When the project was slow to get off the ground, NP took over the building and is using it as a base to purchase produce for the export market and to engage in some agro-processing. WIBDECO, the company that markets Windward Islands' bananas in the UK, later expressed an interest in the project and has now joined in a company with NP to operate the facility.

NP has also been trying to operate the supermarket set up by the Marketing Corporation and mentioned earlier. It has now been agreed to privatize it.

To summarize, Cims' grandmother's faith and tenacity encouraged him to sit the Entrance Examination to BGS although he had no idea how his school expenses would be met. While there, he had many anxious and embarrassing moments when his mother was late in sending what little she could afford to keep him in school. Mr. A. C. Cyrus helped him to stay in secondary school in unspecified ways; and although he occasionally faltered, he worked indefatigably and utilized unusual methods to recover and enjoy the rewards of an exceptional promotion and an outstanding School Certificate performance. This latter, with assistance from a headmaster who appreciated his effort, brought him relief from some of the burden of constant financial worry. During his University of the West Indies years, another mentor, similarly impressed, supported his unflagging exertion; and he left the University well-prepared to aid his country's economic progress.

His work in the Civil Service quickly paid off and, despite an early expression of doubt by an Englishman who held the highest position in government, in about five years, he had obtained the highest Civil Service position in his homeland. On the way, he had impressed still others in influential positions who ensured that other opportunities were available to him when he did not fit in with the plans of a new Government. He used his opportunities on these occasions to gain further formal education and to work in positions that afforded him great experience while exposing him to many problem-solving approaches. His current contributions to his nation draw greatly on all of the knowledge he has accumulated. And in 2002, he was awarded a CMG (Companion of the Order of St. Michael and St. George). Yet, the honor conferred by his country on him falls short of what he deserves. He has certainly contributed more to St. Vincent than many who have been knighted; and he continues to busily occupy himself in helping to meet the tremendous needs of the nation.

Cims has made time to engage in considerable writing, mostly in newspapers, aimed at helping Vincentians to better understand the economics and history of the country. He is sole author of two monographs and coauthor of a third:

1. The Role of Government in the Agricultural Development of St. Vincent (His M. Sc. Thesis).
2. A Manual on Project Planning for Small Economies. Prepared for the Commonwealth Secretariat.
3. The Rise and Fall of the Black Caribs (Garifuna). Earle Kirby coauthor.

He and Kathy have two sons, Alistaire Hugo, a qualified Computer Technologist, and Jerome Gregor, an Attorney at Law.

Dr. Roy Austin was US Ambassador to Trinidad and Tobago from 2001-08. He was also formerly Associate Professor of Sociology at Penn State University, Pennsylvania, USA for many years. He was born in St. Vincent and the Grenadines but is now retired and lives in Pennsylvania.

Caribbean Trailblazers: St. Vincent and the Grenadines

10.   **GEORGE A. MCINTOSH**
By
Kenneth John

[Editors' Note: For another perspective on George McIntosh, especially his legislative agenda, see Rupert John: Pioneers in Nation Building in a Caribbean Mini-State; 2009, KINGS-SVG Publishers.]

George Augustus McIntosh was born on March 6, 1886 in Kingstown, St. Vincent and the Grenadines, a faithful product of his times and his own social environment.

Among the influences on the life of George McIntosh were the socialist preachments of J. Elliot Sprott, the Liberal editor of *The Sentry* newspaper; the racial message of Marcus Garvey whose organ , *Negro World*, penetrated the Colonial curtain despite its being banned in St. Vincent in 1920; the promise of the Russian Revolution (1917) which was thought to have delivered power to the people; the general ferment of ideas generated by members of the local Ex-Servicemen League who had been "exposed" to Libertarian ideas while fighting overseas in the First World War.

There is a sense in which it can be said that George McIntosh was thrown up by the events of the day. The times were hard and the island was experiencing its worse economic days. King Sugar had been dethroned; the estate system was bankrupt and the mass of people were barely eking out an existence. Given the benefit of hindsight, Emancipation was seen only as a cold legal fact, one newspaper noting that:

The emancipated found themselves in a worse position than when in slavery, for the planters had lost all interest in them as a chattel and native industry was crushed by the importation of foreign labor. Political aspirations were promptly checked and the plantocracy reigned supreme[1].

As if these were not enough, between 1895 and 1902, nature dealt the colony three telling blows in rapid succession in the form of a flood, a hurricane and a devastating volcanic eruption. If not before, it became imperative to embark upon schemes to establish an independent peasantry such as was recommended by the Royal Commission in 1897. For in an effort to cut losses, estates simply left large tracts of land lying idle, thus at once aggravating the unemployment problem, worsening still further the island's economic plight and demoralizing the bulk of the citizenry. It was heartless planter response like these that prompted the *Sentry* newspaper to tow a line which must have made an impression on the young McIntosh:

Caribbean Trailblazers: St. Vincent and the Grenadines

Nor do we admit that, under every possible circumstance, a man has a right to do what he likes with his property. That is a fallacy which has long since been exploded. Property has duties as well as rights. The right to accumulate land to any extent by purchase or otherwise, carries with it an equal obligation to cultivate that land for the general good. Land primitively belongs to the people and no man has any right to more of it than he can himself cultivate[2].

Trained in the old Colonial Constitutional School, McIntosh believed that he could best make an impact on the system by having men of his own color hack their way through the social jungle to the Legislative Council. It bears recalling that there were no elected representatives in St. Vincent (1877-1925). The Colony enjoyed – if "enjoyed" is the word – what was deceptively known as a pure form of Crown Colony Government, in which the seat of Government was monopolized by the Governor and his handpicked team, a system that was deliberately introduced to checkmate the people of African ancestry from gaining access to the policy making body of the island. In 1919, McIntosh joined forces with the Black Intelligentsia to create a political vehicle known as the Representative Government Association (RGA) with the slogan "Crown Colony Rule Must Go" after the fashion of similar bodies in the sister islands.

It was clear from the outset that the RGA had tapped heavily on the emergent Vincentian Middle Class and that perhaps as a consequence, the aims and objectives of the group were tepid and geared primarily to their own advancement as a class. With one or two exceptions (certainly Cipriani in Trinidad and McIntosh for a time), members of these Associations were not unduly concerned with the welfare of the so-called "barefooted man". Among the membership of the local body, the legal field, the teaching profession, journalists and the merchant class featured prominently. In later times, they would be categorized as House Slaves, Fanon's "Black Faces, White Masks", the sort of people who inspired Lloyd Best's coinage "Afro-Saxon". They were the much lauded "Get-Up-And-Get" type who had cut through a path in the Colonial World and yearned for Massa's stamp of recognition of their newly won status in the form of membership of the Legislative Council. And the British Overseers were not averse to drafting such bodies within the fold for, as one member of the Wood Commission was to put it in 1922:

"This colored population possessing something of the European mind in the African body, constitutes the Middle Class and furnishes an increasingly large contingent of the professional classes, notably the law, medicine and journalism. They are obviously of a higher capacity than the pure African".

George A. McIntosh

Arthur Lewis also had a word to say about the RGA's"

"These Associations were narrowly middle-class in their aims; they wished particularly to see more middle class representation on the legislative councils and to increase the number of posts in the civil service to which educated Negroes could be appointed. Mass support was easily obtainable for such liberal ends, the urban workers willingly associating themselves in meetings, demonstrations and petitions with the demand for constitutional reform and racial equality in the civil service."

The truth is that George McIntosh had been caught on the horns of the traditional colonial dilemma. He could try to build a grass-roots organization, canvas support from the disadvantaged section of the community and confront the system. Instead, he chose the line of weaker resistance, gain respectability by enlisting black intellectual moderates and even solicit the support of planters who might provide him with the necessary air cover if and when he tried to manipulate the system. The result was that in 1922, the RGA struck up an alliance with other groups to form the "Citizens' Committee" which made representations before the Wood Commission for an advanced constitution of sorts. The proud boast of the Committee was that it spoke for:

"all classes and pointed out that, included in the deputation, were landed proprietors, members of Council, leading merchants and professional men of the island, and the principal clergy of the different denominations".

Naturally, the demands of the Citizens Committee were vague and limited, and the British escaped with the introduction of the elected principle, that was so hemmed in by considerations of property and education as to be meaningless in a colonial setting. The same old faces continued to rule but now with a semblance of legitimacy accorded by the magic of the ballot. In fact, it would appear that qualifications for membership of the House were prohibitively high for men of the caliber of McIntosh who had to be content with a peripheral political role through his influence in the RGA. The elections of 1925, 1928 and 1931 returned White Planters and Mulatto Merchants.

In 1932 however, there was a conference of West Indian Progressives in Dominica to discuss the question of West Indian Federation – always dear to McIntosh's heart – and the necessary prerequisite of more responsible government. The RGA delegates at this conference were Robert Anderson and Ebenezer Duncan, editors of *The Vincentian* and *The Investigator* newspapers respectively. It would seem that McIntosh was not thought to be good ambassadorial material given his tendency to radicalism. Although that conference, mistrusting the capacity of the ordinary man to analyze political events, shelved the issue of Adult Suffrage of which McIntosh, like Cypriani, was an ardent exponent, it did manage to secure an increase from three to five in the elected representatives with lowered qualifications. These changes were sufficient to usher McIntosh formally into the system in 1936 but, before that, the upheavals of 1935 had happened.

This short paper can only give a very graphic picture of the social and economic picture which formed the human background to the events of 1935. Briefly, the people were once again suffering grinding poverty that was intensified by the effects on a fragile colonial economy of world recession in general and metropolitan decline in particular. The Estate system still creaked along, upheld by a constitutional scaffolding in which the planters were still the main plank. Local racial tensions had become abrasive in the face of the Italian affront to the Black people of Abyssinia and the general connivance of the White World with this monumental insolence. Perhaps the White conception of the Black masses at the time was best captured in the statement attributed to a former Chief Justice of St. Vincent in 1932. In explaining the cause of the colonies' economic plight, Willoughby Bullock remarked that:

"The Negro will not work, as Nature provides him with the necessaries of life so far as food is concerned. Two flour bags will make a suit of clothes and it is always possible to beg a couple of kerosene tins to help him in the construction of a palm-thatched hut"

One year after the events of 1935, the Administrator of the Colony presented this unflattering picture of the island in a typical British understatement:

"To a newcomer to St. Vincent, such as myself, the colony presents certain very unsatisfactory features. Land is most unevenly distributed. The housing of a great part of the peasant and laboring populations is deplorable. In the villages, most of the houses are built of mud and wattle with cane trash roofs or of odd pieces of wood with corrugated iron roofs. Most of the houses are badly built and the thatching, where it exists, is poor".

George McIntosh's role in the social upheaval that was triggered off by the appallingly low social and economic situation was very dubious. The truth is that the people had moved ahead of McIntosh in assuming a new militancy and resorting to violence as a means of redressing their historical grievances. Initially, however, the people had some confidence in McIntosh who they believed could be used as their sympathetic spokesman before Officialdom. When they realized that McIntosh was not being taken seriously by the Administration, the people, to the dismay of McIntosh and other members of the R.G.A., took to the streets. The rest is history

The ensuing "Riot" so-called, was put down by a heavy hand. The leading lights among the people were sentenced to some of the longest prison terms handed down in the then Empire. Most members of the R.G.A., were swift to disassociate themselves from the insurrectionists who in one notorious reference were called "a bunch of uncivilized savages." The Kingstown Board which the R.G.A. controlled passed a Resolution of condemning the uprising; a few R.G.A. members had actually shot down people in the name of King and Empire; some had offered themselves as Special Constables to help police in troubled areas. Ebenezer Duncan, the historian, was later to refer to the episode as "a blot on our history"; and the planter-element in the R.G.A. cut away from McIntosh, and sent a Resolution to Colonial Office requesting that, in the circumstances, an immediate brake be applied to the Constitution Assembly-line. The fear, apparently, was that in the prevailing scheme of things, control of the island was likely to fall to the Left Wing, comparatively speaking , of the R.G.A. According to the Governor's interpretation of events, "their attitude, not unnaturally, is that any form of administration is better than one which would increase the influence of men of the McIntosh type."

Given the prejudices, preconceptions and predilections of the Colony's official class, it was natural for them to believe that the uprising could not have been a spontaneous movement generated from below, which in fact it was. For them, it had to have middle-class leadership. And officialdom picked on McIntosh who had often exhorted the workers "to fight for their rights", spouted the rhetoric of the Left, wore a flaming red-tie, was known to read "subversive" literature, and defiantly displayed a large photograph of Stalin in a prominent place in his druggist shop.

The Government analysis was simplistic: McIntosh "is mainly responsible for staging the whole business". He was arrested and spent nine days in jail after which he was acquitted following the mockery of a truncated trial.

The political fall out from the uprising was significant. First, it split the R.G.A., the planters abandoning and avoiding McIntosh like the plague; it gave the people a "respectable" leader in McIntosh with a foothold in the House; and it forced McIntosh into seeing that the people wanted more militant leadership and that a presence in the legislature without a bread-and-butter organization, was like a shadow without substance. So it was that McIntosh took with him the more radical section of the defunct R.G.A. and formed the Workingman's Co-operative Association on the 2nd March 1936, partly in response to the social forces about him, partly on the instruction of Cipriani under whose benign influence he had progressively fallen.

It was through the Workingmen's Association that McIntosh realized himself, and through its policy that one can glean something of the philosophy of the man. First of all, McIntosh had broad socialist leanings. As he was to say in the House in 1946; "Socialism is the only way that we can hope to oust the capitalist system and bring people to a decent standard of living." As late as 1955, McIntosh was persuaded to admit that "I like communism." A general framework of socialist doctrine must therefore be accepted if one is to assess most of the political conduct of McIntosh and his followers. Perhaps the basic ideology of the man was best summed up in an election speech he made in 1936.

"I will do all that lies in my power to see these hungry and oppressed people get some land. I am bound to the working class. I belong to the common people. I am one of them. I want no titles, no M.B.E. or O.B.E. What St. Vincent needs are men with human hearts and no letter of the alphabet can make up for that."[10]

Because St. Vincent is an agricultural community, McIntosh felt that he must first tackle the skewed distribution of land from which he believed most of the social ills stemmed. For him, the lopsided distribution of land was:

"the root of all West Indian problems. To it can be attributed
  directly the poverty of the masses of the people, reflected...in
  inadequate wages, insanitary housing, illiteracy etc. What is
  now most urgently needed in the West Indies is that the
  abolition of slavery be taken a step further by destroying the
  economic foundations of slavery and redistributing the land
   more equitably."[11]

Naturally, McIntosh drew fire from the "Vincentian" newspaper, the mouth piece of the Planters. But strengthened in the knowledge that his movement was part of an entity that transcended the narrow boundaries of St. Vincent, McIntosh was emboldened to dismiss such critics with biting sarcasm:

"A certain newspaper that represents the interest of the
  Proprietor class may write all the piffle imaginable but
  that will not stop the labour and trade union movement
  of the world..."[12]

McIntosh's unceasing toils in this area were directly responsible for the Land Settlement Scheme of 1946 in North Leeward, though it needs to be said that his dream of creating an independent peasantry was shattered and the "Settlement" remained virtually a State capitalist enterprise until 20 years or so ago when it was given practical recognition.

McIntosh next confronted the problem of trade union organization, noting that:

> *"agricultural labourers are hard to organize (thus)...*
> *The onus is on the State to provide minimum wage-*
> *fixing machinery and to legislate regarding hours*
> *of work and child labour, workingmen's compensation,*
> *housing etc. if the labourer is not to be exploited by*
> *a small clique of planters".*[13]

McIntosh worked assiduously to get the necessary legislation enacted, and it is no fault of his that such laws when they were enacted had been more honoured in the breach that in the observance.

Sooner or later, any advocate of serious social change was bound to run into conflict with organized religion as was represented by the orthodox middle class churches. McIntosh was no apologist of the status quo, unconcerned about the plight of the Vincentian man. In a fit of righteous indignation, he declared:

> *"Our civilization is all wrong, - our Religion is a farce...*
> *Why do the churches waste time to read the parable of*
> *Dives and Lazarus. All the mad struggle in the world*
> *would cease when fear of poverty has vanished. Then*
> *and not till then will a truly Christian civilization become*
> *possible."*[14]

Still, McIntosh was a respecter of religious freedom and he was appalled when the conservative element in the Council voted out his motion to make legal the practice of Shakerism in 1939. McIntosh rightly saw this negation as yet another example of the big fisted methods by which colonialism set out to obliterate every vestige of African or indigenous cultural forms. He took the opportunity once more to show the linkage between the religious and economic hierarchy in the colony in making damning reference to:

> *"the capitalists and all large landowners who grab all the land*
> *and hold it for the exercise of power in all directions. They*
> *influence even the churches and make so-called Religion serve*
> *their purposes, in disregard for the feelings, wishes or desires*
> *of the great majority."*[15]

Until 1946, there was an uncanny consistency in the policies of George McIntosh. Even after that year when he began to go back on many of the things for which he previously stood, glimpses of the old McIntosh would sporadically reassert themselves. Two such "flashes" are recorded here because of their contemporary relevance. He wanted the people to get their priorities right on the matter of Secondary Education, observing that:

> *"These visionaries...are not advocating a free secondary education for all Vincentian children; they are specially concerned with what happens to their own children. Before we talk about secondary education at all, thinking Vincentians should make it a concern of theirs to see that all children, especially the children of poor parents, receive an education. In fact we should have compulsory (primary) education in St. Vincent."*[16]

And on the very vexed question of West Indian two-party politics, McIntosh commented scathingly in 1958:

> *"In Jamaica, there is a Labour Party in power and a Labour Party in opposition, and so it appears to be throughout the West Indies. They are devoid of principle or policy and have but one aim, getting a few in power who are able to deceive the poor illiterate masses, and so these parties, although they are all supposed to be Labour parties, continue with one object, that of cutting each other's throat..."*[17]

As mentioned above, it is an historical fact that McIntosh played false to his earlier ideas in the post-1946 period. By then, he had become the darling of the planter class, an unbeliever in true democracy, a convert to elitist politics. It is beyond the scope of this contribution to analyse the reasons for the change. Suffice it to say that it is this very enigma of the man which explains why he has such a cross-sectional fan club in the island. The young generation harp on the exciting period of the 1930's and 1940's when McIntosh preached fire and brimstone and could utter a clarion call to the people in very Marxist terms, such as:

> *"Working people, awake from your slumber and be not satisfied to live in misery and squalour! The change of conditions lies in the hands of the working people."*[18]

George A. McIntosh

It is clear that the trip to the Festival of Britain in 1951, coupled with the total electoral defeat of his Party, undid all that, leaving its scars on the psyche of our Hero.

Mention has already been made of his blistering attack on the Two-Party system in which he claimed that "The World looks on with amazement at our stupidity, marveling at our childish behaviour, all the result of our wonderful but unique party system.

To be sure, McIntosh, before setting off for England on the eve of the 1951 elections, had sounded a public note of warning that "Misleaders have sprung up to traverse the road prepared by us."

After his twin defeats in General Elections in 1951and 1954, McIntosh switched his theatre of action to the Kingstown Town Board where he had won a seat from 1923 continuing on to 1960, and had been Chairman on about a dozen occasions.

Suddenly, the tribune of the people who had struggled for the universal franchise with regard to Central Government, argued for the retention of the nominated element at the level of the Kingstown Town Board in order to neutralize any democratic stampede:

> "...Let us have adult suffrage for the Kingstown Board, yes.
> But let us have stabilizing influence as exercised by the House
> of Lords with a measure of dignity thrown in, for when one
> visits the House of Lords, the difference is striking, and if all
> sections and interests are to be represented, as they should be,
> for God's sake, don't leave it only in the hands of the ignorant
> and the uncultured, for however much we may talk of democracy
> in these parts, we find that the rule of the majority is the rule of
> ignorance and while we are trying to make the world safe for
> democracy, let us try to make democracy safe for the world," [19]

Having awakened the sleeping masses, the conclusion has to be drawn that McIntosh became frightened of their muscle and potential strength and would not be comforted until he could lay them back to rest. It was during this process of beating a retreat from the socialist banner that the Establishment befriended McIntosh, that "The Vincentian" decided to extol his "virtues:, that the Labour Party embraced him. Perhaps there is a sense in which, from a people's point of view, George McIntosh is both friend and foe, saint and sinner, hero and villain. Perhaps it is this quality, too, which makes him such an interesting study. For in George McIntosh we see at work the conflicts and complexities of the human condition, the inconsistencies which bedevil man (especially the colonized) as he tries to come to grips with his social environment and hammer out an appropriate philosophy.

George McIntosh died on the 1st November 1963, and was paid glowing tribute in the following editorial of "The Vincentian" newspaper.

"In the halls of West Indian fame, the names of Crichlow, Cipriani, Marryshow, Rawle and others must be inscribed. There along with them the name of George Augustus McIntosh must also be written; nay, his should find a special niche, for it was that little man who brought dignity and respect to the common man of St. Vincent. It was he who made them realize that their labours were worth that which would permit them to live in some degree of comfort. It was that little man who made employers realize that they needed the worker as much as the worker needed them, and it is George Augustus McIntosh that the credit must go for awakening a political consciousness in St.Vincent. He got nothing for it. His life and work will, however, never be forgotten. His was a noble service to this Colony."[21]

REFERENCES
1. The Sentinel newspaper, Kingstown, 1st July 1887.
2. The Sentry newspaper, Kingstown, 22nd October 1897.
3. Ormsby – Gore in an interview with the Observer (London) and reported locally in the Times newspaper, 4th May 1922.
4. Labour in The West Indies, London, 1939.
5. See The Wood Commission Report, June 1922 Cmd 1967. Her Majesty's Stationery Office, London
6. See Proceedings on The West Indian Conference held at Roseau, Dominica, October-November 1932. Printed by "Voice" Printery Castries, St. Lucia.
7. Attributed to Willoughby-Bullock, The Port-Of-Spain Gazette,, (Trinidad), 12th September 1932.
8. The Vincentian Newspaper (incorporating The Sentry), 19th December 1936.
9. Flambeau Magazine September 1967 "1935 Revisited", an article by Oswald Peters and Kenneth John for a concise account of the "Riot".
10. The Times, 27th February 1937.
11. The Times, 11th February 1939.
12. The Times, 24th June 1939.
13. The Vincentian, 28th April 1947.
14. The Times, 11th February 1939.
15. The Times, 4th November 1939.
16. The Vincentian, 28th April 1947.

17. The Vincentian, 28th June 1958.
18. The Times, 11th February 1939.
19. The Vincentian, 28th June 1958.
20. The Vincentian, 18th April 1959.
21. The Vincentian, 6th November 1963.

Dr. Kenneth John is an attorney and political scientist. He resides in St. Vincent and the Grenadines.

Caribbean Trailblazers: St. Vincent and the Grenadines

11. KERWYN L. MORRIS
By
Kenneth John

A Man of Many Parts

Kerwyn Leslie Morris was born on May 19, 1939 in St. Vincent and the Grenadines to Joseph H. Morris and Sydney Eileen Rosalie Morris, nee Anderson. His death in 2007 fell most appropriately on National Heroes Day, March 14. No official day of mourning was announced, but the people took centre-stage with a quiet dignity which saw a national outpouring of grief over a fallen son.

The good deeds done by Kerwyn to his fellowmen were generally unrecorded, on a one-to-one basis, and rendered naturally without pomp, show or fan-fare.

Kerwyn certainly believed in the adage, from whom much is given, much is demanded. He was multi-talented in so many fields, and he tried always to spread his bountiful gifts among his folk.

Kerwyn had himself been lucky to possess a grandfather, the venerable Robert Anderson, who at least opened Kerwyn to many influences, though it had been the grandson's choice as to which direction he leapt off the old man's shoulder.

Kerwyn for example, would have learnt primitive research methods from the author of the St Vincent handbooks, and the journalist's craft from the original owner and publisher of "The Vincentian" newspaper.

Anderson's skill as a photographer was probably reflected later in Kerwyn's mastery of under-sea photography which he had developed as an adjunct to his professional interest in fisheries.

Most of his adult life, Kerwyn chose to live in a modest home in Edinboro, whose location at the water's edge had been its principal attraction, giving easy access for the satisfaction of his twin loves-swimming and fishing.

But Kerwyn put his distance from Andy on the question of dress. The old man had been a British trained Solicitor out-fitted with stiff wing collar and the rest. Kerwyn dressed, especially in his "Black Power" days with dashiki and sandals. He was suited up only on rare occasions, a compromise to his "social" standing, or in deference to his bureaucrat's role.

At the Boys Grammar School (B.G.S.), St. Vincent which Kerwyn entered in 1952, he was a better-than-average student who enjoyed school-life to the full. He took a very active part in extra-curricular activities, especially the cadets, and soccer where he was called Puskas after the skipper of the Hungarian team that shook the world in the mid-1950's.

Kerwyn displayed a like dazzling wizardry in 1955 until cut down by a bout of typhoid.

It was on the athletic field, however, that he fairly shone. I recalled, with John Horne, the day he threw the cricket ball way beyond the arena, and was deprived of a record throw, for its distance could not be ascertained, far less measured.

For about two years, he was champion of the sprints at the School's annual athletic meet. In 1956, at the Windward Islands Inter-School tournament, he was edged out by Percival DeGannes of Grenada in the 100 yards dash, but got back his own in the 200.

Kerwyn wanted to pursue studies in Cambridge Higher School Certificate (the equivalent of London's A level) sciences but at the time, there was a lack of science teachers and facilities at the Grammar School, so he transferred to the Grenada Boys' Secondary School. There, he took out his revenge in the sprints on one Mosanto who had been the rival sprinter from the St. Mary's College. DeGannes had left School, and was then teaching in St. Vincent and the Grenadines (SVG).

Later, Kerwyn decided to pursue studies in marine biology in Canada, where he joined his school mates such as Alfie Roberts and Arnhim Eustace. His early mastery of the key-board was to serve him in good stead, enabling him to entertain with a wide repertoire at night clubs to earn the wherewithal to pay for his upkeep and student fees.

During the 1960's he got caught up with the Black Power Movement in Canada, which formed part of a global left-wing politics, suggesting radical answers to Black Caribbean countries like St. Vincent in the terminal stages of colonialism.

There was a link of sorts back home with some members of the Kingstown Study Group, publishers of a radical magazine "Flambeau" (1964-1968) which provided an outlet for the Canadian brothers. All three Vincentians, Arnhim Eustace, Alphonso Roberts, Kerwyn Morris together with an Antiguan friend, Timothy Hector, were accommodated by "Flambeau".

Roberts and Morris were regular contributors, the titles to the latter's articles being self-explanatory. They are: "King Jaja's Exile to St. Vincent"; "On Afro-West Indian Thinking", (which was published in a collection of reputable works by Comitas and Lowenthal: "Independence, Unity and Non-Alignment"); "Historical Materialism and Caribbean Destiny"; "He Defended Euro-American Imperialism and Exploitation."

Above all, Kerwyn's flaming radicalism inspired him to produce his solo flight into verse which was captured by "Flambeau" in the poem "The Black Reconstruction".

"We shall return from our short exile to reconstruct.

We shall brave the red labels the black bourgeoisie opportunists
place on our backs
We will die with our backs to the wall,
All for the love of Hairoun.

Cowards would tremble in their shoes.
Exploiters of man shall fall back astounded.
Stooges of the brass crown shall be out to shame
And their tin medal dumped in the new incinerator.
Chatoyer will collect them all.

In their rightful stead shall be
The Award of Toussaint L'Overture and
The order of Marcus Garvey.
Sheriff (Haile Selassie" shall be praised, and
Negritude shall prevail"

On his return to SVG in the late 1960's, Kerwyn moved positively into the world of music in which he had been accepted as an adept performer. His band, Latinnaires, specializing in calypso and the Latin beat took St. Vincent to unprecedented heights. In short he was a Frankie McIntosh operating on the local scene.

Kerwyn assisted calypsonians, Becket among them, with their tunes particularly at the carnival season, served as arranger to several young groups; provided music for the Kingstown Chorale which he joined, attending a Carifesta or two in the process.

Above all, the Latinnaires cut albums featuring such maestros as Syl Mc Intosh, a Vincentian-Canadian Ace tenor saxophonist, who mastered such unforgettable renditions of "The first time ever I saw your face", and Lord Hawkes "Oui Pani". For his own part, noted musicologist, Frankie Mc Intosh at Kerwyn's funeral service played bewitchingly on the piano "A Little more oil in your lamp keeps it burning" and "Georgia On My Mind".

This intermittent musical interlude in his life was played even while Kerwyn taught at his alma mater, the BGS, and engaged in moulding young minds as to how to take on greater responsibility. Altogether, Kerwyn taught at the Grammar School, at the Girls' High School in its own right, at St. Martin's, while establishing a presence at various evening classes.

Then the chickens came home to roost with the Sir George Williams affair back in Canada and the problems with Anguilla on our doorstep in the Caribbean. Kerwyn Morris and Parnel Campbell coming from the troublous environment of the Grammar School teamed up with former members of "the Flambeau Group" to emerge with the Educational Forum of the People, 1969, a protest movement.

The following year, 1970, a police party raided the homes of Parnel Campbell, John Cato and Kerwyn Morris "in search of guns, ammunition and subversive literature." Kerwyn had reached home at the dawn from a dance at which he played in Bequia to find his home ransacked, many of his prized books carted away, and his wife, Madge Pollard-Whittle and her three infant children, Marcia-Ann, Zhinga, Osei Patrice, distraught and traumatized, drifting listlessly in the neighbourhood.

Forum members had to see the lighter side of things in order to ease the pain of the reality. John Cato selected himself for the job. At the next Forum meeting he told the crowd: "They come looking for guns. But, comrade, the only gun I have, is the one in my pants." To uproarious laughter of the masses!

In a matter of months, both Kerwyn Morris and Parnel Campbell were dismissed from the Government Teaching Service. Parnel took to giving lessons in motor-car driving to earn a living and ultimately to work out a strategy whereby he might attend U.W.I. as a law student. Morris sought refuge in fishing full-time, not only for the money which he made from it, but for the peace of mind which he claimed he derived from being so tranquil and at rest when alone in the serenity of the deep.

There was a glimmer of hope, so far as the fortunes of Kerwyn were concerned, when "Son" Mitchell led a coalition Government following the defeat of Labour in the 1972 elections.

The Forum, though not competing, had actually run an anti-Labour campaign, and were close to Mitchell who had summoned Campbell enjoying a break from his law studies in Barbados, Kerwyn and myself to be at hand to render advice during the critical post-election negotiations in 1972, in which, so a calypso bard tells it in "First Time," "Two Parties run but none didn't win."

Kerwyn was reinstated at the B.G.S. but the Alliance Government was short-lived being defeated after a vote of no-confidence by "the strongest Government in the world", which is how Premier Cato described his Labour-Party victory.

Between 1974 and 1980, Kerwyn tossed about hither, thither and yon in turbulent waters. During the period, the E.F.P. graduated into the Democratic Freedom Movement (D.F.M.) which was mauled at the polls in 1974. Then it merged with Yulimo to form the United People's Movement (U.P.M.) which bravely contested the 1979 election but failed to win a seat.

Finally, the D.F.M. withdrew from the merger and died a quiet death. Some members joined the burgeoning New Democratic Party (N.D.P.) which won the 1984 election with six erstwhile members of the D.F.M. As for Kerwyn, he managed to survive it all, with his political stocks intact.

Kerwyn Morris

With the more congenial N.D.P. Government in power, Kerwyn was able to work assiduously at Fisheries where he had been promoted to Chief Fisheries Officer.

The close bond between him and Mitchell who like most Grenadines men, shared a particular interest in the fishing industry, tightened. Fisherman's Day rapidly grew in importance to become virtually institutionalized. And the fish trawlers from Japan ensured the proper development of the industry.

At his death, the Fisheries division felt sufficiently moved to present a "paper", on Kerwyn's contribution, in fact demonstrating that he was way ahead of his time. "Mr. Morris had great vision for the fisheries sector. He lobbied and worked hard to obtain increased human, financial and technical capacity to develop the fishing industry and its stakeholders. He tried to dispel negative perception associated with the fishing industry and sought recognition for the entire sector. He was of the firm belief that the fisheries sector had the potential to become a major revenue earner and that it was essential to have trained personnel at all levels, using the best available scientific and technical tools to realize this potential".

At about this time, Kerwyn probably joined the N.D.P formally and was taken aboard several government bodies, notably the Radio 705.

With the N.D.P having entrenched itself politically by its return in 1989 with all elected seats, coupled by a third successive term (10 to 3) in 1994, it seemed to have been plain sailing for Kerwyn.

Finally, on the death of N.D.P's General Secretary, Stuart Nanton, Kerwyn was persuaded to replace him, incidentally rejoining the old firm of Morris and Campbell who had taken over the chairmanship of the party.

Towards the last several years of his life, Kerwyn gracefully resigned as General Secretary of the N.D.P and increasingly withdrew into himself and a small coterie of friends. The reason was almost certainly because he was plagued by prostate cancer, which caused him two or three visits to the U.S.A seeking medical assistance.

In the end, as usually happens, the disease got the better of the patient. Kerwyn died peacefully on National Heroes day, March 14, 2007. After a beautiful service in which his life-long friend John Horne featured as the eulogist, the sea for which he had demonstrated an undying love finally claimed his body.

Fellow-fishermen turned out in their boats to pay their last respects. They tossed their lighted lanterns in a final salute to accompany their hero, as they say, to his watery grave. The whole awe-inspiring and solemn scene recalled the days of yore when a fallen Viking, in Nordic tradition, was sent home to Valhalla.

Dr. Kenneth John is a lawyer and political scientist. He writes a weekly column in the "The Vincentian" newspaper in St. Vincent and the Grenadines where he presently resides.

The Editor acknowledges some information about Kerwyn's family background from Dr. Paula Nanton.

12.   **NORA EMILY PEACOCKE**
                              By
                       Nan Peacocke[1]

On an August morning in 1991 at our house at Dorchester Hill, St. Vincent and the Grenadines, my father Max Audibert Peacocke and I watched on CNN the collapse of the USSR.. Occasionally I shouted details from the images of milling crowds to my mother, Nora, who was downstairs in the kitchen preparing breakfast. The State Committee of the State of Emergency had initiated a coup against *perestroika* on August 19th and had moved to take control of mass media by scripting their "Appeal to the Soviet People". The anti-coup forces, led by Boris Yeltsin, responded with an "Appeal to the Citizens of Russia"[2]. Across the Soviet Union and around the world, newspapers, radio and especially television, brought the drama into homes. In Moscow and Leningrad, barricades went up, tanks crept downtown, pro-democracy rallies washed the streets. A florid Yeltsin gestured for the cameras atop a tank, upturning a famous pose by Lenin. Anxious-looking soldiers pondered propaganda flyers while children, perched among the great guns of the Soviet war machine, waved cheerfully at the world.

At a certain moment some men climbed on to the roof of a building on Red Square and began tugging at a flagpole. We shouted to Nora to leave the stove and come. She appeared, still holding the wooden spoon with which she was about to scramble eggs, just in time to see the men pull down the Soviet flag. As we watched, the celebrants untied the red flag from the mast, tossed it aside and replaced it with another, red, white and blue. With that act, that particular chapter in the "war of scripts, images and symbols"[3] was concluded.

Nora was aghast, "Oh God, Max; they're hoisting the tricolor!" She sat down beside him suddenly, as though her legs had failed her. I asked her what she meant. "The Russian tricolor; it's the flag of the Tsars" she explained.

CNN pronounced the end of the Cold War and the triumph of capitalism. Out with the hammer and sickle! In with MacDonald's golden arches.

Nora shook her head, "Well, all I can say is, capital is really consolidating."

I had the sense to look away from the goddam TV, as Max called it, and study her face. What constellation of ability, a basic education and just plain living-in-the-world equipped Nora Emily Peacocke with that clarity, I wondered. I'll attempt to answer that question here, in this reflection, two decades after that incident, as, in my memory, Max and I follow her and her wooden scepter to the kitchen.

Nora was born on November 3rd, 1912, just before the 1st World War. She was five years old at the time of the Russian Revolution in 1917. It is useful to reflect on details of a life in the context of changing political events of the times. Whatever one's perspective on the outcome of the Soviet experiment from the vantage point of now, there is no denying the appalling conditions in which the Russian peasantry wallowed in the early decades of the 20th century or the global reach of the revolutionary ideas articulated in that crucible. Meanwhile, in the West Indies the trajectory of post emancipation found the people of the region at the door of a 1st World War. The colonial administration needed young men of the colony of St Vincent to sign up and they did. Their reasons for joining varied. The majority of the island's population, though legally in possession of 'formal freedom' since 1834, was exploited, disadvantaged, still disenfranchised agricultural labour. For young black men of this class, the 1st global war, like its successor, was the only kind of opportunity that the continuing machinations of European power provided. Those who survived and returned to St Vincent brought with them skills and experience of the wider world. Not only would they change their bargaining position, so to speak, in their relations with St Vincent's more socially advantaged groups, their knowledge clarified the modern political direction the island would take. My reading of the Grant household in which Nora and her siblings grew up is one where questions of public good and representative government were not removed from everyday happenings but were understood to be integral to the struggles and wishes of the age.[4]

Even if you subscribe to the conviction that genetics, not culture, is entirely responsible for a person's characteristics, it's worth considering that character is learned in response to one's environment; that 'the difference between right and wrong' we are taught as children is not merely absorbed by rote or the occasional slap but through example. If children can piece together happenings around them into the ethical shapes we take as adults, we can look at some broad strokes of the social evolution of St Vincent that directed Nora through her 81 years.

Parents

Born in Montrose, Kingstown to Ellen Elfreda (Nellie) Grant *nee* Mackie and Walter Grant, Nora was the third of her mother's five children: Alexander, Dorothy, Nora, Freda and Douglas. Their older brother, Albert McGregor, Walter's son by his deceased first wife, Amy Thompson, became Nellie's son. I regret that I remember little of my grandmother. She had a heredity condition, acute angle glaucoma that made her blind in her early forties.[5] She nevertheless outlived her husband and, I suspect, suffered the acute loneliness known by widows bereft of a deep companionship. That her children migrated to other islands must also have made the isolation caused by her blindness more acute. Nora's few verbalized reminiscences of her mother were usually coupled with memories of her father: that they had a cocktail every evening before dinner, that they travelled to Barbados to see an ophthalmologist. Of Walter, Nora was more effusive. When I was small, running to her with a bruised knee or 'coconut' on the head acquired in the rough and tumble of life, Nora would 'kiss it better' and repeat words, she told me, her father had said to her when she was small and hurt, 'Take your daddy's heart'.

Anecdotes about our grandfather, called 'Dad' by his children and grandchildren, carry that same endearing note. "Dad was always cheerful and affectionate. I well remember sitting on his lap while he sang to me a number of different songs but especially these two:

> *"I will give you a paper of pins*
> *if you can tell me how love begins"*

and,

> *"Daisy, Daisy give me your answer do*
> *I'm half crazy all for the love of you."*

And the fact that he could hardly carry a tune did not deter him![6]

Sir Rupert John quotes from a tribute to Walter which suggests that his generous nature reached beyond his interactions with his family into his dealings as a businessman and a Christian. "His affable disposition won for him the esteem of all sections of the community".[7]

In writing about him, Sir Rupert states that his compassion, kindness and generosity to those less fortunate than himself, along with his commitment to public service, prevented him from making a financial success of his businesses.[8] (John 160)

"W. M. Grant was born 13 February 1874, the eldest of 7 children of McGregor Grant and Rachel (nee) Romney. Although McGregor was an overseer on an estate, his salary was very small and Walter left school at age 14 to help support the family. Nevertheless he was an avid reader (of the classics as well as of the London Times and The Manchester Guardian, and of course, the Bible) and made rapid progress as a businessman and entrepreneur."

The record of Walter Grant's service is impressive but what Sir Rupert's investigations reveal most strikingly about the man is his insistent, self-confident voice speaking up for representative democracy. As a legislator in the days before adult suffrage, he was nevertheless "an outspoken critic or strong supporter as circumstances warranted and never seemed to compromise his integrity" (John 164). He was fearless in challenging the Administration when he determined officials were not acting in the best interest of the people and unafraid to name names[9] and he held himself accountable to the electorate rather than to colonial authority. For example, in his reply to the address by the Administrator at the first meeting of the Legislature in May 1928, he informed the Council that "the electorate of the island expected great things of them during the next three years; that the electorate would be watching their actions on the Council and would not tolerate any wavering on their part in putting forward proposals for the good of the island or in opposing measures not calculated to be in its best interest." (John 165)

By no means do I attribute Nora's best qualities exclusively to her father's influence but it has to be said that when reading of my grandfather, who died before I was born, I see flashes of 'Dad' that, clearly, he passed on to his daughter. She would not be intimidated. In Jamaica in the 1960s, Nora held the post of Information Officer at Scientific Research Council. At one point she discovered that a leading politician was making use of the Council's printing press to reproduce his political party's propaganda. Nora refused to allow the operatives access to SRC's press on the grounds that the equipment belonged to a statutory body of the Jamaican government; hence, was funded by Jamaican taxpayers and could not legitimately be used for partisan ends. As far as I know, she had little support for her stand by her colleagues; one remark I recall was, "Mrs Peacocke, that's a hot potato I wouldn't want to touch". Mrs Peacocke, by contrast, picked up the potato and aimed accurately, it appears. The politician desisted and the printery resumed its proper use.

The Girls' High School

Walter and Nellie were not wealthy but they found the means to educate their children – not only their sons – at the best institutions of the day. Alexander and Douglas attended the Grammar School. The Grant sisters attended the Girls High School (GHS, currently celebrating its centenary) which was opened in 1911 by the Vincentian Ince sisters – "the only school in the country where girls had the opportunity of obtaining a secondary education.[10] Despite their advantages, the rewards for girls' education were circumscribed by rules that had yet to be overturned. Dorothy Grant[11] famously sat her Senior Cambridge Certificate exams at the age of 14 coming first in the island but was not awarded the Island Scholarship on the grounds that she was female. Though it must have been understood at the time by all concerned that scholarships went exclusively to boys and assuming that young Dorothy was merely testing her abilities against her peers 'just for so', the outrage with which this injustice to Dorothy was greeted by the family suggests they did not passively accept what today would be widely condemned as gender discrimination. Indeed, the 'wrong of it', carries on through the retelling of the story as a marker of the past from which, in this case, the Ince sisters, their successors, the Went sisters and their kind have helped to liberate Vincentian women.

Nora attended GHS between 1924 and 1929. She left with a Senior Cambridge Certificate, a love of reading and a capacity for critical thought. Decades later, Nora's tribute to her headmistress, Muriel Went, demonstrates, both in substance and in style, Went's effectiveness as a teacher. Nora writes:

"We got to know about the unorthodox sexual tendencies of Byron, the mental problems of the unfortunate Lambs, the tyranny of Elizabeth Barrett Browning's father and, on the lighter side, that William Shakespeare's wife, formerly Anne Hathaway, was a determined lady, of whom the great poet was wont to say – Anne hath a way"[12].

If you are inclined to scoff at the colonial content of the lessons, Nora has this to say:

Some will ask, "How has the sum of knowledge from all these things contributed to your wisdom? Most of the facts you were taught have no bearing whatsoever on the life of a West Indian woman! Maybe not. But take it from a West Indian woman who was exposed to Muriel Went's approach to education. After nearly three quarters of a century of living I can say with absolute truth that my 'way of life' has been linked inextricably and beneficially to the way I was taught to use the power of thought which I possess, appreciate the 'beauties of language' and utilize the comradeship of books.

The St Vincent Department of Agriculture

Certainly, Nora's education in 'the classics' equipped her for a hearty working life. Despite the absence of science in the GHS curriculum at the time, she was taught the basics of how to understand a subject and became a successful writer in both technical and political fields. The earliest knowledge I have of her career was in Colonial St Vincent's Department of Agriculture. I can attest from the many stories about people and events from that period of her life that she related to family and friends over the years, often humorously, that her experiences at the Cotton Station established for her, standards of competence, commitment and pride in nation by which she measured herself as a citizen. At her funeral at Kingstown's Anglican Cathedral on Christmas Eve 1993, its halls decked with masses of flowers,

Carlton Williams[13] with whom she worked at the Cotton Station in those early years, paid tribute to her and gave my brother, Trevor and me a hitherto unseen picture of a young woman in trousers and sunhat, intelligent, dedicated to her work, respectful in her interactions with all and unafraid to speak.

Fortunately, Nora could not sit before a computer, as I am at this moment, looking for connections between 'St Vincent' and 'Sea Island Cotton' – she would surely suffer a second death. I can find little reference to St Vincent's substantial role in the scientific research and development of Sea Island cotton.[14] Fortunately, print sources of that history exist. Among these is a copy of *A Plan of Development for the Colony of St Vincent* (1946–1956), of which I was told by its author, Ciprian Bernard ('Chest') Gibbs[15] that Nora was responsible for writing substantial portions of the section on Agriculture.

The history of Sea Island cotton shares with arrowroot, sugar and other crops the legacy of economic dependency which ties our region to the invisible hands of great powers that determine markets and development policy. Like arrowroot, St. Vincent Superfine strain of Sea Island cotton, classified as v.135, gave the Colony a virtual monopoly in world markets.[16] The strain was bred for St. Vincent conditions and, as in the case of Arrowroot, peculiarities of soil and climate created the conditions for the Colony's dominance in these areas. Unfortunately, as with Arrowroot, production could not keep pace with demand. Local interest in the crop declined during the war years due to labour shortages and rising production costs, and exports decreased.

In Nora's telling, the story of St Vincent's cotton industry reached allegorical proportions. She saw Vincentian involvement in cotton research as important to the link between scientific research and agricultural production. Our loss of control in this arena was symptomatic, in her view, of the decline of St. Vincent agriculture in general, which in turn she ascribed to lack of sovereignty.[17] Nora understood that the relationship between sovereignty and land is a driving force in the culture of SVG. Though she was encouraged that banana production afforded small farmers a greater degree of independence and profitability and hence, democratized economic wealth, she fretted that as, with Sea Island cotton, arrowroot and coconut oil, St Vincent would continue to lose its advantage to other territories. She blamed past and present tendencies for this situation: the historical favouring of Barbados by the British throughout colonial rule, she said, robbed St Vincent of the industries it established; secondly, she decried the lack of political vision on the part of our politicians to take a stronger stand on agriculture. In her opinion, they too easily capitulated to the macro-economic dictates of the big powers and needed to focus policy and resources, including education, on agriculture. These sorts of opinions would place her in the path of aspiring political leaders when she returned to live in St Vincent with Max in 1973 to take up the job of editor of the *Vincentian*. However, I must tell you first of the intervening years in territories of the Caribbean rim before returning to St Vincent.

Max and Nora

Nora ended a short lived marriage to fellow Vincentian, Bertram Hadley when she was 27. Max Peacocke came into her life in 1947. A civil engineer from Trinidad, Max was contracted by the Colonial Government to prepare the topographic survey for the development of Kingstown's water system. Max was already married and had a son and two daughters.[18] I understand from my cousins that Max and Nora met at the invitation of Nora's brother-in-law, Adrian Date, husband to her older sister, Dorothy. Adrian in his capacity as acting Administrator, of St Vincent felt obliged to have the fellow to a meal at Government House and suggested that Nora might be a pleasant companion for the evening. It appears that Adrian was correct in his judgement.

Max and Nora moved around the region for the next two decades during which time I was born in Guyana and Trevor Michael in Venezuela. Trevor and I were raised by a pair of nonconformists. The stands they took politically, their general caring for people, animals and each other, the lasting friendships they formed with young and old, and their steadfast nurturing of their children's better natures gave us a kind of wealth that cannot be spent whatever the costs life's journey entails. Trevor and I have made our living in fields related to our parents' regionalism, Trevor in languages and me as a writer. Trevor named his son Max.

Our parents' private non-conformity seems to echo the public longing for a broader social upheaval that, at the time, was shaping new forms of politics and artistic production all over the Caribbean neighbourhood. For example, referring to the transition of Trinidad carnival bands from bamboo and bottle to steel pans in the 1930s, Errol Hill writes, "The tempo of the age required a more strident beat".[18a] Hill's words resonate with phenomena of Caribbean Cultural Revolution in the first half of the 20th century – Aime Cesaire became Mayor of Forte de France in 1945, the same year that Fidel Castro began to study Law at the University of Havana. The 1950s saw Martin Carter publish *The Hill of Fire Glows Red* (1951), George Lamming, *The Castle of My Skin* (1953), VS Naipaul, *The Mystic Masseur* (1957) and Louise Bennett and Ranny Williams brought the oral poetic culture of the Jamaican people to radio. Derek Walcott was writing for both the Trinidad *Guardian* and Jamaica's *Public Opinion* during the 50s.

While in Trinidad between 1948 and 1952, Nora worked at the Caribbean Commission with Dr Eric Williams. He had published *Capitalism and Slavery* in 1944 and had returned to Trinidad in 1948, appointed to the post of Deputy Chairman of the Commission and where he held a series of educational lectures that had a profound impact on Nora's political consciousness.[19]

Some of my earliest memories are infused with images of Maracas Bay and carnival but also of the adults around me during this period. I remember well 'the man with the telephone in his ear' and many of my parents colleagues and friends[20]. I believe that the intensity of my recollection of Trinidad has to do with the avant guard aura of a new politics. Certainly conversations generated by their reading of CLR James and by their engagement with Eric Williams' ideas could have meant nothing to a four-year old, any more than I could understand the meaning of, "Nora, Nora, Nora, I beg you to leave Lord Kitchener". However, when I heard the calypso I was thrilled that my mother might be the subject of a song and I remember the roar of laughter with which Nora and friends responded to my enquiry "Is he singing about you?" I didn't get the meaning but I got the mood. For Nora, the Caribbean Commission experience contextualized her work in the St Vincent's Colonial Department of Agriculture that had shaped her 20s and 30s into a broader, federal vision. Indeed Max, Nora and their friends remained strong Federationists throughout.

Nora's three years in Venezuela were her least happy. In the first year we lived in an American oil company camp with other expatriates, mostly Americans, but as soon as he could, Max moved us to a house out on the savannah several miles from the nearest town. Being a social animal, Nora found life in a country where she could not speak the language isolating. These were the years when she came to understand that it would not be possible for her to live the restricted life in which women in love can find themselves surprised. She wanted to share her life with Max but she wanted to work to 'give back' as she said, from the many advantages she, like her siblings, had been allowed by chance or history. "It's not life that counts; it's the courage you bring to it", she wrote me once.

Trevor and I moved to Jamaica with Nora in 1956. An exchange between her and the Immigration Officer in the Arrivals Station at Palisades Airport is telling. The officer searched her passport in vain for an entry visa. He said, "You can't waltz into Jamaica just like that." She said, "How you mean? I thought we were in a Federation". He paused, looked at her, at the baby in her arms and the eight-year-old at her side. He said, "I think I read something about it in the paper. Pass through!"

Max would finish his contract in Venezuela and join us the following year. They had chosen to settle in Jamaica where they could *both* find employment. Another factor in the decision, at least in Nora's view, was that

Jamaica had the potential to influence the direction of the new federal society in terms of both population size and institutional capacity. Nora was big on 'institutional capacity', by which she meant the chemistry of a large, highly qualified civil service, innovative autonomous bodies with a broad-based cultural vision such as the Institute of Jamaica, and political leadership committed to social justice. She imagined the demise of British control as meaning the advance of a Federal model of governance – the island territories under the leadership of Norman Manley, Grantley Adams and Eric Williams with Belize and Guyana large and rich enough to anchor the whole against the economic predators to which our Caribbean is vulnerable.

Nora quickly found a job as a writer with *Public Opinion* weekly with O.T. Fairclough, one of the founders of the People's National Party. Mr Fairclough, like Dr Williams', broadened Nora's intellectual capacity to disavow colonialism while seeking to extract from that history a native Caribbean socialism that could nurture sovereign political institutions. Fairclough opened Nora's eyes to a uniquely Jamaican sensibility regarding the intersection of class and race. For example, she told me that conversations with Fairclough caused her to discard her views on Marcus Garvey. Not only had she been misinformed about Garvey's philosophy and what was at stake for the Jamaican masses in his leadership but she conceded that her ignorance of Garveyism was part and parcel of a colonial ideology she had imagined herself to be free of and, indeed, was indicative of the self-blinding privileges that accompany middle class status and 'light skin'.

Experience she gained through *Public Opinion* and as editor for another publication, *The Sugar Worker,* brought her talents as a writer into the familiar ground, from her Cotton Station days of agricultural workers, extension officers and technocrats and, importantly, into the immediate proximity of journalism as an arena of political agency that would be crucial years later when she became editor of the *Vincentian*. She also found fellow spirits of the fearless variety, as with prophetic soul of John Maxwell,[21] who lay down in the street to protest Norman Manley's decision to call a referendum over Jamaica's continued participation in Federation, which, Maxwell thought politically unwise.

Oh 'The Referendum'! Max and Nora followed Manley's campaign step-by-step along with other PNP pro-Federation stalwarts. Into the optimism of the speeches and rallies a note of opposition would rear its head – uninvited and unnerving. At that time we lived in a rural area of the Parish of St Catherine. One day my father stopped the car to buy bread at a shop in Slogoville. People were passing around 'Federation No' flyers illustrated with a photograph of anchor chains reputed by some to be from a Russian ship, by others from the 'Federal Maple' and 'Palm'[22]. The flyer and the talk around the shop ran along the lines that Federation would lead Black people back into slavery, as witnessed by the anchor chains of the said boats.

Furthermore, Manley's communist sympathies would require a poor farmer with two goats to give one up to an even poorer farmer for the greater good.

On the fated day we met on Madge and Carmen Smith's politically seasoned veranda to await the results of the referendum. The night began with encouraging returns from polls in the corporate area of the capital, Kingston. The gathering began to anticipate a win for Manley over the anti-Federation, Jamaica Labour Party, Alexander Bustamante – except for Max. A better mathematician, he calculated that the proportion of the urban vote returns, coming as it did from teachers, policemen, the urban middle class in general did not indicate enough of a margin to carry 'Federation Yes'. The utopians dismissed his predictions at the outset but solemnity descended as the rural returns proved him sadly correct. I was 13 years old but until that night, I had not seen my mother weep.

As with all magnificent illusions we can never know what might have been, but the collapse of Federation signaled the end of a particular trajectory of nationalism that came out of the combination of many forces, two of which I want to acknowledge here. First, the political inventiveness of West Indies 'Free Coloureds', of whom one of its descendants, Walter Grant is a stalwart example. That class, even before enfranchisement, cleverly managed whatever material advantages they could extract from their circumstances (and formal education for *both* sexes was crucial among these) to broaden their say in community, country and government. Consequently, their offspring were well placed to intensify their influence in the era immediately after widespread strikes and riots across the region in the 1930s to which the colonial government had responded with the Moyne Commission. Lord Moyne, a Fabian socialist, recommended sweeping policy changes toward self-government for Caribbean territories. This second, ideological, element offered a growing educated middle class a way to navigate between the unmet demands of the majority of impoverished Black fellow citizens and the impotence of a fading empire impatient to be free of its exhausted colonies.

Return to St Vincent

It's no exaggeration to say that the break-up of the Federation was devastating to my parents and their colleagues. It certainly confirmed a long stated agreement between Nora and Max that they would return to St Vincent in the future. Her way was 'to get on with it' and she did. They returned in 1973. Max built their house at Dorchester Hill, worked briefly as an engineer with the government and quit. Nora stepped into the editor's post at the *Vincentian* when Weston Lewis died, entering the strongest and longest test of her working life.

Nora E. Peacocke

The *Vincentian* was first published in 1919 (Nora would have been eight years old). Launched by men of property and business, an independent newspaper in the then colony was part of the recognition that print media technology was making it possible (and opportune) to disseminate ideas among those with access to and interests in modern arenas of political representation. It is well understood that newspapers in general and certainly the *Vincentian* had (and have) the interests of particular classes and groups at play. However, while we recognize those realities, it is also true that the principle of editorial independence was then – and even now in our 21st century reality of corporate media ownership – bandied about, if often hypocritically, as a necessity within capitalist society and that the composition of readership alters over time.

Nora and her generation had been drivers of the bigger idea of the 'public' that newspapers would serve. Public media had, since the 1930s, expanded well beyond the property-owning elites of the *Vincentian's* founding decade into the politically dynamic alliance between organized labour and newly-developing political parties.[23] Nora had fully inculcated the principles Walter had inspired in her childhood but she had also honed her talents as a writer and editor in scope and complexity through her association with the political leadership of Trinidad and Jamaica. She was idealistic; she was courageous but by the time she came home, the times were a-changing.

Idealism needs an object and the leadership and means to inspire and deliver that object. Emancipation was such an object and, over its long struggle, produced many inspired leaders capable of 'seizing the time'. Though such times were incremental and spread across centuries, the leadership for Emancipation articulated the goal and delivered. Self-government was the object of movements spanning the decades between the 1940s till our territories arrived at political independence. Caribbean political leadership for Self-government came from organized labour emboldened by social unrest in the first part of the 20th century:

[The disturbances of the 1930s were] a turning point for the labour movement and influenced the character of organized labour for the following 20 or 30 years (Alexander 2004). From this period, there is a strong association of trade union leaders with leaders of new political parties ... Labour and political movements both identified self-government as a goal and means of achieving their social and economic aims. There was widespread support for a small group of charismatic leaders who were generally middle class (Cooke)[24]

As editor of the *Vincentian*, Nora found herself in difficult terrain. She was a seeker for the kind of charismatic political leadership she had encountered in the likes of Williams, Manley and others during the anti-colonial era. At the same time she was determined to carry forward the role of the paper as an instrument of freedom of speech and this related dimension of her idealism brought her into conflict with the younger generation of leaders, men whose declared political goals she admired but whose actions she scrutinized and, on occasion, as the *Vincentian's* editor, would not give uncritical support. Nora wanted to believe in their leadership but, for Nora, freedom of editorial opinion, including letters to the editor, must be unencumbered except by legal overview. She saw herself as a custodian of the small piece of the fourth estate whose job was to assist the development of democratic institutions – as always, locating herself within the wider national space to which, she believed, each of us has a responsibility.

Would no one rid them of this troublesome editor?

The formation of the New Democratic Party (NDP) and the run-up to the NDP's election victory over Milton Cato's St Vincent Labour Party in 1984, brought exciting days. Nora, already considered a nuisance by the then Prime Minister, Mr Cato, was operating the paper under severe financial difficulty, all government notices having been withheld from the *Vincentian* as punishment for bringing to light certain incidents that the party in power at the time found to be, in today's media jargon, 'inconvenient to their narrative'. Nora had placed her editorial behind the NDP and its leader, the agronomist, James Mitchell.

I remember well on the day of the NDP win, witnessing the 'carylla phenomenon'. Among the jubilant crowds who came to greet Mr. Mitchell at the Grenadines Wharf, many descended from the hills carrying baskets of carylla, symbolic of the new hope that Mitchell's platform on agriculture brought to a key block within the electorate.[25] One man, noticing Nora in the throng, shouted to the world in general, "They think they could shut up we editor – but they couldn't shut she up!" Nora's gratitude for his public affirmation was evident in her face and would sustain her when, in his turn, Prime Minister Mitchell was moved to bring libel suits against her and the paper. I can only add that however 'unrealistic' (a charge I've often heard) Nora's expectation that political leaders should commit to the responsibility of a free press in the ongoing process of Caribbean modernization, the fact that men at the helm of political power found it advisable to restrict independent commentary confirms the truth of her conviction that St Vincent is not too small to have big principles and moreover, the state is served well to the degree that these are embraced.

In understanding Nora, we need to contextualize her life and work within changing conjunctures; between what we understand about the era of movements for Self-government and the conjuncture of the present that is, as yet, not clear to us. The political leadership of the two great Caribbean movements that took us out of colonialism had clear goals: first, ending enslavement/indenture and next, attaining self-government. Anti-colonial leadership found various ways to organize the material conditions of the times to achieve these goals. Also, and most significantly, the leaders of those earlier times did not have the pressures exerted on our leaders today – a circumstance where politicians everywhere on the planet are vulnerable to the availability of huge quantities of money, the sources of which create levels of environmental exploitation and human displacement on an unprecedented global scale; pressures Nora spotted that morning in 1991 when the flag of the Tsars returned to signal that 'capital is really consolidating'.

Conclusion

Nora was an idealist and poorly served by the political system she believed in. Yet, like many imaginative people, she envisioned possibilities that political pragmatists sometimes misread; consequently, her editorials have held water and carry value for the future. For one, the notion that in postcolonial states, particularly small ones, basic food security makes sense; it makes sense to design a cohesive regional agricultural policy and to invest in scientific research that can be applied to wider problems such as economic production and global markets. It makes sense to invest in the education of citizens – sound, broad-based, publicly funded primary and secondary schools and the highest standards of training at tertiary level. It makes sense for states to seek out Caribbean scholarship that enhances stronger communities and to give economically disadvantaged women power in decision making. It makes sense to secure women's 'traditional' obligations to children and the elderly at the very centre of economic and social policy design; and to seek from men the means to strengthen men's too often absent but essential nurture of caring, reciprocal, cultural values.

I can't review Nora's contributions without a final backward glance at the loss of her cherished political love –West Indies Federation.. That the Federation (1958 to 1962) died in its infancy may have foretold the Caribbean's impending displacement within an international system long ruled by Anglo-American power, now in decline.[26] Changes in that conjuncture are now upon us as: "the linked processes of globalization and economic liberalization have weakened the coherence and stability of many Caribbean states"[27] and as China's trade relations with the region assume greater importance. It remains to be seen whether these developments bode well for those who pride themselves on 'going it alone' or if the winds of change now will renew the desire Nora and many of her splendid generation so fervently held – "to dwell together in unity." [28]

End Notes

[1]   I am grateful to Sir Rupert John for his meticulous, *Pioneers in Nation-Building in a Caribbean Mini-State* (2009) for his recognition of Walter McGregor Grant; and to KINGS-SVG Publishers whose documentation of the history of our island irrigates the neglected fields traversed by those determined men and women who nurtured the accomplishments gained through their predecessors' struggles. These ordinary citizens of St Vincent and The Grenadines interpreted and responded to the immense reconfigurations of global power that shaped the 20th century with courage and inventiveness. They were guided by the relationship between self-interest and service to the collective, to social freedom and economic justice.

May we of the 21st century tend to our fields with such hands.

[2]   *Slavic Review* Vol 52 No 4 (Winter 1993) pp 811, 812.

http://www.stanford.edu/~gfreidin/Publications/Televort1.pdf Retrieved Nov 21 2010.

[3] Ibid *Slavic Review, p* 828.

[4]   The term is from Karl Marx, who defined critical theory as "the self-clarification of the struggles and wishes of the age".

[5]   Josephine Allen, Walter and Nellie's granddaughter recalls visiting Nellie at her house on Middle Street in Kingstown. There was easy access between the then Southbridge Hotel, run by Walter's sisters ("The Aunts") and Nellie's house. Josephine remembers watching in childish fright as stilt men paraded past Nellie's house at carnival.

[6]   Alison Parchment, Walter and Nellie's granddaughter, e-mail dated Nov 30, 2010.

[7] The *Vincentian* newspaper of 9 June, 1945, a tribute to W.M. Grant on his death, quoted. By Sir Rupert John.

[8]   Sir Rupert describes his remarkable first speech as a member of the Legislative Council in September 1924. The question before the Council was, "Is the Medical Service of this Colony satisfactory to Government? If not what steps are being taken to make it so?" (John 161)   Walter, responding to the reply of the Administrator, Sir Robert Walter, first

described the reply as "evasive, or rather, as no answer to the question at all", before going on to state that "the community in general was dissatisfied with the medical service of the colony, and that it was his view that Government could not be held blameless." He went further and named, as an example, the case of a Distract Medical Officer, Dr. W.A.S. George, who was away on extended leave for eighteen months while the district remained without the services of a doctor. (John 162)

[9] Nora E Peacocke "My Headmistress", *GHS School Magazine.* Date not available.

[10] Dorothy married Adrian Date of Grenada. She died in 1979.

[11] The paragraph from "My Headmistress" reads in full:

"My Head was the nearest to a 'born teacher' that I have ever encountered. Although no top-flight academic herself, she truly appreciated knowledge. She taught us to love reading, so that books became our friends and getting to know about the people and things related in the various stories recounted in their pages was a pleasure. What we learned about the writers increased our interest further. Miss Went knew it would and that sort of information was often forthcoming in the classes which my group of G.H.S. students had the good fortune to attend. We got to know about the unorthodox sexual tendencies of Byron, the mental problems of the unfortunate Lambs, the tyranny of Elizabeth Barrett Browning's father and, on the lighter side, that William Shakespeare's wife, formerly Anne Hathaway, was a determined lady, of whom the great poet was wont to say, "Anne hath a way!" The anecdote about Sir Philip Sidney refusing a drink of water that he sorely longed for when he was dying on the battle field, and having it presented instead to an ordinary wounded soldier with the words, 'His need is greater than mine,' brought the little known poet into focus. 'Elegy Written in a Country Churchyard', Thomas Gray's great poem, took on an added meaning when we heard that the young General Wolfe, who led his soldiers in the scaling of the Heights of Abraham to capture Quebec (and so Canada) for the British from the French, declared sadly the night before his success (and death) "1 rather be the author of 'Gray's Elegy in a Country Churchyard' than the man to capture Quebec tomorrow."

[12] Carlton Williams would later become Chief Agricultural Officer

[13] A Ramani. *ELS Cotton in India – An Analysis*: "In the next stage, Sujata was crossed with St.Vincent Sea Island seeds and an extraordinary variety was produced which had a staple length of over 1-1/2 inch, stelo strength of 32 gtex (equal to 40gpt on HVI). This by any standard was the

finest cotton ever produced in India. The first three alphabets of each variety (Sujata and Vincent) were used to the name the variety as SUVIN". http://cottonbangladash.com/April2006/ELS.htm Retrieved Dec 05 2010.

[14] C.B. Gibbs, a Grenadian, served in senior positions in the St Vincent civil service from 1943 to 1953, when he acted as Administrator. See Chapter 5, pp 41-56 by P. Antrobus in *Caribbean Trailblazers* , Eds. Baldwin King and Cheryl Phills King, 2010.

[15] Ciprian Bernard Gibbs: *A Plan of Development for the Colony of St Vincent* (1946–1956) p 29.

[16] Historical circumstances that determined distribution of land have always been at the heart of political struggles in St Vincent. Garifuna strategies to disrupt and manage encroaching French/English occupation during the 16th century carried on until 1797; the long travails of African enslavement and Indian Indenture; the eventual demise of the plantation system and the rise of an independent peasantry, as Karl John notes in his case study of land reform in St Vincent 1890–2000, attest to this fact.

[17] Max's children with his first wife are Yann Garcien, Sally Friedberg and Jennifer Peacocke.

[18a] Errol Hill. *The Trinidad Carnival.* 1972 & 1997 London: New Beacon Books p47.

[18] Nora and Max had already left for Venezuela, where Max surveyed with the Schlumberger Oil Company when Eric Williams launched his Caribbean-transforming 'University of Woodford Square' public lectures on world history attracting huge audiences from across the diverse social configurations that make up Trinidad and pushing forward the independence agenda for the entire Anglophone region.

[19] The 'telephone' referred to Dr Williams hearing aid. He also kept a sign on the wall behind his desk that read, "speak loudly". Among my parents friends I remember Keith and Dink Gordon (Dink *nee* King was a teacher at the Girl's High School before her marriage to Keith Gordon of St.Lucia), Monty Braithwaite, and Victor Woodstock.

[20] John Maxwell died on December 11, 2010.

[21] The 'Federal Maple' and 'Federal Palm' were gifts to the Federation of the West Indies by another Federal State of the Commonwealth, Canada.

Nora E. Peacocke

[22] G.C.H Thomas' novel, *Ruler in Hiroona,* McMillan Caribbean (2003) is a riveting account of this period.

[23] Ian Cooke, The Society For Caribbean Studies Annual Conference Papers. Ed. Sandra Courtman. Vol 7 2006 ISSN 1471–2024

[24] Thanks to my cousin, Nicola Williams for recalling Marcus DeFreitas' role in promoting the medical properties of carylla during the campaign.

[25] Regarding the granting of independence to Caribbean territories during the 1960s to 1980s: "Sutton argues 'the process of decolonization was largely [ad hoc] and represented the Caribbean expression of the wider policy of liquidation of empire. It was not fed by any special interest or concern with the Caribbean per se and had no particular distinguishing features except one: that decolonization should be compatible with US interests in the region' (Sutton 2001 p43)" quoted in Clegg, "Out With The Old, In With The New" The Society for Caribbean Studies Annual Conference Papers edited by Sandra Courtman. Vol 7, 2006; ISSN 1471-2024, pdf, p2.

[26] Peter Clegg "Out With The Old, In With The New" The Society for Caribbean Studies Annual Conference Papers edited by Sandra Courtman. Vol 7, 2006; ISSN 1471-2024, pdf, pp1-2.

[27] Motto of the Federation of The West Indies.

Nan Peacocke is a writer and poet. She resides in Peterborough, Ontario, Canada.

Caribbean Trailblazers: St. Vincent and the Grenadines

13.   **PATRICK E. PRESCOD**
By
Fred Prescod

Introduction

Patrick Eugene Prescod was born on the 17th March 1932 at Georgetown, St. Vincent. Pat, as he was fondly known, was brought up in a family rich in musical talent. His grandmother, Clara Bacchus whom he frequently visited, was organist and choir leader in the Methodist Church at New Grounds. She also gave private music lessons on her harmonium keyboard instrument at home. Both of his parents were musically inclined. His father, C.W. Prescod played the violin, and his mother, Louise Prescod was organist for the Georgetown Methodist Church, as well as being a piano teacher. His older brother, Ben was an accomplished pianist, who played both classics and jazz. An older sister, Clara played the violin, while another sister, Norma was accomplished on the piano and organ. Norma was also a talented mezzo-soprano singer. A third sister, Cynthia also played the piano. Pat himself exhibited a very early aptitude for music. At the tender age of five, he would go to the piano and repeat bars of music by ear from pieces recently played by his older brother, Ben. Later he would play, again by ear, hymns that he heard his mother play on the organ at church.

Early Education – Academic, Musical and Extracurricular Activities

Pat received his primary education at the Georgetown Government Primary School. He continued to demonstrate an ability to grasp and display remarkable all-round talents in music. He was a good student and later on, his general academic performance enabled him to gain entrance to the St. Vincent Grammar School in Kingstown.

At the Grammar School, which he entered in 1944, Pat distinguished himself as a good student, while also participating in many extracurricular school activities. His favorite subject was English and in 1951 he was awarded the Bain Gray Essay Prize. As a prefect in the sixth form, he was well liked and respected by staff and students alike. Musically, he benefited greatly from his experiences as a member of the school choir under the direction of the late Dr. Cooper Jacobs, who was succeeded by the late Mr. Henry Williams and subsequently by the late Mr. E. Mc G "Shake" Keane.

In his later years at the Grammar School, Pat became the choir's accompanist on piano; and on joining the teaching staff at his Alma Mater in 1952, after Mr. Keane's departure for the U.K., Pat took over the directorship of the choir. During his time with the choir, he had been introduced to the basic tonic sol-fa system of vocal music, and the knowledge gained through this, and in part singing, proved subsequently to be invaluable. Pat's other pursuits included his role as troop leader of the Grammar School Scout Troup and his active membership in the school's Debating Society. By and large his disposition was pleasant and he always enjoyed a good joke. He had an infectious laugh and was a great storyteller. His younger siblings and close relatives remember with some degree of nostalgia the pleasure they derived from listening to his humorous stories, told over and over, while they hung on his every word and gesture.

However, Pat's activities were not limited to sedentary pursuits, as he also excelled on the sports field. At the school's annual athletic sports in 1948 and 1949, he placed first in the hurdles event and won certificates in other events such as the shot put, all with very little training. Generally, Pat loved the outdoors. During school vacations, he would sea-bathe in the rough Atlantic waters in Georgetown. At other times, he would hike from New Grounds to Georgetown, or vice versa, a distance of about six miles. At New Grounds he would trek through the rough and hilly terrain of his grandmother's estate.

Pat graduated from the Grammar School in 1951. Subsequently, he was appointed non-graduate master at the School and taught French, English and Music there for six years. During that time, he directed the Grammar School choir and helped train the Girl's High School choir as well. Many years later, former students would recount their intriguing introduction to part singing, and some still recall many of the songs they were taught. Others fondly reminisce about the annual caroling excursions around Kingstown and suburbs during the Christmas season.

During his years in Kingstown, Pat took formal piano lessons from Miss Eunice Horne, who in those days was St. Vincent's leading piano teacher. Later, after Miss Horne's retirement, on his own he sat for the various levels of music exams offered in St. Vincent by London's Trinity College of Music and the Associated Board of the Royal Schools of Music (ABRSM). In 1957 he became the first Vincentian locally to gain distinction in piano performance at the Final Grade 8 Level Examination of the ABRSM.

In the Methodist Church

In Kingstown, as was the case previously in Georgetown and at New Grounds, Pat was brought up in the Methodist Church, where he regularly attended morning and evening church service as well as afternoon Sunday school. He was subsequently received into the membership of the Methodist Church in December 1947. His musical talent led him to begin learning to play the church's pipe organ, which he soon mastered. He would later on become the organist for the Sunday school, and assistant organist to the long-standing church organist, Miss Winnie Wilson. In 1963, after the passing of Miss Wilson, Pat was appointed Church Organist and after some time eventually assumed the added responsibility as Choir Director. During the ensuing years, the choir attempted many ambitious programs including excerpts from Handel's Messiah and other works of the great masters, such as Bach, Mozart, Beethoven, Haydn, and others. Although retiring officially at the end of 1999, he continued his contributions to the musical life of the Methodist Church through the organizing of various musical events from time to time; these included workshops for choirs and church musicians, concerts and festivals, plus recitals and other performances by local and visiting soloists and musical groups. A wide cross section of the community has continued to look forward to the annual midweek lunchtime concerts (begun in 1999) held at the Methodist Church in Kingstown and featuring appropriate music during the Lenten season.

The Consummate Musician

Extremely modest and reticent, Pat gave further evidence of his musical talents when in 1954 at age 22 he went to Trinidad to enter the Trinidad and Tobago National Music Festival. He swept all before him and walked away with first place in the Piano Solo Class. In addition he won the Championship trophy for Best Pianoforte Performance overall. He also accompanied on piano two other Vincentian performers, namely Dietrich Thomas who won in the Under 14 Violin Class and Doris Robinson who placed 3rd in the Soprano Solo Class. The adjudicator was Dr. Herbert Wiseman of the U.K.

In 1956 he decided to share his passion for music with others who had a similar love, this time in the area of choral music. The result was that Pat established and directed a mixed choir, which he named the Kingstown Choral Group. In April of the same year he entered the choir in St. Vincent's first Music Festival, and their stirring performance won them first place in the choral category from six already established choirs. The adjudicator was Dr. Vernon Evans, then Music Officer of Trinidad and Tobago.

Pat's busy schedule of teaching at the Grammar School and operating as Musical Director of the Kingstown Choral Group did not deter him from other musical activities. He served as Chair of the Music Festival Committee that organized St. Vincent's first Music Festival in 1956 and thereafter he remained an active member while also fulfilling the role of official accompanist (piano) at successive festivals. Over the years his home was always a hub of musical activity and the venue for long hours of rehearsals for vocal and instrumental soloists, duets, trios, quartets, and of course the Kingstown Choral Group, later to be known as the Kingstown

Chorale. Additionally in the years between music festivals, which were usually held at intervals of two to four years, he was frequently called on to accompany vocalists and other musicians for performances at a variety of events, and this would include amateur and professional visiting musicians. Further there was a growing demand for him to play piano solos at several concerts and other such events.

Pat eventually opened a music studio at his home to offer piano and voice lessons. Needless to say, he was quickly swamped with applicants, who saw him as a role model and naturally had aspirations of great achievements in music. Indeed many of his students achieved high marks in the Trinity College and Royal Schools music exams and have gone on to contribute significantly to the musical life of St. Vincent and the Grenadines at home and abroad.

Higher Education and Training

In 1958, Pat was awarded a scholarship to study music, and he entered Trinity College of Music in London, England. He graduated from Trinity College in 1962 with the diploma G.T.C.L. (Graduate of Trinity College London) having previously satisfied the requirements for the Licentiate Diploma in School Music (L.R.S.M.) from the A.B.R.S.M. and returned home to begin an illustrious career of distinguished national and regional service in the field of music.

Some of the treasured memories he frequently shares concerning his stay in the U.K. and his time at Trinity College of Music are:

i.   His fruitful interaction with eminent musicians whose books he had previously read or studied assiduously at home in St. Vincent.

ii.   The excitement of listening to some of the world famous choirs, orchestras and soloists live, and the added privilege as a music student to sit in on their rehearsals before the final performance.

iii.   His own participation in the Trinity College Choir under the direction of the late Charles Kennedy Scott, one of England's vocal and choral experts of all time.

iv.   His participation in a joint choir consisting of students of the four major Music Colleges in London, viz. The Royal Academy, The Royal College, The Guildhall School of Music and the Trinity College of Music, who, along with their combined orchestras, presented a memorable concert at the Royal Albert Hall, London, under the baton of the eminent Sir Malcolm Sargeant in February 1961.

Having gained considerable and valuable musical knowledge, techniques, experience and exposure abroad, Pat was now anxious to share his insights with all and sundry in his homeland.

In October 1962, he was appointed to the new post of Music Officer in the Ministry of Education and was given the responsibility for the development of music in schools and educational institutions.

As the sole member of the Ministry's Music Department, he set about his task with enthusiasm, developing programs for teachers through workshops at various centers, visiting schools and later introducing radio programs to complement the classroom teaching. He instituted an annual schools' music festival in 1965 giving more scope for performance, and for the revival of folk music. He also introduced the descant recorder as an aid to the reading of musical notation and as a preparation for progression to larger wind instruments like the clarinet. In subsequent years, the work of the Music Department benefitted from the contributions of many other talented and dedicated musicians including Lois Williams, Olsen Peters, Gloria Jack, Joel Miguel, Ian Glaude, Vin Stewart and Joffre Venner.

A Creative and Fulfilling Period

On his return from the U.K., Pat revived the Kingstown Choral Group, resumed his service to the Methodist Church as organist, and restarted his private tutoring at his home. Further he answered ever-increasing requests for his services in the wider community. These requests included serving on judges' panels for calypso and steelband competitions as well as being involved in the staging of various musical events run by volunteer organizations. During this period too, he served as Musical Director for the production of the Gilbert and Sullivan operettas, *"The Mikado"* in 1965 and the *"The Gondoliers"* in 1966. The productions were staged by the St. Vincent Light Operatic Group. By 1970, the positive effects of Pat's work with the Kingstown Choral Group began to become evident in the improved standard of performance and the first full-length choral presentation, *"November Serenade"*, was staged at the Peace Memorial Hall that year. This production became an annual feature, eagerly anticipated by the Vincentian public. The Group's timetable thereafter was a rather demanding one, as can be seen from the following record:

1970	November Serenade I
1971	November Serenade II
1972	Carifesta (Guyana)
	Carifesta Program repeated in St. Vincent
1973	Concert tour to Trinidad
1974	(i) "Moods of Music" at the Peace Memorial Hall
	(ii) St. Vincent Music Festival
1977	(i) "Moods of Music" repeated on Concert tour
	to St. Lucia

	(ii) "Sing Noel" – Christmas Concert at St. George's Cathedral, Kingstown
1976	(i) St. Vincent Music Festival
	(ii) Production of L.P. record "We kind a music"
1977	Christmas Concert, "Peace, Love and Joy" at St. George's Cathedral
1977	This was the year also, when Pat was invited to adjudicate at the Grenada National Music Festival. This enabled him to once again become aware of musical trends and developments in another Caribbean country .

In the Choir's 40th Anniversary Magazine in 1996, Pat wrote:

"This period was for me the most creative and fulfilling, and yet most frustrating and demanding – physically and emotionally. There were times when sleepless nights gave birth to new musical ideas and adventurous compositions and choral arrangements; when the drive to recapture heights of excellence experienced abroad became relentless and compelling; when weary hours were spent drumming out choral parts at the piano in a never ending succession of rehearsals; when thirty-odd tired voices were often coaxed and cajoled into repeating a musical phrase for 'just a few times more' so that some particular nuance of choral interpretation could be perfected".

The decades of the 60's and 70's were exciting times in the Caribbean and of great significance. Issues relating to identity, self-determination and national development dominated. Intellectuals spoke and wrote with passion, politicians agitated and the "man-in-the-street" wanted his place in the sun. These stirrings soon created powerful vibrations that found sympathetic utterance in the realms of politics, religion and culture, and the reality of this phenomenon began to show its influence on the creative and performing arts in the region. With Jamaica and Trinidad gaining political independence in 1962 after the unfortunate demise of the West Indies Federation, the other Caribbean territories followed in quick succession with St. Vincent and the Grenadines achieving its independence in October 1979. At this time too, there was the increase in interest in our African roots. Small wonder then that Pat who had always had a quiet fascination with the 'boom drum' serenaders at Christmas time, the rhythmic chants of the Spiritual Baptists and the songs and stories of the Vincentian countryside, consciously turned his attention to expressing some of these hidden vibrations in his creative work. Two important events provided him the opportunity, viz.

i. The Caribbean Festival of Arts (Carifesta) 1972 in Guyana

Patrick E. Prescod

ii.   The Inauguration of the Caribbean Conference of
      Churches in 1973

The Kingstown Choral Group (renamed the Kingstown Chorale) was
invited to represent St. Vincent at Carifesta I. This was an historic event and
the challenge led to a feverish search for exclusively Vincentian musical
material. This resulted in Pat's creation of the folk operetta, "Sarah and
Dalfus" from local folk songs, and a representation in song and drama of a
Vincentian "Tea meeting". Also for the first time, as far as is known, a
conventional choir was including calypsos in its repertoire. A medley of
patriotic songs of St. Vincent and the Grenadines was also included.

The choir was well received at Carifesta and was invited to Trinidad the
following year (1973) to appear in concert with the Marionettes, one of that
country's leading choirs. The Kingstown Chorale once again presented a
repertoire of Vincentian music, including *"Hairoun my Home"*, with words
by the late Tim Daisy set to music by Pat Prescod; also *"Ding Dong"*, a
calypso by the late Caribbean Hawke in which the voices imitated the sound
of a steel band, and *"Mas in May"*, a calypso by the late Lord Kitchener of
Trinidad. The audience was taken by surprise and the press was most
generous in their comments, especially as the leading choirs in Trinidad, it
appeared, had not yet included calypso in their repertoire.

Caribbean Church Music

In November 1973, The Caribbean Conference of Churches (CCC) was
inaugurated. This organization was the umbrella body of the ecumenical
movement in the Caribbean, and its objective was to serve the Churches in
the Caribbean in the cause of unity, renewal and joint action through its two
subsidiary agencies – Christian Action for Development in the Caribbean
(CADEC) and Action for the Renewal of the Church (ARC). At its
inauguration there were thirty-three member churches from countries in the
Caribbean and the Americas.

In 1976, CADEC had sponsored the production of the L.P. record "We
Kind a Music" by the Kingstown Chorale. The repertoire consisted of
classical, popular, folk, calypso, patriotic songs, and religious songs. In this
production, Pat had taken the choir on a new path with his arrangement of
the Caribbean items. The repertoire also included the hymn "The Right Hand
of God" with words by Patrick Prescod and music by Noel Dexter of
Jamaica. This hymn had been adopted by the CCC at its inauguration as its
theme song. It has since been translated into several languages and included
in the hymn books of many Christian denominations worldwide.

In 1978 the CCC requested Pat's services to fill the position of Regional
Coordinator of its Caribbean Church Music Program. This necessitated

secondment from his position as Music Officer with the St. Vincent and the Grenadines Government, which agreed to release him for two years. During this period, based at the Trinidad headquarters, he traveled throughout the region meeting with pastors, church musicians, composers and authors with a view to compiling and arranging a collection of hymns by Caribbean writers for use in the churches of the region and abroad. These efforts resulted in 1981 in the publication of *'Sing a New Song No 3'*.

An ardent lover of steelpan music, Pat took the opportunity while in Trinidad to visit the main pan yards from time to time. In St. Vincent he had already broken new ground by having the Starlift Steel Orchestra accompany the Kingstown Chorale at their Christmas Concert at St. George's Cathedral in 1975. He had also worked closely with many of the local pannists and encouraged the playing of the classics as a means of developing variety in their repertoire and also in developing music reading skills, sensitivity and technical dexterity. Because of his training in the Western European musical tradition, he naturally sought every opportunity to encourage the integration of contrasting cultural strands.

Resumption of a Hectic Musical Schedule

After his stint with the CCC, Pat returned to St. Vincent to resume his hectic musical life. Two of his main areas of preoccupation at this time were:

i.   Organizing a Festival of Caribbean Hymns involving choirs and instrumentalists from the Anglican, Methodist and Roman Catholic Churches, the Salvation Army, the Lowmans Leeward Anglican School, the Girls' High School and the Kingstown Chorale. The Festival took place at the Methodist Church, Kingstown late in 1980 and was put together in conjunction with the St. Vincent Christian Council.

ii.   Preparing and rehearsing the Kingstown Chorale for the Celebration of its 25th Anniversary in 1981.

Both these projects were well received by capacity audiences. Unfortunately, however, after the 25th Anniversary Celebrations the Chorale experienced a period of dormancy but resumed its activities in 1983 with a name change to the New Kingstown Chorale. During this period though, Pat's involvement as Organist and Choir Director at the Methodist Church, his execution of the musical program at the Ministry of Education, his tutoring of private students and his service to the wider community intensified. Also, he again played a pivotal role in the St. Vincent and the Grenadines National Competitive Music Festivals of 1981, 1984 and 1986. Once again his home became a hub of musical activity as individuals and groups rehearsed late into the night for several months leading up to these festivals. His last major productions as Musical Director of the New Kingstown Chorale were *"Christmas is yours, Christmas is mine"* in 1985, *"To music"* in 1988 and *"Incarnation"* in 1989, at which time he gently passed the Music Director's baton to Mrs. Jeanne Horne. Nevertheless, he still remained intimately involved with the Chorale in a supportive and advisory capacity and traveled with the group on their North American tour in 1992, assisting with choral arranging, piano accompanying, and conducting.

In 1990 some of his young enthusiastic voice students who had done well at the Trinity College music exams and who had sung together at a student's concert, decided that they wanted to stay together as a small female ensemble under the name "Cantemus". This group participated in the 1991 St. Vincent Music Festival and excelled. Pat found himself once again in a familiar nurturing role for this new musical baby which he piloted through the first nine years of its existence, and which later in 2006 had the distinction of capturing the Mary Evans Cup at the championships in the Trinidad and Tobago Music Festival under the direction of Mrs. Donna Clarke.

Important Developments in Pat's Musical Journey

Two other important developments, which had some impact on Pat's musical journey, were:

i.   His retirement from the post of Music Officer in the
        Ministry of Education in December 1986 and
ii.   His relocation in 1995 from his Higginson Street home to
        Cane Garden

Pat's retirement from the Ministry of Education created the opportunity for added dimensions to his service not only to the Kingstown Methodist Church, but to the other Methodist churches and churches of other denominations throughout St. Vincent and the Grenadines, as well as to individuals and organizations such as the St. Vincent and the Grenadines Music Association. He also extended his hours of private music teaching.

At the Kingstown Methodist Church, apart from his duties as Organist and Choir Director, he became involved in the organization of musical events such as concerts, festivals and workshops, and in 1987 identified at the church a number of musically talented young people whom he brought together to form the group *"New Life Singers"*. This group contributed meaningfully to the worship at the church for many years, and its members benefited greatly from the experience. Later, some of these young people graduated to the senior church choir, which at the time was extending its membership and repertoire.

The Prescod home at the corner of Higginson and Grenville (Back) Streets in Kingstown had been for many years a familiar landmark from which the sound of music and clicking typewriters emanated every day of the week. Every St. Vincent-based member of the family taught. The patriarch, C.W. Prescod, before his passing in January 1980, had taught shorthand, typewriting and book keeping (this of course was in an era before the advent of the computer, the cellular phone, and other communication tools of the 21st century); Mrs. Louise Prescod taught piano until the age of 90; Clara taught the violin, English, and mathematics; Cynthia taught commercial subjects and piano, and Pat taught piano, musical theory, and voice. Therefore when in 1995 the family relocated to Cane Garden, there was a cessation of activities at that location.

By September 1996, Pat however reopened his music teaching studio at a location at White Chapel, Kingstown. Journeying daily from Cane Garden, he conducted classes at White Chapel with the help of a few of his past students.

On many occasions the studio produced concerts at which students displayed their skills before their parents, relatives and friends. These concerts allowed the students to share their talents while gaining confidence. One of the special features of these concerts was the performance of a choir consisting of the parents and relatives of the students. In 1999 also, students of the St. Lucia School of Music were invited to perform as guest artistes. Similarly, in 2001 a music student from the Barbados Community College performed as guest artiste in flute. These performances gave the visiting students added exposure and helped to motivate the local students.

In 2002 however, because of health challenges and domestic emergencies, Pat decided to discontinue his teaching at the White Chapel location and he made the necessary arrangements to do his teaching at his home at Cane Garden on a less strenuous timetable. Consequently he turned over the White Chapel studio to Floyd Parris, one of his former students.

In 2009 Pat had the distinct pleasure of seeing one of his advanced students, Victor M. Job exceed his own 1957 record by becoming the first student locally to achieve a pass with distinction in piano performance at the diploma level (Dip. A.B.R.S.M.). This was in an examination conducted by a visiting representative of the Associated Board of the Royal Schools of Music.

At the time of writing, at age 79, Pat still maintains his musical passion although, because of health challenges, he is unable to keep up his former hectic pace. Nevertheless, he still does some limited teaching, continues to exercise his mentoring role and delights in encouraging and motivating all who come within the scope of his influence to attain worthwhile goals and make a positive contribution to their community. At this time he is also compiling a selection of his musical compositions over the years.

Religious Conviction

Unfailingly, Pat has always placed, at the top of his priority list, the nurturing of his own Christian faith and he has believed in the power of prayer, the confession and forgiveness of sins, the necessity for active Christian fellowship and service and the practice of Christian love. In September 2010 he published *"A Selection of Favourite Memorable Texts and Topics From The Holy Bible"*. Indeed he has often quoted the following lines from his late mother's favorite hymn by Joseph Hart, 1712 – 1768:

"We'll praise Him for all that is past
And trust Him for all that's to come."

A Selection of Pat's Compositions and Arrangements

Words only
- *The Right Hand of God* – (Music by Noel Dexter)
- Theme Song for Inauguration of the Caribbean Conference of Churches – 1973

Music Only
- *Per Ardua ad Alta* – St. Vincent Girls High School (Words: Yvonne Gaynes)
- *Hairoun My Home* – Words from a poem by the late Tim Daisy – 1973
- *In Your Hands* – Words by the late Rev. Allan Kirton – 1980
- *Righteousness Exalteth a Nation* – words based on Proverbs 14:34

Words and Music
- *God Bless Our Homeland* – Patriotic Song
St. Vincent – 1969
- *Per Aspera ad Astra* – St. Vincent Grammar School Song – 1964
- *Participation in God's World* – Caribbean Conference of Churches Theme Song – 1991
- *Vision 2002* (words 1996)/
Mission! The Kingdom of God (words revised 2011) – The Methodist Church St. Vincent Renewal Song

Choral Arrangements

- *We kind a Music* – The Mighty Sparrow – Trinidad Calypso
- *Ding Dong* – Caribbean Hawke – Vincentian Calypso
- *Mas in May* – Lord Kitchener – Trinidad Calypso
- *Lovely Isle* – H. W. Hall (Patriotic Song, St. Vincent)
- *I love the blest Hairoona* – E. Mc. G. "Shake" Kean (Patriotic Song, St. Vincent)
- *Massa say no wuk today* – Vincentian work song (for male voices)

Some Expressions of Appreciation
To Patrick E. Prescod

Certificates, Plaques and Medals

- 1981, From the Caribbean Conference of Churches
"For outstanding service to regional ecumenism"

- 1994, From the Ministry of Education – St. Vincent and the Grenadines
"Award presented for dedicated service to education"

- 2000, From the Department of Culture – St. Vincent and the Grenadines
"For contribution to music and culture"

- 2000, From the St. Vincent and the Grenadines Music Association
"For sterling contribution to the development of music in St. Vincent and the Grenadines"

- 2006, From the Kingstown Chorale, 50th Anniversary Award
"Presented in recognition of your visionary leadership, pioneering spirit and continued assistance and mentoring over the years"

- 2007, O.B.E. (Officer of the Most Excellent Order of the British Empire)
From Her Majesty the Queen
"For distinguished service to music and education"

- 2007, From the Methodist Church, Kingstown/Chateaubelair Circuit
"For his sterling contribution to the development of music in St. Vincent and the Grenadines and the Caribbean"

- 2010, From the Starlift Steel Orchestra

"For his dedication to music and salutes him as an inspiration to generations of Vincentian musicians"

Fred Prescod is a Vincentian-born horticulturist by profession. He lives in Hamilton, Ontario, Canada.

Caribbean Trailblazers: St. Vincent and the Grenadines

14.   **ALPHONSO "ALFIE" ROBERTS**
By
Kenneth John

Cricket genius, political titan

Alphonso "Alfie" Roberts was born in St. Vincent and the Grenadines on September 18, 1937 to Theodore and Naomi Roberts. He was born a sportsman. Cricket had become his first love. But he was also good in track and field, and the records show that in the year 1953 when he made the national cricket team at 15 years old; he also broke the Grammar School Pole vault record for his age-group.

In the early 1950's too, Alfie was one of the leading footballers for his school, playing a dashing centre forward and paving the path for other youths, notably Creswell Durrant and Carl "Pee Wee" Glen, to follow.

From early on, Alfie took to cricket like a duck to water. As Frankie Thomas describes it, he was of the same mould as Lawrence Rowe. The majesty of his all-round stroke-play was poetry in motion. The Windward Islands never saw the likes of him before, or since, though Irvin Shillingford reached within striking distance.

By any objective standard, Alfie remains simply the most accomplished batsman ever produced in the Windward Islands. And yet in the early nineties in a competition sponsored by Bottlers Limited in Dominica for selection of the strongest Windwards post-war team, Alfie did not make it to the batting line-up. There were Irvin Shillingford, Shane Julien, Val Felix and Evelyn Gresham, none of whom, save Irvin, could walk in Alfie's shadow.

Alfie cut his cricket teeth as a "park-boy" on the "small wicket" at Victoria Park, Kingstown along with Vincent Hadaway, Ian Neverson and Caspar Quammie and the seasoned brigade of Eldon Bramble, Sylvester Noel and George Hinds. These games were " a dollar-a-side", protective gear was forbidden and, ironically, they separated the men from the boys. At thirteen years, Alfie was counted among the men of the "Park Boys"!

In fact, backyard cricket apart, I first saw Alfie in action on the "small wicket" one Saturday morning when he was about thirteen years old. He had filled a vacancy in a Roman Catholic School team, and he and Martin Barnard put up a stout resistance against an older team, to the astonishment of onlookers.

Next came Grammar School where Alfie met Lester Huggins, Raymond Liverpool, and Phil Ambris in Reeves House Juniors. But the precocious youngster, still in short pants, was invited in his first year to play for the Senior Team with the likes of George T. Browne who went on to become an International umpire.

Only fourteen years old, Alfie went to Grenada for the Inter-School tournament in 1952 with two other promising youths in the persons of Vin Cuffy and Eddie Griffith – as the Grammar School's most exciting batsman. Roberts did not come off with the bat, yielding pride of place to opener Errol Daisley, but he returned the best bowling figures!

On his return from Grenada in 1952, he was expressing to me his dislike of his Grenadian nickname "Zagada" when heart-throb Betty Sandy rode up to us on her bicycle and innocently enquired "Alfie, what is your nickname – Zig-what?" He turned all colours of the rainbow.

At fifteen years, Roberts became the youngest Windward Islander to play Cork Cup Tournament. He made the home-team in 1953, easily meshing with the big guns – Eldon Bramble, Ardon Daisley, Cayley Bonadie, Ian Neverson and Frankie Thomas – in a batting arsenal of awesome fire-power.

Immediately, Roberts as well as Grenada's Evelyn Gresham caught the eye of Berkeley Gaskin, then in a star-search mission on behalf of the West Indies Cricket Board. They were both selected on one of the early Windward Islands teams that played against John Trim's British Guiana team in St. Lucia in June 1953.

Next year, in the first innings of the first match against Grenada in the Windwards School Tournament held in St. Lucia, Roberts failed to score in the first innings going by the familiar run-out route in a mix up with his friend Ian Hadley.

Roland Ogilvie fairly pulverized the Vincentian attack and St. Vincent's next turn at the crease became academic owing to limited time. Skipper Vin Cuffy therefore sent in Roberts to open with his boon companion, wicket-keeper batsman Ken Boyea. Roberts obliged with an exhilarating exhibition of batsmanship at its finest, completing an unbeaten half century that became Castries second fire of note.

At about that time, Alfie moved in a trio of close companions, Ken Boyea and Alfred "Vites" Herbert completing the charmed circle.

Alfie again failed against Hutton's M.C.C. in Grenada later that year. The laurels went to his cricket twin, opener Ian Neverson, who hooked for six the first ball of the match bowled by Freddie Truman and carried his bat through for 90 not out!

However, in the following year against Ian Johnson's Aussies, Roberts polished off a superb 77 against Lindwall, Davidson and company.

He confirmed his ascendancy in 1956 with high scores at home against a strong Trinidad club side, "Sunbridge", that contained West Indian spin-bowler Wilfred Ferguson and other hopefuls rapping on the door of West Indies Test selection such as Leo John, Syl Olliver and George Alexander.

Later in 1956 Roberts proceeded to play for the Windward-Leeward team that gave Trinidad a run for its money on home-soil, thanks to the bowling of fellow Vincentian John DaSilva who ripped through the defences of Stollmeyer, John and the rest in a repeat performance of the Sunbridge match.

By that time, Roberts had been preparing for his Higher School Certicate exams at Queen's.Royal.College. in Trinidad to which he had been awarded a scholarship, courtesy the Bermudez Biscuit Company, on the recommendation of cricket great, Everton Weekes while talent-scouting for the Cricket Board in the sub-region.

Ian Neverson subsequently obtained employment at a Bermudez factory in Trinidad where he impressed with his cricket until an industrial accident cut short a promising career.

Roberts, on the other hand, displayed his glittering wares in Trinidad where he played for a local side as well as the national team. He gained selection on the touring party for New Zealand in 1956, aged eighteen years.

In New Zealand, Roberts played in a solitary Test, the one that we lost, and was the last man out in the first innings for 28 in a total of 145, making second top score.

In the second innings he made a duck when the West Indies were skittled out for 77.

In the same match Garfield Sobers and Collie Smith made 1 and 1 and 2 and 0 respectively. Their average for the four Tests in which they played was 16.2 and 15.6.

In his celebrated classic on West Indies cricket, Michael Manley approvingly noted that: "In spite of these statistics however, the selectors persevered with these two young men...with both it was obviously only a matter of time."

As to Roberts, not a word. Not even to indicate that he was the first Windward Islander to reach Test level. So it was that a budding cricket prodigy was unceremoniously dumped after a single opportunity without a soul to speak up for him.

1957 was a bad year for Windward Islands cricket. And Alfie was omitted from the touring party to England which carried a disinterred Andy Gantaume, for instance.

Roberts' privileged stay in Trinidad was over. They were through with him. The dream was over and he had to look after a livelihood and a life in general.

So Alfie returned to St. Vincent and played for his club Malverns with Frank Mason, Ardon Daisley, Hudson Soso, Caspar Quammie et al. He dominated the Windwards circuit hitting a record score at the time of 163, not out, and establishing a partnership record with his school-mate Foster Huggins.

He took the opportunity to do a spot of coaching at the Anglican Primary School which he had attended for his primary education, as well as tried to influence the administration of the game by taking it over, which proved short-lived.

Roberts viewed the West Indies cricket scene askance, entertaining little hope of staging a come-back .With the entrenchment of Sobers and Collie Smith, the emergence of Basil Butcher and Seymour Nurse, and Worrell's influence on the wane, Roberts probably felt that no one would again be concerned about small-island cricket talent. So he hung up his boots for good, and left for Canada where unlike fellow migrants Garnet Brisbane and Ashford Lewis, he never lifted a bat again. Brisbane, in fact, went on to captain the Canadian National Cricket Team.

Instead, Roberts plunged into the world of academia. Ultimately, he became an authority on Black History, a don in the politics of underdevelopment, and a student of Marxist philosophy, specializing in the teachings of C.L.R. James and Franz Fanon who significantly were Black West Indians, hailing respectively from the islands of Trinidad and Tobago and Martinque. He moved and had his being in circles that included the cerebral Timothy Hector of Antigua, the firebrand Rosie Douglas of Dominica, Jamaica's Bobby Hill, Anne Cools of Barbados and Canada, the ideologue Franklyn Harvey of Grenada and his own home-town boy George Richardson of St. Vincent and the Grenadines (SVG).

Alfie kept in touch with Left and Liberation movements all over the world. He was associated with the student uprising at Sir George Williams University in 1969. And he organized in Montreal countless numbers of seminars, symposia, workshops and lectures on his pet subjects.

Alfie flooded kindred souls in the Third World with up-to-date literature. In Canada, Alfie often engaged in all-night rap sessions discussing the problems of race and neocolonialism. His own home resembled a full-scale library, documentation centre and archives rolled into one.

Vincentians and other Caribbean people visiting the Montreal chapter of the Black Diaspora were expected to call on the shrine that was Alfie's home as the high-point of the pilgrimage. Some over-nighted and drank deeply of the intoxicating spring of socialist thought.

Alfie maintained contact with SVG by sending articles to the "Flambeau" magazine of the 1960's such as "Why we must think for ourselves" which was earth-shattering in its disturbance of our settled way of life, including our ready acceptance of Black neo-slavery.

Alfie did not mince words. He simply told it as it was, as in his Flambeau contribution on constitutional change: "The rights of the people must remain inviolate."

On the date of his death on July 24, 1996, I received a document faxed by our mutual friend George Richardson expressing Alfie's thoughts on a local honours award system!

Throughout his life, he maintained dialogue with Everton Weekes who had been instrumental in the development of his cricket, attesting to his acute sense of gratitude.

Alfie would enquire always of friends and associates of the past, however humble – Sinclair Warner and Ashers, an agricultural labourer who played for Union Estates and St. Vincent in the 1950's. He died leaving an unfinished booklet on Leon "Congo" Bonadie who led the local champions Kingstown Cricket Club, that held the Fraser-Neckles Cup, the symbol of cricket supremacy in contemporary St. Vincent. It took a decade for it to be hoisted by the Grammar School featuring Alfie in 1954 in a bruising Goliath and David encounter.

In the end, I prefer to remember the little moments of joy I shared growing up with Alfie in the early 1950's. At thirteen years old, we never missed the weekly public meetings of the 8th Army of Liberation featuring Joshua's anti-colonial speeches, and on his death-bed, Alfie recalled those evenings.

I would swear that Alfie's first century or two were cracked playing with limes and coconut bat in his back yard at Bottom Town, within earshot of his future stomping ground at the Victoria Park.

Fancying himself a trend-setter in dress, Alfie once gave Mr. A.C. Cyrus outlandish measurements for a suit he wished. Mr. Cyrus simply called out the dimensions to his staff who erupted in laughter. Alfie was thus persuaded to opt for a more sober cut, but left the tailorshop fuming.

I recall, too when he and I descended from the Anglican Communion table endeavouring to walk as lightly as possible, so as not to attract attention. Both our parents in an effort to stretch the life of the soles of our shoes had gotten shoe-maker Drakes to attach small iron cubes called "Blakeys" that reverberated like "D Dan on the beat" but saved our soles though, perhaps, not our souls!

Or when Alfie turned my dance instructor. It was simplicity itself. Put one foot to the left and draw the other along side, like a series of attention and stand-at-ease. And so Alfie and I with partner would circumscribe the entire dance floor.

Actually, Alfie married Pat Cambridge who in her school-days was a happy girl, a heart throb to many a lad. I recall Ian Hadley being her coveted partner in the Meringue dance Band we once put out at Carnival.

In later life, Pat turned out to be a serious student in her own right and a compatible help-mate who stood by her husband through thick and thin, until death do us part- which it did, months apart, with Pat going ahead.

With Alfie's passing, the Third World lost an exciting scholar, the Caribbean a committed son, and St. Vincent and the Grenadines a true patriot.

I am distinctly the poorer for the loss of a great friend. But always his memory can be dredged for inspiration, sustenance and hope. A group of us, led by Oscar Allen, has promised to rescue his memory from obscurity, perhaps with a view to enlisting him at least in a local Hall of fame.

Dr. Kenneth John is a lawyer and political scientist. He also writes a weekly column in the *The Vincentian* newspaper of St. Vincent and the Grenadines where he resides.

15. **NELCIA ROBINSON**
By
Carleen Marshall

In pointing the way for others, I am carrying on the legacy of my mother, a Garifuna queen whose kindness at a low point in my life spurred me on to leadership. I wear her mantle with pride- A *Garifuna Queen, Nelcia Robinson, 2002.*

In 1947 Caspar and Maria Marshall welcomed the ninth of their thirteen children. They named the little girl Nelcia Celeste, the name Nelcia chosen in honour of educator Nelcia John who was highly respected by Caspar Marshall; himself an educator. However, when her mother's friends saw her they exclaimed "What a pretty baby-This is a Layou blossom!" giving rise to her pet name "Layou blossom". She was always aware of being different, growing up as the ninth child in a family of thirteen. Her birth order had something to do with the older ones seeing her as mediator between the younger ones and their parents and vice versa; daring to ask questions the others would not ask. Her questions always seemed to bring peace. Her parents or siblings would be so astonished that she even dared to ask that they would either carefully give her an answer, or burst out laughing and dismiss the matter. One instance was when they wanted to go to the beach and their father would not allow it. She reminded him that he had taught them "All work and no play make Jack a dull boy"

Her early years were spent in Layou until the family moved to Chauncey when her father was transferred to the Questelles Government School. Long before it was fashionable, head teacher Caspar Marshall, loathe to trust anyone but himself and his wife to his children's primary education, had them homeschooled. He would leave their full quota of work before he set off to school and upon his return the Marshall children would be put through their drills. A hard task master, he instilled in his children a high sense of discipline, search for excellence, dedication and self esteem. In respect to time, he would say "Punctuality is the politeness of kings". Nelcia decided that not only kings had that right. He would also say "A cat may look at a king" in reference to fear and subservience, a guiding theme that was central in Nelcia's recognition of her self-worth and that of others.

When his children attained secondary school age, he would enroll them at the school where he was stationed in order for them to sit the entrance examinations. His unorthodox method proved successful as all thirteen won scholarships to the premier secondary institutions. At the Questelles Government School, a motto on the walls was "A little learning is a dangerous thing, drink deep or touch not the Pierian Spring". Her curiosity was piqued by this Pierian Spring and upon enquiry her father explained that it was a fount of knowledge. Her thirst for knowledge and natural intelligence so impressed the late Thomas Saunders that he predicted a great future for her.

At age 10, she, like her 4 older sisters, won a scholarship to the St Vincent and the Grenadines Girls' High School. She dreamt huge dreams, dreams that would see her passing the Senior Cambridge examinations, becoming qualified to set the Higher School Certificate and winning an Island Scholarship. Success in these ventures would be the ticket to a University education. At the Girls' High School, the enquiring mind that would challenge the status quo was evident. Principal Barbara Heddle's edict of not venturing past a particular tree was ignored since sharing a snack with younger brother Anselm was more important. She performed well in her studies showing an affinity for Math and Science. In fact she was so strong in these subjects that Mrs. Smith, a mistress at the school recommended she be allowed to continue to take Science. The Girls' High School at that time did not teach science beyond fourth form. As a consequence she and some classmates were sent to the Grammar School for classes where much to the dismay of Winston Baptiste the science master, she regularly came out ahead of the boys. At age sixteen, while preparing for the examinations she became pregnant.

As a result she was unable to continue her formal education. For one who wanted to drink deep, the waters of the spring had been cut off-or so she thought. She had not reckoned with the strength of her mother who insisted that she be allowed to write the examinations. Thus began a program of self –imposed and self-directed home study which led to her gaining six passes in English Language, English Literature, History, Biology, Mathematics and French. With her secondary school certificate she was now qualified for a job in Teaching or the Civil Service. Since she was legally too young for work in those fields her mother sent her to learn typing so that she would have a marketable skill. The Government Service was her first place of employment and was a rich spring of learning. At that time, every entrant to the Public Service had to learn to type but she was already an adept typist since she had taken classes during the eight months wait for her appointment. This skill placed her in the secretarial grade where she was exposed to all the important government ministries and departments, and most importantly the intellectuals.

One such intellectual was Mr. C.I Martin, a brilliant economist fresh from the University of the West Indies. Prior to the advent of Mr. Martin she was something of a dilemma to her supervisors as she completed her assignments quickly and therefore appeared to have nothing to do. When Mr. Martin appeared on staff, with new ideas and long reports to be typed she was delivered to him and so began a career of twenty formidable years. Her thirst for knowledge led her to not only read the entire documents she was assigned to type but to seek additional information. This so impressed him that she was given more responsibility. Whenever he was he was transferred to high and sensitive posts, he requested that his Secretary accompany him. This continued until he left to take up employment with the United Nations. Over the years she was formally trained as a Secretary, including the skill of shorthand. This added skill allowed Mr. Martin to loan her to the House of Parliament, a testimony to the accuracy of her minutes. Within the Public Service, while serving under Mr. Frank Thomas at the Service Commissions Department, she was responsible for giving a test to the persons applying for jobs as typist, stenographers, and secretaries and was assigned as a Tutor at the Technical College. For every new venture undertaken by the governments in terms of Corporations and Companies, her formidable typing skills ensured that she was the "start up" secretarial and administrative support.

Still asking questions, one day she enquired of a new boss, Mr. Medford Scott, also the Financial Secretary, the necessity of the old people on welfare and those who had done road work having to come to town for their money, and his slowness in signing the claims. In her opinion, by the time the claims were approved much of the money had gone in transportation! He was surprised by her candour, but shortly after, he authorized her to sign claims, and then mildly complained that she was sending them out too quickly. She was further pleased when systems of payment were set up at rural post offices and police stations so that the aged and low waged persons would not have to come to town for their allowance.

As the years passed, responsibilities and knowledge grew but wages did not. One day she realized that she was trapped by her skill; her spring had become her pond. She rebelled by going on strike and was promoted in name only, since she still had to perform the secretarial functions. This situation continued for several years, until at age 37 she tendered her resignation from the Public Service. At that point, she realized that what she had perceived as great was little and this little learning was indeed a dangerous thing. This was the time when she subconsciously began to de-skill herself of the typing function. She credits the latent effects of crises of early motherhood, divorce and societal pressures with her inability to earlier discern her bondage and break free. Coupled with this was the fact that she enjoyed her work-learning and facilitating learning as well as the economic need to work. Perhaps subconsciously, she was also telling society that she was progressing despite the odds.

Her community role and activism, shaped by her relationship with God and a belief that she was called to be of service to others had emerged alongside her civil service career. A popular figure with her trademark straw basket, Sister Nel as she was affectionately called was particularly concerned with bringing education and skills to young people who had dropped out of school. Many of these young people had not had a chance of secondary education or had dropped out because their parents could not afford to maintain them in school. This meant that they were twice disadvantaged as gaining employment would be more difficult. At a time when mothers had an economic need to work, there was a growing need for preschool centres. Unaware of the requirements but having the requisite space, she opened her "school". The additional motive for opening this "school" was that some of her young school drop-outs would be employed.

To her amazement, she received a visit from two early childhood education coordinators from the Ministry of Education and VINSAVE who gently informed her that she had adequate space and ventilation but the wrong furniture. In addition, her teachers needed training. However, the school would remain open provided she agreed to the necessary changes. She, of course, agreed and the coordinators used their resources to provide the training and equipment. The centre became a model and the pride of the village and is still in existence. She then became the first chairperson of the pre-school services committee, the body overseeing over 100 pre-school centers in the island. In the process, she became fully trained in childhood education. Due to her impressive secretarial skills, the Governor General requested her services to serve on the Committee for the United Nations Year of the disabled. This facilitated her involvement in working with people with disabilities and specifically as Secretary to the national and regional councils of and for the blind.

Her earliest group was formed in 1970 when she gathered a group of young men and women and taught them to read, write and type. This group attracted the attention of the National Youth Council who encouraged her to make the group an affiliate. The result was that in 1975, she was elected Secretary of the National Youth Council. Two important outcomes of that period was her leadership in the composing of the National Youth Song 'Youths of this Nation, Let's arise' and the establishment of a Radio program, both of which exist today. Around this time, operating from her home in Questelles, the Dorcas Typing School was formally started, equipping hundreds with a skill. It attracted clientele from many sections of the country, prompting one village elder to say to her "You have brought light into this village". Sis Nel had, to all intents and purposes, launched her own Education Revolution. That same year, 1975, was declared the International Year of Women, and her voice was audible. Having experienced the results of gender inequality when her education was curtailed due to pregnancy, the crises of domestic violence and divorce, she spoke with passion on these issues.

In 1981, the Youth group decided that they wanted a playing field. Several acres of land, formerly an estate used for agriculture, were lying unused. The South Leeward Playing Field Committee was formed under her leadership. One weekend, the group went ahead and marked out the playing field. Thus began a long battle with politicians and investors on allocation of the land. They of course had "squatted", but led by the indefatigable Nelcia, they lobbied the government on the recreational needs of youth, and won the right to use the land. Here, her secretarial skills, learnt almost two decades ago, were critical as she documented everything, wrote the letters, press releases and spoke on the radio program. Today, the Campden Park playing field is home to all sports- basketball, netball, cricket, football, tennis, and athletics.

Faith in God has always been a driving force in her life and an ecumenical study group she helped to form, remains a group with a critical mission in her life. This group brought together youth from different religious beliefs but united in a common goal. They would search the scriptures and define passages according to the burning issues of the day. Then, a public folk mass would be organized at strategic venues in the villages and deliver their "sermons" to the accompaniment of relevant songs and drumming. It was an act of resistance that drew the attention of the churches, the wealthy and the oppressed. The "sermons" were always published in the progressive weekly newspaper, and broadcast on the National Youth Council's radio programme. The ecumenical study group hosted a regional/work study camp and she was invited to be the rapporteur for the opening conference. She involved herself in the work aspect of this group which was the building of a community center. Emerging from this was exposure to national and regional development concerns and a position with the Caribbean Conference of Churches, through the local Christian Council, as coordinator of an integrated rural development project.

When she was in the Public Service, she had joined the United People's Movement, a political party which advocated social justice. After resigning from her job, she became a candidate for the 1984 general elections in the South Leeward constituency. This event was at the same time a culmination of awareness of oppression in the society, the need to change it and a launch into an exciting new career. The opinion leaders were not of that view. To them, she was taking her tendency to be different too far-'bordering on madness' even. In speaking out on the social issues of illiteracy, unemployment and violence, she earned the solidarity of the oppressed and the anger of politicians. It was then she realized that she was the agent of change she wished to see. Therefore her entry into politics was not "madness" but a conscious decision to get national visibility and to challenge the existing policies and structures.

In 1984, she was the single female candidate in her political party, and when she was announced, the other parties had not yet named female candidates. Since Hon. Ivy Joshua's defeat in 1974, it was Prelena John who had contested for a third Party, and Hon. Valcina Ash had won her seat in a by-election for the St. Vincent Labour Party. Her entry into the political realm shocked the two older parties, not because she was female, but the fact that she had the potential to win her seat. In addition, with gender issues surfacing, it was the view of many that they were compelled to field female candidates. She was a public speaker who changed the campaigns from slander of opponents to education and empowerment of people. The public attended her meetings in droves, but did not see how a single seat from her party would help their cause. As a result she did not win her seat. She then proceeded to further shock the society by being the first to go into the community the day following the elections to thank those who had voted for her. Although not elected, she assured the community that she would show them the true meaning of representation. The constituents however pushed their representatives to implement her manifesto. 1984 was not a fulfillment of George Orwell's prophecy but instead a critical turning point in her life. It was a blossoming of her actions for change built through years of dedication and the formal launch of her work in human services as a vocation.

Following the general elections of 1984, she became Coordinator of the newly established Committee for Development of Women, a nongovernmental organization located within Projects Promotions. This organization's mission was to build awareness among women of the policies that under-develop them and to work for change in the areas of education, employment and health. It was in fact the seat of the first Women's Desk in St. Vincent & The Grenadines. The political mission of the organization won the attention of development agencies which provided funding for research and action programs. Women were advocating for, and marching for bread and roses- work with fair wages and full enjoyment of human rights. During this period she developed a theme song for the organization- 'Women's Voice" which was used in the Women's Bureau Radio program for several years. The organization challenged the government on issues of equal pay for equal work, maternity leave, the recognition of domestic violence as a crime, child maintenance, inheritance and citizenship rights. Having endured an abusive marriage, eradicating domestic violence was dear to her heart since despite the presence of medical and physical evidence of abuse, she had great difficulty getting the police to listen to her case. It took a silent protest which involved sitting out at the Police station for one week and inevitably being told to go home, and an appeal to the Governor General to bring attention to her plight. The result was an arrest and court restraining order in force to this day.

The networks of rural women had now found expression of their issues through her voice, and in 1984, she was elected President of the National Council of Women; a position she currently holds and has held on three separate occasions. With this position she also became an executive member of the Caribbean Women's Association. In 1985 the organization became the national representative for the Caribbean Association for Feminist Research and Action (CAFRA), a regional social movement dedicated to challenging the structures that oppress women. In 1987, the organization was the institutional base for research on women in agriculture. The findings of this research led to women's contribution in agriculture being recorded in the Gross National Product (GNP).

In 1985, the National Children's Homes ran a training program for social workers. She was asked to supervise the work practice component for one student. Little did she know that this was another turning point in her life. The organizers continued to ask her to supervise students and in 1989, decided to set up Marion House; a social work facility in St Vincent and the Grenadines. She was asked to be the coordinator but declined preferring instead to be a Board member. As co-founder of the facility she served as a voluntary community outreach worker. Under the umbrella of Marion House, she drank again from the Pierian Spring pursuing a certificate course in social work from the University of the West Indies through distance teaching. She also served as President of the Association of Social workers and coordinated the first training program in community care of the elderly, with support from Help Age International. So effective was the awareness building that the area of Geriatrics was added to the Curriculum of the St. Vincent & The Grenadines School of Nursing. Around this period, she added another facet to her portfolio-that of poet. Drawing on her personal experiences and those garnered on her many travels, she published two anthologies which met with favorable reviews.

As a recipient of the Partners of the Americas Fellowship in International Development, she was required to do a community project. She chose the Glebe, a large village in the suburbs of the "rural" township of Barrouallie. In her first community meeting to discuss needs, it was reinforced that one of the main problems was water supply. She therefore intended to use her grant to bring a larger pipeline to the village. The project was well publicized and ignited significant reaction so much so that at the next meeting, the parliamentary representative was present. Although she had not won a seat, she was regarded as an opposition politician and was perceived to be treading on the representative's turf. Her grant was sufficient for a single pipeline. His resources brought a large pipeline, and extended pipelines throughout the village, so that homes could have pipe borne water. In the 1980's as a Partners fellow in International development, she visited Ecuador, Dominican Republic and Washington DC to undergo training, and was in Mexico in 1983 undergoing training in building requirements for Early Childhood Education Centres, the only Caribbean Participant in the company of male architects from Latin America.

Caribbean Trailblazers: St. Vincent and the Grenadines

When she moved to Upper Questelles, she was again touched by the literacy and employment needs of the community people with whom she interacted. With the idea of opening a facility, she looked around for suitable space and located a building, which the caretaker said she could use for a small rent. A community group was co-opted to rehabilitate an abandoned building. After clearing the surroundings, a fundraising drive was organized which acquired materials and paint to renovate the building. The second phase was acquiring furniture and equipment through donations from the public. In 1986, the Caspar and Maria Marshall Centre for Adult Education opened its doors. It offered classes in English, mathematics, typing, sewing, tie-dyeing, craft and photography. The centre was also a voice for community concerns and issues, and was the venue for community events. The operation of the centre added value to the building which to her dismay was clandestinely sold in 1993.The result was that the services of the centre had to be spread across two locations in order to meet the needs of a large clientele. The Centre has also spawned several other services at community and governmental levels. One Graduate of the Centre, now a successful Seamstress, Caterer and small business woman, was highly indignant when she nominated Sister Nel for consideration as an "Unsung Hero", and was told she did not qualify. The Graduate was not at all mollified when Sister Nel told her that her satisfaction came from seeing results, such as her achievement.

The operation of the centre also opened the doors for her becoming President of the Association of the forty adult education centres in the country. – The National Association for Mass Education (NAME). She was then a member of the Caribbean Regional Council for Adult Education and benefitted from extensive training under both programs. The country's historical context was an important part of adult education learning. Research into this area led to her appointment as Coordinator of the first Caribbean conference of indigenous peoples in 1987, and subsequent coordination of the Caribbean Organization of Indigenous Peoples. Her interest in the Garifuna peoples had been sparked by tales recounted to her by her mother who was of Garifuna stock. The exploits of Paramount Chief Joseph Chatoyer so intrigued her that she joyously claimed the indigenous identity, privately deciding that her mother was a descendant of the chiefs- a Garifuna queen. Therefore, her involvement with the Garifuna peoples of Belize and her commitment to the indigenous cause was not mere coincidence but a natural progression of her childhood interest.

From 1993-1995, she was actively engaged in lobbying work nationally and at the United Nations in the following important social issues:

-Sustainable development of Small Island Developing States
- The conference on population and development

Nelcia Robinson

-The fourth World Conference on women.

These conferences exposed her to broader development issues and strengthened her political work. The year 1995 was a milestone in her life. As the national representative for the Caribbean Association for Feminist Research and Action she was offered the position of Regional Coordinator. This was a triumph in achievement, but she was reluctant to take up the post since it required her to relocate to Trinidad and Tobago .After much negotiation, she was persuaded. This job opened the floodgates of another Pierian Spring leading to extensive regional and international travels and lending her voice to more and more issues. As the first Chairperson of the Commonwealth Civil Society Advisory Committee she spoke on behalf of Civil Society at the Commonwealth Peoples Forum and Heads of Government Meetings in Malta and Uganda, as well as at Commonwealth Finance Ministers Meetings in Sri Lanka, Barbados, St. Lucia, and Brunei Darussalam. She was also active at the 8th Women's Affairs Ministers Meeting in Uganda, and the 9th in Barbados, at which time she was Chair of the Commonwealth Women's Network. As Coordinator of the International Gender and Trade Network she was present at major trade organizations around the WTO in Seattle and Qatar and the FTAA in Miami. As a trainer, she visited Ireland on several occasions to conduct training on the Beijing platform for Action, Trade liberalization and Women's involvement in politics.

However, her career was again threatened as she did not possess a university degree. Not only was she in danger of not having her contract renewed, she was facing a greater disaster. Having broken ties with her homeland for over five years; a new job would definitely require a degree. She had considered returning to school at several points in her career but the requirement for an advanced secondary school certificate, and no provision for experience to be computed for formal entry qualification was a barrier. In 2002, she found a college that met her particular needs; taking account of life experiences as against a high school certificate. In the process she learnt new methodologies, language and behaviours. She also discovered that she had a Caribbean story to tell. Drinking from the Pierian Spring exposed her need to break down reservations about the computer, important technology to which she had closed her mind. The little girl whose dreams of a university education had been abruptly cut would finally graduate in 2006, a proud recipient of a Bachelor's Degree from the Springfield College, Massachusetts, through its Human Services Division in Miami. In 2005, the Caribbean Court of Justice was inaugurated in Trinidad. Nelcia Robinson, following consultations with regional non-governmental organizations was one of three persons chosen to represent civil society; nominated jointly by the Secretary General of the Caricom Community and the Director General of the OECS for a period of three years. This term was renewed for a further three years up to 2009.

In 2009, she was ignominiously forced out of CAFRA, suffering the indignity of being barred entrance to the Office's headquarters; a building she had secured for the organization without having to face a mortgage and high interest rates. The clandestine manner in which her removal was exacted was a bitter pill to swallow. It was premised on the assumption that she was using her position in the organization to advance on the regional and international scene. A weaker person would have lost faith in the sisterhood of women but she understood that even the safest of harbours could come under threat from storm winds. Her Father had always said as he watched her swim upstream – "Nel is made of sterner stuff". .Like the slave foremothers, she was without material possessions, but carried the culture, wisdom, and knowledge in the vast storehouse of memory as she headed home to St Vincent.

On her arrival in St Vincent and the Grenadines, she was greeted by the news that the government had named her Goodwill ambassador. This honour, in recognition of her devotion to community service, gender equality, and contribution to poverty eradication, guaranteed her a diplomatic passport. She was to be further vindicated when it came out that she had earned her positions on regional and international boards independent of CAFRA. In the course of a few months she had drunk from the cup of despair and of triumph

Nel has been the recipient of several awards, including the prestigious "Woman of Great Esteem" awarded under the endorsement of the United States Congress. Her hobbies include reading, storytelling and writing poetry, a lot in the mode of "Praise Singer" which reflect the life and soul of the region and Nelcia herself. Her poems "My Caribbean", "Young Woman, Rolling Water, Warigabaga and Chatoyer's Children" aptly sum up her passion. This mother of four, grandmother of seven and remarried since 2006 appears to no longer maintain the same frenetic pace of previous years., but like the meandering river, she is revisiting and rebuilding where there are waste places. Her path is now one of active Mentorship, as can be seen in the Margaret & Nelcia Foundation for the Advancement of Young Women, the Jochebed Project for the Advancement of Young Men, and the Youth Project – Tomorrow's Women and Men. She confidently asserts that it is still her duty to point the way for others.

Carleen Marshall is a civil servant. She works and lives in St. Vincent and the Grenadines.

16.   **RANDOLPH BERTIE RUSSELL**
By
Gwendoline Russell

Randolph Bertie Russell as a businessman, former Parliamentarian and Member of Government has made a significant contribution to the social, economic and political life of St.Vincent and the Grenadines.

He was the second child, first son of Stephen and Virginia Russell nee Alexander. He was born on the 22nd November 1927 at Questelles, (pronounced Kay-tells) on the south-western coast of St. Vincent. He attended the Questelles Government School until his parents moved to Kingstown to live and he then went on to the Intermediate High School, which at the time, was run by the Eustace Family.

After leaving school, he and his younger brother, Linton, studied motor mechanics at Marshall's Garage at Arnos Vale. At that time in the 1940's many young men were leaving for Aruba where Largo Oil Company was employing people to work in their refineries. At the age of 19, Rannie, as he is widely known by, travelled to Aruba to seek such employment. Because of his mechanical knowledge he was trained and given the job of relieving pumpman on ships transporting oil from Venezuela to Aruba. His job was to operate the pumps discharging the oil from the ship to the holding tanks at the Refinery. He held this job for five years in spite of the fact that he suffered badly from sea sickness.

In 1952 at the age of 24, he returned to St. Vincent and, with his uncle, Luther Robertson, who was at the time working in Aruba, his uncle's father and a few others, purchased the Lyric Cinema and hotel building in the same compound in Kingstown from Henry Wilson. They then registered a company, the Lyric Theatres Limited. Rannie was appointed as Managing Director and made such a success of that cinema that very soon he was able to establish another cinema in Mesopotamia and build another in Georgetown which opened in January 1956.

In 1956 he married Gwendoline "June" Williams and they have three children: Stephen the oldest who returned to St Vincent after college in Canada, and Dale and Kirk in the United States. They have been blessed with nine grandchildren.

After the opening of the cinema in Georgetown, Rannie's entrepreneurial spirit led him, now supported by his wife, to venture into other areas of commerce. He set up the Lyric Trading Company which became the agent for several international companies.

By this time, the refineries in Aruba were closing down and many Vincentian workers were laid off and returned to St. Vincent and the Grenadines. The Company applied for the agency to supply seamen for National Bulk Carriers of New York, owners of ships which transported oil to various parts of the world. Mr Cyril Rich, their representative, came to St. Vincent and was so impressed with the arrangements we, at Lyric Trading, had made and the seamen we had invited to meet him that he immediately started sending for the men to man the ships. That was in 1958/59.

The first group of men included such stalwart seamen as Wycliffe Hutchinson and his brother, the Wilson brothers and others from Union Island. Transportation was really difficult in those days so to meet the deadline for the men to leave, Rannie hired a boat to go for them. The Chief Minister at the time, Ebenezer Theodore Joshua, was very much in favour of the scheme but we were under Colonial rule at the time and apparently, the Administrator had the final say. According to Administrator Giles, only Government could send men abroad for employment through the Labour Department, that we were encroaching on their authority and that they were not prepared to grant permission to export seamen. Rannie told the Administrator that he had a number of men already lined up to leave to catch ships in various parts of the world and we could not at that time stop the men from leaving. The Administrator was very determined and arrogant but since Rannie had the backing of the Chief Minister who was glad that men were getting gainful employment, he told the Administrator: "When I send the men to the airport tomorrow, you send and stop them". Of course it would have been foolhardy for the Administrator to do any such thing and so began a process that gave employment over many years to many thousands of able bodied men not only from the Grenadines but also from mainland St. Vincent. I would venture to state that this undertaking greatly assisted in the social and economic development of the Grenadines.

Rannie also ventured into real estate. Mrs. Emily Rodriguez, a close friend, offered to sell him her large seaside property at Villa. He purchased the property in the name of Lyric Theatres Ltd. The property had four small buildings which he rented mainly to families on vacation. By this time Rannie had started building the gas station known today as Banfield's Service Station which was later sold to Esso.

In 1960 with the approval of the Company, he demolished the old hotel building next to the cinema and began construction of the building which on completion became the most modern and up to date supermarket in the state.

In 1962 Rannie's uncle, Luther Robertson, who was a major shareholder in the Company gave up his job in Aruba, where the job situation was getting bad in any case, and came home to help in the running of the business.

Around 1964, Rannie was persuaded to purchase shares in the St. Vincent Agricultural Credit and Loan Bank Limited, a local bank that was established in 1909. He was elected as a Director and two years later was appointed Chairman of the Board, a position he still holds.

Randolph Bertie Russell

It soon became clear that he and his uncle could not work harmoniously together and Rannie decided that he would be happier on his own. As he had already started building the cinema at Stoney Ground, they came to an agreement that he would have that cinema and a lump sum for his shares in the Lyric Theatres Ltd. He and his wife formed a Company called "The Westindia Development Company Limited". He completed the cinema, which a friend from Film Centre in Trinidad named "The Russell Cinema". It was opened on 12th December 1964 and continued operating until 2001 when changing times demanded smaller cinemas, and the advent of videos and DVD's forced its closure. However throughout the years since the cinema was closed, many people had been asking that it be reopened. When the Cinerama cinemas were closed in 2008, Rannie did just that. He converted the very large cinema building into two smaller ones or plexes, as they are now called, and reopened in October 2009.

When he and his wife visited New York in June 1964 to purchase equipment for the cinema, they were offered an ice cream freezer and deep freeze at reasonable prices. Even though they had no immediate plans for the equipment, they bought them. This purchase turned out to be the start of what became a factory producing milk and ice cream. The production of milk did not continue for very long but the Russell Ice Cream, choc ice and popsicles became a household name for many years until powdered ice cream mix became available on the market and many people started making ice cream in their homes and selling in vans on the market. This, as well as the closing of the cinema, our biggest outlet, damage to vehicles by careless drivers, theft by employees who covered it up by sabotaging cold storage equipment and rising costs, particularly electricity, resulted in the closing of the factory.

In 1973, Rannie, his wife and a friend along with others, started The West Indian Insurance Company Ltd. Rannie is the Chairman and Managing Director of this Company which is well known by the trade name "Sentry Insurance".

One of his biggest ventures was the establishment of the Coca Cola Bottling Plant here in St. Vincent and the Grenadines in 1973. Rannie obtained the Coca Cola Franchise for his Company, built the plant, obtained the equipment, bottles, sugar and other ingredients and with the assistance of the Coca Cola Company set up the Plant to bottle the Coca Cola drink. This business was run successfully until it was left solely in the hands of a Manager. By the time he left, that business was in financial difficulties and rather than face the enormous cost of purchasing new bottles and new equipment, the Company sold the franchise, the equipment and bottles to the St. Vincent Brewery in 1994. Rannie then converted the bottling plant building into a Shopping Mall with fourteen shops and a restaurant along with two other large areas which he rented to others to run their own businesses. One such business was a supermarket in which he was a shareholder. When the Manager left the country, it was found that the business was very heavily in debt and the stock was unable to cover the debt. He took over the debt and the supermarket.

By 1997, with all the vehicular traffic going to and fro, it became quite stressful, living in the area of the Mall where our home was located. Rannie decided to build an apartment on to The Tropic Breeze Hotel which he had purchased in 1992. Eventually the house at Stoney Ground was converted into a supermarket. In 2003 the supermarket was turned over to Fine Foods Limited which now runs the very successful Aunt Jobe's Market.

Rannie has always been interested in real estate and it is this that has greatly financed his undertakings. His purchases included land at Wallilabou Bay. Our son Stephen who now owns that property, developed it to such an extent with a restaurant, bar and hotel that Disney chose it for the filming of their very popular movie "Pirates of the Caribbean" and National Geographic has just completed filming there.

Political Life

Rannie was always interested in politics and agreed to run for membership of the Kingstown Town Board when he was asked by the St. Vincent Labour Party (SVLP) in 1967. He was elected and two years later he became the Chairman of the Board. He did an excellent job as Chairman ensuring that the city and surrounding areas were kept clean, the roads repaired in a timely manner and he was always available to people who needed to see him. He gave a full annual report to the people of Kingstown at a party given by the Board every "Old Year's night". It was no wonder then that when he and Hudson Tannis contested the two Parliamentary seats in Kingstown in 1972 for the SVLP they won, even though the People's Political Party (PPP) had considered them safe seats for their Party. That was the election when each Party won six seats out of thirteen and Mr James Mitchell (later Sir James Mitchell) won the Grenadines seat as an Independent member. That was a very tense time for the State. The night after the election, PPP supporters were enraged and they took to the streets shouting and knocking pans. When they passed our Company's office at Stoney Ground, some workers were in the office. The crowd threw stones at them through the glass windows breaking them. The Labour Party supporters, who were at his home at Stoney Ground retaliated when the PPP supporters returned on their way back to Largo Heights and started throwing bottles. The riot squad had to be called out that night.

After days of tension and no sign of a compromise, the Governor Sir Rupert John called on the Labour Party which had been in power before the election, to form a Government. However, before that could be done, Mr

Mitchell gave his support to the PPP giving that Party the majority of elected members. When the new Alliance Government finally emerged, Mr James Mitchell was named Premier with added responsibilities for Agriculture, Trade and Tourism and Ebenezer Joshua, the leader of the PPP, became the Minister of Finance. After the election, Mr Joshua was so annoyed that he said that if the Chairman of the Kingstown Town Board could be so popular that SVLP could win the two seats in the city, he would dissolve Local Government. To make matters worse, the Board raised wages for the workers by one dollar over the minimum wage and Local Government was dissolved soon after. To this day, Local Government has not been re-instated in spite of the many promises to do so.

It was not long before rumours began surfacing that tension was growing among the parties in the Alliance Government. Joshua began publicly voicing his dissatisfaction and frustrations. Finally on the 18th September 1974, a resolution of no confidence in the Government was passed in the House of Assembly paving the way for new General Elections on the 9th December 1974. Rannie won his seat again for the SVLP and was appointed Minister of Health, Housing, Local Government, Community Development and Co-operatives in a SVLP Government

Up to today, people still tell him he was the best Minister of Health the country has ever had. When he became the Minister, he found out that on most nights, the hospital had mainly student nurses on duty and that senior nurses worked from 8.00am to 4.00pm daily. He set up rules and regulations whereby there were always some senior nurses on duty 24 hours a day. He introduced an action station for the efficient running of the hospital. When complaints came to him about the exorbitant extra charges patients facing surgery were called upon to pay, he called the surgeon into his office and made it clear to him that such practice was unacceptable and had to stop. He ensured that the distribution of drugs to the various clinics was properly monitored and arrived at their destination. When complaints came to him that patients were complaining about the meals served to them at the hospital, he often passed there at lunchtime to check the food in the kitchen. Many a night, long after midnight, people used to call and ask him if he could get the ambulance for them as they could not get to the hospital. He would then send his Company's watchman to the hospital to pass on the message.

He was a very caring Minister and considered it his responsibility to ensure that people throughout the island had the best health care that the country could offer. When people needed further medical treatment abroad in the Caribbean, he often arranged for them to go at Government's expense.

When he found out that the Nurses' Training School consisted of two rooms at the back of the nurses' hostel, he got funds through a visiting Minister of the United Kingdom Government and had the old tuberculosis hospital at Largo Height converted into the School of Nursing and Allied Health Sciences. After its opening, the school was constantly used for the training of nurses, seminars and workshops on health issues. At the time, Bassy Alexander asked him what was he opening a Nursing School for when after three batches he'll have no jobs for them. Rannie replied that they would be able to get employment abroad as there was a need for nurses all over the world. He told Bassy: "When those nurses go away and work, do you know how much money will come back to the country?" (remittances). Thirty years later, Bassy had to admit that it was a brilliant and progressive move at the time and that Rannie was a man of foresight as, since then, many nurses had found employment in the United States and elsewhere.

Bassy also recalled that thirty five years ago, Rannie had tried to get the Milton Cato Government, of which he was a part, to work towards the building of an International Airport for the country. Rannie had suggested to Cabinet that an area suitable for the airport be identified and that the Government should put two bulldozers and two men to start cutting the airstrip. He told Cabinet the country would hardly feel the cost as the Public Works Department would absorb the added expense. He said that it might take several years, but once the airstrip was cut and paved, he was sure a country like Canada, who was at the time giving financial assistance to other countries in the Caribbean for the same reason, would assist with the construction of a Terminal Building. Argyle was the natural choice and there were no houses built there then, so the cost would have been affordable.

The Kingstown Medical College was one of his major achievements as Minister of Health. He was introduced to Doctor Charles Modica, then Chancellor of St. George's University in Grenada at a cocktail party at Government House one night and immediately asked him to set up a branch of the University here in St. Vincent. Dr. Modica agreed to his request and, after some difficulty obtaining Cabinet approval, the Kingstown Medical College came into being in January 1979. At the Opening Ceremony, Dr. Modica said: "The person with whom I had the pleasure of working in this past year is the Minister of Health, Mr. Randolph Russell. Mr. Russell is, in my opinion, the model of what every Government Official in the world should stand for. Mr. Russell loves his country as most men love their own families. I have never witnessed such an intense effort made by a Government Official in developing plans for an Institution of any type. As a token of our appreciation, we have decided to name one of our scholarships in his honour" (The Star, Saturday, February 3, 1979)

The Kingstown Medical College was of great benefit to the economy of St. Vincent and the Grenadines for almost thirty years. It also benefitted many young people who obtained scholarships and those who were able to take advantage of the more affordable cost of studying medicine.

Randolph Bertie Russell

At that time, there were no resident doctors in places like Owia, Sandy Bay, Canouan and other Grenadine islands and transportation to those places was difficult. Seeking to ease the situation in those areas, Rannie submitted a project to Dr. Hector Acuna of WHO/PAHO at a Conference of Caribbean Health Ministers for the training of Family Nurse Practitioners, a new kind of training aimed at improving the quality of primary–care services. Newspapers in the MDC's – Jamaica, Barbados, Trinidad & Tobago and Guyana, and even our own newspaper "The Vincentian" were up in arms against him. Apparently the MDC's were getting funds to assist the Less Developed Countries but that was not happening so, of course, they were annoyed. The Project was approved and funded by the United Nations Fund for Population Activity (UNFPA) and managed by PAHO/WHO. Rannie was asked where he would like to have the Project located and of course he chose St. Vincent & the Grenadines. Senior nurses from Anguilla, Antigua, Dominica, Grenada, Montserrat, St. Kitts –Nevis, St Lucia & host country St. Vincent and the Grenadines all participated in the training. Governments of participating countries were supposed to take over the project in 1985 but, unfortunately, did not and it was discontinued.

Housing schemes for people of the lower income bracket were established, under his Ministry, at Glen, Campden Park and Redemption Sharpes. Many people were able to acquire a property in those days at a very low cost through the Central Housing and Planning Authority and most were able to do so at extended terms.

In the industrial sector he was foremost in the establishment of the Campden Park Industrial Estate.

Rannie also arranged for the area known as "Monkey Hill" above New Montrose to be subdivided into housing lots. Many people bought the land and built small wooden houses. Some who had built expensive homes protested strongly that the development would devalue their properties. Bassy Alexander recalled saying to him "Why did Government allow those people to mess up that area?" Rannie told him "Don't say that, our Vincentians have ambition and in time you will see lovely houses up there some of them better than those of the rich. Do you _ecogni how many of those (people) will be paying taxes, light bills, water bills?" The proof is there to be seen today.

In his constituency of East Kingstown and under his direction, Community Centres at Rockies and Redemption Sharpes were built by people in those areas who willingly and freely gave of their time and expertise in those self-help projects. He obtained a number of industrial sewing machines for training young people as well as equipment for making pottery, for the Redemption Sharpes Centre.

He also cut roads connecting Green Hill to Redemption Sharpes and Sharpes over to Rockies and Sion Hill. Later on, these roads were paved for vehicular traffic.

In Community Development, Rannie introduced a smocking project which gave a small wage to many people throughout the island. Women throughout the State were to be seen along the roadside in small groups chatting and smocking away. The garment factory which supplied the materials and paid for the smocking, had markets in the United States. It was a joy to Rannie when he went into a store in Atlanta, Georgia and saw garments with the label "Produced in St. Vincent and the Grenadines".

When the Soufriere volcano erupted in 1979, as Minister of Health, Rannie was able to get much needed assistance from abroad. He requested the help of Dr. Modica, the Chancellor of the Kingstown Medical College and through him obtained the services of an associate of the college. The Brother's Brother Foundation of the USA who, through their various representatives in the USA and Canada, obtained and shipped to us blankets, camp cots, stoves, cooking utensils, foodstuff, an abundance of clothing, new and used, and galvanize for roofs. In Canada, to get their goods to us as quickly as possible, Ken Davis, at Rannie's request contacted Barney Dawson, the Canadian Minister of Health at the time and requested his assistance in getting supplies to us. Barney Dawson on being told of the urgency of the situation, arranged for a Hercules aircraft to transport the goods to us here in St. Vincent.

Doctor Hinson, then Head of The Brother's Brother Foundation, also mobilized a team of medical personnel, obtained medical supplies and came to St. Vincent to inoculate those in the Centres as a precaution against certain infectious diseases.

Cable and Wireless had offered free calls to all Ministers of Government and Rannie took full advantage of the offer and made calls to various parts of the world for assistance for the people of the country in their hour of need. He even called the Red Cross in Geneva. He was in constant touch with Dr. Hinson in Pittsburgh and Ken Davis in Canada. His telephone calls _ecogni thousands of dollars as he was in constant contact with Dr. Hinson, Ken Davis and others. The amount was so high that Cable and Wireless submitted their bill to Cabinet which agreed to pay it since the calls had benefitted the country tremendously.

In 1979 St. Vincent attained Political Independence from Great Britain. At midnight on 26th October 1979, the British flag was lowered and the new flag was raised and the country became known as Saint Vincent and the Grenadines. Rannie, as a Minister in the Cabinet was part of the entire process.

During his first term, in addition to his substantive Ministry, he also acted as Minister of Agriculture, Minister of Communication and Works and at least one time as Premier during the absence of those Ministers from the State. He again won his seat in the elections of 1979 and continued as the Minister of Health. The rebuilding of the hospital in its first phase was the next major project of his Ministry and he took great interest in its construction.

However by 1981, he had gotten very frustrated with the slow pace, the lack of initiative, no move to compulsory education and what he considered corruption by the Government and he resigned as a Minister. In his letter of resignation, he again alluded to the need for a larger airport. He said: " Our airport needs relocating if we are to accommodate larger planes and to make it safe for landing. Regardless of how much money we spend to lengthen the airstrip, it is not going to change it from a downwind takeoff to an upwind one and no large hotel is going to move in. No real tourist development will take place".

James Mitchell had been the Leader of the Opposition supported by the only other independent member, Calder Williams, Parliamentary Representative for North Leeward. Calder offered his support to Rannie if he would join the Opposition as its Leader. Rannie accepted and became the Leader of the Opposition. He was a very effective leader who was not afraid to attack the Government on its policies. Even though they were few in number in the Opposition, he tabled a Resolution for the lands at Lauders Estate to be subdivided and sold to the people at a low price. The Resolution fell for lack of support. It was a vain hope that the Government would have been considerate enough to support the people in that area.

About 2 years after, Calder once again gave his support to James Mitchell who then became the Leader of the Opposition and Rannie remained as a member until the General Elections of 1984 when he lost his seat. The people had by this time become very frustrated with the Labour Party Government and openly voiced their opposition to many of their policies. Thus it was no great surprise that in the General Elections of 1984, the little known New Democratic Party launched by James Mitchell in 1975, came into its own and won the majority of seats in the election and formed the new Government.

For the next ten years, Rannie devoted himself to his business. In 1994, not liking what was happening in the country, a group of prominent citizens invited him to join their group of concerned citizens. This resulted in the St. Vincent Labour Party joining The Movement for National Unity headed by Dr. Ralph Gonsalves. This coalition became the Unity Labour Party. Rannie was persuaded to run for the Central Kingstown constituency in the General Elections of 1994. He did not win but in those three weeks of campaigning, he regained a lot of his earlier support.

He concentrated on his business after that, turning the old bottling plant and other buildings into a shopping centre. He also dabbled in real estate. He bought and renovated the Tropic Breeze Hotel which is located on the hill overlooking Arnos Vale Airport. This hotel is still in operation and is also in much demand for weddings, parties, family reunions and the like.

In 2006, he _ecogniz that there was no place where people who had given yeoman service in this country were being _ecognized. He therefore set up, at his own expense, a "Hall of Fame" in the Russell Centre with pictures of people who had given outstanding service to the country. Many Vincentians who returned on a visit have said to him that visiting the Hall of Fame with all the pictures there, was the highlight of their visit.

His wife has, over the years, been very much involved in the Girl Guides Movement and she has always had tremendous support from him in her many activities especially in the building of the first phase of the Guide Headquarters Building. He gave much advice on the actual construction of the building and allowed his own Company's workmen to install the electricity, the welding of the steel beams and much of the transporting of materials at no cost.

At 83 years of age he remains fit and fairly agile and is still willing to venture into new businesses and embrace new ideas. His latest venture is the establishment of a spacious True Value store in the Russell Shopping Centre, ably assisted by his oldest son, Stephen. This store is unique for SVG with light hardware, electrical and plumbing materials, household goods, lawn and garden equipment and tools, pet supplies, ornaments and toys all under the same roof.

Randolph Russell has served his country ably and well. He has done much in the way of development and has provided, (and continues to provide) employment for many people over the years. He is often sought out for advice on various matters, advice which he is always willing to give.

He is one of a kind, always ready with fresh ideas and new plans. May he continue to be blessed with good health to pursue those endeavours for many years to come.

Gwendoline Russell is a business woman. She resides in St. Vincent and the Grenadines.

17.   **GEORGE OWEN WALKER**
By
Yvonne Walker Andrew

Foreword

Throughout his life, our father, Owen Walker, did everything he could to keep his family and political lives separate. In the early days of Vincentian politics, politicians were subject to stone throwing, roadblocks and ambushes. Dad shielded us from the turmoil of the time as best he could. In fact, much of what we know of his political life we learned from behind the scenes. In researching this article, we have sifted through Dad's meticulous files, his recorded speeches, and the recollections of his political contemporaries. Looking back, Owen Walker's family and political lives were two sides of the same coin. In both, he exhibited the qualities of a true Caribbean trailblazer.

As we reflect on the events of our father's life and the character of the man behind them, we must say we knew from a very young age that Owen Walker was an extraordinary human being. Few men possessed the combination of vision, courage, and selflessness we saw in our father. He harnessed these qualities to empower his people and help a young nation come into its own.

We still remember heading to the beach at Layou behind his shop. There Dad taught us all how to swim. He would have us lie on his outstretched arms and say, "paddle and kick your arms and legs as fast as you can." With our hands and legs in full motion, he would slowly remove his support from under us. Although we initially panicked at the loss of our security blanket, he would encourage us to continue paddling and before we knew it we were swimming on our own. This was who Owen Walker was to the people of Saint Vincent – a guiding hand who helped people achieve more than they thought possible. Even though he was not an elected representative, he knew how to assist those in need.

On days when Dad drove us to school, the twenty minute drive sometimes took twice as long, because many people would stop him along the way to share their wants, needs and numerous issues that they were facing. We could gauge what sort of reception he received at the public meetings by his good or bad mood. We also got up early in the morning to inspect any new dents on the car when he held meetings in hostile territory. Yet we always saw him as fearless; he never backed down from any confrontation and would always say what was on his mind. He taught us all never to settle, but fight to the end for what we believed was right. For him, nothing was impossible to accomplish. His life was a demonstration of this ethic. This legacy has helped shape our view of the world and lives on in all of us. No wonder that on Labour Day, 1994, he was proclaimed the World's Greatest Father and Grandfather by his family. Everyone who knew Dad or "Cap" as he was affectionately called, knew of his love and passion for the people of Saint Vincent and the Grenadines. This sometimes required him to sacrifice a lot of family time. We wished we had more time with him, but we knew his work was changing things for the better, and he was fortunate to have a strong, loving and caring wife Esther taking care of the family.

Mom was his rock and no task was too daunting for her. In her unique way, she was a trailblazer. She never took political sides and therefore got along with everyone. She drove the passenger bus if need be and would transport people to the hospital or to Kingstown to travel overseas by boat to England. She made it easier for him to reach out to others who were less fortunate.

Although he was gone often, and would come home late at night, we always knew when he returned home, because he would come to our rooms, count the 14 feet and kiss us all before he went to bed. He told stories to make a point and one always learned something from those experiences. Of course we were not wealthy, but Dad made us feel as such. He always reminded us that we were the happiest children in Saint Vincent and we in turn felt and acted that way. He was however a strict disciplinarian.

He always generated employment for the people of Layou. These small jobs were often their only source of income. Sometimes he had to get labourers from as far as Georgetown to reap his arrowroot, when, for political reasons, the people of Layou would refuse to work for him. But with Mom at his side, the task was usually accomplished with ease.

One of our most enduring images of Dad is of him toiling under the hot Caribbean sun in the fields in Layou. His sons were always a step away from him as he imparted his knowledge to them. Dad loved farming and planted just about everything – peanuts, bananas, arrowroot, tobacco, cotton, fruits, flowers and vegetables. He also raised a variety of livestock. Rarely did we ever have to buy fruits and produce from the market. All the while – with every constituent rally, political campaign or business endeavour – he sowed the seeds of prosperity for St. Vincent and the Grenadines.

Early Beginnings

George Owen Walker was born on November 18, 1923 in Richmond Vale, Saint Vincent where his father was overseer of the estate. He was the second child and first boy of Matilda "Only" Jack and Charles "Bob" Owen Walker of Layou. He had three siblings – Belle, Ralph and Eric. He was solemnized in the Methodist Church at Chateaubelair on December 30, 1923.

At the age of three his parents returned to Layou, where he attended the Layou Government School from Stage One to Standard Six until the age of

15. He apprenticed as a tailor while also learning from his mother, herself a skilled seamstress. In 1940, his entire family migrated to Aruba.

He immediately enrolled in night school while working at various jobs during the day. In 1943 he landed a job with Lago Oil & Transport Co., Ltd. As a seaman on their oil tankers. He quickly was promoted to boatswain and supervised all the deck personnel. He travelled extensively to Europe and the United States, and had many stories to tell about the dangers at sea during the war and the prejudices he encountered in the segregated U.S. South. In Aruba, he met and married Esther Bain of Grenada on July 16, 1949. Two of their daughters were born in Aruba.

In 1953, having been laid off by Lago, Walker had the choice of returning to Saint Vincent or starting a new life in the U.S. At that time, the process of immigrating to the U.S. was easier than today. Many of his relatives had already made the trip, and it would have been easy for him to follow. However, Walker's health was a concern at the time, as he was recovering from stomach ulcer surgery. In addition, in his travels to the U.S. on Lago oil tankers, he experienced blatant racism in the South that made him question how much one could achieve in such a discriminatory environment. He made the decision to return to Saint Vincent.

Upon his return to Saint Vincent, Walker seized at the many opportunities to improve the standard of living of his fellow Vincentians. Saint Vincent was light years behind the progress he had seen in his travels and while living in Aruba. He first went into the retail business, opening a general store beneath his parents' home in Layou while his home and shop were being built. Later, he opened the first gas station on the Leeward side of the island and began a bus service between Layou and Kingstown. At that time, the only mode of transportation for area residents into Kingstown was a bi-weekly vessel that also carried coal and provisions from Cumberland in North Leeward. Most of his business ventures merely broke even, however they provided critical services to the local people and helped support Walker's growing family.

Early Political Years

Around the time of his return to Saint Vincent, adult suffrage had recently (1951) been achieved in the islands and political parties were being formed. He got involved with the Layou Town Board. In 1957, Walker tossed his hat into the political ring, lending his support to the newly-formed (1955) Saint Vincent Labour Party (SVLP) headed by R. Milton Cato. By 1958, he shifted to the People's Political Party (PPP) led by Ebenezer Theodore Joshua – either because he found the Labour Party too elitist and conservative or because he sympathised with the grassroots populist PPP. (John 2000)

His early years with PPP were spent in the role of trade unionist, as he joined with E.T. Joshua in the fight for decent wages for labourers especially the estate workers at Mt. Bentick, Georgetown and for freedom of worship for the Spiritual Baptists ("Shakers"). "Walker will be remembered for the work he did during the hey-day of PPP and its Trade Union arm, the Federated Industrial and Agricultural Workers' Union (FIAWU) together with other stalwarts such as youthful Duff Walker James." (London 2000)

In 1961, he became Secretary General of the PPP, assuming the former role of his nephew Duff. As Secretary General, he organized the political meetings and travelled the length and breadth of the island, sympathetic to the plight of the working class. As Ambassador Layne recalled in his eulogy, "he often said that he belonged to a rare breed of Vincentian politician who could speak in any village, or part of the country, with equal facility." (Layne 2000)

At this time, there developed a rivalry between himself and Herman Fraser Young, the then representative of South Leeward and a member of the Labour Party. The rivalry lasted many years, during which he ran against Young and lost. It wasn't until 1966 that they were able to work together, when Walker was instrumental in getting Young to join the PPP. Under PPP, Young contested the election and lost to J.L. Eustace. However, PPP won by a slim margin and appointed Walker as a Nominated Member of the Legislative Council of Saint Vincent.

PPP lost the majority in parliament when Samuel E. Slater crossed the floor and joined with the opposition SVLP in 1967. On March 17, 1967, Walker was appointed by Hywel George, the then Administrator, as Minister for Social Services and Education. This caused much consternation: "the petit bourgeois in alliance with the ruling circles, then on a mission to impose their will on the country through deceit and base treachery, protested his appointment... They said Walker was unlettered and uneducated... The sons and daughters of the petit bourgeois, then in the Grammar and High Schools, found themselves boycotting classes and making their displeasure known to Walker's appointment in obedience to their mummies and daddies." (London 2000) This appointment was short-lived, as elections were called in May 1967 and PPP lost 6 to 3 to the SVLP. Despite this setback, "the exploits of Walker and others led by Ebenezer Theodore Joshua, broke the shackles of estate serfdom and child labour and challenged British Colonialism, ushering in a new era of self-governance and constitutional development." (London 2000)

Walker continued as Secretary General of PPP, holding Wednesday night meetings at the Market Square to rally the constituents leading up to the next election. Always an avid observer, he served as sub-editor and reporter of the party's newspaper, *The Voice of Saint Vincent*. "Walker virtually replaced a tiring Joshua as the cutting edge of the PPP during the violent elections of 1967 when the Colonial State had picked its own side whose path they wished to smooth as successor to the departing British overlords." (John 2000) In 1969, Saint Vincent gained Associate Statehood headed by Premier R. Milton Cato.

The 1972 elections resulted in a draw, six seats each for PPP and SVLP, and one seat for the independent candidate, James F. Mitchell. Walker advised E.T. Joshua to go back to the polls and let the people decide. Instead, Joshua made a deal with Mitchell which allowed Mitchell to become Premier under an Alliance Government.

E.T. Joshua and his wife Ivy soon became uncomfortable with the situation of playing second fiddle to Mitchell and they crossed the floor to join ranks with the Labour Party. Elections were called in 1974 and the Labour Party, led by Milton Cato, won.

In October of that same year, as Secretary General of PPP, Walker invited James Mitchell to be a member of the PPP's Executive Committee and to assist in running its affairs. Mitchell accepted on the grounds that the Joshuas be expelled from the PPP. In 1975, however, Mitchell decided to start his own party, the New Democratic Party (NDP). Walker joined Mitchell in this venture as the first Secretary General of NDP.

Years in America

In the midst of these political changes, Walker's family life saw many transitions. In 1972, his two eldest daughters migrated to the U.S., to further their studies. In 1974, he and his wife Esther celebrated 25 years of marriage with a lavish party at their residence in Layou. By 1978, his six remaining children had migrated to the U.S.

In 1979, Walker left Saint Vincent to join his family residing in Brooklyn, New York. He worked with the Rockefeller Group which ensured his family the best tickets to the Rockefeller Christmas Spectacular. He loved his job and got numerous awards from his superiors for excellence and going beyond the call of duty. By example, he instilled a strong work ethic, always prompt and cheerful, even through the harsh New York City winters to which he was not accustomed. He spent his free time at home with his children, always stressing the importance of education as the means to freedom from financial stress. As his children grew and met their spouses, his home was once again filled with the cries and laughter of children, this time his grandchildren. With them he displayed a softer, gentler, more playful side. When they were sick, he rubbed their tummies to make them feel better. He allowed desserts to be eaten even before dinner was finished. He sat by while they kneeled down at the end of the day to hear his grandchildren thank God for their blessings which always included him.

Although he was residing in America, he still felt a strong sense of duty to his homeland. During his employment with the Rockefeller establishment, he had conversations with David Rockefeller about investing in Saint Vincent and the Grenadines. He kept in constant contact with Mitchell during this time and never missed out on the excitement of an election. He returned to Saint Vincent for the 1979 and 1984 campaigns. In 1984 NDP formed the Government with 10 of the 13 seats. Walker returned to his job in the U.S. immediately after the general elections. His goal was to get vested for his retirement. In hindsight, that was a wise decision as it helped him to maintain his political independence.

In 1986, the Governor-General Sir Lambert Eustace appointed Walker to the Constituency Boundaries Commission, acting under the advice of Prime Minister Mitchell. Two new seats were added, bringing the total to fifteen and in 1989 helped to secure a clean sweep of all 15 seats for the NDP.

Later Political Years

At the age of 65, he retired from his job in the U.S. and immediately returned to his homeland. Acting Governor-General Henry H. Williams, acting on the advice of Prime Minister Mitchell, appointed Walker as Senator on June 23, 1989. In July of that year he and his wife lovingly celebrated 40 years of marriage. He was appointed to various boards, commissions and authorities. He was particularly proud of his contribution to the Port Authority and the Arrowroot Association. At the legislative sessions his agenda was focused on improving life in his homeland. For example, he was an advocate of parking meters in Kingstown to ease traffic congestion, a problem that still exists today. In 1992, he and Senator Robinson went to Taiwan on a goodwill mission. He related what an awesome experience it was, and learned much from the Taiwanese people. He also visited the McCormick Company in the U.S to promote the arrowroot industry.

Ambassador Layne in his eulogy summed up some of Walker's characteristics as follows: "Walker maintained his philosophical principles throughout his life. In victory and defeat, in power and out of power, he was resolutely, 'a man of the people,' always accessible and willing to offer advice and assistance. He was jovial and gregarious, but most decisively, he was an indomitable political operative, fearless in battle, and yes, he also possessed a devastating political style on the hustings. He was a treasured ally, and a feared opponent. Whatever one's feelings about Comrade Walker, he demonstrated time and time again that he was a force to be reckoned with in the political life in Saint Vincent and the Grenadines. His influence could not be underestimated or ignored. One did so at one's own peril. " (Layne 2000)

In 1994, his relationship with the NDP began to fray. At the time, he complained to Mitchell that some members of the present NDP Central Committee had shown him open hostility and humiliation on several occasions, but his complaints fell on deaf ears. In particular, he felt that the Central Leeward constituency was being underserved by the then representative Herbert Young. He "kept his mouth shut" (hard to believe but true) for the entire campaign, until NDP held a political meeting in Layou, and some of his former allies heaped unwarranted accusations against him. In his own words: "I had to clear my name," so on the eve of elections he made a solo two-hour speech in Layou. Eloquently and sometimes comically he set the records straight and he gave his support to Louis Straker, the United Labour Party candidate. In the 1994 elections, NDP won 12 of 15 seats, but Young lost his seat to Straker.

Things continued to sour between Walker and NDP. He felt the Party that he was an integral part of for nearly 20 years had abandoned him. "Unfortunately, unhappy differences not uncommon to the human as well as the political family had arisen to tear Walker away from the NDP in 1994. Disconsolate and distraught, the wandering Walker even tried to find solace in the restoration of a PPP which had long died and been born again in the NDP." (John 2000)

In August 1995, Walker along with Terrence Parris, Cameron Codougan and others attempted to resurrect the PPP. The then Prime Minister, Sir James Mitchell, compared Walker's efforts at rebuilding the PPP to the king's men trying to put Humpty Dumpty together again. Walker openly protested some of the NDP policies of the day. He and his colleagues would set up picket lines with placards in front of the Prime Minister's office.

PPP developed a Policy Statement of what they hoped to accomplish. Of utmost importance was employment for the people of the countryside. PPP also opposed the building of the Market at its current site, instead they suggested that it be built on the reclamation site next to the fish and meat markets; and the current location should be a National Square with beautiful trees, water fountain, flowers and benches for relaxation where every Vincentian could enjoy with pride, its beauty. (Walker was probably envisioning a Rockefeller Center in Saint Vincent.) PPP also wanted the cruise ship berth built in Layou, Barrouallie or Chateaubelair. Always looking for new prospects for his homeland, in September 1995 Walker travelled to Hawaii to look into the purchasing of sugar mills in the hopes of restoring the sugar industry to Saint Vincent.

Edgerton Richards Jr. sought an alliance between his party – The African Liberation Party and PPP. Richards suggested that the new party be called the "People's Liberation Party." That alliance was not in the stars.

On September 26, 1996, Walker met with a disciplinary committee (Alphonso Dennie, Chairman, Alwyn Gould and Leon Mason) set up by the Central Executive of NDP to inquire into his conduct and behaviour. Walker vehemently defended his actions. At an NDP committee hearing, he reiterated his contributions to NDP, noting that,

As the first Secretary General of the Party who had contributed in no small measure to the structure of the Party, and who was one of the main cornerstones in its construction, he deserved to have been better treated... He emphasized that he was not well treated by the hierarchy of the Party, and that he was virtually forced out of the Party, and had to rebel and show dissatisfaction in the way he did... He noted that with all the political vendetta exhibited by both sides, and all the outpourings of ill will, our President and Political Leader at no time said anything derogatory of him, and this he considered a mark of political maturity and deep human friendship. (Dennie 1996)

At this hearing, at Walker's request a meeting was set up between Mitchell and himself.

By the elections of 1998, Walker and NDP reconciled and NDP won by a slim margin (8 to 7). As Dr. Kenneth John aptly puts it: "It was a great homecoming when Walker returned to the fold on the eve of the last elections in 1998, and rejoined the family which greeted him with the killing of the fatted calf. Walker formed part of a team that enjoyed a satisfying victory against untold odds of a Party he had helped to form and build by the sweat of his brow nearly a quarter century ago. It was the beginning of a new era." (John 2000)

At a cocktail party at the Prime Minister's residence, Walker was overheard telling the current Prime Minister Ralph Gonsalves that his time will soon come, no need to rush things. This has proved to be prophetic as the elections following were all won by the party led by Gonsalves.

The Final Days

On July 16, 1999 Walker celebrated 50 years of marriage to his bride, Esther. Surrounded by family and friends, he was regaled in a beautiful banquet hall by a lavish gala including speeches, songs, and dances performed by the family created by their love. This was a very timely event, as it would be one of the last celebrations the family would experience together.

In December 1999, he was diagnosed with brain cancer. Walker, surrounded by his family, passed away February 10, 2000 in New York. He was eulogized by people of every walk of life. His friends Othniel Sylvester and Carlos Maloney along with Ambassadors Layne and Wilson eulogized him. Acting Prime Minister Arnhin Eustace sent condolences to his wife Esther. At a memorial service held in Layou a month after his passing, he was eulogized by Alphonso Dennie and Parnell Campbell.

"George Owen Walker had completed his political agenda towards the close of the century. There were no more walls of Jericho to shout down. The old order had passed, and a new one was in the offing. From all accounts, Owen Walker was at peace with himself and his family when he responded to the call of a higher duty." (John 2000)

Bibliography

Dennie, Alphonso. "Report of a committee set up by the NDP Central Executive." Kingstown, 26 September 1996.

John, Dr. Kenneth. "A Thumb-Nail Sketch of the Political Life of George Owen Walker." Searchlight 18 February 2000.

Layne, Ambassador Kinsgley. "Letter read at the funeral of George Owen Walker." New York, USA, 15 February 2000.

London, Caspar. "Brief note on George Owen Walker." The News 25 February 2000.

Yvonne Walker Andrew lives in Queens , New York, USA.

Caribbean Trailblazers: St. Vincent and the Grenadines

18.   **DANIEL WILLIAMS**
By
Kenneth John

Poet of the people, Politician of the Street

In the late 1940's there sprang up in St. Vincent and the Grenadines (SVG), a trio of poets who did this country proud. They were Ellsworth "Shake" Keane, Daniel Williams and Owen Campbell.

These were colonial days when life was rough and the three youngsters, barely out of the Boys' Grammar School, devised a tool wherewith to confront the backwardness of their society. For a few years they published poems in "The Vincentian", the sole outlet at the time.

Then the said writers would turn around and criticize themselves in a classic case of operation bootstrap in which this triumvirate laid bare in verse those innermost feelings that helped them to come to terms with their environment.

Two of the writers, Danny and Shake formed another charmed circle that included Richard John and Cecil Cyrus that discussed world politics, usually on moonlit nights at King George the Fifth playing field at Arnos Vale. The latter two, retired doyens of the medical profession, are still around to tell the tale.

As for the literary three, with no way to turn to, they began playing games amongst themselves. I vividly recall that Danny was carried away by Campbell's "Washer Women". Campbell in turn thought that the "Shake" was the first among equals, while Shake deferred always to Danny especially for his early work:

LOOK AT THE SUN

Look at the sun threading his eye
With the shade and stitching patterns
On the grass or photographing the
Tree by my window in the film
in my room-see the wind blowing
The mature print on my picture partition
Then hear the drizzle of stale leaves
On the emerald sheet of the ground green
Nursed from the crystal breast of the dew
watch the panther sun stalk the tall
Acres of heaven and dissolve into night
Scattered with a shoreful of boundary stones.
Then to plot the graph of the sky

And encompass the stars, to join the lines
And solve the ethereal equation.
To scan the fleet of the wind
Or to find the painful element in joy.
And the light side of darkness where the hill steepens.

Williams and Keane later read their poems over the BBC and all three poets gained entry to anthologies published of poets in the Black World. Williams in particular was recommended reading at the University of Ibadan, among others.

A few of us in St. Vincent did what little we could to shore up these, and other stalwarts, who ran the danger not only of lack of appreciation, but also non-recognition and down-right condemnation in our cultural waste-land. "Shake" made a cover story of an unpretentious local publication "Horizon", (1960) and all three, along with Tim Daisy, featured particularly in a Special Issue of Flambeau magazine, published in 1967 and in Forum magazine published February 1972. In the latter issue I had made use of my first opportunity to utter mon cri de Coeur concerning Danny's demise while I was pursuing post-graduate studies abroad. Within three months of my return in November 1971, I had penned the following in Forum of February, 1972, put this way:

"One year has passed since we lost our dear beloved brother, Danny Williams. It has been a dreadful loss to us, the poor and disprivileged people and those who are prepared to stand by their side.

Socialist thinker, democratic philosopher, brilliant poet, and people's lawyer, Daniel etched out a permanent place in the hearts of the down-trodden masses, and today his name lives on as a house-hold word in the wattle-and-daubs, the slums in the Towns. But we who are left must not mourn. The struggle is unceasing and demands our all.

If we do love our brother, we must show it by advancing the cause for which he stood – the realization of a just State where the livelihood of everyone is secured, his happiness ensured and his dignity maximized. In loving memory of Daniel Williams, we here rededicate ourselves to that cause."

Cecil Blazer Williams was the only other person who had had the decency and presence of mind to put in print an appreciation of Williams in his publication "N.A.M. SPEAKS", albeit five years after the event (1976). He had a word also for Tim Daisy who had died. I write here a more generalized account of the Daniel Williams I knew, especially in his latter years when he was a sub-editor of the Flambeau and became a close friend of mine.

As an adolescent, I had always been impressed by the radicalism, brilliance and forthrightness of the youthful lawyer- poet, Danny Williams. One day after my return from U.W.I in 1964 I went to visit Danny in my search of kindred souls wherewith to form the Kingstown Literary Society and the Flambeau magazine.

I approached Danny Williams' law chambers in Egmont Street and there put the matter to him with which he readily agreed. Subsequently, when we got to know each other better, this is how he described that first meeting.

Danny said that he had been looking out of his window when he saw me on the side-walk, and buried his head to avoid eye contact. His untested opinion of me was that of a brash and arrogant youngster returning home armed with a degree, ready to lord it over his people. He sat down further to ponder his thoughts and was startled by a knocking on the door, and in I walked with my suggestion of forming Flambeau.

When we started the group, in order to protect it from degenerating into a social club, we had agreed that no drinks (except water) will be served during meetings which were held in rotation at members' homes. When Danny's turn came to host, he greeted us with a fine selection of alcoholic beverages to prime us before the serious argumentation that invariably followed.

My objection to drinks earned me a dressing down by Danny who reminded me that it was his home which the law holds to be his castle. No outsider, including the head of the group, could tell him what to do.

On another occasion, Danny observed that a fellow member of the group, Clem Iton, who was short of stature, was having a heated discussion with me. At the end of it, Danny drew me aside and poking his finger in my chest, volunteered the following advice:

"Don't ever argue with Clem from a sitting position. Clem delights in talking across to you at eye level. So when I talk to him, I always rise to my 6 ft. 2 in. forcing him to stand up. I then sternly look down at him, not forgetting to place one hand condescendingly on his shoulder. In short time, Clem's voice is reduced to a whisper and the vibrancy of his argument falls flat."

The Kingstown Study Group which had gone on to publish "Flambeau" had folded up in 1968, three years before the death of Danny. Those of us surviving decided to re-publish the Flambeau articles with encouragement and under the auspices of Baldwin King, a former member of the "Flambeau" group, and his wife, Cheryl. This we did in three volumes – *Search For Identity, Quest For Caribbean Unity and Home Sweet Home*. We were struck by their persistent contemporary relevance. Their shelf life must be the envy of fellow manufacturers of food for the mind.

When I landed back home from England in November 1971, I could only think of the law firm - Williams and John - that I had dreamt of establishing with Danny. The least I could do to honour his memory was to reopen his Chambers, secure his office telephone number-61827- which I possess to this day, and wear his lawyer's wig which his dear wife, Agnes, graciously presented to me

The original Flambeau presented a fairly wide array of Danny's poems. In "Mixture" he speaks of a woman he dearly loved but could not reach because of social barriers. She had not been the pure, unadulterated product of home-land Africa. She was hybridized, a faithful representative of the myriad races that form the "Mixture" that is the West Indies.

"Down in your brown face,
In the negro-white of your hair
And along the high ridge of your nose
I could hear the murmuring of another race
Out of place."
"You were mixture;
Cosmopolitan
Tanned with the heat and the cold
Nomad features
Chiseled in Spain by the English,
With a French finish."

"Cane Garden" represents a view from the suburbs of Kingstown in the direction of New Montrose where there was a new middle-class housing scheme of Civil Servants. How Danny enjoyed taunting this type, pulling at their stuffy noses, as it were.

"The city is a cemetery lit with candles,
We are the dead; and hope our bones.
Each night is the all saint's day and
We are the prefabricated saints,
Pious
In the nightgowns and prepared prayers."

One gets nearer to the basic philosophy of Danny Williams as is expressed in "Song of the Peasant"

To the peasant we owe our very existence
in these colonial lands of battered agriculture.
In fact, "The peasant is a green blade of grass,
Is keeper to the deep dark keys

376

Of the earth, locks and unlocks the ground
Spews an underworld
Is heart of the earth, Soil of the Soil
The peasant is King of the islands.
Yet we, ladies in lace, gentlemen in silk
Pass him without a glance, without obeisance. "

Like most colonial children, Danny felt the pull of the metropolis and in his earlier days, compared living in both climes that showed no disadvantage to the local scene, only the understandable difference. All this is beautifully captured in "We who do not know the snow". But as he often does, he closes the poem by stressing the common humanity of mankind wherever and however situated.

"And yet who does not know the prick of pain
The light in the candle of a child's eye
And the slow draw of dusk across the sky".

I remember well the emphasis by restraint contained in those last three lines, for Professor Figueroa had edited them out in an anthology which consequently ran hollow, a case of Hamlet without the Prince of Denmark. On reading the abridged version Danny, as impassioned as ever, raved and ranted over the gratuitous removal of his gem which starved his poem of vibrancy, and global symmetry.

Danny had always thought that the colonial needed to make a trip to the metropolis in order properly to find his true bearing and locate himself. Especially when his friend "Shake" was about to make the journey, Danny advised the roving spirit:

"You Must Go Out"

"Into the cold unanswering world
My dear, not prodigal;
Frugal, you must seek light
Where is no light,
And call to the cold dumb world
In syllables of sorrow.
But you must go out, out in the scalding century
Where the feeble are cinders and the boisterous
Construct hollow room for martyrs-
But you must keep company with words and the place of the skull
Intimate with dead

377

Caribbean Trailblazers: St. Vincent and the Grenadines

I tell you; for few have enjoyed the kind of kinship
Until they were forced.
But he is our guardian, and has prepared our board,
Begotten our laughter
Now that we find dying easier to do than living together
Go out, but secure your feelings;
Tie them up with strong chords of indifference
Or you will lose them.
In the grey twilight yawning tired with years and torpid seasons
Put them away
Or they will freeze in frigid breeze and snows of reason
Yes, you must go out
Into the damp dark whirling world
With your soul braced under the tight waistcoat
You must swing pendulum hands under
Minatory minutes ticking lines into your face
And they will tell you that time passes out.
That tempus fugit: forget it. You take word-
Time is stagnant as a vacuum, empty as ghosts
But for us who are weathered and torn asunder,
As we drift across the jagged edge of years bowed
Our hands brittle at each sun break

Go into the nefarious
Out into the callous world go.
Make exposure with the mind, and take snap- shots
You develop them in the distant corners of the soul
And in these fertile acres sow;
But you must go out
Into the cold and answering world
And find scripture in stone; see light
Where is no light, and here hold
Faith where there is no hope; into the bleak
Cold, into the hard unfeeling world, knocking the bruised hand,
You Must Go Out.

The poet himself did his stint in England and returned home about 1958 and helped form the Flambeau group six years later. In fact he felt then that he had already made his statement in full, over the BBC when he studied in England and was persuaded to write only "His is the Ebon Fibre" around 1966 as a final fillip to his genre of "Black Powerism", his last word on the concept of negritude.

In the mid-1960's during the racial ferment in the U.S.A. and beyond Danny Williams held firm to a belief in the Black cause. He often said at times that he felt relieved that young Blacks seemed to be catching up with him!

Apart from using the medium of Flambeau and the meetings of the group to ventilate and advocate his views, he assisted me as U.W.I. Resident Tutor to spread the gospel of Black Nationalism over the entire country.

I recall at a session sponsored by the Barrouallie Fisherman's Cooperative, he straightened out the position held by an English priest who thought that we limply lay on the boughs of black slavery, blaming that bestial institution for everything under the sun.

Danny's response was as impassioned as it was rational. I refer to that speech partly because the young Adrian Fraser who had been present in the audience has always felt that it provided the beginnings of his own search for an identity and formed his intellectual baptism into things political.

Danny was a permanent fixture on my UWI panel team that went about the country spreading the word of the University. One such panel took place at Langley Park at the school whose Headmaster, Alphonso Dennie, had been invited to join the panel with us to judge a public speaking contest.

When time came for the judgment, Dennie asked me in confidence how I rated the various speakers. Apparently Danny had heard the request and suggested that I should not reveal the contents of my score sheet. For, he said, Dennie just wanted to agree with us so that it could be announced that the three judges are of one mind and so declared. This was typical Danny, always creating laughter.

Naturally, Danny's outspokenness and widely expressed views on Race did not endear him to the remnants of the plantocracy, a sprinkling of British officialdom or the fairly large mass of perspiring colonials who subscribed meekly to British over-lordship. Unbeknown to him, his well intentioned middle-class friends had tried to gain him membership of the arch-conservative and stiff-necked Kingstown Club. But the planters and reactionaries turned up in full to black-ball him when the vote was taken.

On another matter, a mutual friend sought legal advice from Danny, concerning a constant nuisance of a white foreign neighbor who harbored racist grudges. Danny's advice was that our friend should call the neighbor to the boundary fence as if amicably to settle the matter. He should ensure that no other person was around. Then suddenly, he should unleash a back-handed slap on the neighbor with all the force he could muster. Danny was told that, far from settling the matter peacefully, he would put our friend in trouble. No, said Danny; the offended party would not dare go to Court to say he had been sharply slapped by a black native. Problem solved.

Danny Williams, in spite of it all, was not a racist at heart. He explained that he was racist by policy, and will change only when he encountered a level playing-field. He also made allowances for individual instances. He cited the case of the merchant, Fred J. Dare who invited Williams to buy a car from him on one-hundred percent credit, to start off his life as a lawyer. Fred J. Dare was a Syrian Jew.

In the Flambeau Group, Danny consistently maintained a radical stance, backed up by persons such as Kerwyn Morris and particularly Clement Iton who produced articles that were right up his street. Iton's *"Of Colour of Skin and St. Vincent"* and Morris' *"On Afro-West Indian Thinking"* were highly favoured by Williams.

When my turn came to make my own pilgrimage to Britain and keep a rendez-vous with the British connection, Danny toasted me at an impromptu gathering which met one evening in 1967 at Kerwyn's home. Armed with a full glass of rum in hand, Danny delivered, ex tempore, a two-hour speech, which he called, "The Return Journey" that was sheer brilliance, and probably bespoke of more than a spark of genius.

It followed that in the practice of his profession of law that he would be radical with an affinity for the masses and, for that reason, a sympathizer though not an active supporter of Joshua's P.P.P.

On the other hand, Danny had his own "inner cabinet" where he kept court – Othniel Sylvester, Clement Iton, Kenneth Adams, Barney Jacobs and I - Danny always expressed puzzlement as to how I gained membership of that august body!

 Kenneth Adams had been a struggling businessman who had a night-club called "Flambeau" which name was thought appropriate for the publication of our group, with motto: "Instead of cursing the darkness, one lights a Flambeau."

On any occasion that I was present at the Flambeau club,when Danny who was a regular visitor turned up, the management would greet him with the Irish tune Danny Boy in which he delighted. Apart from the music, I believe that the song reminded him of his fellow-bohemian poet from Ireland, Dylan Thomas whose poem was frequently cited by Danny- *"Do not go gently into that dread night"*.

As editor of "Flambeau", I was able to persuade Danny not only to write a new poem but also to produce an article for our publication. He obliged with *"The Democratic Process and the Single Party in the New States,"* which revealed issues that had preoccupied him for a considerable time.

Danny was uncompromising in his suggestion that the Single Party system is the recommended salvation of these islands:

"The priorities in such states are economic planning, education and social services. The best minds in such states are required to work together towards the national goals, which are primarily to raise the standard of living by training their citizens in industry and the technical skills of the

modern age. Indeed, then, there is only one party, the party of exploited and underprivileged, the party of those who must unlearn the propaganda and the half truths of their colonialist training, and formulate a pattern of thinking indigenous to them, and appropriate to their unfortunate situation."

In Williams' view:

"Since the competitive two-party system has emerged on what I would call "the Lazarus-Dives Line" with their innate ideologies, the opposition or other party, would comprise those who found their entrenched position under colonial rule threatened with the demise of colonialism. The planters who own large portions of the country, and who descend directly or otherwise from white overlords on sugar estates as an economic proposition are expected to form part of the other party, since the nationalist party must of necessity threaten their privileged position. But if the planters form no opposing Party, then who is this other party and from where does it emanate? This other party must, indeed, be the tool of the other group, acting covertly.

There is evidence that, in some of these islands, the planter group encourages the two party system by dividing the working class into two camps, aided and abetted by our own unscrupulous, but perhaps more correctly, our more unthinking and naïve politicians. It is not unusual in some areas to see laboring people in the most straightened circumstances on opposing sides, completely unaware, as naturally they must be, of why they are opposing each other."

In fact Williams' argument proceeded logically in demonstrating that

"The colonialist teaching was designed to create division and dissension among the colonial people. It advocated a socio-economic class structure based on the bizarre and unnatural tabulation of human existence into middle, upper and lower classes. Illogically, the first class is always the middle one, the bourgeois – to which the supporters of this formula usually claim to belong. They never belong to the upper class, jetsam from the privileged positions of the landed gentry of the colonialist period. Most certainly they never belong to the lower class, that amorphous body of human debris which the economic mill ground into sub-humanity. It is to that class their forbears belonged, not them."

Daniel Williams died tragically in a motor-car accident February 1971, in his mid-forties, before he had warmed to his pet subject, that of truly liberating his people, his potential unrealized, his dreams unfulfilled.

381

Probably Danny had written his own epitaph in his "Letter For a Friend."

"It is not always dark
Often I have seen day with dawn
Like a rag dusting out the night
And the stars retreat into the deep sky;
Seen the houses come out of hiding
And the day awake, shake itself,
Resume its business.

It is not always dark.

This letter is emotions overdue
But I must let you know that I call sorrow synonym
For joy confuse pain and pleasure
Nicknamed love necessity

So when uncertainties ago the season
Was fitful I prayed that he would
Jamaica us, and when fears ago we
Daemocles and Soufriere hung a threat
He did not spill us as I hoped
So that love could come like a thief
And circumstances chisel friendship out of ashes.

So burn no holes in your cheek
With tears my friend
The dead are more secure than we
Past the spite in the sun and the farcical smile.
The habit of living and the dry jest in the
Cracking wind; for earthquakes do not shake
Them though the earth cracks
But we crack at each tumble of the sky.

Resuscitation begins in the dark
And out of the night the light is begot;
Eternity is the stretch
And time the boundary stone.
But on the edge of the heart
Wisdom is weak"

Then the poet declared in the very last stanza – was it in a moment of weakness or triumph- that came within touching distance of a cry of despair.

"And I too have paid my bill for sorrow
Cashed my share of tears
Known the currency of the salt cheek
And learnt that grief is no miser.

Shake Keane did come as a breath of fresh air but his stay in SVG was short-lived and pock-marked by politics. But he did continue to lift Saint Vincent and the Grenadines culturally as he, Danny and others were committed to do since the late 1940's. We owe them a debt of gratitude.

Dr. Kenneth John is a political scientist and attorney. He resides in St. Vincent and the Grenadines.

.
.

Daniel Williams